Library of
Davidson College

Rhine Crossings

RHINE CROSSINGS

France and Germany in Love and War

Edited by
Aminia M. Brueggemann
and
Peter Schulman

State University of New York Press

Published by
State University of New York Press, Albany

© 2005 State University of New York

All rights reserved

Printed in the United States of America

No part of this book may be used or reproduced
in any manner whatsoever without written permission.
No part of this book may be stored in a retrieval system
or transmitted in any form or by any means including
electronic, electrostatic, magnetic tape, mechanical,
photocopying, recording, or otherwise without the prior
permission in writing of the publisher.

For information, address State University of New York Press,
90 State Street, Suite 700, Albany, NY 12207

Production by Judith Block
Marketing by Michael Campochiaro

Library of Congress Cataloging in Publication Data

Rhine crossings : France and Germany in love and war / edited by Aminia M.
Brueggemann and Peter Schulman.
  p. cm.
  Includes bibliographical references and index.
  ISBN 0-7914-6437-7 (hardcover : alk. paper)
  1. Literature, Comparative—German and French. 2. Literature, Comparative—French and German. 3. Germany—Foreign relations—France. 4. France—Foreign relations—Germany. 5. National characteristics, German, in literature. 6. National characteristics, French, in literature. I. Brueggemann, Aminia M., 1961– II. Schulman, Peter, 1964–
  PT123.F7R45 2005
  830.9'358—dc22
                                                           2004014214

10 9 8 7 6 5 4 3 2 1

Contents

Part I.
Introduction

France and Germany: A Tempestuous Affair
    Aminia M. Brueggemann and Peter Schulman   3

Part II.
Pre-Romantic Currents

Chapter 1
Re-constructing a "Gendered" *Bildung*: Mme de Staël's and Sophie von la Roche's Epistolary Fiction
    Beatrice Guenther   19

Chapter 2
"*Vous appellés cela betrügen?*": Slippery French Morals and German Bourgeois Virtues in Selected Writings by G. E. Lessing
    Heidi M. Schlipphacke   35

Chapter 3
The Dying Poet: Scenarios of a Christianized Heine
    Sarah Juliette Sasson   67

Part III
From Fin de Siècle to Modernist Connections

Chapter 4
Girls, Girls, Girls: Re-Membering the Body
    Terri J. Gordon   87

Chapter 5
Hygiene, Hard Work, and the Pursuit of Style in Baudelaire
and Nietzsche
    Andrea Gogröf-Voorhees   119

Chapter 6
Pierrette, assassine assassinée: The Portrait of Lulu in Two Tableaux
    Jennifer Forrest   141

Chapter 7
Benjamin Between Berlin and Paris: The Metaphorics of the City
    Michael Payne   165

Chapter 8
À fleur du dialogue: Georges Bataille, Karl Blossfeldt, and
the Language of Flowers
    Kimberley Healey   173

Part IV
World War II and Its Legacy

Chapter 9
An Unwanted Connection: Aristide Maillol and Nazism
    William J. Cloonan   193

Chapter 10
Of Heroes and Traitors: Two Early Films by René Clément
    Philip Watts   211

Chapter 11
Between Collaboration and Resistance: Ernst Jünger in
Paris, 1941–44
    Elliot Neaman   229

Part V
Postmodern Reflections

Chapter 12
Romy Schneider, *La Passante du Sans-Souci:* Discourses of
Vergangenheitsbewältigung, Feminism, and Myth
    Nina Zimnik   251

Chapter 13
History/Paris-Berlin/History
    Sande Cohen   273

Contributors   297

Index   301

Part I
Introduction

FRANCE AND GERMANY
A Tempestuous Affair
Aminia M. Brueggemann and Peter Schulman

François Truffaut's famous film, *Jules et Jim*, which depicts a fiery love triangle between a young French writer, a German poet, and a seductive yet troubled femme fatale from the belle époque until 1933, captures the volatile dynamic that has characterized the French-German symbiosis throughout many centuries. Caught in an intense relationship oscillating between love and hate, France and Germany have engaged in a dialectic marked both by aggression and mistrust, on the one hand, and a mutual fascination and respect, on the other. In this book, we explore the explosive and ongoing exchange between the two nations as they struggle not only with their individual identities, but also with their collective European ones. *Rhine Crossings* takes us on a journey from the literary salons of the eighteenth century to the trenches of the twentieth, from love-hate interactions to ones of cooperation and peace, from literature, to politics, to history. Indeed, this book spans several time frames and discourses as it investigates this unique and charged relationship.

Beginning with the intense cultural exchanges that characterized the French and German artistic worlds in the Middle Ages, France and Germany have punctuated European civilization by their two different outlooks on life and society. Taking, as a paradigmatic example, two radically different twelfth-century "takes" on the grail legend—Wolfram von Eschenbach's *Parzifal* and Chrétien de Troye's *Perceval le Gallois*—significant clichés have emerged and have been sustained, even magnified throughout centuries. Certain iconic representations have not only been perpetuated, but also have fed the propaganda machines which stoked three bloody and increasingly brutal Franco-German wars. Indeed, two significant cultural stereotypes have emerged from the contrast between the two national interpretations of the Perceval legend alone: on the one hand, the image of the German warrior driven by ironclad notions of honor and battle; on the other, the more playful French knight who is more preoccupied with the subtleties of chivalry and romance than his more somber German counterpart. Yet, it was the disagreement of the two European superpowers in 1519 that laid the foundation to the so-called *Erbfeindschaft* between Germany and France when Spain and France decided to fight for dominance on German territory. When the German dukes favored Karl of Spain and his money, France became one of Germany's bitter enemies—simply because the political situation demanded it.

During the course of the nineteenth century, the legacy of the odd German-French medieval dialectical match resurfaced, when French and German artists rediscovered their respective "others" through the prisms of a romanticized Middle Ages. Friedrich Schlegel, for example, was moved to catholic conversion after visiting Notre-Dame de Paris while, in *Le Génie du Christianisme*, Chateaubriand fused notions of a universal Christianity with Gothic architecture. Victor Hugo also looked eastward, towards the ruins of gothic castles on the Rhine for inspiration in *Le Rhin*. The Rhine was a literary gold mine for Hugo who saw catalysts for the fantastic and the mystical in its dreamlike landscape. Gérard de Nerval would be so enchanted with Germany's past that he would even declare: *"La vieille Allemagne, notre mère à tous, Teutonia!"* (*Old Germany, the mother of us all, Teutonia!*)[1] The German and French attitudes toward each other moved like a pendulum between hatred and fascination: For example, Frederick II, King of Prussia, wrote letters of enthusiasm to Voltaire, and the Bavarian rulers commissioned smaller copies of Versailles built in their country. If, in the eighteenth-century, Voltaire, for example, did no great service to Franco-German relations in his parody of what was for him the quintessential German with an unpronounceable Teutonic name, the blustering Baron Thunderten-Tronck, Mme de Staël's seminal work, *De l'Allemagne*, written in 1800, more than made up for her fellow countryman's caricature. *De l'Allemagne* was one of the first major French works to spawn a genuine appreciation of Germany. It in fact sparked a huge literary attraction to Germany among French writers and artists. Similarly, Melchior Grimm's letters about Paris (from 1753–1793) enchanted and encouraged generations of Germans to seek out their French neighbors. German poets would flock to Paris and even write their poems in French. The German *"Wesen"* and the French *"Esprit"* would merge in a maelstrom of creativity that would find its peak in the twentieth century during the thirty year interval between 1900 and 1930 documented by the Paris-Berlin exhibit at the Pompidou Center in 1978.[2]

Indeed, there was an incredible amount of interdisciplinary creative traffic between Paris and Berlin since Mme de Staël and Grimm. In the mid-nineteenth century, for example, the eminent literary critic Charles-Augustin Sainte-Beuve dreamed of an ideal Académie Française whose members would all be German while Heinrich Heine, who saw intense parallels between the French Revolution and German philosophy, proclaimed the Rhine the "Jordan" that separated the "promised land of liberty" from the land of the Philistines. German music also found a home in the Parisian cultural *milieu*. In J. K. Huysmans's novel *A Rebour*, it is by listening to Wagner that Des Esseintes is able to flee what he perceives as the ugliness of the French bourgeoisie. In real life, it was in fact Jacques Offenbach, born in Cologne, who became the toast of Paris under Napoleon III while Hector Berlioz, fascinated with Goethe's *Faust*, became a huge success in Berlin. Similarly, Gérard de Nerval became obsessed with Albrecht Dürer, and wrote of an ideal poetic space where Mozart and Weber are playing in the background while Goethe admired Eugène Delacroix's masterful representation of Faust, and goes so far as to say that even though the French may have been critical of Delacroix's enthusiasm, he could always find a home in Germany. "Delacroix has surpassed my own vision," Goethe wrote, "[. . .] readers [of Faust] will find all of this quite lively and superior to what they might have expected."[3]

The traffic between France and Germany hardly let up in the twentieth century. Walter Benjamin's captivation with Paris led to his extraordinary work on Baudelaire and fin de siècle Europe; Rainer Maria Rilke moved to Paris, even wrote poems in French and featured it in *The Notebooks of Malte Laurids Brigge;* Guillaume Apollinaire's boat trip along the Rhine inspired him to write his Rhénane poetry. In the art world of the early twentieth century, Berlin became the center for French art, as it celebrated exhibits by Henri Matisse, Charles-Eugène Delaunay, and Raoul Duffy at the expense of German artists, while in Paris, German artists flocked to Le Dôme, the famous Montparnasse café, to exchange ideas and techniques as Paris became their subject and muse.

It is with the birth of DADA and surrealism, however, that the most intense exchanges took place. As a reaction to the nationalism and boundaries that allowed the carnage of World War I to take place, the Dadaists and Surrealists forged an international interchange which meant to destroy the artificial constructs that drove a wedge between the two countries. A veritable explosion of cross-cultural and interdisciplinary activity was hatched in the interwar period, for example, as Tristan Tzara, Francis Picabia, Paul Eluard, Pierre Reverdy engaged in lengthy correspondences and discussions with Hans Arp, Carl Einstein, Hugo Ball, and Franz Jung. Outside the Dada/Surrealist worlds, other writers developed historic connections as well: Thomas Mann and André Gide, for example; Stephan Zweig and Romain Rolland. French writers wrote novels with German protagonists, such as Jacques Rivière's *L'Allemand*, or with protagonists in the disputed Alsace-Lorraine region such as Jean Giraudoux's novel *Siegfried et le Limousin*. In cinema, G. W. Pabst made the most potent films on war and resolution between France in Germany with his *Westfront 1918* (1930), a harrowing account of soldiers at the front during the last days of World War I which ends with a delirious and dying German soldier holding the hand of a French soldier as he cries out: *"Moi, camarade . . . pas enemie"* (I am a friend, not an enemy). With the Franco-German production of *Kameradschaft* (1931), Pabst's portrayal of French and German miners uniting to help some French miners trapped in a mine accident at the French/German border vividly showed the possibilities of cooperation and healing after the trauma of World War I. Pabst's versatile and empathetic understanding of French and German culture reached its peak in the 1931 Franco-German-American production of *The Three Penny Opera* which he shot both in German and in French with two different casts but using the same sets.

Since Napoleon's rule, however, clichés and foe images continuously crept into French-German politics and public opinion until the twentieth century. According to Joseph Rovan, the first quarrel between Karl and Franz I, and the Second World War bracketed twenty-three military French-German conflicts, which played themselves out mainly on German territory.[4] German-Franco relations were being reduced to interplay between victory and defeat, humiliation and revenge. The railway car of Compiègne—witness of German surrender during the First World War and the French defeat during the Second World War—serves as one of the most potent symbols of this ominous catenation.

Yet, beyond politics there is always art and the artists. World War II would usher in an obviously intense and complex artistic production between the two countries. Literary production was particularly ambiguous in France. On the one hand, such clandestine works of resistance as Vercors's *Le Silence de la Mer* urged French readers not to be taken in by the seemingly nice, "good" Germans behind whom lurked the horrors of Hitler and Nazism; on the other, pro-Fascist writers such as Robert Brasillach (who would be the first writer to be hanged after the war for war crimes) and Lucien Rebatet wrote pro-German novels and newspaper articles. The notorious Céline produced horrific anti-Semitic pamphlets such as the infamous *Bagatelles pour un massacre*, but used his modernist, dizzying literary style to depict his flight from France towards Germany as he joined a host of collaborators during the German retreat in his trilogy *D'un château l'autre*, *Nord*, and *Rigodon*. In Germany, there were writers such as Ernst Jünger who wrote graphically about his war experiences in occupied France and the slippery figure, Otto Abetz, the German Francophile diplomat who became very close to Pierre Laval during his term as Hitler's ambassador to France during the Vichy years. He was neither trusted by the Germans, who sent him back to Berlin shortly after the American landing in North Africa, because they were suspicious of his close ties to France, nor by the French who sentenced him to forced labor after the war for war crimes: he was involved in the deportation of French Jews and the assassination of Georges Mandel in 1944.

After 1945, Germany and France were forced to confront two different situations: Germany lost its national unity, experienced a moral discreditment, and had to be ruled by allied forces. France was able to retain its borders as well as its historic self-esteem and a sense of entitlement of being a great power. Although France led a tough policy, its attempts to revive Germany's cultural infrastructure encouraged Germany to catch up to contemporary cultural trends. At first, mainly brave and socially engaged private citizens attempted to overcome deeply embedded historical fears. On a regional level, town twinnings soon offered a forum for the renewed German-French dialogue. Within the framework of a European community, politicians of both countries attempted to bridge the gap. In 1963, the Elysée-contract—signed by Konrad Adenauer and Charles de Gaulle, ensuring continuing French-German cooperation—underscored this attempt by making international law out of the flourishing French-German relationship. The "mutual declaration,"[5] which accompanied the contract, reinforced the conviction that the reconciliation between the French and German people not only marked the end of a centuries old rivalry, but also represented a historical event which rebuilt the relationship of both countries. The caricaturist Klaus Pielert interpreted the contract as a marriage between Marianne and Michel, the national stereotypes. The proud fathers of the couple, de Gaulle and Adenauer, followed closely. Nowadays, regular political consultations, military cooperations, and youth exchanges characterize the daily life of these neighboring countries.

As Germany climbed economically out of the ruins of the Second World War towards the economic boom led by the strong German currency (*Deutsche Mark*) entering the so-called phase of the *Wirtschaftswunder* (economic miracle) and France emerged from its confused wartime past with thirty years of prosperity known as the *trente glorieuses*, the French and German cultural symbiosis was slower in coming. Yet, less than ten years after the war, Alain Resnais probed the immediate trauma of the apocalyptic scars of the Holocaust and Hiroshima with his landmark films, *Night and Fog* (1952), the most detailed and vivid documentary on the Holocaust the world had seen up until that point, and *Hiroshima mon amour* (1961), with a screenplay by the novelist Marguerite Duras, about a French woman and a Japanese man who have an affair in Hiroshima as they try to heal the respective anguish that they had buried after the war. On a more lighter note, François Truffaut's *Jules et Jim* (1962) would serve as a metaphoric coming to terms with the French-German relationship, as it represented a beautiful but troubled love triangle between a German, a Frenchman, and a seductive French woman.

It was with Marcel Ophül's groundbreaking epic documentary, *Le Chagrin et la Pitié* (1969) that France really began to confront its Vichy past that De Gaulle had seemingly swept under the rug after the Allied victory in order to promote an internal healing within France. Ophüls opened a floodgate of French introspection that led the way in the 1980s and 1990s to the famous trials of war criminals such as Maurice Papon and Klaus Barbie (about whom Ophüls would film another documentary, *Hotel Terminus*, in 1988).

Working together with the French cinematographer Henri Alekan and the Austrian writer Peter Handke, the German film director Wim Wenders accomplished the act of combining present and past, as well as the multicultural and multilingual aspects of Germany in his film *Wings of Desire* (1987). In Wender's film, the war-scarred and still divided city of Berlin provides the backdrop for an unusual love story between an angel and a French trapeze artist. Berlin becomes "a spatial link between the past and present, where history is preserved in the flesh of its inhabitants."[6] *Wings of Desire* goes beyond the simple telling of a love story but rather it zeros in on the weight of material history, the traces of the past, the fluidity of borders, and the beauty of transient humanity.

It is both encouraging and at the same time an almost logical and obvious culmination of the French-German codependency that despite so many centuries of Franco-German violence, trauma, destruction, and reconstruction, the Centre Pompidou held it's extraordinary exhibit, titled *Paris-Berlin*, in 1978, and that both countries declared the fall of 1996 as a French and German season during which a series of cultural exchanges, exhibits, film, and music festivals, culminating in a paradigmatic exhibit titled *Marianne et Germania, 1789–1889, A Century of Franco-German Passions*, were held jointly in Paris and Berlin.

Today, cooperation and competition distinguish the economic relations. In 1945, France was dominated by agriculture, after 1945, France became the leading supplier of advanced technologies in air and space, traffic systems, and energy technology. In fact, France has become one of the most important export partners of Germany's industry. Yet, in spite of all this economic activity, consumers of both countries continue to identify their products in terms of national characteristics. Product advertisements still use the established clichés: *Savoir-vivre*, the French way of living a joyful and sensual life, continues to be juxtaposed with *savoir-faire*, German perfectionism and organizational talent.

Germany's unification and the changes within Eastern Europe proved to be another challenge for the French-German friendship. Latent distrust towards a seemingly overpowering Germany burdened bilateral relations. The *"D-Mark-Diktat"* and France's nuclear experiments caused irritations on both sides. Yet, after a period of initial hesitation, France has emerged as an active partner within the German unification process while also taking advantage of opportunities to invest in the new German states. The German-French cooperation in air and space technology (Aerospaciale and DASA) provided new and vital impulses for cooperation. Jacques Chirac's state visit in June 2000 in Berlin, the first state visit of a French president since the German unification, was a diplomatic highpoint of France-German relations in the past decade. As he declared:

> It is now more than half a century that we have been working together. Between us, reconciliation is a fact. It is self-evident. A reality of daily life which is so much a part of our landscape that we no longer perceive its true dimension.
> ... What France and Germany have experienced and undergone in history is unlike anything else. Better than any other nation, they grasp the deep meaning of peace and of the European enterprise. They alone, by forcing the pace of things, could give the signal for a great coming together in Europe. Together, as their voyage of mutual rediscovery has grown more intense, as the commitment of their peoples has deepened, they have moved the idea of Europe forward. [*Seit mehr als einem halben Jahrhundert arbeiten wir Hand in Hand. Zwischen uns ist die Aussöhnung abgeschlossen. . . . Was Deutschland und Frankreich im Laufe ihrer Geschichte erlebt und erlitten haben, ist ohnegleichen. . . . Nur sie vermögen Europa voranzubringen, sei es bei der Verwirklichung seiner Ziele, bei der Ausweitung seiner Grenzen oder bei seiner Verankerung in den Herzen . . .*][7]

In August 2003, the French Minister of Foreign Affairs, Dominique de Villepin, met his German counterpart, Joschka Fischer, in order to discuss many subjects on which France and Germany cooperate such as their common stand on Iraq, the Middle East peace process, and the results of the European Convention. Apparently, the Franco-German alliance has developed into such a strong bond that Dominique de Villepin privately voiced his thoughts that the two countries—having the economies and populations within the European Union—could merge into one union.[8] Perhaps Einstein's comment that prejudices are harder to crack than atomic nucleuses is slowly being contradicted.

Although France and Germany have had a long and storied affair, this present volume does not attempt to provide an exhaustive historical or political analysis of the Franco-German dynamic throughout the centuries. We have endeavored, instead, to offer a mosaic of different insights and connections that have not hitherto been covered by historians or literary critics. By branching out from the early sentimental eighteenth-century epistolary beginnings to the vanguards of film and photography, *Rhine Crossings* seeks to cross various disciplines as well as the geographical boundaries that have come between these two nations.

In chapter 1, Beatrice Guenther explores the paradigmatic commonalities that have characterized Madame de Staël's and Sophie von la Roche's epistolary fiction. While Madame de Staël is widely considered as having inspired a new appreciation of Germany among the French through her seminal work, *De l'Allemagne*, Guenther reveals how de Staël's epistolary fiction can also shed light on and contribute to French-German sensibilities. Similarly, Guenther explains how, thirty years later, Sophie von la Roche, who is considered Germany's first female novelist, picks up on and has a dialogue with de Staël's theories of education which she integrates into her own fiction. For Guenther, the two writers demonstrate how acts of reading and education help women shape their own judgment and conduct as well as affect the communities around them in a positive manner while using national characteristics as a form of stereotypical shorthand; in fact they call into question assumptions of social place and national rootedness.

In chapter 2, Heidi M. Schlipphacke examines the surprisingly contradictory nature of G. E. Lessing's reception of France and the French. Perhaps carried away by his wish to create a national German theater independent from the firmly established French academy, Lessing instrumentalizes and ultimately exploits France by equating France with decadence and ridicule.

In chapter 3, Sarah Juliette Sasson attempts to trace the French reception of Heinrich Heine as a source of errors or illusions. Heine, who regarded Paris as the capital of *esprit* and creativity, was also blessed with a "Voltairian" irony that secured his place in the French literary landscape. Yet, it appears that not only his writing, but also his persona was being interpreted by enthusiastic critics thus transforming the poet into a mere *image*.

In chapter 4, Terri J. Gordon undertakes a study of the cabaret revue, the troupes of girls that stormed the stages of Paris and Berlin in the interwar period. A testimony to the prosperity of the Roaring Twenties, the revue was comprised of troupes of girls that performed in perfectly synchronized units, giving rise to reiterated images in the French and German press of the military body and the mass-produced machine. By taking up the image of the "femme-machine" in mass culture and a number of works by avant-garde artists Man Ray and Hans Bellmer, Gordon argues that the displacement of the (male) machine and/or male soldier onto the body of woman reveals culturally disjunctive responses to the trauma of the war. The similar reception in the press in Paris and Berlin suggests that the revue held a common appeal for the inhabitants of the two cities. Unlike the psychic and social fragmentation expressed in the machine art of Dada and surrealist photomontage, the revue produces images of health and wholeness, symbolically putting the individual and military body back together again. In this sense re-membering is forgetting.

In chapter 5, Andrea Gogröf-Voorhees focuses on Charles Pierre Baudelaire's and Friedrich Nietzsche's strategies of resistance to physical and cultural decline. The article shows how Baudelaire and Nietzsche, swimming against the tide of their times, defend values such as originality, courage, honesty, will power, beauty, and style in an increasingly modernized age, characterized by a misguided optimism and the erroneous belief that technological and scientific progress guarantees moral improvement. Baudelaire and Nietzsche see original art and thought being buried under frenzied activity that leads nowhere but to chaos, mediocrity, and emptiness. Their strong work ethics reflect an understanding of work as a self-paced activity through which one expresses and resolves inner conflicts and channels one's creative energies. Their insistence on hygiene grows from a deep concern to cultivate those qualities within us that we wish to promote. Whether these qualities are "good" or "bad" is not for them the question as much as the strength of character and taste that determines one's choice. The aesthetic expression of this choice and taste is precisely what Baudelaire and Nietzsche call "style." As Nietzsche pointed out, "to give style to one's character, is a rare art."

In chapter 6, Jennifer Forrest examines the effort to take Frank Wedekind at his word on what he was trying to do in his creation of Lulu (e.g., the eternal woman), combined with that of associating his ideals with both the era's great philosophical dialogues (Nietzsche, Schopenhauer) and Western literary and artistic archetypes (Pandora, Eve, Antoine Watteau's paintings depicting Gilles) has led to grand pronouncements on his often awkward yet earnest treatment of "serious" subjects. However, failure to analyze seriously Wedekind's German Lulu in terms of French popular culture leaves critics unsatisfactorily scrambling for ways to reconcile the multiple stylistic and ideological currents composing the plays. This essay explores how instrumental the late-nineteenth-century Parisian circus and pantomime were in Wedekind's creation of his fin de siècle femme fatale.

In chapter 7, Michael Payne looks at the productive and continuing tension between aesthetics and ideology as found in Walter Benjamin's unfinished writings on Paris and Berlin. Payne compares Benjamin's associations with Paris and the "aesthetic" (including Baudelaire, speculation, playfulness, and flaneurism) to his associations with Berlin and Bertolt Brecht's Marxist critique of ideology. Payne also underlines the importance of Benjamin's discourse on these two cities on the continuing discussion between critical and cultural theorists today.

In chapter 8, Kimberley Healey demonstrates how a little known interdisciplinary collaboration between the German photographer Karl Blossfelt and the controversial French writer and essayist Georges Bataille led to an original artistic communication between the two writers at a time when dialogue between their respective countries was at a standstill with the looming approach of World War II. Healey argues that, through a unique "language of flowers," the two artists were able to merge their idiosyncratic aesthetics into a language that defied the usual stereotypical production that was emerging from the two nations at that time. Healey contends that Bataille and Blossfeldt's textual and visual dialogue was at odds with conventional representations of nature between the wars which ideologically tended to reject and embrace nature and the natural in various ways. Through a botanical language, Bataille and Blossfeldt were able to transcend the "unnatural" nationalistic barriers of the era by creating a multilayered and multiangled critical voice of their own.

In chapter 9, William J. Cloonan brings attention to the life and works of the French sculptor Aristide Maillol and his ambiguous role during the German occupation. As Cloonan examines Maillol's friendship with the German sculptor Arno Brecker, he suggests that while Maillol's work found favor in the Reich, and Maillol had certain affinities with the German regime, he was not a Nazi or a Nazi sympathizer. Rather, Cloonan contends that Maillol simply echoed a political and artistic conservatism that had already been widespread and accepted in France and Europe as a whole between the wars.

In chapter 10, Philip Watts examines the period immediately after World War II as he reassesses two films the popular French filmmaker made right after the war. One, *La Bataille du rail*, released in 1946, was a documentary-style account of French resisters triumphing over the Germans, while *Les Maudits*, released a year later, depicted the flight of Fascists and collaborators as they headed for South America in a submarine. Watts compares the contrasting reception of each film (*La Bataille du rail* was a great success while *Les Maudits* had been excoriated). Through a cinematographic and historical analysis of these films, Watts provides key insights not only into how history is represented by Clément during France's fragile period right after the war, but also into the relationship between aesthetics and politics through the eyes of a nation desperately attempting to come to terms with its traumatic past.

In chapter 11, Elliot Neaman attempts to solve the puzzle of the high status of German writer and World War I hero Ernst Jünger in France. On the one hand, Jünger was part of the military occupying force that was responsible for the shooting of hostages and other coercive acts against the citizens of Paris from 1940–1944. On the other hand, Jünger's diaries from 1942 onward, published after the war, revealed a man who carried out his official duties even though he was deeply disturbed by the atrocities committed during the war in the name of the German people. This paper suggests that the postwar French reception of Jünger reflected the ambivalence of the French people themselves, faced with the dilemma of either accepting the Vichy regime's cozy relationship with the German occupiers, even if that meant tolerating the deportation of Jews and other crimes against humanity, or resisting the regime and risking imprisonment or death. Jünger's diaries provided a soothing justification for cultural collaboration between the two nations and an interpretation of the roots of fascism that blamed modernity and mass democracy, thus resonating with a long tradition of anti-Enlightenment, conservative thought in France.

In chapter 12, Nina Zimnik examines the myth of Romy Schneider through the complex Franco-German reception of her 1982 film, Jacques Ruffio's *La Passante du Sans-Souci*. As Zimnik delves into Schneider's own past, which was filled with abusive relationships linked to Germany's wartime crimes, and her present, a life as a German émigré in Paris, a city in which she felt absolutely free, Zimnik draws a more general parallel between the film and the actress. For Zimnik, the release of *La Passante*, as well as a conspicuously edited version of the film shown relatively recently on German television, point to the ways Schneider's life was mythologized in a manner that revitalized the romantic Francophile gaze of Germans wanting to escape the problems of postwar Germany. For Zimnik, the "mythology" centered around Romy Schneider's life and acceptance in France was similar to the passerby she plays as she seemingly embodies a certain "coming to terms with the past" that was reflected in a generation of women in the 1970s. Through the many symbolic "branches" of Ruffio's film, Zimnik traces the ways in which Romy Schneider's "star essence" could be seen as a focal point for German and French attempts to grapple with the Holocaust.

In chapter 13, Sande Cohen's paper discusses four conceptions of history that are often associated with Parisian radicalism of the 1930s and the German slide into nihilism of the same period: Simone Weil's critique of "uprootedness," Alexandre Kojeve's installation of history at an end, Hannah Arendt's attempt to recover "taste" and judgment after Nazism, and Walter Benjamin's notion of history as messianism and social urgency. These writers are juxtaposed for having made conceptions of history that have helped bring the very concept of history to a state of paralysis: it is easier today to speak of "history-for" rather than "history-of." These writers invoked conceptions of history as a response to some of the terrors of the twentieth century; one of the implications is that today intellectuals and writers do not have the "resource" of historical theory at their disposal.

NOTES

1. Quoted by Wolfgang Leiner, "De la vision française de l'Allemagne" in *Marianne et Germania, 1789–1889: Un siècle de passions franco-allemandes* (Paris: Musée du Petit Palais, 1998), pp. 41–47.

2. For a full view of this exhibit see *Paris-Berlin* (Paris: Centre Georges Pompidou/Gallimard, 1992). This book version of the exhibit gives detailed analyses and graphic imagery of the links and contrasts between France and Germany in art, architecture, graphic design, literature, industrial art, cinema, theater, and music. It is indeed one of the most comprehensive works on this subject.

3. Quoted by Anna Czarnocka in *Marianne et Germania, 1789–1889: Un siecle de passions franco-allemandes* (Paris: Musée du Petit Palais, 1998), p. 188.

4. Joseph Rovan and Georges Suffert, "A New Row between an Old Couple," in *When the Wall came down: Reactions to German Unification*, eds. H. James and M. Stone (New York: Routledge and Kegan Paul, 1992).

5. Compare http://www.documentarciv.de/brd/elysee1963.html.

6. *The Cinema of Wim Wenders* ed. Roger F. Cook and Gerd Gemünden (Detroit: Wayne State University Press, 1997), p. 164.

7. Staatspräsident Jacques Chirac, addressing the German parlament on June 27, 2000. For further information see http://www.bundestag.de.

8. For further information, see the *New York Times* articles, "France and Germany Flex Muscles on Charter" by Elaine Sciolino. *New York Times*, 10 December 2003.

Part II
Pre-Romantic Currents

Chapter 1

Re-constructing a "Gendered" *Bildung*

Mme de Staël's and Sophie von la Roche's Epistolary Fiction

Beatrice Guenther

About thirty years separate Sophie von la Roche's *Die Geschichte des Fräuleins von Sternheim* (1771) and Mme de Staël's *Delphine*, published in 1802. Despite both historical and geographical differences, however, several provocative intersections suggest themselves—which will, I hope, illuminate the larger question of this collection of essays: the French-German connection. The two novelists' works waver between Enlightenment ideals and a sensibility associated with romanticism or its precursors in Germany: *Empfindsamkeit*[1] (sensibility) and *Sturm und Drang* (storm and stress). Both writers also transcended their national borders, finding translators to introduce their works to readers across the Rhein.[2] Sophie von la Roche is credited with being Germany's first female novelist, besides being recognized in England, France, and Switzerland,[3] whereas there is surely no need to explain Staël's cultural prominence as author, literary and social critic, and flamboyant personality of late eighteenth- and early-nineteenth-century Europe. Of greatest interest to me, however, is that both writers actively concerned themselves with the education of women and both chose educated, female characters as the protagonists of their novels.

If we are to see how both Staël and la Roche helped to stretch and redefine assumptions about how women were to be educated, our first move must be to explore the status quo that they challenged through their epistolary fiction. In fact, although it would be a mistake to treat the status quo as a homogenous and simple set of conventions, for the purpose of this chapter, it does make sense to use Jean-Jacques Rousseau's widely read *Émile, ou traité de l'éducation* (1762) as a foil to la Roche's *Sternheim* and de Staël's *Delphine*. This move seems particularly appropriate in light of the fact that Staël gently mocks her mentor's work: "... *l'espèce de soin que Rousseau exige de l'instituteur pour suppléer à l'instruction ... obligerait chaque homme à consacrer sa vie entière à l'éducation d'un autre ...*" [... the kind of care Rousseau demands from the teacher in order to provide instruction ... would oblige each man to devote his entire life to the instruction of another].[4]

Book V of *Émile*,[5] which develops at length the portrait of an ideal woman—Sophie, who is bred to become a model wife and mother—ends, not surprisingly, with the news that Sophie is expecting her first child. The text covers multiple subjects, such as Sophie's physical and moral attributes, the means of regulating Sophie's appetite, her relationship to clothing and cleanliness, her understanding of religion and approach to household chores—all this in order to lay out the characteristics of a proper or, rather, "safe" mate. Two premises govern the elaborate plan set forth by Rousseau: (1) that men and women are constituted differently ("*l'homme et la femme ne sont ni ne doivent être constitués de même, de caractère ni de tempérament*") [man and woman are not and should not be constituted in the same manner–neither in character nor in temperament (E, V, 440)]; and (2) in that men's relation to the opposite sex is governed by desire whereas women's relation to men is governed by desire and by need, women's education must reflect this difference in mutual dependence (E, V, 439)]. One of Rousseau's fundamental assumptions—and one that is perhaps most difficult to consider seriously at this point in time—reads:

> *Ainsi toute l'éducation des femmes doit être relative aux hommes. Leur plaire, leur être utiles, se faire aimer et honorer d'eux, les élever jeunes, les soigner grands, les conseiller, les consoler, leur rendre la vie agréable et douce: voilà les devoirs des femmes dans tous les temps ... tous les préceptes [qui s'écarteraient de ce principe] ... ne serviront de rien pour leur bonheur ni pour le nôtre* (E, V, 440). [Thus, the whole education of women must be relative to men. Pleasing them, being useful to them, making themselves loved and honored by them, raising them when young, caring for them when grown, advising them, consoling them, making their lives

agreeable and sweet: these are the duties of women at all times. . . . All precepts [which would diverge from this principle] . . . would provide them with nothing—neither for their happiness nor for our own.]

According to Rousseau, the female mind knows nothing but should be like cultivated earth, ready to receive grain in order to yield some unidentified crop (E, V, 503). The aggressive rhetoric in this passage likens the mind's subjective capacities to a passive, to-be-worked-upon object and slyly suggests that the work of a woman's mind simply reproduces the unreflected, involuntary work of her womb.

The reasons behind this need to bind women's intelligence are not too difficult to identify. According to Rousseau, females' precocious linguistic ability (E, V, 447, 469) seems to give them an unfair advantage over boys and men; their ability to dissemble and deceive can only be outwitted by disregarding what their mouths say. In short, eyes, complexion, and respiration communicate more truly than a woman's tongue (E, V, 469). Rousseau also cautions men to avoid a woman who might prefer to "shine" rather than to please—who might, indeed, prefer the role of teacher over disciple to her mate, who might establish a literary court at home over which she can preside (E, V, 501). In order to contain this threat, Rousseau advises educators to withhold books from girls; their source of knowledge should consist ideally of conversations with their fathers and mothers, their own reflections, and observations resulting from their limited knowledge of the world (E, V, 484). The goal seems to be to create a woman able to think (*réfléchir*) and engage or entertain her husband without being knowledgeable.

Rousseau does diverge from his dogmatic pronouncements when he allows his Sophie to read one book, *Aventures de Télémaque* (1699)[6]—and this more ambiguous moment shall be the last example drawn from *Émile*, an example whose explicit purpose in the text is undercut by its narrative function. When Sophie first reads *Télémaque*, her imagination is fired by the protagonist, causing her to fall in love with an idealized, fictional being, her overexcited sensibility and imagination potentially causing her to succumb to her deathly obsession (E, V, 495). Rousseau "playfully" imagines Sophie wedded to that fatal obsession, which destroys her life and replaces the wedding altar with a tomb—before abandoning that plotline. When, however, Sophie meets Emile, her future husband, her knowledge of *Télémaque* actually seems to prepare her ability to love her mate. In effect, through the narrative triangulation of desire, Sophie seems to have been socialized to fall in love with her "proper" mate (E, V, 510). Despite the explicit injunction against reading, then, Rousseau's text seems to create an ambiguous space for reading books—even narratives or prose poems—within the program of female education.

The contrast of la Roche's and de Staël's ideal female education with Rousseau's is of necessity rather complex, since one needs to take into account a double focus in both women's works. The education enjoyed by the propertied Delphine or Sophie von Sternheim cannot be read as an ideal *Bildung* meant to be accessible to all women[7]—and this is especially true in *Sternheim*, where multiple plans to organize schools for destitute girls are all informed by very precise, utilitarian goals, meant ultimately to reconcile the young female students with their lower social station, their proper place.[8]

If one focuses on the education of the exceptional woman, however, it becomes clear that la Roche and de Staël emphatically reject Rousseau's censorship of books—and indeed, an education meant to produce dependent submission. In *Sternheim*, Sophie's critique of court life—its egotism, decadence, and disregard for humanitarian values—seems to stem in part from her familiarity with moral teachings she has gleaned from books.[9] The books are confiscated by Sophie's court-obsessed aunt, but this removal only serves to prove that Sophie's autonomous, moral sense, resulting in large part from her readings, is no longer in need of "leaders and interpreters" in order to lay bare the shortcomings of courtly life. Most significantly, the work *Sternheim* is itself written to advance the development of virtue and wisdom among the mothers and daughters of the German nation—this according to the novel's editor, Christoph Martin Wieland, who took it upon himself to publish la Roche's work anonymously (St, 10).

In *Delphine*, on the other hand, the importance of reading is not dramatized explicitly. However, throughout de Staël's own literary career, she writes an impassioned defence of the importance of reading. In "De l'étude" ("On Studying"), part of her 1796 study of *De l'influence des passions sur le bonheur des individus et des nations* [*On the Influence of Passions on the Happiness of Individuals and Nations*], she argues that an individual perfects him/herself by contemplating the ideas of others, such reflection ultimately permitting a greater detachment from the self, clearing the way for a more global understanding of the universe.[10] In her *Essai sur les fictions* [*Essay on Fictions*] (1795), Staël adds the insight that texts construct a community of like-minded sensitive souls able to offset the pull of a blunted, mediocre *Zeitgeist*. According to de Staël:

> ... *sans cesse condamnées, [les âmes] se croiroient seules au monde, elles détesteroient bientôt leur propre nature qui les isole, si quelques ouvrages passionnés et mélancoliques ne leur faisoient pas trouver dans la solitude, quelques rayons du bonheur qui leur échappe au milieu du monde.*[11]
> [... condemned incessantly, (these souls) would believe themselves alone in the world, they would soon detest their own nature which isolates them, that is, if several impassioned and melancholic works would not allow them to discover in their solitude some rays of happiness that escape them in the midst of people.]

Even as late as 1810, in her *De l'Allemagne* [*On Germany*], Staël recommends the study of foreign languages as the core of any educational program. Through translation, the student learns to recognize analogies and probabilities (*vraisemblances*)—an activity, she argues, that can truly develop the faculty of thought. She goes on to claim that the study of grammar gradually permits the student to grasp the metaphysics of thought: *"l'exactitude du raisonnement et l'indépendence de la pensée"* [accuracy in reasoning and independence of thought (DA, 142)].[12] We can conclude: where Rousseau saw in the transgressive act of reading the threat of pathological individuality but, paradoxically, also the potential socialization of girls, la Roche and, particularly, de Staël discover in the act of reading the emergence of an individual consciousness, able to judge and transcend inadequate social conventions. Through the contrast with Rousseau's *Émile*—where the needs of the individual seem for the most part rather at odds with the needs of community—we should consider, then, how the two women writers reconcile the refining of an autonomous consciousness with the female subject's integration within a larger social frame.

The next step in this study must be to juxtapose the characteristics of la Roche's Sternheim and Staël's Delphine, a step that should make clear how both novelists redefine—in contrast to Rousseau—what should constitute the goals of women's education. De Staël and la Roche both choose to represent protagonists who are educated but existing on the margins of family. Sternheim is initially represented as the product of her parents' utopian world but spends much of the novel, after her parents' death, unhappily resisting the inadequate supervision of her guardians, her aunt, and uncle von Löbau. Moreover, as Monika Nenon points out, la Roche's novel continually lays out alternative life choices, that is, "*Selbsterfüllung durch Berufsarbeit*" (self-preservation through vocational work) [N, 93], for the female characters are leary of marriage. Delphine, on the other hand, is introduced as alone from the start. As a widowed and wealthy orphan, she is bound to her friends, sister-in-law, and community by her interpretation of what constitutes honor and friendship—even if much of the novel does circle around her unhappy liaison with Léonce. Both texts foreground women who must rely on their own wits and judgment in order to maneuver their way through rather complex social situations. And, as if these narrative scenarios are not sufficient to critique implicitly Rousseau's principle that women's education must be informed by their subordination to and dependence on men, both de Staël and la Roche incorporate episodes into their novels, where the protagonist is cut off from her social context and must learn to survive on her own—either in the bleak, lead-mined mountains of Scotland or in the barren no-man's-land between France and Switzerland. The two novelists seem to explore the extreme limits of their protagonist's self-sufficiency, that is, the effectiveness of their education, to help them survive on their own.

The two writers do seem to share the strategy of imagining a woman's life uncircumscribed by Rousseau's restrictive pedagogical principles. Nonetheless, the simple fact that Delphine chooses to exile herself whereas Sternheim is kidnapped, thus forced to submit to a life of hardship, signals that de Staël's and la Roche's projects don't mirror one another perfectly. Sternheim's experiences in the Scottish mountains counterbalance her earlier willful decision to flee court life. Her earlier flight away from courtly decadence paradoxically had placed her under the control of a character, who embodies most clearly the vices of court life: egotism, decadence, and lack of integrity. Whereas Sternheim recognizes that her misdirected sensibility (*Empfindsamkeit*) caused her to privilege self-love over her concern for others (St, 214), which in turn had destroyed an important facet of her being—her function as role model for other women ("*Wohltätigkeit des Beispiels*," 215)—her exile rehabilitates her reputation. During her exile—limited to her own moral and intellectual resources—Sternheim moves quickly from despair to the recognition that her persecutor's power to alter her external circumstances will not extend to altering her basic convictions ("*Gesinnungen,*" 305). The moral test of endurance, facilitated by the writing of diary entries (the *Selbstklärungsprozess*), helps to distill these inner (learned) principles: the love of virtue; the carrying out of one's duties; and the joy of doing good (St, 305–6, 315). In effect, the individual, thrown back upon her resources, seems to rediscover the power of community. Through Sternheim's self-abdicating love for the abandoned and illegitimate five-year-old daughter of her persecutor, she learns to communicate with, then understand, value, and ultimately transform into allies the Scottish family holding her hostage. Sternheim's educational program—aimed at shaping and guiding the Scottish host's daughter and her new five-year-old charge—does more than train the girls to improve their lot in life; it also helps to instill her own values into the foreign community around her: an expanded love of God; enlightenment of their reason; and the control (calming) of their heart (St, 314–5).

On one level, this metamorphosis of community through education connects the beginning of the novel with its end. Sternheim is following the example of her father's utopian social innovations, in which all social elements—including the poor, old, and infirm—are given a function and a place within the community. It is this social model which Sternheim will also reproduce on English soil, once she is married to Lord Seymour at the end of the novel. One might conclude, then, that the function of education in *Sternheim* is to provide the individual with moral fortitude in order to transform the world into a utopian, humane, if still hierarchical, community (St, 41).

The fusion of individual and social goals is not a completely stable one, however. Self-love—or at least self-interest—motivates Sternheim's education of the Scottish world around her. Educating those less fortunate than herself is not the primary goal she sets herself; instead, she uses the education of her host's daughter as a signifier meant to signal to the unsuspecting local gentry that she is out of place and in need of rescuing (St, 312, 315).

A second ambiguity present both in the exile episode and the ending of the novel is the question of social hierarchy. Numerous episodes in the text foreground how education is a tool to reconcile individuals with their social station (St, 41). And yet, the two characters who repeatedly justify the social status quo are themselves emblematic of its antithesis. Sternheim's father is himself a parvenu, accepted into the ranks of nobility because of his military prowess and through his marriage to a more established, legitimate branch of aristocracy. Sternheim—besides being neither fully German nor English—thematizes explicitly her own mixed status. Reevaluating her past, she recognizes: "*Aber sie dachten, es wäre nicht viel an einem Mädchen aus einer ungleichen Ehe verloren*" (St, 211) [But they thought that much was not lost (by ruining) a girl issuing from an unequal marriage]. And if one thinks back to the exile episode, one can recognize that the example of the educated Scottish daughter can also be read as the symbol of (limited) social mobility of the girl rather than the fixing of her social station. Once again in *Sternheim*, the individual's desires and mobility through the process of education implicitly contradict the explicit needs of community to reproduce its social hierarchy.

In *Delphine*, it is primarily the inadequate intellectual education of women that comes under fire. Through the example of Delphine's cousin, Matilde, and Matilde's mother, Mme de Vernon, we recognize two pitfalls: first, to withhold education from girls, considered "toys,"[13] becomes the leading cause for the development of egotism, duplicity, and the breakdown of the individual and the community surrounding her. This is borne out most clearly through the example of Mme de Vernon. The second trap for women—the traditional Catholic schooling, through which Matilde learns to submit her will to "all the yokes of female destiny" (D, I: 39–40, 333)—leads to the loss of sensibility, autonomous thought, and judgment. Through the character of Delphine, on the other hand, de Staël explores an alternative solution to the educational crisis for women. Delphine's exemplary formation permits her to "*voi[r] tout par ses propres lumières, soumet[tre] sa conduite à ses propres idées, et dédaigne[r] souvent les maximes reçues*" (D, I: 26) [to see everything through the filter of her own wisdom, submit her conduct to her own ideas and to hold accepted ideas (commonplaces) in contempt].[14] Moreover, as Doris Kadish points out, Delphine places high value on the feminine exercise of authority,[15] carefully placing the education of her own ward, Isore, in the hands of another enlightened woman (besides passing her fortune on to younger women) before her death.[16]

The shift, however, to Delphine's intellectual and emotional trial—her self-imposed exile from Paris—hardly brings to light a self-confident, autonomous woman. The six fragments that Delphine writes during her self-imposed exile almost seem to bear out—on an explicit level—Rousseau's belief that women's *raison d'être* lies in their attachment to men.[17] Delphine's texts, addressed to herself, lament her unfulfilled desire for Léonce, her unmitigated misery. With markedly less enthusiasm than Sternheim, Delphine attempts to devote her energies to her young ward, Isore. At this point in the novel, however, she sees the educational project as rather futile: "... *mais développer son âme ou l'étouffer, l'exalter par des sentiments généreux, ou la courber sous de froids calculs, n'est-ce pas une alternative presque semblable*" [but developing her soul or stifling it, exalting it through generous sentiments or forcing it to stoop through cold calculation, aren't these two alternatives almost similar (D, 168)]?

Delphine's preoccupation with her own unhappiness is not at odds, however, with the larger framework of de Staël's historical optimism—her belief in the ever-continuing perfectibility of the human race. In *De la littérature considérée dans ses rapports avec les institutions sociales* [*On Literature and its Relation to Social Institutions*] (1800), de Staël argues that melancholy imagination responds to the limits imposed by human destiny and life by conjuring up infinity [*en faisant rêver l'infini*].[18] Staël develops the connection of melancholy and the infinite in *De l'Allemagne* [*On Germany*], written in 1810. In the later text, it is the darker, negative aspects of life that permit more profound reflection—an exploration of immortality, of ideas and objects without limits (DA, II: 293). Delphine's own morose reflections indicate that her renunciation of Léonce, resulting in solitude and melancholy, in fact provide her with deeper insights into the human condition:

> *Oh! que l'homme aurait peur, s'il existait un livre qui dévoilât véritablement le malheur; un livre qui fît connaître ce que l'on a toujours craint de représenter, les faiblesses, les misères qui se traînent après les grands revers; les ennuis dont le désespoir ne guérit pas; le dégoût que n'amortit point l'âpreté de la souffrance ... et tous les contrastes et toutes les conséquences qui ne s'accordent que pour faire du mal, et déchirent à la fois un même coeur par tous les genres de peines!* (D, II: 166–67) [Oh! how man would be frightened if a book existed that would truly unveil misfortune; a book

that would make known what one has always feared to represent, weaknesses or miseries which drag themselves along after great setbacks; troubles whose despair can't be cured; the disgust that doesn't deaden the bitter harshness of suffering . . . and all the contrasts and consequences which are only in harmony in order to hurt and which tear to pieces the same heart through all forms of pain!]

Delphine's moral test of endurance—in contrast to Sternheim's—is to submit fully to her grief and to broaden her comprehension of the human mind by exploring the intensity of her own thoughts and emotions. The fragments are filled with her discovery of paradoxes that show up the gap between moral precepts and individual experience: the superiority of slight hope—even over reason-fueled courage, patience, and resignation (D, II: 163); the relativity of moral guilt, to be determined by the degree of sensibility of which each individual is capable (D, II: 173–74); and even the limits of education, in light of each individual's particular sensibility and circumstances.

Les êtres distingués voudraient adapter le sort commun à leurs désirs; ils tourmentent la destinée humaine, pour la forcer à répondre à leurs voeux ardents . . . que voulez-vous faire de ces âmes de feu qui se dévorent elles-mêmes? . . . Quelle vérité, quelle leçon doivent-elles servir à consacrer? (D, II: 168–69) [Refined beings would like to adapt common fate to their desires; they torment human destiny in order to force it to comply with their burning wishes . . . what do you want to make of these souls of fire that devour themselves? . . . To which truth, which lesson must they devote themselves?]

If—on an explicit level—Delphine's sufferings seem to emphasize the centrality of her lover in her life, the subject of her melancholy-induced deliberations ultimately privileges her moral independence by drawing attention to the gap between social structure and individual uniqueness. The impossibility of fully codifying human behavior implicitly gives primacy to an open-ended educational program that will ultimately protect the uniqueness of the individual and her sensibility.

What of the Germany/France—or more appropriately here—the Weimar/Paris connection, however? To what extent do la Roche's and de Staël's representations of educated women reflect and reproduce cultural distinctions? On the surface, both novelists do use national identity as shorthand in their texts. In *Sternheim*, French characteristics are disparaged as corrupting German ones. The French *mentalité*[19] is dismissed as being preoccupied with marquises, fashion, manners, and a superficial knowledge of texts (St, 129), whereas the true (if rare) German genius is represented as benevolent, capable of transforming error into an occasion for intellectual discovery as well as able to depict nuanced moral shadings when representing very different characters (St, 132). De Staël's text also makes use of national characteristics as shorthand. It contrasts Delphine's French republican ideals with Léonce's feudal, reactionary beliefs, stemming from his half-French, half-Spanish heritage (D, I: 24), and this opposition seems to permit the denigration of Spanish values as convention-driven thought, exclusively preoccupied with public reputation and the claims of family honor. Even here, however, the antithesis of Spanish and French characteristics hardly masks de Staël's strategy of attempting to cast the aristocratic, royalist position as profoundly "anti-French," as "other."[20]

Despite the explicit bias in both texts, it is important to recognize the connection the novelists make between national characteristics and culturally learned habits of thought. For both la Roche and de Staël, ideology seems to play a more decisive role than blood, land, or history in determining cultural difference.[21] In effect, it is interesting to read both texts with the hindsight provided by Suzanne Nash's fascinating reading of de Staël's *De l'Allemagne*. "One of the most important stakes of [de Staël's] German story is the separation she would establish between individual 'national' cultures and an ideology of 'nationalism' . . . a specifically nineteenth-century phenomenon that fuses nationality (a cultural group's speaking the same language and sharing the same customs) with patriotism, that is, loyalty to a sovereign patriotic state. Mme de Staël's concept of nationhood was different. It derived from the popular revolutionary point of view that a 'nation' was not based on ethnicity but on a shared commitment to individual freedom and the common good as opposed to privilege and particular interests (N, 19)."[22]

Sophie von la Roche writes well before Mme de Staël drafts her "*patrie de la pensée*" (N, 17) or "homeland for the mind" (N, 27); nonetheless, her novel seems to contribute to such a reading of nationhood—especially in the symmetry of its beginning and end. The novel begins with the mapping of Sternheim's mixed heritage and ends with her grafting innovative German social structures onto an English context. Moreover, by the end of the novel, Sternheim has finally broken free of her infatuation with England and its customs: "*Mein Enthusiasmus für England ist endlich erloschen; es ist nicht das Vaterland meiner Seele*" (St, 334) [My enthusiasm for England is finally extinguished; it is not the fatherland of my soul]—and this, ironically, when it becomes clear that she will live out her days in England as Lady Seymour. As if this were not enough, the novel ends with the news that her two sons will be continuing two branches of an established, noble English family—reproducing, in effect, Sternheim's own dual national heritage and the double vision it entails. Symbolically, la Roche's novel helps set the stage for de Staël's European vision of 1810. As Nash puts it: . . . [Staël's] text on Germany sets out to "de-racinate" not only French neoclassicism, but certain outgrowths of German national culture for importation and hybridization, if not transplantation and imitation, abroad (N, 17).

I am tempted to conclude: a certain refusal to identify too closely with nationalism, that is, an implicit skepticism vis-à-vis a patriarchal definition of community is present in both la Roche's and de Staël's works. Even in the more general context of national difference, it is the individual's intellectual and cultural complexities that dominate—either by being linked to her radical potential to define communal values, the primacy of individual freedom (as in *De l'Allemagne*), or represented as her ability to disrupt the clear-cut distinctions separating one culture from another.

I don't want to overemphasize the parallels between de Staël's and la Roche's novels; they do define the interrelationship of female self and community differently. La Roche tends, paradoxically, to highlight *Bildung* in a nineteenth-century way (with a few key exceptions), as the passing down of norms to facilitate the integration of the individual into a pre-existing, class-based society, whereas de Staël seems to draw on an earlier Enlightenment ideology that might allow an individual to develop his or her inherent abilities.[23] Still, the overlap between de Staël's and la Roche's representations does extend beyond their conceptualizing cultural difference as a question of *mentalité*. Both contribute to imagining a space for female experience that emphatically calls into question Rousseau's assumption that female education should be geared to teaching women submission to and dependence on a male partner.[24] And while both novelists imagine a space marked by exile and grim crisis, that space also does symbolize a place where women—in defiance of prevailing traditions—might hone their own judgment in order to define both their own conduct and their intellectual goals.

Notes

1. Monika Nenon, *Autorenschaft und Frauenbildung: Das Beispiel Sophie von La Roche* (Würzburg: Koenigshausen und Neumann, 1988), pp. 81–82, p. 138. Monika Nenon points out that the most important elements of *Empfindsamkeit* are the virtues of compassion and sympathy, that is, the capacity for moral sentiments or feelings. Nenon also identifies the three fundamental elements that should determine—according to la Roche—female conduct: *Herz* (heart), *Verstand* (intellect), and *Tugend* (virtue).

2. Madame de la Fite translated la Roche's *Sternheim* in 1773–74, and Sophie Mereau is one German translator of de Staël's works. All translations in this chapter from the French and the German are my own.

3. Helga Meise, "Der Frauenroman: Erprobungen der 'Weiblichkeit'" and Reinhard Nickisch's "Briefkultur: Entwicklung und sozialgeschichtliche Bedeutung des Frauenbriefs im 18. Jahrhundert," in Brinker-Gabler's *Deutsche Literatur von Frauen, Band I. Vom Mittelalter bis zum Ende des 18. Jahrhunderts* (München: Beck, 1988), p. 439, 409.

4. Mme de Staël, *De l'Allemagne, Tome I* (Paris: Garnier-Flammarion, 1968), p. 144. Subsequent references to this work will be cited as (DA, page no.) in the body of this chapter.

5. Jean-Jacques Rousseau, *Émile, ou le traité de l'education* (Paris: Librarie de Firmin Didot, 1846), p. 77. It is worth recalling that Rousseau suggests waiting until the age of twelve before educating a male child; education until this age should remain "negative."

L'éducation consiste, non point à enseigner la vertu ni la vérité, mais à garantir le coeur du vice et l'esprit de l'erreur. Si vous pouviez ne rien faire et ne rien laisser faire; si vous pouviez amener votre élève sain et robuste à l'âge de douze ans . . . dès vos premières leçons les yeux de son entendement s'ouvriraient à la raison; sans préjugés, sans habitudes, il n'aurait rien en lui qui pût contrarier l'effet de vos soins" [Education does not consist in teaching virtue or the truth; it consists in protecting the heart from vice and the mind from error. If you could do nothing and allow nothing to be done; if you could bring your student—healthy and robust—to the age of twelve years . . . from his first lessons, the "eyes" of his comprehension would open to reason; without prejudices or habits, there would be nothing to thwart the effect of your care.] Subsequent references to this text will be cited as (E, V, [indicating the volume number] page no.).

6. In *Télémaque*, principles of good government are explored (the welfare and happiness of subjects should be of first concern to the king; the law is above the king; Mentor deplores the folly and cruelty of war; and one is innocent until proven guilty). In Fénélon's *Traité de l'éducation des filles* [*Treatise on the education of girls*] (1687), he argues that girls are not to read novels, plays, books on theology and philosophy, and that they are to be trained to be submissive spouses and good housewives.

7. Joan Kelly's critique of the *querelle des femmes* in her *Women, History, and Theory* articulates the drawbacks of such a method very clearly: "The power of women of rank was a weak foundation on which to rest hopes for women's ultimate emancipation . . ." (p. 93). Looking to "enlightenment and traditional sources of power" blinded early feminists to the powerful potential of the lower- and middle-class women—as it obscured those women's sufferings (pp. 93–4).

8. Monika Nenon points out that la Roche emphasizes class (*Stand*) over nature as determining education in contrast to Rousseau (Monika Nenon, p. 84).

9. Sophie von la Roche, *Geschichte des Fräuleins von Sternheim*, herausgegeben von B. Becker-Cantarino (Stuttgart: Reclam, 1983), p. 81, 277. Upon her arrival in England, Sternheim spends time reading historical, journalistic, and religious texts as a way to become acquainted with the *Nationalgeist* in England. Subsequent references to the novel will be indicated as (St, page no.).

10. Mme de Staël, "De l'étude" in *De l'influence des passions sur le bonheur des individus et des nations* in her *Oeuvres complètes*, 17 tomes, published by Auguste Louis Staël-Holstein (Paris: Treuttel et Wuertz, 1820–1821), p. 251, 254.

11. Mme de Staël, "Essai sur les fictions" in her *Oeuvres complètes*, 17 tomes (Paris: Treuttel et Wuertz, 1820–1821), p. 215.

12. It is interesting to contrast this educational program to the one issuing from the *querelle des femmes*, where it was a question of recovering "a true image of women—an image that could be safely internalized, to mobilize women's powers." The earlier feminists used "history mainly to find precedents

for women's governance (and hence their right to self-rule) and for their learning (of which they felt newly and unjustly deprived)" [Kelly, 83]. One strong example of such feminism is, of course, Christine de Pizan's *La cité des dames*.

13. Mme de Staël, *Delphine, Tomes I and II*, ed. Claudine Herrmann (Paris: des femmes, 1981), I: 330. This text will be referred to as (D, I, or D, II, page no.) in the body of the chapter.

14. Delphine describes her own education on D, I: 31–2 and 33, emphasizing her freedom from public opinion.

15. Kadish shows how the "anti-maternal" current in *Delphine* is tempered. "Although Stael's mothers too are censured, the narrative expression of the censure is feminized: that is to say, women's voices do the censuring, and thus their voices are empowered not only to deceive, as they often are in nineteenth-century novels, but also to propose alternatives to such deception" (90). In addition, Kadish points out, "the aristocratic women are presented as victims of the regressive social forces that bring down progressive efforts such as revolution" (96). The possibility of "successful maternity" is, in short, entertained and used as "a marker of successful politics" (98). Doris Kadish, "Censuring Maternity: *Delphine* and *La Rabouilleuse*" in her *Politicizing Gender. Narrative Strategies in the Aftermath of the French Revolution* (New Brunswick: Rutgers University Press, 1991).

16. Kadish, *Politicizing Gender*, p. 100.

17. Marie-Claire Vallois argues, in contrast, that *Delphine* is mostly about the impossibility of a feminine autobiography, an impossibility which becomes visible through the fragmented quality of Delphine's prose during her exile. Marie-Claire Vallois, "Voyage au pays des doubles: Ruines et mélancolies chez Mme de Staël" in *L'Esprit créateur* 25 (1985): 75–85.

18. Mme de Staël, *De la littérature considérée dans ses rapports avec les institutions sociales* (Paris: Flammarion, 1991), p. 361.

19. *Le Petit Robert* defines *mentalité* as: *"Ensemble des croyances et habitudes d'esprit qui informent et commandent la pensée d'une collectivité, et qui sont communes à chaque membre de cette collectivité."*

20. Eve Sourian elucidates the political allegory in *Delphine* by pointing out that the French Revolution is not only the historical framework of the novel, but also its subject (p. 43). She goes on to argue that "Delphine's democratic morality [is] based on honesty and integrity" whereas Léonce's value system resides on an "aristocratic concept of honor born of feudal society" (p. 44). Eve

Sourian, "*Delphine* and the Principles of 1789: 'Freedom, Beloved Freedom'" in Gutwirth's et al *Germaine de Staël. Crossing the Borders* (New Brunswick: Rutgers University Press, 1991), pp. 42–51.

21. It is interesting to note, along with Monika Nenon, that la Roche wrote several travelogues but that these texts focus on a very particular cultural goal: "*Es liegt ihr daran, zu erfahren, wie Frauen in anderen Ländern leben, welche Sitten und Gewohnheiten sie pflegen und wie hoch ihr Bildungsstandard ist*" [She is primarily concerned with learning how women live in different countries, which customs and habits they cultivate, and how high their standard of education is] (Nenon, 186). Her travel writings are primarily directed toward constructing a Frauengeschichte.

22. Suzanne Nash, "Nationalism and Cultural Diversity in Mme de Staël's *De l'Allemagne*, in *Kaleidoscope. Essays on Nineteenth Century French Literature in Honor of Thomas H. Goetz*, eds. G. Falconer and M. Donaldson-Evans (Toronto: Centre d'Etudes Romantiques Joseph Sablé, 1996), pp. 15–34.

23. These two definitions of *Bildung* are drawn from Rolf Selbmann's *Der deutsche Bildungsroman* (Stuttgart: Metzler Verlag, 1984), p. 2.

24. Again, Nenon is helpful in showing that Sternheim, while ending with and thus privileging marriage, does throw into relief the importance of a feminine, self-fulfilled and fulfilling lifestyle. The proliferation of unmarried and widowed women in the novel does seem to support Nenon's argument (NM, 95, 99).

Chapter 2

"*Vous appellés cela betrügen?*"
Slippery French Morals and German Bourgeois Virtues in Selected Writings by G. E. Lessing

Heidi M. Schlipphacke

The unnamed traveler in G. E. Lessing's comedy *Die Juden* [*The Jews*] (1749) espouses the moral of the text with the following line: "*Ich bin kein Freund allgemeiner Urtheile über ganze Völker*" (LM, I: 386) [I am no friend of generalizations concerning entire cultures].[1] Such is the lesson of the spirit of the Enlightenment in the eighteenth century—a rational tolerance of people of all cultures and classes. The respected traveler in *Die Juden* confesses that he is a Jew, and this revelation provides the opportunity for the education of the other figures. After overcoming his initial shock at the startling news: "*Ein Jude? grausamer Zufall!*" [A Jew? What a cruel coincidence. (LM, I: 410)], the Christian baron takes a step toward reconsidering his prejudice: "*O wie achtungswürdig wären die Juden, wenn sie alle Ihnen glichen!*" (LM, I: 411) [O how worthy of respect the Jews would be if they were all like you!] The early one-act comedy reflects Lessing's message of religious and cultural tolerance that informs his canonical drama *Nathan der Weise* [*Nathan the Wise*] (1779)—a drama in which Christians, Jews, and Muslims learn to respect and love one another. If one understands the words of the Jewish traveler in *Die Juden* to be a reflection of Lessing's own views on prejudice, then the polemics against France and the French that permeate a number of his writings would constitute an ideological contradiction. Lessing's frequent attacks on France and French aesthetics potentially call into question Lessing's revulsion to cultural and religious stereotypes. Beginning with his early theoretical writings and culminating in those works that coincide with the end of the Seven Years War (1756–63)—*Hamburgische Dramaturgie* [*Hamburg Dramaturgy*] (1767–68) and the comedy *Minna von Barnhelm* (1767)—Lessing's polemical attack on the French threatens to undermine the tolerant message of his best-known works. His frequent use of terms such as "*Galanterie*," (gallantry) "*Eitelkeit*," (conceit) and "*falsche Delikatesse*" (false delicacy) (LM, IX: 360) to describe French authors and manners reflects a polemics that cannot resist the use and abuse of national stereotypes.[2]

The following essay will explore the contradictory nature of Lessing's reception of France and the French. Whereas the use of negative stereotypes of the French in the *Hamburgische Dramaturgie* can be understood in part as a product of Lessing's attempt to construct a national German theater separate from the solidly established French academy, the representation of France and ridiculous French figures in his dramatic works seems, at times, to be unnecessarily negative. The line between polemics and ridicule becomes, especially in selected literary works, uncomfortably thin. Indeed, the infamous French Major Riccault in *Minna von Barnhelm* functions, I argue, not to further the plot in any way, but rather as a figure of ridicule, a negative example against which the German figures appear to be all the more honorable. In fact, critics have discussed the extent to which Lessing's final comedy balances tenuously on the border between comedy and tragedy. Riccault's function, I suggest, is to produce artificially the laughter from the audience necessary to a comedic work. In this sense, Lessing's representation of France and French figures—in *Minna* and selected other dramas—as stereotypical objects of ridicule contradicts the Enlightenment message of tolerance that he otherwise espouses.

In order to provide a context for my analysis of *Minna*, I will give not only a brief historical background of Lessing's relationship to France and French authors, but also his polemics against French classicism. Lessing's most scathing criticism of the French is achieved in the *Hamburgische Dramaturgie*, a series of reviews of dramas that provides a forum within which Lessing articulates his vision of a revived national German theater. However, Lessing's polemics against the French are, as will be shown, ambiguous and often contradictory. An analysis of *Minna*, however, will reveal less ambiguity with respect to France.

While Lessing's criticisms of the French in his theoretical works are often mitigated, these same stereotypes remain unquestioned in Lessing's dramas; here, French decadence and pompousness are often funny and even repulsive, but the relationship between these qualities and French national identity is never really questioned. Lessing's seemingly simplistic use of a French "other" in his dramas contradicts his otherwise "enlightened" engagement with difference.

I.

In an attempt to understand Lessing's polemical stance vis-à-vis France and French aesthetics, literary critics have pointed to the historical background of the Seven Years War (1756–63).[3] Although France and Prussia fought on opposite sides during the Seven Years War, Frederick the Great, the celebrated Prussian king, retained close ties with the established French academy. In his essay detailing Lessing's criticism of French classicist aesthetics, "Laokoon oder Lessings Kritik am französisch-preußischen Akademismus" [Laokoon or Lessing's Critique of the Franco-Prussian Academy], Gerhard Bartsch elucidates the extent to which Frederick identified with the French language and culture:

Unter der Regentschaft Friedrichs, der seiner Vorliebe für französische Kultur so weit folgte, daß er nie richtig deutsch sprechen lernte und 1756 Gottsched gestand: "Ich habe von Jugend auf kein deutsches Buch gelesen und ich rede es wie ein Kutscher", wurde die Akademie der Wissenschaften eine Institution der französischen Kolonie in Berlin, wie die führenden Namen Voltaire, Maupertuis und La Mettrie verraten. In Umkehrung der Gründungsabsicht Leibniz', nämlich die deutsche Sprache, Kultur und Geschichte zu pflegen, wurden nur Franzosen zur Akademie zugelassen, die in ihrer Landessprache vortrugen und veröffentlichten (21). [Under the regency of Frederick, who pursued his love of French culture to such an extent that he never really learned to speak German and confessed to Gottsched in 1756: "From my youth on I have read not one German book, and I speak it like a coachman." The Academy of Sciences became an institution of the French colony in Berlin, as the leading names Voltaire, Maupertuis and La Mettrie reveal. In a reversal of the growing plan of Leibnitz—that is, to nurture the German language, culture and history—only Frenchmen were allowed into the Academy, and they gave lectures and published in their native language.]

Frederick actively supported the founding of a literary academy in Berlin, but Bartsch shows that this academy was not primarily "German" in nature. Not only were well-known French authors such as Voltaire chosen to lead the academy, but Frederick himself identified strongly with the French language and culture.[4] Perhaps this is one reason why the argumentative Lessing turned down a position at the university in Königsberg—"*weil er dort eine jährliche Lobrede hätte auf den König halten müssen*" (Bartsch, 22) [because he would have had to give a yearly speech praising the king]. Frederick was distasteful to Lessing in large part due to his love of France. In the fifty-ninth piece of the *Hamburgische Dramaturgie*, Lessing laments: "*Denn leider gibt es Deutsche, die noch weit französischer sind, als die Franzosen*" (LM, X: 31) [For there are unfortunately Germans who are more French than the French themselves.]

As Gisela F. Ritchie has pointed out in her essay "Spuren des französischen Dramas bei Lessing" [*Traces of the French Drama in Lessing*], French was the language of the elite in the middle of the eighteenth century in Germany. In fact, well-educated Germans were more fluent in French than they were in German (120). Moreover, the "Akademie der Wissenschaften" in Berlin, along with others in the German states, was modeled after the French academy that was established in Paris in 1635 by Cardinal Richelieu (Bartsch, 6). This institution had the task of retaining the purity of the French language and elucidating a practical aesthetics for artists and craftsmen. More importantly, French dramatists such as Pierre Corneille, Jean Racine, Louis-Ferdinand Destouches, and others had a role in shaping the course of French letters via the academy.

Since the French academy was more established than any literary movement in Germany during the middle of the eighteenth century, it was French authors who had the most profound influence on the blossoming literary community in the German states. Whereas Johann Christoph Gottsched, the dramatist and author of *Versuch einer critischen Dichtkunst vor die Deutschen* (1730) [Attempt at a Critical Poetics for the Germans],[5] embraced the French model for tragedy based upon Aristotelian poetics, Lessing rejected the French model. It is not the task of this essay to elucidate the parameters of the French classicist aesthetics that Lessing rejects.[6] Rather, I will explore Lessing's radical and sometimes contradictory polemics against a generalized notion of

French aesthetics and culture in order to pinpoint his functionalization of France and French figures for his own theoretical and aesthetic purposes. Thus, Lessing's rejection of the French classicists and France in general strikes me as reactionary and functional and, in this sense, offers an example of how an otherwise enlightened thinker makes use of a cultural "other" in his works.[7]

II.

Perhaps the most often cited passages concerning Lessing's rejection of French classicism are contained in the seventeenth *Literaturbrief* [letter on literature] from the volume *Briefe die neueste Literatur betreffend* [Letters Concerning the Newest Literature]. These letters, published in 1759, provide a forum for Lessing to analyze the literary trends of the day.[8] The seventeenth letter underscores Lessing's radical break from the "Critische Dichtkunst" of Gottsched whose aesthetics were derived from the French classicists.[9] The letter begins in Lessing's famous rhetorical style:

> *Niemand, sagen die Verfasser der Bibliothek, wird leugnen, daß die deutsche Schaubühne einen großen Teil ihrer ersten Verbesserung dem Herrn Professor Gottsched zu danken habe. Ich bin dieser Niemand; ich leugne es geradezu. Es wäre zu wünschen, daß sich Herr Gottsched niemals mit dem Theater vermengt hätte* (LM,VIII: 41). [Nobody, say the editors of the *Biboliothek*, will deny that the German stage is indebted to Professor Gottsched for a great deal of its first improvements. I am this Nobody; I deny it outright. It would be desirable that Mr. Gottsched had never become involved with the theater.]

The seventeenth *Literaturbrief* signals Lessing's rejection of Gottsched's reception of the Greeks since this reception is based upon the French model. Thus, Lessing reduces Gottsched's work to an attempt to mimic the French theater:

> *Er verstand ein wenig Französisch und fing an zu übersetzen; er ermunterte alles, was reimen und Oui Monsieur verstehen konnte, gleichfalls zu übersetzen; [. . .] er wollte nicht sowohl unser altes Theater verbessern, als der Schöpfer eines ganz neuen sein. Und was für eines neuen? Eines französierenden; ohne zu untersuchen, ob dieses französierende Theater der*

deutschen Denkungsart angemessen sei oder nicht (LM, VIII: 42). [He understood a little French and began to translate. He likewise encouraged everyone who could rhyme or understand "Oui Monsieur" to translate—in short he didn't want to improve our old theater so much as he wanted to be the creator of a brand new one. And what kind of a new one? a Frenchifying one; without researching whether this Frenchifying theater was suitable to the German mentality or not.]

For Lessing, Gottsched's crime did not consist in his desire to revive a national German theater; rather, it consisted in his desire to "Frenchify" a German theater that, according to Lessing, had little in common with the French model.[10] In other words, Gottsched's theater lacked originality and, it is suggested, the taste befitting the German public.[11]

The present participle *"französierend"* can loosely be translated as "Frenchifying." Lessing's use of this word reveals his tendency to polemicize without a clear argument. Rather, the manner in which he uses the term *"französierend"* condemns an entire nation while simultaneously disallowing a rational argument. Indeed, nowhere in the seventeenth *Literaturbrief* does Lessing provide a clear basis for his scorn of Gottsched and the French theater. Instead, he introduces a third nationality into the equation that functions as a positive "other" vis-à-vis France: England. Thus, without providing a systematic criticism of French classicism, Lessing pits France against England and Shakespeare against Corneille and Racine. Moreover, far from providing a coherent reason as to why Shakespeare is superior to the French dramatists, Lessing suggests that it is a matter of taste.

Wenn man die Meisterstücke des Shakespeare, mit einigen bescheidenen Veränderungen, unsern Deutschen übersetzt hätte, ich weiß gewiß, es würde von bessern Folgen gewesen sein, als daß man sie mit den Corneille und Racine so bekannt gemacht hat. Erstlich würde das Volk an jenem weit mehr Geschmack gefunden haben, als es an diesen nicht finden kann; und zweitens würde jener ganz andere Köpfe unter uns erweckt haben, als man von diesen zu rühmen weiß. Denn ein Genie kann nur von einem Genie entzündet werden (LM, III: 43); [If one had translated the masterpieces of Shakespeare for our German citizens with a few minor changes, I am certain it would have brought about better consequences than those stemming from the fact that they have been so well acquainted with Corneille and Racine. Firstly, the people would have found much better taste in the former than they can find in the latter; and secondly, the former would have inspired vastly different minds than one knows were inspired by the latter. For genius can only be sparked by another genius.]

Shakespeare's superiority over Corneille and Racine, one suspects, is a product not least of all of an accident of birth: Shakespeare was no Frenchman and his works are thus unlikely to "Frenchify" their public. Lessing resorts to the concepts of taste (*Geschmack*) and genius (*Genie*)—concepts which can be used to condemn or ennoble, but which cannot be pinned down in terms of rules or methods. Rather, it is Lessing himself who assumes the authority of one who can recognize genius. Ostensibly, the German-speaking people would recognize genius were it to be presented to them; the French, on the other hand, have, according to Lessing, long mistaken mediocrity for genius.

This polemical strain appears again in the eighty-first piece of the *Hamburgische Dramaturgie* when Lessing asks the question: "*Will ich denn nun aber damit sagen, daß kein Franzose fähig sei, ein wirklich rührendes tragisches Werk zu machen?*" (LM, X: 127) [Do I mean to assert by all this that no Frenchman is capable of writing a really touching tragical play?][12] At this point, the author presents a short lesson on tolerance and prejudice. "*Ich würde mich schämen, wenn mir das nur eingekommen wäre*" (LM, X: 127). [I should be ashamed of myself if I had even thought this (Lange, 202).] However, the question is implicitly asked in the seventeenth *Literaturbrief*, and the explicit answer is, indeed, that a culture that Frenchifies could not produce a work of genius. Although Lessing qualifies his discussion by choosing to attack specific French dramatists, his diatribe ultimately condemns an entire culture:

> *Auch nach den Mustern der Alten die Sache zu entscheiden, ist Shakespeare ein weit größerer tragischer Dichter als Corneille; obgleich dieser die Alten sehr wohl, und jener fast gar nicht gekannt hat. Corneille kömmt ihnen in der mechanischen Einrichtung, und Shakespeare in dem Wesentlichen näher. Der Engländer erreicht den Zweck der Tragödie fast immer, so sonderbare und ihm eigene Wege er auch wählet; und der Franzose erreicht ihn fast niemals, ob er gleich die gebahnten Wege der Alten betrifft* (LM, VIII: 43). [Even if we judge based upon the rules of the Ancients, Shakespeare is a much greater tragedian than Corneille, although the latter was very familiar with the Ancients and the former

almost not at all. Corneille approaches them in terms of mechanics and Shakespeare resembles them more closely in essence. The Englishman achieves the goal of tragedy almost always, despite the unusual and eccentric methods he chooses. And the Frenchman achieves this almost never, even though he follows the established methods of the Ancients.]

Rather than comparing the two dramatists, Shakespeare and Corneille, in specific terms based on examples, Lessing shifts from using their names to their nationalities. Thus, while *der Engländer* refers directly to Shakespeare, it also connotes that Shakespeare's nationality is perhaps his most important characteristic. Likewise, Corneille is replaced by *der Franzose*, revealing that the dramatist's nationality plays, for Lessing, no small part in his inferiority to Shakespeare. Moreover, Lessing follows his criticism of Corneille with one of Voltaire, suggesting that one "*Franzose*" is as bad as the next.

If the seventeenth *Literaturbrief* can be said to level any coherent criticism against the French classicists, then it is the accusation of being too rigid. Corneille, Racine, and even Voltaire have all failed to produce a work of "genius," one that is entirely original. In the above citation, Corneille is not accused of ignorance of the Greeks. In fact, in the *Hamburgische Dramaturgie* (75–83), Lessing credits Corneille with understanding the letter of Aristotle's poetics without comprehending its spirit; this is precisely the criticism in the seventeenth *Literaturbrief*. The "Frenchman" is highly educated, but he lacks a heart. According to Lessing, Corneille achieves a mechanical fidelity to Aristotle while the less educated Shakespeare breaks the rules yet achieves the ends of genius. The Frenchman is correct, but the Englishman has a heart.

III.

In the *Hamburgische Dramaturgie* (1767–68), Lessing continues to criticize the French classicists for their rigid reception of Aristotle's poetics and for their lack of affect. The "pieces" of the *Hamburgische Dramaturgie* were conceived as reviews of plays that were performed at the newly opened theater in Hamburg where Lessing was employed as a critic. However, the individual reviews make up only a part of the *Hamburgische Dramaturgie*; the analyses of the plays themselves provide Lessing with the material through which he can provide a somewhat more systematic discussion of drama and aesthetics than is achieved in the *Briefe die neueste Literatur betreffend*. In the *Hamburgische Dramaturgie*, Lessing's criticism of the "Frenchmen" is more differentiated. While he continues to accuse Racine, Voltaire and, especially, Corneille of a lack of understanding when it comes to Aristotle, he also praises these authors at times. Perhaps more importantly, in the middle of his deconstruction of Corneille's Aristotle reception (piece 81), Lessing reflects on the evil of prejudice and the equality of all national cultures.

Despite Lessing's tendency to condemn prejudice in the abstract, the *Hamburgische Dramaturgie* nevertheless reproduces the general criticism leveled in the seventeenth *Literaturbrief*. Here, Lessing continues to accuse the French classicists of a mechanical knowledge that does not translate into genius. Just as Lessing criticizes Corneille for a mechanical but not spiritual fidelity to Aristotle in the seventeenth *Literaturbrief*, so does he level the same criticism against Racine in the fifty-ninth piece. Here, Lessing suggests that the French dramatists and, by extension, the French, are "unnatural." According to Lessing, Racine's kings and queens speak in a highly stylized manner that reflects a lack of a human element:

> *Ich habe es lange schon geglaubt, daß der Hof der Ort eben nicht ist, wo ein Dichter die Natur studieren kann. Aber wenn Pomp und Etikette aus Menschen Maschinen macht, so ist es das Werk des Dichters, aus diesen Maschinen wieder Menschen zu machen* (LM, X: 32). [I have believed for a long time that the court is precisely not the place where a poet can study nature. But when pomp and etiquette create machines out of people, then it is the work of the poet to create humans again from these machines.]

Lessing suggests that, like the dramas of Corneille, Racine's works adhere to a strict form without providing a human content. "*Pomp*" and "*Etikette*" are impressive, but these qualities alienate the audience rather than stimulating affective responses. Once again, *die Franzosen* are accused of following the Aristotelian rules of drama without understanding the essence of these rules.

The theme of the slavish French adherence to form at all costs recurs again and again in the *Hamburgische Dramaturgie*. Thus, in the forty-fifth piece, Lessing ridicules Voltaire's retention of Aristotle's unity of time in his play *Merope*. According to Lessing, Voltaire heaps event upon event within an improbably short span of time in order to remain true to a rule that is undermined through the sheer improbability of the resulting action. Such is also the gist of Lessing's criticism of the "*tyrannische Regeln*" (tyrannical rules) and the tendency of *die Franzosen* to subordinate themselves to these rules without understanding the larger vision underlying the rules themselves.[13]

The use of the terms "*tyrannische[n]*" and "*Gehorsam*" (obedience) implies that Lessing attributes not only a certain rigidity to *die Franzosen*, but also political conservatism. Indeed, Gerhard Bartsch has shown how Lessing's merciless polemics against the established French academy simultaneously reflects the author's liberal politics:[14]

> *Er (Lessing) durchschaute, daß die "freyen Künste" der Akademie ja nicht im luftleeren Raum angesiedelt waren und die systematische philosophische Begründung einer "reinen Kunst" ja nicht artistischer Selbstzweck war. Je rationaler die Kunst erklärt wurde, desto deutlicher erschien für Lessing auch ihre Kehrseite, nämlich ihre Abhängigkeit vom Träger dieser Ratio, d.h. von wem diese lehrbare Kunst eingesetzt wurde und damit ideologisch benutzbar war* (Bartsch, 7). [He (Lessing) perceived that the "free arts" of the Academy were not created in a void, and the systematic philosophical foundation of a "pure art" was not an artistic end in itself. The more rational the terms used to explain the art, the more clearly Lessing saw its reversal—namely, its dependence upon the carrier of this ratio: in other words, he who introduced this art form and to whom it was thus ideologically useful.]

Lessing's implicit criticism of the political servitude of *die Franzosen* in the *Hamburgische Dramaturgie* is underscored by his scorn for the choice of royalty and nobility as subjects of tragedy. Not only do Racine's kings and queens speak in an unnatural tone, but the court is not, according to Lessing, the proper context for a modern tragedy. For Lessing, the success of a tragedy can be measured by the degree of pity and fear it inspires in the audience (pieces 74–83). Kings and queens, according to Lessing, inspire rather awe than pity, an emotion that reflects a fear for one's own fate. In this sense, Lessing advocates a dramatic aesthetics in line with the French dramatist Denis Diderot: both dramatists envisioned the bourgeois citizen as the hero of their dramas. It is therefore ironic that Lessing praises Diderot's aesthetic theories and simultaneously condemns the aesthetic and moral tendencies of the entire French nation—as if Diderot himself were only an anomaly and not truly "French."

> *Man lasse aber diese Betrachtungen den Franzosen, von ihren Diderots und Marmontels, noch so eingeschärft werden: es scheint doch nicht, daß das bürgerliche Trauerspiel darum bei ihnen besonders in Schwang kommen werde. Die Nation ist zu eitel, ist in Titel und andere äußerliche Vorzüge zu verliebt; bis auf den gemeinsten Mann will alles mit Vornehmern umgehen; und Gesellschaft mit seinesgleichen ist so viel als schlechte Gesellschaft. Zwar ein glückliches Genie vermag viel über sein Volk; die Natur hat nirgends ihre Rechte aufgegeben, und sie erwartet vielleicht auch dort nur den Dichter, der sie in aller ihrer Wahrheit und Stärke zu zeigen verstehet* (LM, IX: 240) [But no matter how much their Diderots and Marmontels preach this to the French, it does not seem as though domestic tragedies were coming into vogue among them. The nation is too vain, too much enamoured of titles and other external favors; even the humblest man desires to consort with aristocrats and considers the society of his equals as bad society. True, a happy genius can exert great influence over his nation. Nature has nowhere resigned her rights and she is perhaps only waiting there for the poet who is to exhibit her in all her truth and strength. (Lange, 40)]

Once again, it is the French nation itself that is not human enough to embrace the bourgeois tragedy. Although Lessing admits that it is not unthinkable that the country would be moved by a true genius (vielleicht auch dort) [perhaps even there], the reader suspects that this is only a rhetorical nod to the improbable. French classical drama and, by extension, the French nation are too fixated on form and appearances to appreciate a drama more concerned with human emotions. As Lessing proclaims in the eightieth piece, *"die Franzosen [haben] noch kein Theater. Kein tragisches gewiß nicht! Denn auch die Eindrücke, welche die französische Tragödie macht, sind so flach und kalt!"* (LM, X: 124). [The French have as yet no theatre, certainly no tragic one. The impressions produced by French tragedy are so shallow, so cold (Lange, 199).] Along these lines, Lessing deems Voltaire's tragedy *Semiramis* "*kalt*" (cold) (LM, X: 127). Despite the reflections of dramatists such as Voltaire and Diderot (LM, X: 409) on the limitations of the French theater, these figures remain themselves French, and Lessing ultimately refuses to separate cultural stereotypes from aesthetics. Even when he praises the work of a French dramatist, as is the case in the eighty-fourth piece in which Lessing reviews Diderot's *Der Hausvater*, Lessing laments the inability of a French public to appreciate a work of art: "[. . .] *(ein) vortreffliche(s) Stück, welches den Franzosen nur so so gefällt—wenigstens hat es mit Müh' und Not kaum ein—oder zweimal auf dem Pariser Theater erscheinen dürfen—*" (LM, X: 140) [Since this excellent play—it only pleased the Parisians moderately—at least with a lot of effort was allowed to appear once or twice on the Parisian theater]. Thus, despite his debt to Diderot, Lessing nevertheless retains the cultural stereotype that condemns *die Franzosen* simultaneously to rigidity and moral laxity.[15]

The tension between a rigorous adherence to rules and a miscomprehension of these same rules resulting in, for Lessing, decadence, permeates Lessing's projection of *die Franzosen* throughout the *Hamburgische Dramaturgie*. In the forty-sixth piece, he once again faults the French for a superficial knowledge of rules that forecloses true comprehension: "*Ein anderes ist, sich mit den Regeln abfinden; ein anderes, sie wirklich beobachten. Jenes tun die Franzosen; dieses scheinen nur die Alten verstanden zu haben*" (LM, X: 377) [It is one thing to resign oneself to the rules and another to really observe them. The French do the former while it appears that only the Ancients have understood the latter]. *Die Franzosen* are educated, but nevertheless do not comprehend the essential truths of Aristotelian poetics. Indeed, *die Franzosen* function well as a projection screen against which Lessing can structure his own brand of dramatic aesthetics based on affect rather than form. Thus, in the seventy-fourth to eighty-third pieces, Lessing presents his own aesthetics based on the necessary affective attributes of pity (*Mitleid*) and fear (*Furcht*). In these pieces, Lessing presents a reading of Aristotle's *Poetics* in which he claims to comprehend the "spirit" of Artistotle where the French had merely understood its letter.[16]

In his formulation of a theory of dramatic aesthetics, Lessing continues to make use of a French counterpart. Thus, it is the dramatist Corneille against whom Lessing presents his interpretations of Aristotle. Lessing's polemical style seems to require a figure against whom he can argue, even when this model of argumentation entails contradiction. Thus, in his criticism of Corneille's interpretation of Aristotle, Lessing complains of Corneille's free reading of Aristotle. In other words, here is an example where *der Franzose* has not followed the rules, yet Lessing is not primarily interested in consistency. Where Corneille interprets Aristotle freely, arguing that a tragedy can stimulate either pity or fear, but must not necessarily produce both in the audience, Lessing is aghast. Indeed, he reiterates the argumentative sentence: *"Das ist grundfalsch!"* [That is entirely false] (LM, X: 105). And upon what does Lessing base his objection to Corneille? For Lessing, Corneille not only miscomprehends Aristotle; more importantly, he interprets Aristotle with too much freedom:

> *Die Regeln des Aristoteles sind alle auf die höchste Wirkung der Tragödie kulkuliert. Was macht aber Corneille damit? Er trägt sie falsch und schielend genug vor; und weil er sie doch noch viel zu strenge findet: so suchet er, bei einer nach der andern, quelque modération, quelque favorable interprétation* (LM, X: 129); [The rules of Aristotle are all calculated to produce the greatest tragic effect. What does Corneille do with them? He brings them forward falsely and inaccurately and because he still finds them too severe, he endeavors with one and the other to introduce *quelque modération, quelque favorable interprétation.* (Lange, 203)]

The reader of the *Hamburgische Dramaturgie* might wonder at this point if the author has suddenly changed his viewpoint. Whereas up until this point the French dramatists are criticized for their *too* strict adherence to the rules of the Ancients, Corneille is chastised for his loose interpretation of Aristotle. The criticism of *die Franzosen* as rigid and superficial is now juxtaposed with a potentially contradictory criticism, namely, that *die Franzosen* do *not* follow the letter of the established aesthetic rules, but rather interpret them according to a given context.

Despite the individual inconsistencies, Lessing is consistent in his use of *die Franzosen* as a projected "other" throughout the *Hamburgische Dramaturgie*. In fact, the inconsistencies reveal the extent to which the French are instrumentalized by Lessing in order to plant the seeds for a national German theater. However, this is not to say that a plurality of projections negates the force of Lessing's instrumentalization of *die Franzosen*. Lessing's insistence on a conflation of the French nation with certain negative stereotypes is tautological and is never successfully deconstructed in the *Hamburgische Dramaturgie*. Although the adjective *"französisch"* refers on the one hand to certain negative qualities that might or might not belong to an actual Frenchman, Lessing's insistence on the use of a national term underscores the prejudice that underlies its use. Thus, when Lessing suggests in the fifty-ninth piece that some Frenchmen might be worse than others and that some Germans might even be worse than the French, he nevertheless retains the national term as a referent for negative characteristics.[17]

The literary critics who have addressed Lessing's relationship to France have generally taken an apologetic stance. Both Gerhard Bartsch and Gonthier-Louis Fink ultimately attribute Lessing's criticism of the French to his polemical style, and, even, to a higher purpose—the construction of a national German theater. For Fink, Lessing is the Enlightenment thinker who preaches a message of tolerance, and his polemics against the French do not call this status into question. Indeed, even in the *Hamburgische Dramaturgie,* Lessing seems to withdraw his sword for a moment when he asks the rhetorical question in the eighty-first piece: "*Will ich denn nun aber sagen, daß kein Franzose fähig sei, ein wirklich rührendes tragisches Werk zu machen? daß der volatile Geist der Nation einer solchen Arbeit nicht gewachsen sei?*" (LM, X: 127) [Do I mean to assert by all this that no Frenchman is capable of writing a really touching tragical play? that the volatile spirit of the nation is unable to grapple with such a task?] Here, in the midst of his indictment of Corneille, Lessing seems to reflect upon his own instrumentalization of the French. Throughout the first eighty pieces of the *Hamburgische Dramaturgie*, with few exceptions, Lessing has indeed suggested that *die Franzosen* are incapable of producing a truly moving drama, or, were an exceptional Frenchman such as Diderot to produce such a work as *Der Hausvater*, the French themselves would not recognize its greatness. However, Lessing seems to reject everything he has already written when he answers his own question:

> *Ich würde mich schämen, wenn mir das nur eingekommen wäre. Deutschland hat sich noch durch keinen Bouhours lächerlich gemacht. Und ich, für mein Teil, hätte nun gleich die wenigste Anlage dazu. Denn ich bin sehr überzeugt, daß kein Volk in der Welt irgendeine Gabe des Geistes vorzüglich vor andern Völkern erhalten habe. Man sagt zwar: der tiefsinnige Engländer, der witzige Franzose. Aber wer hat denn die Teilung gemacht? Die Natur gewiß nicht, die alles unter alle gleich verteilet. Es gibt evensoviel witzige Engländer als witzige Franzosen, und ebensoviel*

tiefsinnige Franzosen, als tiefsinnige Engländer; der Praß von dem Volke aber ist keines von beidem (LM, X: 127) [I should be ashamed of myself if I had even thought this. Germany has not as yet made herself ridiculous by any Bouhours and I, for my part, have not the least inclination towards the part. I am convinced that no people in the world have been specially endowed with any mental gift superior to that of any other people. It is true we say the meditative Englishman, the witty Frenchman. But who made this distinction? Certainly not nature, who divided all things equally among all. There are as many witty Englishmen as Frenchmen and as many meditative Frenchmen as meditative Englishmen, while the bulk of the people is neither one nor the other.] (Lange, 202)

With this answer, Lessing seems to mouth the words of the traveler in *Die Juden* and the Enlightenment moral of *Nathan der Weise*. National stereotypes, Lessing seems to suggest here, are founded upon ignorance and cannot be extended to an entire culture.

Although Lessing feels compelled to thematize his own projections of *die Franzosen*, I suggest that he does not, with this one disclaimer, overcome a methodology that makes polemic use of a French "other." Indeed, even the enlightened response to his own question begins with a snide comment about Bouhours, the Frenchman who claimed that Germans had no sense of "*Esprit*" (Fink, 105). Moreover, as Lessing continues to reflect upon his reception of France and the French, his writing slips quickly into the old stereotypes:

Ich will bloß sagen, was die Franzosen gar wohl haben könnten, daß sie es noch nicht haben: die wahre Tragödie. Und warum noch nicht haben?— Dazu hätte sich der Herr von Voltaire selbst besser kennen müssen, wenn er es hätte treffen wollen. Ich meine, sie haben es noch nicht; weil sie es schon lange gehabt zu haben glauben. Und in diesem Glauben werden sie nun freilich durch etwas bestärkt, das sie vorzüglich vor allen Völkern haben; aber es ist keine Gabe der Natur: durch ihre Eitelkeit (LM, X: 127f). [What then do I mean? I mean to say that the French might very well have what as yet they have not got, a true tragedy; and why have they not got it? Voltaire ought to have known himself very much better if he meant to alight on the reason. I mean they have not got it because they deem they have had it for a long time; in this belief they are certainly confirmed by something they possess beyond all other nations, by their vanity, but this is no gift of nature.] (Lange, 202).]

What began as a seemingly sincere reflection on the unproductive nature of national stereotypes has degenerated into a diatribe on French conceit. Although Lessing thematizes his own prejudices within the *Hamburgische Dramaturgie* and contradicts his own assertions about *die Franzosen* within the text, the above reflection ultimately does not change the fact that the text consistently instrumentalizes *die Franzosen* as a negative "other." Contradictions and reflections aside, Lessing's tautological use of the concept of "Frenchness" as a negative modifier always refers back to the country whose national theater and language were oppressive to Lessing.

IV.

The representation of France and French figures in Lessing's dramas are, I suggest, not in the least ambiguous. Whereas his general criticism of *die Franzosen* can be summarized as a tension between a too rigid adherence to rules and a miscomprehension of the spirit of these rules on the part of the French, this projection is, I argue, even more simplified in Lessing's dramas. Although France and French figures do not play a major role in Lessing's dramas—comedies or tragedies—, minor scenes reveal an even less differentiated image of Frenchness in Lessing's dramas than in the *Hamburgische Dramaturgie*. Thus, where Lessing ultimately questions his own prejudices in the *Hamburgische Dramaturgie*, no such reflection takes place in the dramas. Rather, I suggest, the appearance of France and/or French figures constructs an image of Frenchness that is by no means rigid; instead, France and French figures are associated with "lawlessness" and decadence. Whereas Lessing's projection of *die Franzosen* in the *Hamburgische Dramaturgie* constructs a loose image of slavish devotion to meaningless rules, this stereotype is overturned via minor figures in Lessing's dramas.[18] An even more simplistic projection deems *die Franzosen* ridiculous and decadent. Although this image partially contradicts the stereotype put forth in the *Hamburgische Dramaturgie*, it nonetheless perpetuates the gesture that instrumentalizes France as a negative "other."

France appears as a negative signifier in Lessing's first domestic drama, *Miß Sara Sampson* (1755)—a play that is also considered to be the first German bourgeois tragedy. In the drama, a virtuous young woman, Sara, has been seduced by the wayward but reforming Mellefont, who has taken her away from her father without his consent. Sara's greatest wish is to be married to Mellefont, whom she loves, since she believes that each day outside of the bonds of marriage constitutes a sin against God and her father. In fact, her moral rectitude leads her to the contradictory decision of refusing to marry Mellefont if this sacred act is to take place in the "barbaric" locality of France.[19]

Sara's arguments in this scene are unnecessarily convoluted. Indeed, I suggest that the introduction of the "France problem" contributes very little to the movement of the drama. Sara's role as a model for vulnerable bourgeois feminine virtue is based primarily on her insistence on marriage regardless of the opinions of the world. Indeed, her aversion to France cannot even be solely a product of her filial love, since she has left her father to be with Mellefont, and she assumes that this father would not support her marriage to him in any country. Her aversion to France appears to be superfluous to the general plot of the drama.

France functions as a negative mirror for German virtue in *Miß Sara Sampson*. This gesture is repeated in minor scenes in three of Lessing's comedies: *Der Freygeist* (1749), *Die Juden* (1749), and *Minna von Barnhelm oder das Soldatenglück* (1767).[20] In both early comedies *Der Freygeist* and *Die Juden*, France and Frenchness occur as negative tropes associated with two servants (Johann and Christian).[21] In each case, the servant is represented as ignorant, and both men see France as an exotic ideal. In both comedies, France is the topic of a seemingly marginal conversation between servants, and these particular scenes contribute little to the movement of the plot. They do, however, encode France and Frenchmen with the barbaric, ridiculous, and pompous qualities that make them ideal comic figures. The topic of France in these dramas is seemingly arbitrary and gratuitous. However, within the context of Lessing's subtext on France, it serves two purposes: it establishes the comic figures as fools, and it once again locates France as the cultural ideal of such fools.

V.

The above marginal references to France provide the groundwork for Lessing's instumentalization of France and Frenchmen in the *Hambur-*

gische Dramaturgie and his last and most successful comedy *Minna von Barnhelm* (1767). France is associated with decadence and insubstantial pomp, and the figures who exoticize this country are themselves fools—serving ultimately to point to the superiority of their Germanic masters. Although the use of France in these dramas seems to be gratuitous, Lessing constructs an intertextual narrative of France and Frenchmen as ridiculous and, ultimately, comedic. In fact, this is, I suggest, the function of the Major Riccault de la Marlinière in *Minna von Barnhelm*.[22] Riccault is the best-known French figure in Lessing's dramatic work, and this figure epitomizes Lessing's intertextual construction of France and Frenchmen as ridiculous and funny—as negative mirrors of a more virtuous and serious Germany.

An entire scene is devoted to the Frenchman Major Riccault in *Minna von Barnhelm*. While Riccault basically embodies the characteristics associated with France in the earlier dramas and, later, in the *Hamburgische Dramaturgie*, he commands a greater presence than the references to France in the earlier dramas. For this reason, critics have oscillated between an interpretation of Riccault's function as superfluous[23] and an understanding of Riccault as a negative image of the virtuous Tellheim and even Minna.[24] Fritz Martini sees Riccault as the figure who introduces the concept of "play" into the drama—a concept that Minna utilizes in her discourse with Tellheim.[25] Riccault certainly functions in part along the lines of the France-loving servants in the earlier comedies, as a ridiculous figure against whom Tellheim can be judged.[26] Moreover, his presence does not, I contend, further the plot of the drama in any way. In this sense, Riccault is as gratuitous as any of the nods to France in Lessing's earlier works. Indeed, based on Lessing's discussion of plot (*Handlung*) in his theoretical writings on the fable ("Abhandlungen über die Fabel" [1759]), Riccault's presence in the drama remains a riddle. Lessing insists that a good plot contains nothing superfluous or gratuitous (LM, VII: 429). However, I will show that the figure Riccault does nothing to further the plot of the drama, and is in no way instrumental to the outcome. Instead, I put forth the hypothesis that Riccault's function is rather generic. In other words, comedic and ridiculous figures in Lessing's texts are often associated in some way with France, and the Frenchman Riccault serves to keep *Minna von Barnhelm* funny.

Critics of *Minna von Barnhelm* have consistently discussed the generic status of the drama. Indeed, Judith Aikin, Heinz Stolte, and

Karl Guthke have all suggested that the figure Tellheim is tragic while Minna is a comic figure.[27] These attempts to reconcile the drama to its proper genre (*Lustspiel*) reveal the extent to which Lessing's final comedy wavers on a tenuous border between comedy and tragedy.[28] Although the outcome is ultimately happy (Minna and Tellheim become engaged to be married), scenes and figures in the drama often seem more tragic than comic. Figures such as the recently widowed and impoverished Lady Marloff are neither ridiculous nor comic.

The relative virtue of all figures in *Minna von Barnhelm* except for Riccault threatens to undermine the comedic nature of the drama according to Lessing's own conception of comedy. In the *Hamburgische Dramaturgie*, Lessing defines what he considers to be the function of comedy (LM, IX: 303–04): For Lessing, a successful comedy is funny, and the laughter of the audience should lead its members to reflect upon their own behavior. In this sense, a comedy should function as a moral warning to the virtuous and licentious alike: those behaviors which strike the audience as ridiculous and funny are precisely those that one should avoid emulating. In fact, people do not want to be laughed at. The laughter itself reminds one of his/her own real and potential vices via the funny figures who commit these sins on the stage. Thus, Lessing suggests that it is not necessary for figures in the play itself to be reformed. It is ultimately the reception of the comedy that is crucial, and successful reception is based upon laughter. Those who laugh at the comical rogues and fools on the stage will, according to Lessing, be more likely to avoid the same behaviors in their own lives.

In the *Hamburgische Dramaturgie*, Lessing connects the necessary laughter of the audience with the immoral and ridiculous behavior of comedic figures.[29] While the servants in *Die Juden* and *Der Freygeist* represent comedic figures in this sense, *Minna von Barnhelm* is notably lacking in this kind of comedic figure.[30] Although all characters have weaknesses of some sort, only one of them is truly ridiculous in the manner Lessing describes in the *Hamburgische Dramaturgie*—Riccault de la Marlinière.[31] The hero of the play, which takes place in the aftermath of the Seven Years War, is Tellheim, a recently discharged officer and Minna's wayward beloved who is prone to the weakness of rigidity; however, critics have emphasized the heroic and tragic nature of this figure. Indeed, Tellheim's resistance to Minna rests upon his desire to be a suitable and honorable husband to her—a role that is called into question by an examination of Prussian officials into money lost during Tellheim's tenure as officiator over Minna's town in Saxony. Tellheim is, however, free of all guilt, and true to Minna in all regards. Minna herself is a witty and faithful lover, certainly more playful than Tellheim, but no less serious in her desire to be legally wed to him.

Whereas the servants and minor figures in earlier comedies are sometimes themselves ridiculous and debauched, all minor figures in *Minna von Barnhelm* with the exception of Riccault are likable and, in essence, good. In fact, Tellheim's servant "Just" is so loyal that he begs to remain with Tellheim even without pay. Although he is clearly prone to drinking and fighting, this servant, in contrast to his counterparts in *Der Freygeist* and *Die Juden*, has acquired solid values. The same can be said of Tellheim's good friend and former guard, Paul Werner. While prone to a mercenary existence as a soldier, Paul Werner is nonetheless a true friend to Tellheim, offering all of his money to his impoverished friend. Franziska, Minna's maid, who replaces the "Lisettes" of Lessing's earlier comedies, is likewise true to her mistress.[32] In fact, whereas the earlier Lisettes thrive on good-natured pranks, Franziska is more serious than Minna herself. It is she who decides that Riccault is nothing but a *Spitzbube* (rogue) (LM, II: 233), and she resists Minna's games with Tellheim at each turn. The same can be said of the other minor figures in the drama: the proprietor of the guest house is greedy, but ultimately honest and good. Even Lady Marloff, who mourns the loss of her husband who had been a friend of Tellheim, is so good that she desires to pay her husband's debts to Tellheim despite the fact that she herself is in dire need of money. Strohschneider-Kohrs has even suggested that the dialectical relationships between the figures are crystallized in the economic metaphors—in the constant tension between *geben* (give) and nehmen (take) (102).

Indeed, everyone in the play is desirous of giving others money except for the Frenchman Riccault. Based upon Lessing's definition of the function of comedy, I contend that Riccault is the only truly funny figure in the comedy, and thus the only figure capable of creating a laughter in the audience that would remind its members of their own flaws. It is, I suggest, Riccault who brings the drama back to the realm of comedy, although he certainly contributes little to the plot. It can likewise not be seen as accidental that Riccault is French. An intertextual conception of France and Frenchness that runs through Lessing's works lends a ridiculous, debauched, and therefore comedic nature to Riccault by virtue of his French origins.

The figure Major Riccault de la Marlinière appears in a single scene in the drama (IV: 2), and his first words are in French: "*Est-il permis, Monsier le Major?*" (LM, II: 227). Franziska responds to him as to a monster: "*Was will das? Will das zu uns?*" (LM, II: 227). [What is that? Is that for us?" (Meech, 154)]. Riccault is looking for Major Tellheim so that he can impart to him the good news of Tellheim's pardon by the Prussian officials. However, those critics who have argued that Riccault serves as a necessary messenger in the drama should take into account the response to this news.[33] Minna's response to Riccault's news is to be pleased, but she does not ask any further questions of Riccault. Indeed, when the news is brought in an official form by a "*Feldjäger,*" (soldier), Minna is just as astonished as if she had never heard it: "*Franziska, hörst du?—Der Chevalier hat doch wahr geredet!*" (LM, II: 251) [Do you hear that, Franziska? . . . The chevalier was speaking the truth after all! (Meech, 179)]. Her response at this moment reveals that neither Franziska nor Minna had believed a word spoken by Riccault, and this is why it does not occur to Minna to tell Tellheim the good news. In this sense, Riccault does not further the plot as a necessary messenger, since his message falls upon deaf ears; he is immediately perceived by Minna and Franziska as a frivolous Frenchmen, and as such incapable of telling the truth.

Riccault attempts to convey his message to Minna mostly in French intermingled with tortured German. Although Minna admits that she can speak French, as all educated young women could at the time, she refuses to speak it on German-speaking soil. Thus, in response to Riccault's question: "*Sie sprek nit Französisch, Ihro Gnad?*" (LM, II: 228), [You speak not French, your Grace? (Meech, 155)], Minna reflects a national sentiment that refuses to allow Germany to be colonized by the French language: "*Mein Herr, in Frankreich würde ich es zu sprechen suchen. Aber warum hier? Ich höre ja, daß Sie mich verstehen, mein Herr. Und ich, mein Herr, werde Sie gewiß auch verstehen; sprechen Sie, wie es Ihnen beliebt*" (LM, II: 228) [Mein Herr, I would try to speak it in France. But why here? I can see that you understand me, mein Herr. And I, mein Herr, will most certainly understand you. Speak as you like best (Meech, 155)]. Minna embodies here a national superiority, since she can speak French, but chooses to converse in German, and the

Frenchman Riccault is rendered yet more ridiculous by his attempts to speak German: *"Gutt, gutt! Ik kan auk mik auf deutsch explizier"* (LM, II: 228) [Good, good. I can explain myself in German also . . . (Meech, 155)].³⁴ It is impossible for Riccault to speak a grammatically correct German sentence, or one that does not contain a French word. Thus, although we assume that Minna herself is multilingual, the morally and intellectually inferior Riccault can barely communicate in German.

By Minna's prompting, Riccault reveals himself to be an ideal comedic figure: he is pompous, lacks honor, is a gambler, and desirous of money. More importantly, he is French. His inflated name provides real comedy to an otherwise serious drama with a happy ending:

> *RICCAULT. Mein Namen wünscht Ihro Gnad?—Vous voyés en moi—Ihro Gnad seh in mik le Chevalier Riccault de la Marlinière, Seigneur de Pret-au-vol, de la Branch de Prensd'or—Ihro Gnad steh verwundert, mik aus so ein groß, groß Familie zu hören, qui est véritablement du sang Royal* (LM, II: 229–30). [You wish my name, Your Grace? . . . Vous voyez en moi . . . Your Grace see in me le Chevalier Riccault de la Marlinière, Seigneur de Prêt-au-vol, de la Branche de Prensd'or . . . Your Grace is amazed to hear that I am from such a great, great family, which is certainly of the royal blood . . . (Meech, 156)].

Riccault's name thus reveals his character: thief and money grubber and a representative of the French nobility. However, Riccault is by no means particularly nationalistic, and reveals his inferiority by his lack of loyalty to any particular country. He has served in St. Marino, Poland and Prussia, and admits that he presently lives by gambling: *"Was ein Honnêt-homme von mein Extraction kann anders haben für Resource, als das Spiel?"* (LM, II: 230). [An honnet-homme of my extraction, what other resource can he have but the cards? (Meech, 157)].

Minna feels pity for Riccault, and offers him money to gamble at his discretion. This is the point where Riccault functions as the ridiculous *Spieler* to which Lessing refers in his description of the laughter that comedy stimulates. Every other figure in the drama refuses to accept money. Tellheim is in dire need of funds but will not accept any help from friends or Minna. In fact, this is the central reason why he feels he cannot marry her. All figures in the drama desire a position where they give more than they receive from others, yet Riccault not only hints at his need for money to a total stranger, but greedily accepts all she offers him.[35] In stark contrast to the other figures in the play, Riccault cannot even wait for Minna to finish her sentence before taking her money.

Although Minna, too, is a "player," she is shocked when Riccault suggests that he will cheat (LM, II: 232).[36] Riccault admits he does not comprehend Minna's horror at cheating; in fact, he prefers to think about it as having an impact on one's own luck, taking matters into one's own hands: "*Comment, Mademoiselle? Vous appellés cela betrügen? Corriger la fortune, l'enchainer sous ses doits, être sûr de son fait, das nenn die Deutsch betrügen? betrügen! Oh, was ist die deutsch Sprak für ein arm Sprak! für ein plump Sprak!*" (LM, II: 232) [Comment, Mademoiselle? Vous appellés cela cheating? Corriger la fortune, l'enchainer sous ses doits, être sûr de son fait, that the Germans call cheating? Cheating? Oh the German language she is so poor! so clumsy! (Meech, 159)]. In naming Germans, Riccault underscores the nationalist prejudices that he represents.[37] His French values are in line with those figures from earlier dramas and even with Lessing's comments about *die Franzosen* in the *Hamburgische Dramaturgie*. He is pompous, conceited and, ultimately, ridiculous. He doesn't comprehend true "German" values such as honesty and honor. He derides the German language since he himself is, we are to suppose, too ignorant to learn the language of the country where he works and lives.[38] Even his concept of "play" is corrupt. Thus, as a counterhypothesis to Martini's thesis that Riccault's function is to introduce the important concept of "play" into the drama, I suggest that Minna has been "playing" long before Riccault came upon the scene. She herself admits that she enjoys light gambling, and she has taken Tellheim's ring from the proprietor with the vague intention of using it to trick Tellheim. However, Riccault's concept of "play" shocks her, and serves rather as a negative example for those who enjoy Minna's playful character.

Riccault is "comedic" in Lessing's sense. He stimulates laughter through his vices, many of which are ostensibly a product of his French origins. He is, I assert, the only funny character in the drama, and this is where his function lies. His good news falls on deaf ears, since no one would believe such a rogue, and he likewise never reappears in the drama. Tellheim himself merely asserts that Riccault is no friend of his, and that is the end of the discussion (LM, II: 241). Tellheim and Riccault are polar opposites, and therein lies part of Riccault's function. As the single figure in the comedy at whom one can laugh without risk of identification, Riccault functions as the servants Christoph and Johann do in *Die Juden* and *Der Freygeist*, as negative mirror images of their more honorable masters. Riccault serves to bring humor back into a drama that becomes, at times, very serious. We are to assume that Riccault will never be reformed; indeed, he never returns with money for Minna. However, as Lessing suggests in the *Hamburgische Dramaturgie*, it is not important that rogues like Riccault be reformed. Rather, their function is to make the audience laugh, and to stimulate its members to reflection on their own behavior. Riccault is indeed the only figure in the drama who needs to be reformed, and he carries thus the burden of comedy upon his weak French shoulders.

VI.

Critics have often suggested that Lessing's digressions from the message of cultural and religious tolerance embodied in *Nathan der Weise* are insubstantial.[39] In *Nathan*, members from three religions—Judaism, Christianity, and Islam—are brought together as family, and the three religions are deemed equal. However, this text does not undo the instrumentalization of France and the French in the dramas in question and the *Hamburgische Dramaturgie*. Especially in the dramas, where no mitigating messages of tolerance accompany negative representations of France and the French, Lessing uses these tropes as a negative example and/or as a comedic device. The use of French motifs in the dramas discussed here can be seen as gratuitous in terms of plot enhancement. The Enlightenment hero Lessing constructs an intertextual conception of France and the French which ultimately equates France with decadence, ridicule, and the negative example of a good German. Lessing's use of France in his dramas reflect the thesis put forth by Max Horkheimer and Theodor Adorno in *Dialektik der Aufklärung*: the "progress" associated with the Enlightenment is always predicated upon exploitation. Lessing's instrumentalization of France in his writings is perhaps minor, but it reflects a mechanism of objectification endemic to the project of the Enlightenment.

Notes

All quotations from Lessing's works follow the edition: Gotthold Ephraim Lessing, *Sämmtliche Schriften*, ed. Karl Lachmann (Stuttgart: Göschen, 1886). Henceforth cited only as LM together with the volume and page number.

    1. All translations of the German, unless otherwise noted, are the author's.

    2. See also Gonthier-Louis Fink, "Nationalcharakter und nationale Vorurteile bei Lessing," *Nation und Gelehrtenrepublik: Lessing im europäischen Zusammenhang*, eds. Wilfried Barner and Albert M. Reh (Detroit: Wayne State University Press, 1983), pp. 91–120.

    3. See Robin Harrison's elucidation of the historical background for Lessing's *Minna von Barnhelm* in *Lessing: Minna von Barnhelm* (London: Grant and Cutler, 1985), pp. 9–11.

    4. In his essay, Gerhard Bartsch includes the following anecdote:

Voltaire konnte noch 1750 mitteilen: "Ich befinde mich hier in Frankreich, man spricht nur unsere Sprache. Das Deutsche ist blos für Soldaten und Pferde." Es brauchte einige Generationen, um der deutschen Muttersprache als Bildungsträger und Kulturvermittler überhaupt erst Anerkennung zu verschaffen (17–18) [Voltaire could still report in 1750: "I find myself here in France; one speaks only our language. German is only for soldiers and horses." It took some generations for the German language to receive any recognition as a medium for culture and education.]

    5. Gottsched's text went through four different editions between 1730–1751.

    6. For such an essay, see especially Gerhard Bartsch. Amadou Booker Sadji also addresses Lessing's rejection of French classicism in *Lessing und das französische Theater* (Stuttgart: Hans-Dieter Heinz, 1982).

    7. See also Gonthier-Fink, who describes how Lessing's education was focused in large part on the French language and literary legacy (1983, 99, 100).

    8. Lessing conceived of the idea for the volume together with his friends Friedrich Nicolai and Moses Mendelssohn. However, critics debate the extent to which Nicolai and Mendelssohn were involved in the production of the letters. See Wolfgang Bender, Afterword, *Briefe die neueste Literatur betreffend* by G. E. Lessing (Stuttgart: Reclam, 1972), pp. 483–84.

9. Amadou Booker Sadji asserts the following: "*Allerdings kann man mit Sicherheit feststellen, daß ab der Periode der Veröffentlichung dieser Rezension die Kluft zwischen Lessing und den französischen Tragikern sich in einem unerhörten Tempo vergroßerte, um endlich im 17. Literaturbrief zum endgültigen Bruch zu führen*" (91). ["In any case, one can ascertain with some confidence that, starting with the period of the publication of this review, the gulf between Lessing and the French tragedians increased at a radical pace and led to the ultimate break in the seventeenth letter on literature.]

10. Critics have pointed out that Lessing was not always so critical of Gottsched. See the Notes to *Briefe die neueste Literatur betreffend* (Reclam):

In der "Vorrede" zu den "Beiträgen zur Historie und Aufnahme des Theaters" (1750) schreibt er: "Es sind nun vier Jahr, daß uns bei dem Beschlusse der 'Deutschen Schaubühne' der Herr Professor Gottsched Hoffnung zu einer Historie des Theaters machte. Es ist gewiß, wir sind nicht die einzigen, die der Erfüllung dieses Versprechens mit Vergnügen und mit einem unruhigen Verlangen entgegengesehen haben. Man muß gestehen, daß er sehr geschickt dazu sein würde, und daß seine Verdienste, die er unwidersprechlich um das deutsche Theater hat, dadurch zu ihrer vollkommenen Größe anwachsen würden (422). [Four years have now passed since Professor Gottsched laid claim in the "German Stage" to the hope for the history of the theater. Certainly, we are not the only ones who have looked forward to the fulfillment of this promise with pleasure and with a restless longing. One must agree that he would be very fitting for the job and that his abilities—which cannot be overlooked with regard to the German theater—would develop completely in the process.]

11. Already in the introduction to the "Beiträge zur Historie und Aufnahme des Theaters" (1750) Lessing was suspicious of the German obsession with French theater:

Die einzigen Franzosen hat man durch häufige Übersetzungen sich eigen zu machen gesucht. Dadurch hat man aber unser Theater zu einer Einförmigkeit gebracht, die man auf alle mögliche Art zu vermeiden sich hätte bestreben sollen (LM, IV: 50). [One has attempted to make the works of the French one's own through numerous translations. In this way, however, one has brought our theater to a state of simplicity which one should try by any means to avoid.]

12. Translation author's; however, I consulted the following translation: G. E. Lessing, *Hamburg Dramaturgy*, trans. Victor Lange (New York: Dover, 1962), p. 201.

13. "*so trafen sie (die Franzosen) mit den tyrannischen Regeln, welchen sie ihren völligen Gehorsam aufzukündigen nicht Mut genug hatten, ein Abkommen*" (LM, IX: 378) [they made a truce with the tyrannical rules against which they had not the courage to rebel (Lange, 141)].

14. For a contrasting theory, see Paul Böckmann, "Das Formprinzip des Witzes bei Lessing," *Wege der Forschung: Gotthold Ephraim Lessing*, eds. Gerhard and Sibylle Bauer (Darmstadt: Wissenschaftliche Buchgesellschaft, 1968), pp. 176–96. Böckmann links the German concept of "*Witz*" with the French "*Esprit-Ideal*" and suggests that, after the French Revolution, French is the paradigmatic language of the Enlightenment.

15. See also Sadji on Lessing's reception of Diderot (230–309). Amadou Booker Sadji, *Lessing und das französische Theater* (Stuttgart: Heinz, 1982).

16. See Wolfgang Schadewaldt, "Furcht und Mitleid?" *Hermes* 83 (1955), in which Schadewaldt takes issue with Lessing's supposedly "accurate" interpretation of Aristotle's *Poetics*.

17. "*Denn leider gibt es Deutsche, die noch weit französischer sind, als die Franzosen*" (LM, X: 31) [For there are unfortunately Germans who are more French than the French themselves].

18. In "Spuren des französischen Dramas bei Lessing," *Nation und Gelehrtenrepublik: Lessing im europäischen Zusammenhang*, eds. Wilfried Barner and Albert M. Reh (Detroit: Wayne State University Press, 1983), pp. 120–138. Gisela Ritchie argues that Lessing's dramas were, in fact, greatly influenced by French dramas:

> *Es läßt sich feststellen, daß Lessing trotz seiner Ablehnung des französischen Dramas in dem vielzitierten 17. Literaturbrief und der Hamburgischen Dramaturgie vom 75. bis zum 83. Stück doch gerade für die Charakterisierung seiner unvergeßlichen Frauengestalten von dem französischen Theater mehr übernahm, als man bisher zugegeben hat* (135). [It can be asserted that, despite his rejection of French drama in the oft-cited seventeenth letter on literature and in pieces 75–83 of the *Hamburg Dramaturgy*, Lessing borrowed much more from the French theater when it came to the creation of his unforgettable female figures than one has as yet acknowledged.]

19. *In jeder Welle, die an unser Schiff schlüge, würde mir der Tod entgegenrauschen: jeder Wind würde mir von den väterlichen Küsten Verwünschungen nachbrausen, und der kleinste Sturm würde mich ein Glutgericht über mein*

Haupt zu sein, dünken.—Nein, Mellefont, so ein Barbar können Sie gegen mich nicht sein (LM, II: 278). [Death would roar at me in every wave that struck against the vessel, every wind would howl its curses after me from my native shore, and the slightest storm would seem a sentence of death pronounced upon me. No, Mellefont, you cannot be so cruel to me! (Meech, 19)].

20. In "Apel und Lessing—or: the Ethics of Communication and the Strategies of Comedy," *Lessing Yearbook* 23 (1993): 41–54, Mark W. Roche elaborates on the technique of mirroring in *Minna von Barnhelm*:

> The extraordinary use of mirroring between characters in *Minna* and the play's elaborate portrayal and critique of asymmetrical behavior makes Lessing's comedy a fascinating text for any reader interested in the transcendental pragmatic argument that all behavior should be symmetrical and communicative. The linguistic and theatrical technique of mirroring serves to highlight contradictions in Tellheim's behavior and lead him toward a union with others. Mirroring is a formal analogue to the play's content: Tellheim's self is portrayed through the other characters, just as Tellheim, eventually, finds his own selfhood in others. (43)

21. Fink, "National Characters," pp. 100–01.

22. For an overview of the reception of the figure Riccault, see Peter Christian Giese, "Riccault und das Spiel mit Fortuna in Lessings *Minna von Barnhelm*," *Jahrbuch der deutschen Schillergesellschaft* 28 (1984): 104–117.

23. For examples of the former see especially the early reception of *Minna*. A review of Lessing's drama from 1767 sees Riccault as superfluous: "Den Riccault de la Marlinière wünschten wir ganz aus dem Stück heraus; er ist mehr als überflüssig" [We would wish that Riccault de la Marlinière would be removed completely from the play; he is more than superfluous]. (Hein, Jürgen, *Erläuterungen und Dokumente: G. E. Lessing, Minna von Barnhelm* [Stuttgart: Reclam, 1970], p. 65). The review in the "Deutsche Bibliothek der schönen Wissenschaften," Halle, 1767 was similarly critical of Riccault: "*Was uns am wenigstens in dem Lustspiele gefällt, ist der französische Offizier. Warum mußte dieser just ein Franzose sein? Er kommt bloß, eine Satyre auf sich machen zu lassen*" (Hein, 65) [What we liked least about the comedy was the French officer. Why does he have to be a Frenchman? He appears, only to satirize himself.]

24. Examples of the latter include Simonetta Sanna, "Streitkultur in Lessings *Minna von Barnhelm:* Minnas Fähigkeit versus Franziskas Unfähigkeit zum Streiten als Movens von Handlungsentwicklung und Konflik-

tlösung," *Streitkultur: Strategien des Überzeugens im Werk Lessings*, eds. Wolfram Mauser and Günter Saße (Tübingen: Niemeyer: 1993), pp. 444–57. Sanna argues that Riccault's function is to reveal Minna's ability to be tolerant (454). Likewise, a number of critics view Riccault as the negative mirror image of Tellheim. See, for example, Hans-Georg Werner, "Komödie der Rationalität: Zu Lessings *Minna von Barnhelm*," *Weimarer Beiträge* 25, no. 11 (1979): 39–60 and Mark Roche "Apel und Lessing—or: The Ethics at Communication and the Strategies of Comedy," *Lessing Yearbook* 23 (1993), pp. 41–54. Fink also sees Riccault as the polar opposite of Tellheim: "So stehen Riccault und Tellheim wie Schein und Sein einander gegenüber" (112). [Thus Riccault and Tellheim are polar opposites—the former is appearance where the latter is truth].

25. Ingrid Strohschneider-Kohrs follows this line of argumentation when she suggests that Riccault is aligned with Minna against Tellheim, since both are *Spieler*. "Die überwundenen Komödiantin in Lessings Lustspiel," *Poesie und Reflexion: Aufsätze zur Literatur* (Tübingen: Niemeyer, 1999), pp. 95–115.

26. Wolfgang Wittkowski puts forth the fascinating thesis that Riccault is not only the polar opposite of Tellheim, but also a caricature of Frederick the Great:

> *Der Major geht mit Geld korrekt um, nobel, freigiebig, selbstlos: 'hausväterlich'. Dem Leutnant läßt sich kein Pfennig anvertrauen. Sein Auftreten, unmittelbar bevor Minna ihr Spiel mit dem Major beginnt, setzt ein Zeichen, daß sie, die ja das Spiel um des Spielens willen liebt, ihre Art von Falschspiel zu weit treiben könnte, genau das tut sie dann und gerät dadurch in Schwierigkeiten. Bei Riccault klappt es mit der deutschen Sprache und mit dem Glück nur dürftig. Ist er am Ende, holt er "neue Rekruten." Alles wie bei Friedrich. Sein voller Name bedeutet denn auch "Herr von Diebeslust aus der Linie derer von nimmgold": in der Tat gehört er zu einer zum Verwundern "groß, groß Familie [. . .] qui est véritablement du sang Royal." "Fortune" heißt auch Vermögensverhältnissen mit faulen Mitteln aushelfen. Genau das tat der König.* "Minna von Barnhelm oder die verhinderten Hausväter," *Lessing Yearbook* 19 (1987): 45–66. [The major handles money well—nobly, generously and selflessly: like the paternal head of a household. The lieutenant, on the other hand, can't be trusted with a penny. His appearance, immediately before Minna begins her game with the major, shows that Minna, who plays for the love of play itself, could take her deceptive game too far. In fact, this is what she does, and she experiences difficulties as a result. Riccault can just barely master the German language and his luck. When his luck is up, he calls for "new recruits." Just as with Frederick. His complete name also means

"Sir of Thievery from the line of the Money-Grubbers"; in truth, he belongs to the admirable "great, great family [. . .] that is truly of a royal blood." "Fortune" means also to improve one's financial situation through unethical means. And this is also what the king did.]

27. See Judith P. Aikin, "'Das klingt sehr tragisch!' Lessing's *Minna von Barnhelm* as Embodiment of the Genre Discussion," *Lessing Yearbook* 20 (1988): 15–27. Heinz Stolte articulates the problem as follows: "*Ist die 'Minna von Barnhelm' überhaupt ein Lustspiel? Sie ist es, aber sie ist es nicht wegen der Gestalt des Tellheim, sondern trotz ihr, nicht wegen der sittlichen Strenge dieses preußischen Offiziers, sondern trotz ihr*" [Is *Minna von Barnhelm* really a comedy? Yes, although not through the figure of Tellheim, but rather despite this figure—not due to the moral rectitude of this Prussian officer, but despite this]. ("Lessing's *Minna von Barnhelm*," *Zeitschrift für deutsche Bildung* 17 [1941]: 80). Karl Guthke views the play not as a "*Lustpiel*" but as a tragicomedy. See *Geschichte der deutschen Tragikomödie* (Göttingen: Vandenhoeck and Ruprecht, 1961), p. 62.

28. Martin E. Smith puts forth the convincing thesis that Minna creates a fictional tragedy in which she plays the lead so that she can move Tellheim through pity, "Tellheims Wandlung-eine dichterische Gestaltung von Lessings Mitleidsprinzip," *Acta Germanica* 7 (1972): 39–57.

29. Lessing's notions of the comedic and ridiculous articulated here reflect an engagement with the discussion among his contemporaries. In particular, the English author Henry Fielding conceived of the comedic in a similar manner. In the preface to his comic novel *Joseph Andrews* (1742), Fielding asserts that "affectation [is] the only true source of the Ridiculous." See Henry Fielding, *Joseph Andrews and Shamela* (London: Everyman, 1993), p. 52. Moreover, "hypocritical affectation" seems to Fielding to be the most comical form of the ridiculous, a quality that can very well be attributed to Lessing's Riccault.

30. Judith Aikin attempts to account for the lack of traditionally comic elements in *Minna* by arguing that the comic principle in the play follows a Shakespearean model of optimism. However, Aikin admits that Riccault retains the characteristics of a comic figure (17).

31. In *Die Kunst der Interpretation* (Zurich: np, 1955), Emil Staiger suggests that the Germans found Riccault funny due to their exaggerated respect for French culture (90).

32. Ritchie argues that the "Lisette" figure in Lessing's early comedies stems from the French comedic tradition. For Ritchie, Minna embodies the "*Witz*" modeled by these earlier Lisette figures (134).

33. Giese sees Riccault's act as messenger as his main function in the play (110), and Roche asserts that Riccault, through his message, is ultimately an agent of truth (48).

34. This translation does not render the extent to which Riccault's German is grammatically and stylistically flawed.

35. *DAS FRÄULEIN: Hier habe ich, was ich ohnlängst gewonnen; nur zehn Pistolen—Ich muß mich zwar schämen, so wenig—RICCAULT: Donnés toujours, Mademoiselle, donnés.* (LM, II: 231) [MINNA: I have here something I won only recently, only ten Pistoles . . . I am quite ashamed . . . It is so little . . . RICCAULT: *Donnés toujours, Mademoiselle, donnés.* (Meech, 158)].

36. Giese puts forth the interesting theory that Riccault cannot really be a cheat, since if he were one, he would not be so unlucky (114).

37. Fink points out that Riccault's attempt to poke fun at the German language is a parody of the Frenchman Bouhours' criticism of German:

Lessing benutzt jedoch auch die Gelegenheit, um Bouhours' Verspottung des Deutschen als einer armen, rauhen, "plumpen Sprache" ins Positive zu wenden. So gibt Minna, die sehr wohl Französisch kann, Riccault zu verstehen, daß nur falscher Adelsdünkel dazu verleiten kann, in Deutschland Französisch zu sprechen, selbt mit Franzosen; in ihren Augen ist die deutsche Sprache der französischen mindestens gleichwertig (111). [However, Lessing also takes the opportunity to place a positive spin on Bouhours' joke about the German language as poor, raw and "clumsy." In this way, Minna, who can certainly speak French, makes it clear to Riccault that only a false sense of aristocracy would compel one to speak French in Germany, even with the French. In her eyes, the German language is at least as good as the French.]

38. Fink further suggests that Riccault and the concept of play are meant, in part, to undermine Bouhours' assertion that a German could not have "*Esprit*" (105).

39. See Fink, "National Character," p. 117.

Chapter 3

The Dying Poet

Scenarios of a Christianized Heine

Sarah Juliette Sasson

Der Heine meines Pantheon is keineswegs der parfümierte Jüngling, der mit dem "Buch der Lieder" eine schöngeistige Bourgeoisie in Entzücken versetzte; er ist der gemartete Dichter des "Romanzero," das Gespent aus der Rue d'Amsterdam, das in sich verkrümmte, eingeschnurrte, vielfach gezwickte und gezwackte Männlein, das Lebendigen, oder doch noch halblebendigen Leibes in der Matratzengruft verfault.
—Klaus Mann, *Der Wendepunkt: Ein Lebensbericht*[1]

The 1873 French edition of Heine's *Reisebilder* (published by Michel Lévy Frères) opens with an engraving, in which the poet, lying on an armchair, propped upon pillows, is asleep or perhaps engaged in a melancholic reverie. He represents an exemplary personification of a man resigned to his illness. The caption, which reads Henri Heine and seems to have been written in a shaky hand, leaves the reader with a feeling of intimacy, of sharing, as though allowed some type of private access to the poet's life. The technique used for the reproduction of the signature (the appearance of an autograph and the presence of purposely smeared ink) gives a staged impression of authenticity; the poet has been surprised in his home, in a moment of grievous intimacy; there seems to be no concern for making him appear as something other than a sick, dying man. This particular image seems characteristic of the fashion in which Heine is presented to the nineteenth-century French public. A foreword by Théophile Gautier, a reprint of Heine's obituary previously published in *Le Moniteur*, complements this striking presentation.[2] There, Gautier describes his visits to the dying poet in abundant detail; reading his text is almost like entering into the picture. Heine's death scenario is engraved as an introduction to the reading of his texts.[3]

The French reception of Heine, like that of many other German writers, must be placed in the context of nineteenth-century French-German literary relations. It is primarily defined by the topos of Germany as a mysterious country and an absolute source of exoticism within the framework of Europe; François-René de Chateaubriand, Victor Hugo, Edgar Quinet, and other literary travelers have provided manifold illustrations of this fascination. The French attraction to Germany had become such a commonplace that in 1948 a critic devoted to this notion a whole book, entitled *Les Ecrivains français et le mirage allemand*.[4] Whereas this text's attempt to trace the French reception of German literature as a source of errors or illusions should be situated in its historical context, it demonstrates nevertheless the passion and interest Germany commanded in French literary circles. Jean-Marie Carré writes, for instance:

> In the same way that they had been Goetheans and Kantians, the French became Marxists, Wagnerians, Nietzscheans. But the Germans, they remained German. [*Comme ils avaient été goethéens et kantiens, les Français devinrent marxistes, wagnériens, nietzschéens. Mais les Allemands, eux, restèrent allemands.*][5]

Yet, Heine, who is often situated among the German writers who came to find freedom and liberalism in the Paris of the 1830s, belongs to a category of his own. Although he cannot be separated either from the circles of émigrés or from Jewish intellectuals in France, his overall reception appears nonetheless atypical in retrospect.[6] Indeed, the particular and even privileged conditions of his stay in Paris quickly secured him a preeminent position in the Parisian press; he was so much considered an actor and a participant of French literary life that some even called him "a French writer."[7] Both his allegiance to Paris as the capital of esprit, creativity, and joy and what has been widely described as his *Wahlverwandschaften* with French culture, namely, his "Voltairian" irony, procured him a substantial place in the French cultural and literary landscape. As a consequence, the persona of the writer as much as his poetry became the topic of an ongoing literary feuilleton, echoed not only in journals, but also in memoirs and other fragmented testimonies of literary life at the time.

Heine's reception in France has developed its own grammar. Whereas articles in the first years of his stay focus on his sardonic style, the reception during the *Matratzengruft* years displays striking new features. Effecting a shift from the previous general perception of the poet, it focuses on his illness and thereby draws a revised portrait of the poet's function. Heine's illness is *staged* in a particular manner; Gautier's introduction of *Reisebilder* constitutes one among many examples of what historian Philippe Ariès has described as "framing the drama." In this setting, death is no longer portrayed as part of the mundane; rather it is made public and associated with ostentatious ceremonials and rituals. Emotions are now displayed. "Death was no longer desirable (. . .) but it was admirable in its beauty."[8] Heine's illness and ultimate death fit this pattern of emotion and aestheticizing, yet their representation has developed an imagery of its own. But most importantly, as a radical shift from the earlier reception and as a source of the renewal or transformation of the poet's image as well as his work, the French reading of Heine raises particular questions about his status as a Jewish author.

In Heine's early French reception in the 1830s, the first articles about his poetry, notably in the *Revue des deux mondes*, develop an image of the poet as an iconoclastic ironist. They describe Heine's writing in sparring, combative terminology; his stylistic dexterity calls to mind an image of an arrow hitting its mark with rhetorical precision. Charles Augustin Sainte-Beuve writes for example:

> A man of battle, a rapid skirmisher, an evasive and somewhat cruel archer, he jumped into our midst on our bank of the Rhine, and there, he showed us how he could shoot forth irony and strike at the heart of his own people (. . .). We, with our lucid and precise logic, have . . . difficulty following his broken and jerky rhythms, which are continually interrupted by the rockets of his metaphors.
> [*Homme de guerre, d'escarmouche rapide, archer fuyant et un peu cruel, il s'est jeté parmi nous sur notre rive du Rhin, et de là, il nous a montré comment il savait décocher l'ironie et frapper au cœur des siens qui n'étaient pas des nôtres (. . .). Notre juste et droit sens a . . . quelque peine à le suivre dans sa logique brisée, saccadée, qu'interceptent à chaque fois les fusées de la métaphore.*][9]

Barbey d'Aurevilly employs a similar rhetoric when he characterizes Heine's writing style as "epigrams of phosphorus."[10] Théophile Gautier also describes Heine's speech as "pointed and barbed arrows, sarcastic spears never missing their mark, shooting forth hissing from their red bow" [*des flèches aiguës et barbelées, des dards sarcastiques ne manquant jamais leur but (jaillissant en sifflant de leur arc rouge)*].[11] The constant reference to Heine's stylistic fighting spirit is complemented by an analogy to mythical and classical figures. Heine emerges as a photographic negative of a young divine figure; the comparison to a demon, a "good-natured Mephistopheles" (*un Méphistophélès bon enfant*),[12] emphasizes how the playful, almost jest-like aspect of his irony constitutes a momentous element for his critics. Moreover, Heine's demonization is placed in a context of carnivalesque exultation. Heine epitomizes defiance and provocation, as much as the rituals which define the carnival:

> Imagine Mephistopheles coming out from the underworld, escorted by a battalion of gnomes with bizarre heads, chatting, shouting, dancing, laughing and laughing at everything. [*Imaginez Méphistophélès sortant de dessous terre, escorté d'un bataillon de gnomes à tête bizarre, causant, criant, dansant, riant et riant de tout.*][13]

The carnivalesque theme is also present when the critic Mme d'Agoult, whose nom de plume in *La Revue des deux mondes* was D. Stern, compares his verve to a

> rowdy and licentious muse who frolics about heedless of her colorful dress through intersections and streets, throwing, like Roman carnival masks, flowers or dragées of plaster in the face of passersby who laugh at these escapades.
> [*muse tapageuse et dévergondée qui s'ébat sans grand souci de sa robe bariolée à travers carrefours et rues, jetant comme les masques du carnaval romain, tantôt des fleurs, tantôt des dragées de plâtre à la face des passants qui rient de ses incartades.*][14]

One critic even imagines him in a version of Don Juan's last meal, laughing and jesting as he welcomes the Commander who comes for him.[15] In this sense, Heine's representation resembles that of the Parisian crowds he himself described, the crowds gathered on the boulevards on the eve of the eruption of the cholera epidemic in 1832. While the people sang and reveled, some wearing costumes, others wearing masks replicating the supposed appearance of cholera, the real face of the disease revealed itself:

> ... als plötzlich der lustigste der Arlequine eine allzu große Kühle in den Beinen verspürte und die Maske abnahm und zu aller Welt Verwunderung ein veilchenblaues Gesicht zum Vorschein kam. Man merkte bald, daß solches kein Spaß sei, und das Gelächter verstummte, und mehrere Wagen voll Menschen fuhr man von der Redoute gleich nach dem Hôtel-Dieu, dem Zentralhospitale, wo sie, in ihren abenteuerlichen Maskenkleidern anlangend, gleich verschieden. Da man in der ersten Beschürzung an Ansteckung glaubte und die ältern Gäste des Hôtel-Dieu ein gräßliches Angstgeschrei erhoben, so sind jene Toten, wie man sagt, so schnell beerdigt worden, daß man ihnen nicht einmal die buntscheckigen Narrenkleider auszog, und lustig, wie sie gelebt haben, liegen sie auch lustig im Grabe.
> [... when suddenly the funniest of the harlequins felt too much coldness in his legs, and he took off his mask, and—to everyone's surprise—a violet-colored face appeared. Soon everyone realized that this was no joke, and the laughter grew silent, and several carriages full of people were driven from the Redoute to the Hôtel-Dieu, the main hospital, where they—arriving in their adventurous costumes, immediately passed away. At first, everyone was afraid of contagion and the elderly guests of the Hôtel-Dieu began to scream out of horrible fear so that those corpses were—as it is told—quickly buried without even taking off their variegated carnivalesque clothes, and merrily, as they had lived, they merrily lie in their graves.][16]

In its acute perception of the clash between carnival and genuine death, this description of the genesis of the epidemic captures the essence of the dialectics of Heine's reception in France. Only upon the critics' confrontation with the poet's long illness and death do they find their own equilibrium and vision. In the first years, however, the French reception views Heine as a young character, an impertinent son, a scoffer incessantly poking fun at his victims. He must be young because his writing displays both panache and provocation, which the reception interprets as the metaphor of flirtation with danger, one of the clichés attributed to youth.

Another recurrent comparison applied to Heine is that of a Greek god: the poet conveniently incarnates two opposite aspects, the Apollinian and the Dionysian. The combination of the poet's plumpness and fairness and his characteristic witty style provides an ideal illustration of the Greek duality. Gautier associates Heine with a "Germanic Apollo" (*un Apollon germanique*),[17] or more precisely, "Apollo mixed with a bit of Mephistopheles" (*Apollon mêlé de Méphistophélès*).[18] The supposed affinity between his textual irony and that of Aristophanes also justifies the persistence of the Greek comparison. These common images in the reception of the 1930s and 1940s borrow definite pagan features and combine them with their corollary, Voltairian irony. In fact, Heine's own reference to the small German nightingale, which had built its nest in the wig of Voltaire, becomes one of the most popular quotes in the press. Sensitivity, on the other hand, will be explained through the usual traits characterizing German romantic poetry, a commonplace since the publication of *De l'Allemagne*.

In this first phase, both categories of definition belong to the aesthetic domain. Heine is certainly represented as a demon, but this view also allows him to be elevated by his critics to the status of prodigal child. Moreover, these demonic images rarely take on a moralistic tone. Rather, they spread in the press according to a journalistic logic of indefinite replication. Soon afterwards, they become commonly accepted references. It would be vain to search for textual evidence of these clichés in Heine's texts. Whereas some elements indeed authenticate this representation, such a construction is based on a general image of the poet as beloved provocateur, an exotic yet akin stranger, in short, an adopted child of France. The diversity of Heine's pantheon—the fact that he becomes everybody and personifies everything—can certainly be attributed to a certain rhetorical style of the literary feuilleton. In this regard, Barbey d'Aurevilly's description of Heine is exemplary in its attempt both to seduce and to categorize, but not to explain:

> He is a son of Rabelais and Luther, who, tears in his eyes, marries the buffoonery of these two immense clowns with sentimentality as great as that of Lamartine. He is a sad Ariosto (. . .), he is a gay Dante—has that been seen before?—(. . .) He is a Voltaire, but one with a soul, while Voltaire has only esprit. He is a Goethe, but without the ennui of Goethe (. . .). He is a Hoffmann without pipe smoke. (. . .) He is an ideal Schiller

without the odious philanthropic mockery. And he is finally (. . .) a Rivarol with a colorful metaphysics, but much more complete and much more astonishing than Rivarol.

[*C'est un fils de Rabelais et de Luther, qui, les larmes aux yeux, marie la bouffonnerie de ces deux immenses bouffons à une sentimentalité aussi grande que celle de Lamartine. C'est un Arioste triste (. . .). C'est un Dante gai—cela s'était-il vu?—C'est un Voltaire, mais qui a une âme, quand Voltaire n'a que de l'esprit. C'est un Goethe sans l'ennui de Goethe (. . .) C'est un Hoffmann, mais sans fumée de pipe (. . .). C'est un Schiller idéal, moins l'odieuse philantropaillerie. Et c'est enfin (. . .) un Rivarol de métaphysique pittoresque, mais bien plus complet et plus étonnant que Rivarol.*][19]

The shift which occurs from this initial reception to that of Heine's illness and death is remarkable. How can one explain such an abrupt evolution, from an accumulation of Greek and demonic images to narratives of suffering and atonement? The description of Heine's decade-long illness and ultimate death is developed among critics into a cohesive text. His former character fades away, to be replaced with new, radically different features: from a young Greek god or a semi-demonic jester, the poet becomes instead a Christ-like figure. Describing him on his *Matratzengruft*, Théophile Gautier uses the metaphor of the nailing to the cross to portray the intensity of Heine's physical suffering: For eight years, he remained nailed to the cross of paralysis by nails of suffering [*Il resta huit ans cloué sur la croix de la paralysie, par les clous de la souffrance*].[20]

Similarly Caroline Jaubert, who hosted a salon and later published her recollections of the period, describes the "crown of thorns that fell upon a brilliant genius" (*une couronne d'épines dévolue au génie brillant*).[21] These references to Christ are initially derived from Heine's striking physical metamorphosis, which then becomes the object of manifold descriptions. For Gautier, for example,

> Sickness had diminished him, emaciated him, dissected him, and carved in the statue of the Greek god, with the meticulous patience of an artist of the Middle Ages, a Christ of mere skin and bones, whose nerves, tendons and veins protruded. Thus bared, he was beautiful still. [*La maladie l'avait atténué, émacié, disséqué comme à plaisir et dans la statue du dieu grec taillait avec la patience minutieuse d'un artiste du moyen-âge, un*

> *Christ décharné jusqu'au squelette, où les nerfs, les tendons, les veines apparaissaient en saillie. Ainsi dépouillé, il était beau encore.*]22

Gautier's description follows the aesthetic line taken earlier with Heine as an Apollo. Through the detail of the atrophied sculpture, the text develops the metaphor of a slow and natural carving of the sick body, and one sees the emergence of a figure reduced to its essential traits. The austerity of the medieval reference emphasizes the evolution from the materially grounded to the spiritual. In the same vein, Jules Legras describes Heine's physical evolution into a Christ-like statue, which is justified by the poet's paleness.

> The slightly plump Apollo (. . .) had become a slender figure of Christ on the cross, with remarkable hands of transparent ivory, a radiant face surrounded by long curls, pale lips where paralysis seemed to have fixed the ordinary crease of sarcasm, and a fine nose thinned and accentuated by pain and emaciation. [*L'Apollon un peu gras (. . .) était devenu une maigre image du Christ en croix, avec d'admirables mains d'ivoire transparent, un beau front enthousiaste entouré de boucles longues, des lèvres pâlies, où la paralysie avait comme figé le pli ordinaire du sarcasme, et un nez aux lignes fines, amincies et accusées par la douleur et l'amaigrissement.*]23

This aestheticized comparison between Christ and the poet becomes, in various guises, so widespread that even Heine's brother Gustav will have it in mind and will integrate it into his own portrayal of the poet:

> The features of his face have not changed, so to speak; they have only taken on a more refined and noble appearance. The observation that was made concerning his resemblance to the classic image of the Savior is quite accurate. It's the head of Christ with closed eyes. His entire being is spiritualized. [*Les traits du visage n'ont pas changé pour ainsi dire, ils se sont seulement affinés et ennoblis. L'observation qui a été faite au sujet de sa ressemblance avec l'image classique du sauveur est très exacte. C'est une tête de Christ aux yeux fermés. Tout son être est spiritualisé.*]24

The initial staging of Heine as Christ indeed derives from an aesthetic vision of his physical appearance. His thinness, the growing impression of immateriality emanating from him, and his immobility in a near-grave justify to a large extent this comparison (Gautier describes him morbidly as "nailed alive in his coffin" (*cloué vivant dans sa bière*).[25] This representation is accentuated by the presence of engravings, which repeat in graphic terminology the theme of spiritual ailment. The engraving I described earlier is in fact a reproduction of the famous illustration accompanying Saint-René Taillandier's 1852 article on Heine in *La Revue des deux mondes*; Heine personifies an idea of resignation and serenity in illness.[26] This image powerfully complements the cohesion of the descriptions. At first, it seems to fit perfectly the conventional death scenarios in the nineteenth century outlined by Philippe Ariès. Such scenarios focus on the theatricality of the process: death must be staged. One cannot but notice the importance of staging in, for example, the use of dramatic terminology in the textual description of the poet's death:

> Heine made a point of falling elegantly, a lovely smile on his white lips. He spent his last years draping with dignity the pleats of his mortuary tunic around his poor body, without ever forgetting his role as a witty invalid, without a lamentation, a request for grace, without even the theatrical rigidity of the stoic. [*Heine a mis une coquetterie d'ancien à tomber correctement, un joli sourire sur ses lèvres blanches. Il a passé ses dernières années à draper décemment autour de son pauvre corps les plis d'une tunique mortuaire, sans oublier jamais son rôle de malade spirituel, sans une lamentation, une demande de grâce, sans même la raideur théâtrale du stoïcien.*][27]

The theatrical references, the pleats, the draping, and the notion of roles all convey the impression that the death appears on stage. And indeed the press, which reviewed the death and commented upon it in minute detail, also becomes a locus of theatricality.

In itself, the association between a long and painful illness and the aesthetic and magnified representation of a sick poet is not surprising. What is extraordinary is the radical nature of the shift, which takes place from Heine's early career as a Greek god and a merry Mephistopheles to one who invokes pious representations. Beyond the aesthetic reasons and the obvious similitude of the two types of suffering, the very selection of Christ as a recurrent analogy for the suffering Heine raises the question of the significance of such a choice. Moreover, one could even argue that the difference between the two representations is erased by the use of the same structural traits in the profane and the religious versions. The figure of the young, pagan, and rebellious son would then only have to be translated in Christian terms into another type of son, and the rebellion mutated by virtues of resignation and martyrdom. Caroline Jaubert, for instance, compares Heine's stance toward sickness to the "heroism of the martyr."[28] However, if Heine remains a god in the imagination of his readers, the passage from a pagan god to a Christian one is fundamental enough to be noticed. This new scenario embraces more than a purely rhetorical twist in which Heine's metamorphosis would be justified by common structural features; those of a "son," a young god, whose beauty once of a Greek and almost cherubic type (his stoutness is even described as "somewhat pagan portliness") evolves into an emaciated one.[29] The proliferation of the clichés in the descriptions corroborates their textual potency. However, the fact that the images are borrowed from one another, make use of each other as infinite intertexts and also employ the devices of mise en abyme and self-referentiality, only partly accounts for the seductive passage from God to demon and from demon to Christian god which is effected back and forth in the text. I am not denying that the image is stylistically convincing, as it brings together two extremes and merges them into one ambiguous figure: Imagine the smile of Mephistopheles passing unto the figure of Christ, a Christ finishing his chalice [*Imaginez le sourire de Méphistophélès passant sur la figure du Christ, un Christ achevant de boire son calice*].[30]

Nonetheless, the recurrent staging of Heine as Christ, if it is justified by a common aesthetic representation of the dying poet at the time, cannot be explained solely on these grounds. This staging functions on the literary level in a convincing manner when Gautier, for example, substitutes the austere medieval figure for that of the Greek Epicurean one. But the effect is forceful because the text remains strictly enclosed in the boundaries of literary terminology and figures of style. Gautier's pure aesthetic representation remains, however, atypical. Another far less neutral motif, the expiatory motif, emerges. Whereas the comparison between Heine and Christ takes place in eulogistic and even sublime terms (Meissner, for example, speaks of the beauty of the corpse and of the transfiguration of the face of Heine in death),[31] his illness takes on quite another stature. Behind the serene and resigned figure of the poet appears the shadow of atonement. Heine's years of suffering are presented as a form of silent revenge for his delinquent youth. For example, Camille Selden (*la Mouche*) writes:

> For me, the entire youth of the poet came to be reflected in the miseries of his current life. One sensed the remains of an unhealthy past, of some sort of taste for outmoded playacting that called to mind (. . .) the shouts of laughter of grisettes.
> [*Pour moi, toute la jeunesse du poète venait se réfléchir dans les misères de sa vie actuelle. On y sentait les restes d'un passé malsain, je ne sais quel goût de cabotinage démodé qui rappelait (. . .) les éclats de rire des grisettes. . .*][32]

Selden's sketching of Heine as a sort of Dorian Gray conveys the image of an old sinner, whose atrophied body still carries the traces of his escapades. The body becomes a permanent and significant testimony, a living proof of his debauched youth. The metaphoric stigmata signify a transformation of the physical illness into a spiritual one. It is thus no longer a question of the facility of the aesthetic image; the critics will now interpret any distinctive sign of sickness, thinness or resignation as a mark of spirituality. The spiritualization of the image of the poet has two consequences. On the one hand, through a sort of rhetorical pirouette with pedagogical undertones, it allows for a revised and generally more acceptable image of the iconoclastic ironist to be presented to the public. The *enfant terrible*'s atonement through physical suffering simultaneously permits the reader to come to terms with the most disparaged aspects of his personality and his writing. As Saint-René Taillandier points out, echoing a widespread opinion of the time:

> What will dominate for a long time to come in the judgments of Heine is the regret at seeing such a beautiful poet made delinquent by his penchant for cynicism and mockery. [*Ce qui dominera encore longtemps dans les jugements sur Heine, c'est le regret de voir un si beau poète dévoyé par son penchant au cynisme et à la moquerie.*][33]

Nevertheless, the idea of expiating past provocations through illness cannot pass for a simple manifestation of the (somewhat dated) nineteenth-century approach of "the man and his work." The contrary occurs: Heine's sickness seems to constitute a justification a posteriori of the criticisms aimed at him.

No longer only a question of a sublimated aesthetic suffering, the reception points to the necessity for a brutal and clearly moral process of expiation of a life and an oeuvre considered excessive. It thus becomes impossible to retain solely the aesthetic argument as a valid justification for such an abundance of similar representations. Rather, the insistence on the process of suffering as the only redeeming element, and the fact that this suffering is linked in such a constant way to an evolution to the spiritual, to a positive metaphysical experience, emphasizes the so-called transformation of the poet at the end of his life. Since such a conception clashes with the irony contained in Heine's writings, even the last ones, one must seek an answer outside the text.

The obsession with the figure of the Savior and the absolute necessity for the critics to Christianize Heine in order to worship him more completely only makes sense in the context of the problematic of his identity. This amounts, in fact, to a metaphorical conversion. What has been overshadowed by the diverse representations of Christ is the obvious fact that the portrayal of a Christ figure invokes the classic image of a suffering Jew. It is this image and no other which appears as the most natural and aesthetically most seductive one to a large number of critics. For to unanimously applaud a spiritualized Heine, one could argue, not only constitutes a way to take the sting out of the power of his irony, to the relief of all, but also a tendentious way to approach his Judaism. Although the question of Heine's Jewish identity is not openly addressed in any significant way until much later, in the writings of a Paul Bourget or an Edouard Drumont (and there, only as an exemplum of the Jewish character), the earlier reception subtly approaches this theme through the figure of Christ.[34] It seems that this representation of the Jewish Heine serves as a means of reconciling two essential elements of his identity, Judaism, and suffering through the ideal figure of a martyred Jew, Christ. This rewriting of Heine's image is confirmed when one reads, for example, the critic Emile Montégut, who synthesizes the different components and explicitly writes that the Jewish and suffering Heine is the one that he prefers:

> In soul as in body, Heine was no longer anything but a Jew, and lying on his sick bed, he seemed to me truly like a distant cousin of this Jew so blasphemed not so long ago, but whose kinship he no longer thought to

deny. (. . .) I did not miss the Apollo of Théophile Gautier at all, and need I say it? I would not have wanted to see Heine differently than he thus appeared to me. This mixture of the moribund, the Jew and the adolescent that I had before my eyes presented to me a much more exact image of the genius of Heine than the most flourishing health or the most classic beauty could ever have achieved. [*D'âme comme de corps, Heine n'était plus qu'un Juif, et, étendu sur son lit de souffrance, il me parut véritablement comme comme un arrière-cousin de ce Juif si blasphémé naguère, mais dont il ne songeait plus à nier la parenté. (. . .) Je ne regrettai guère l'Apollon de Théophile Gautier, et dois-je le dire? Je n'aurais pas voulu voir Heine autrement qu'il ne m'apparut alors. Ce mélange de moribond, de Juif et d'adolescent que j'avais sous les yeux me présentait une image bien autrement exacte du génie de Heine que n'aurait pu faire la santé la plus florissante ou la plus classique beauté.*][35]

The Heine-Christ figure, while borrowing the iconography of pain, suffering, and transcendence from the Christian spiritual tradition, does not necessarily have to be identified with the suffering of a religious type. The ancient pagan stoutness from which Heine had to free himself in order to become a slender martyr could have equally been interpreted as a manifestation of Greek destiny. Montégut's review emphasizes what he esteems to be the "true nature" of the poet. The last act of Heine's life is thus marked by the revenge of the Judeo-Christian martyr and the rejection of the Greek image in which Heine delighted; ultimately it reduces him to his Jewish or Nazarean origins.[36]

> The terrible neurosis had avenged the outraged Nazarenism by effacing all traces of the Hellenist and only making the features of the race to which he belonged reappear, in which the spiritualism against which his eloquent impiety had so often risen up dominated. [*La terrible névrose avait vengé le nazarénisme outragé en effaçant toute trace de l'hellénisant et en faisant reparaître seuls les traits de la race à laquelle il appartenait et où domina toujours le spiritualisme exclusif contre lequel son éloquente impiété s'était si souvent élevée.*][37]

In order to measure the irony of such a remark, it suffices to recall Heine's *Ludwig Börne. Eine Denkschrift*, in which he establishes a binary typology between the Greek type [*Menschen von lebensheiterem, entfaltungsstolzem und realistischem Wesen*] and the Nazarean (or

Jewish) type, which itself is associated with the Christian one [*Menschen mit aszetischen, bildfeindlichen, vergeistigungssüchtigen Trieben.*] But Heine's description, far from constituting a return to a poetics of identity, speaks of a natural disposition (*ein Naturell*) or an intellectual attitude [*eine sowohl angeborne als angebildete Geisteisrichtung und Anschauungsweise*], never an ethnic definition.[38]

Although towards the end of the century, and at the beginning of the twentieth century, readings of Heine tend to favor more and more his Jewish origins as an explanation of the specificity of his work, Heine's romantic and post-romantic reception remains intriguing in its haunting imaginary *ekphrasis* of the poet.[39] In an article she wrote in 1867, Camille Selden compares Heine's poetry to Flemish or Italian paintings:

> Through the most extraordinary and most unusual metamorphosis, each idea and each event transforms in his imagination into a painting, everything takes on color, shape and finish (. . .). Walk through the enchanted gallery that appears before your eyes, you will see a Titian next to a Holbein, a courtesan of Giorgione displaying her opulent shoulders next to the lowered head of a Virgin of Albrecht Dürer. [*Par la métamorphose la plus merveilleuse et la plus rare, toute idée et tout événement se transforment aussitôt dans son imagination en un tableau, tout se colore, se précise et se complète (. . .). Parcourez tout au long la merveilleuse galerie qui s'ouvre devant vous vous verrez un Titien auprès d'un Holbein, une courtisane du Giorgione étalant ses épaules opulentes auprès du front baissé d'une Vierge d'Albert Dürer.*][40]

That Camille Selden sees rich pictures in Heine's poetry calls to mind the inverted movement in which the critics saw paintings in the figure of the poet, paintings evoking their idea of the ancient imperative of carpe diem to be replaced by ascetic yet sublime images of a religious character. Because Heine came to incarnate both the luxuriant nature of Italian painting and the severity of its German counterpart, the Christianizing of the poet at the end of his life points to a particular aesthetic vision, that of an asceticism still declared beautiful. In transforming the poet into an *image* interpreted by enthusiastic critics, Heine's unique reception appears as an exercice de style whose visual details comprise a palette of literary strokes still too complex to interpret.

Notes

This article was originally published in *The Germanic Review*, Vol. 74: 4, (Fall 1999) and is being reprinted with the permission of Heldref Publications.

1. Klaus Mann. *Der Wendepunkt. Ein Lebensbericht.* (München: Nymphenburger Verlag, 1969), p. 110. "The Heine of my Olympus is by no means the popular author of the "Book of Songs," but the wretched invalid of his last years in Paris, stricken with disease and poverty; writhing, shrinking, rotting in his bed; pinched and shaken by most hideous pains but still quiveringly alive, still alert and sagacious, in the midst of his agonies." Klaus Mann, *The Turning Point* (New York: Fischer, 1942), p. 208.

2. Gautier, *Le Moniteur*, February 1856.

3. This drawing is a reprint of the famous image of Heine published in *La Revue des deux mondes* in 1852.

4. Jean-Marie Carré. *Les Ecrivains français et le mirage allemand.* (Paris: Boivin et Cie, 1948).

5. Carré, *Les Ecrivains*, XII.

6. For a presentation of the Jewish German circles, see, for example, Michel Espagne, *Les Juifs allemands de Paris à l'époque de Heine. La Translation ashkenaze* (Paris: Presses universitaires de France, 1996).

7. Cf. Claude Porcell's *Heine écrivain français? Les Œuvres de Heine à travers les manuscrits. Genèse, publication, réception* (Ph.D. diss., University of Paris IV—Sorbonne, 1977).

8. Philippe Ariès, *Western Attitudes Toward Death: From the Middle Ages to the Present* (Baltimore: John Hopkins, 1974), pp. 58–9. See also Philippe Ariès, *L'Homme devant la mort* (Paris: Seuil, 1977).

9. Sainte-Beuve. *Premiers lundis* (Paris: Gallimard, coll. La Pléiade, 1956), I: 551–2. This article, a review of *Französische Zustände (De la France)* was first published in *Le National*, in the arts section on 8 August 1833.

10. Barbey d'Aurevilly, *Les Œuvres et les hommes* (Paris: Alphonse Lemerre, 1840), XII: 161.

11. Théophile Gautier, *Portraits et souvenirs littéraires* (Paris: Bibliothèque Charpentier et Fasquelle), p. 109.

12. Philarète Chasles, "Henri Heine," *Revue de Paris* (April 1835): 202.

13. Philibert Audebrand. *Petits Mémoires du XIXe siècle* (Paris: Calmann-Lévy, 1892), p. 12.

14. D. Stern, "Etudes sur l'Allemagne," *La Revue des deux mondes* 8 (1844): 861.

15. Philibert Audebrand, *Petits Mémoires*, p. 27.

16. Heinrich Heine, *Französische Zustände*, Artikel VI (Berlin und Weimar: Aufbau-Verlag, 1986), 4: 94–5.

17. Gautier, *Portraits*, p. 108.

18. Edmond et Jules de Goncourt, *Journal. Mémoires de la vie littéraire* (Paris: Flammarion et Fasquelle, 1904), 2: 210. The Goncourt brothers are quoting Gautier here. (Entry of 20 June 1864).

19. Barbey d'Aurevilly, *Les Poètes. Les Œuvres et les hommes* (Paris: n.p., 1899), 9: 117–8.

20. Gautier. *Portraits*, p. 116.

21. Caroline Jaubert, *Souvenirs* (Paris: J. Hetzel, 1848), p. 318.

22. Gautier, *Portraits*, p. 116.

23. Jules Legras, *Henri Heine Poète* (Paris: Calmann-Lévy, 1897).

24. The French version of Gustav Heine's text appeared in *La Revue de France*, no. 21 November 1, 1924) under the title *"Les Dernières Années de Henri Heine. Notes inédites de son frère Gustave Heine."*

25. Gautier, *Portraits*, p. 118.

26. As Professor Sammons pointed out to me, on the whole history of *La Revue des deux mondes*, only two imprints of this sort were published, one was Heine, the other Carlyle.

27. Emile Hennequin, Etudes de critique scientifique. Ecrivains francisés. (Paris: Librairie académique Didière, 1889), p. 84.

28. Caroline Jaubert, *Souvenirs*, p. 289.

29. Gautier, *Portraits*, p. 110.

30. Camille Selden (*die Mouche*), "Henri Heine et l'Esprit moderne en Allemagne," *Revue nationale et étrangère, politique, scientifique et littéraire* 1 (April 1867): 239.

31. Meißner is quoted by Joseph Dresch in *Heine à Paris, 1831–1956* (Paris: Didier, 1956), p. 143.

32. Camille Selden, *Les derniers Jours de Henri Heine* (Paris: Calmann-Lévy, 1884), p. 12.

33. Saint-René Taillandier, *Ecrivains et poètes modernes* (Paris: Michel Lévy Frères, 1861), p. 152–3.

34. See Edouard Drumont, *La France juive devant l'opinion* (Paris: Marpon et Flammarion, 1886), p. 47.

35. Emile Montégut, "Esquisses littéraires," *La Revue des deux mondes* 15 (May 1884): 245–6.

36. Gautier notes that Heine complained about the vignette published in *La Revue des deux mondes* which made him look like a "Christ painted by Morales." [Je veux être peint en beau, comme les jolies femmes (. . .) substituez mon ancienne image à cette piteuse effigie.] Th. Gautier, *Portraits et souvenirs littéraires* (Paris: Bibliothèque Charpentier Fasquelle), pp. 107–8.

37. Montégut, "Esquisses littéraires," p. 265.

38. Heinrich Heine, *Ludwig Börne. Eine Denkschrift* (Berlin und Weimar: Aufbau-Verlag, 1986), 5: 178.

39. Paul Bourget attributes for example Heine's style to his Jewish origin, thus emphasizing his capacity for assimilation. Paul Bourget, "L'Enfance de Henri Heine," *Revue critique des idées et des livres*, no. 97 (April 25, 1912): 128–29. For a specialist in hygiene and microbiology, a few years later, Heine's writing is to be attributed to the poet's "morbid temperament," therefore to his heredity. Dr Jean Bastard, *Un Malade de talent: Henri Heine* (Lyon: Bosc, 1930).

40. Selden, *Revue nationale*, p. 229.

Part III
From Fin de Siècle
to Modernist Connections

Chapter 4

GIRLS, GIRLS, GIRLS
Re-Membering the Body

Terri J. Gordon

> *The revue caters to the bourgeois need for diversion, more in terms of number than in the nature and design of its programs. It will soon exhaust its store of inspiration. Ever since it undressed the female body to the point of total nudity, its only available mode of variety was quantity; soon there will be more girls than spectators.*
>
> —Walter Benjamin, "Revue oder Theater"

In the 1929 show at the Folies-Bergère in Paris, "*De la Folie Pure*," a sketch entitled "*Les Beautés Mondiales*" offers a potent vision of Germany after World War I. Reproduced as a spread in the *Revue des Folies-Bergère*, the picture features a hyper-stylized tank moving forward slowly on a metal belt. Nineteen giant canons shoot forth at sharp angles from the machine. Light glints off the surface, casting black and white shadows along the metal rods. Gunpowder hangs in a haze in the air. A half-naked woman presides over the machine, a long white stole draped over her black-gloved arms. A row of automated figures marches stiffly in front. The beauty of Essen stands proud and tall. The girls move laterally as if on a conveyer belt. The machine moves inexorably forward. A fantasy of fusion. Of cataclysmic release. A dream of apocalypse. This cultural coupling of *Ares* and *Eros* is by no means unique in the interwar period. Drawing on the utopic vision of the machine common to Italian futurism and Russian constructivism, the music hall of the 1920s gave birth to a new aesthetic, the staging of half-naked dancers in highly ornamental patterns.[1] In his famous 1927 essay, "The Mass Ornament," Siegfried Kracauer understands this phenomenon as the "mass ornament," an abstract, geometric display of "indissoluble female units" whose uniform movements serve as "mathematical demonstrations."[2] The machine aesthetic of the revue, which harkens back to the baroque court ballet and anticipates the Fascist aesthetic that will shape Leni Riefenstahl's Nazi-era films, points to the lasting impact of the Great War in the postwar imagination.[3] As German critic Alfred Polgar writes in a piece entitled "Girls," "There is more than just erotic magic in the appearance and behavior of the girls: there is the magic of militarism. The trained precision, the straight lines, the regular rhythmic beat [. . .] the obedience to invisible but ineluctable orders, the marvelous 'drill', the submersion of the individual into the group, the concentration of bodies into a single collective 'body'."[4]

Considering the recent experience of the war, it is significant to find images of the military projected for pleasurable purposes. Due to the first wide-scale deployment of instruments of modern warfare, World War I took an unprecedented toll in human life, resulting in over nine million dead and over twenty million wounded. The trenches of the Western Front, which extended from the North Sea to Switzerland via Belgium, Flanders, and France, provided an *ethos* of warfare never before experienced.[5] Modris Ecksteins describes the "battle ballet" in the war zones of Verdun, the Somme, and Ypres as an unremitting assault on the senses: a deafening barrage of machine gun and artillery fire and high velocity shells exploding in the air with apocalyptic force.[6] The efficiency of the machine gun allowed defending units to "mow down" their attackers in rows "with the mechanical efficiency of a scythe."[7] A number of accounts of machine gun warfare employ mechanical images, recalling German soldiers falling like "cardboard soldiers" and "shooting-gallery targets."[8] The Great War, which George Mosse calls "war in an age of technology," made manifest the deadly power of modern technology and signaled the victory of the machine over man.[9] As Ernst Jünger writes in his war diaries:

> The war battle is a frightful competition of industries (. . . .) Here, the era from which we come shows its cards. The domination of the machine over men, of the servant over the master, becomes apparent. (. . .) Here, the style of a materialistic generation is uncovered, and technology celebrates a bloody triumph. Here, a bill is paid which seemed old and forgotten.[10]

The bloodiest war in history up to that point, the Great War resulted in at least ten million disabled persons.[11] The weapons employed in the war, from hand grenades to chlorine gas to high velocity shells, lead to a mutilation on a scale never before experienced. More than forty-one thousand soldiers had their arms or legs amputated during the war; thousands more suffered serious injuries to their heads, eyes, and bodies.[12] The Bastille Day celebration in France following the signing of the Treaty of Versailles was marked by a solemn recognition of the suffering of the "lost generation." Kenneth Silver describes the Bastille Day celebration in France in 1919 as follows: "As living testimony to France's heroic suffering, it was the *mutilés de guerre* that led the way—facially disfigured, some blinded, bandaged, many with limbs missing, many others on crutches, all decorated—these were the solemn advance guard of the great procession as depicted by the painter Galtier-Boissière."[13] The dismembered body altered the landscape of the civilian population, serving as a visible mark and reminder of the devastation wrought by the war: "The wartime aesthetics of the male body (. . .) spread into civilian society after the war. The male body was no more than the sum of its various parts and the dismembered man became Everyman."[14]

Given the significant losses suffered in the war and the visible signs of the carnage of the war, why does the military body return so suddenly? And in such a frivolous form? If World War I was the "war to end all wars," the war that discredited notions of chivalry and heroism dating from the Middle Ages, the war that seemed in the end to have been fought for no reason at all, why would a military aesthetic inform the most popular form of entertainment of the period? Why would images of the military and the machine be deployed as light entertainment? And why does this *mise en scène* take shape in the form of young girls, in the form of *femmes-machines*?

This essay suggests that the phenomenon of the revue is intimately connected to the experience of the war, that it is both a consequence of and a response to the trauma of the war. The experience of the war provided a starting point for the most important artistic movements in the period, from avant-garde cinema to *Neue Sachlichkeit* to French surrealism. Images of the *femme-machine* littered the cultural landscape, appearing in films such as Fritz Lang's *Metropolis* (1927), the photography of Man Ray and Hans Bellmer, Dada photomontage and collage, and surrealist art exhibits. In this essay, I examine the girl phenomenon in relation to the historical avant-garde in order to draw out a number of culturally disjunctive responses to trauma. The central theses guiding my analysis are the following: (1) The prevalence of the image of the *femme-machine* in mass culture and avant-garde art points to the trauma of the war in the large sense and the correlated trauma of technology in a smaller sense; (2) The creation of a *femme-machine* is an operation of *displacement*—a displacement of the (male) machine and/or the male soldier onto the body of woman; and (3) This operation of displacement, which reveals a constellation of male fears and fantasies concerning both sexuality and technology (Huyssen), provides a vehicle by which we may understand larger cultural responses to the trauma of the war.[15] This study reveals some important differences in cultural formations, but cross-cultural commonalities. The strikingly similar reception in the press in Paris and Berlin in the interwar period suggests that the revue held a common appeal for the inhabitants of the two cities. While France and Germany exited the war with radically different positions, the citizens of the two countries shared in a sense of disillusionment and irretrievable loss, losses marked by the war memorials and cemeteries remaining on the empty battlefields of northern France and Flanders.[16] This essay argues that the revue provides a very different kind of commemoration, a re-membering which is also a forgetting.

I. *Femmes-machines*

The interwar period witnessed a deluge of troupes of girls, including the Tiller Girls, the Hoffmann Girls, the Fisher Girls, the Jackson Girls, and the Lawrence Girls. The girls performed in the world's major music halls, from Ziegfield's Follies in New York to the *Folies-Bergère* in Paris to the *Theater am Admiralspalast* and the *Grosses Schauspielhaus* in Berlin. Originating in New York and evolving via Paris, the nude revues soon spread to Europe's capitals, finding a particularly inviting audience in Berlin, where German producers such as Hermann Haller, James Klein, and Erik Charell fashioned their shows on the model of the *Folies-Bergère*. A testament to the prosperity of the Roaring Twenties, the shows, called "super-revues" or "hyper-revues," were elaborate productions whose appeal drew largely from the deployment of nudity in numbers. In the program of *"Von Mund zu Mund,"* the 1926 Erik Charell revue, Stefan Grossmann proclaimed, *"Die Welt Wird Nackt!"* [The world will be naked!].[17] For his 1924 revue entitled *"Das hat die Welt noch nicht geseh'n,"* James Klein announced, *"Tausend nackte Frauen!"* [A thousand naked women!][18]

On a formal level, a troupe, which dance critic André Levinson calls "a caterpillar with thirty-two feet,"[19] performs as a perfectly synchronized unit. In lines of twelve, fourteen, or sixteen, the girls execute their steps with geometrical precision, resembling one another like multiplying images in a game of mirrors.[20] Classic moves include the railroad, in which the girls appear to sit on the knees of one another; a domino in which they collapse in a line like bowling-pins; and a conveyor belt, in which they create an undulating pattern resembling a wave.[21] The constant shifting of geometrical patterns produces a kaleidoscopic effect, a multicolored facade of "living facets" in permanent transformation.[22] Not only was the revue based on an aesthetic principle of replication, but a phenomenon of "twins" and "sisters" dominated the stage. The era evinced a strange cultural impulse toward repetition and replication, one that manifested itself on stage in the formal production of twins, doubles, and girls in series.

These "dancing doubles" on stage gave rise to a vision of automation in the press of the period.[23] Articles in the press repeatedly employed mechanical metaphors, comparing the revue girls to automata and human puppets. Legrand-Chabrier, a theater reviewer of the time whose articles on the revue appeared in a column in *La Presse* entitled "Pistes et Plateaux," wrote: "A troop of these girls is like one single girl replicated in the form of six, ten or twelve mechanical dolls."[24] André Levinson compared the girl troupe to a hydra with nodding dolls' heads, a metaphor that captures the self-replicating nature of the impotent mechanism: "Automatons, these girls; but a wondrous Hydra, too, with twelve or twice twelve placid and nodding dolls' heads."[25] One of the more popular illustrated magazines consecrated to the revue was entitled *Jolies Poupées*.

Embodied in this notion of the dancing automaton are aspects of the military and the machine. As Peter Jelavich suggests in his important study of the Weimar revue in *Berlin Cabaret*, the highly mechanized nature of the girls' gestures and the absolute simultaneity of their movements bring to mind both a conveyer belt and a military parade.[26] A photo that appeared in *Le Petit Journal* in December 1932 captures this triple image in the figure of the toy soldier. The shot features a row of little wooden soldiers, under which a caption reads:

> [T]he girls are most certainly living dolls. They have the measured step, the uniform appearance, and a sort of rigidity in the exercises that they are assigned. When they are lined up, they seem to be linked together by an invisible thread commanding an invisible spring.

With their stiff gestures and their uniform appearance, the girls resemble a line of little wooden soldiers heading out to war in a play reality.[27]

LES USINES DU PLAISIR

As early as 1929, Maurice Verne established a link between the revue and the factory, baptizing the revues *usines du plaisir*, female factories engaged in the scientific fabrication of pleasure.[28] "The female nude is raw material like any other article of the factory," Verne writes in a serialized article that appeared in *Paris-Soir* in 1928.[29] The raw material in these industrial pleasure plants, the female nude became a cog in the machine, a *femme-machine* whose movements were regulated by the precise choreography of the revue.[30] Weimar critic Adam Kuckhoff refers to the "machine-like exactness" of the Tiller Girls, whose clock-like movements serve as a "regulating metronome."[31] In a 1931 revue entitled *"L'Usine à Folies,"* the Folies-Bergère evinced a self-consciousness about the mechanized nature of the genre, producing a revue against the backdrop of a factory. A spread of the show reproduced in the September 15, 1931 edition of *Paris Music-Hall* contains the headline: *"Quelques-uns des plus jolis 'produits' de l'Usine à Folies aux Folies-Bergère"* [Some of the prettiest 'products' of the *Usine à Folies* at the *Folies-Bergère*].

The predominant machine metaphor reflected the new industrial production techniques introduced to Europe by Taylorism and Fordism, the American systems of labor management and industrial mass production, respectively.[32] Much like the products of an assembly line and conveyor belt, the girls were produced *en masse* in dancing schools in England and America and exported to foreign stages for consumption, becoming what Walter Benjamin calls a "mass article." If a Tiller Girl fell ill or left the troupe before the end of her engagement, a replacement immediately arrived from the appropriately industrial town of Manchester, England. Titles of articles in the press included: "*Le Fabricant de Girls*" (The Girl Manufacturer) and "*La Fabrication Industrielle des Chorus-Girls*" (The Mass Production of Chorus Girls).[33] John Tiller, the producer of the Tiller Girls, was known to say of his girls, "I rent them by the yard."[34] Al Bert, producer of the "Bringjoy Girls," claimed his job consisted in the mass production of girls "made in England."[35] A series of photos entitled "Les Girls?" which appeared in the January 15, 1929 edition of *Paris Music-Hall* makes an explicit connection between Fordism and Girl production, comparing the manufacture of revue girls to that of mass-produced automobiles: "*Comme les autos Citroën, (elles) se fabriquent en série, par six, dix, douze ou seize. Généralement made in England*" [Like Citroëns, (they) are fabricated in series of six, ten, twelve or sixteen. Generally made in England].

Not only were the dancers products of a thriving Girl industry, but their performances reflected the uniformity and replication characteristic of mass production as well. For Walter Benjamin, the staging of repetition in the revue is exemplary of the "dialectic of commodity production in advanced capitalism," in which the new is constantly replaced by the ever-the-same.[36] A note in *Das Passagen-Werk*, "'*Les Sept Vieillards*' on the subject of eternal sameness. Chorus girls," points to a relationship between the revue girls and the "*sept vieillards*" in Charles Baudelaire's poem of the same name in the "*Tableaux parisiens*" section of *Les Fleurs du mal*.[37] In "*Les Sept Vieillards*," Baudelaire paints a macabre portrait of an "infernal procession" of seven old men whose uncanny repetition ends up derouting the mind of the poet entirely.[38] The sinister quality of the old man arises from his incessant multiplication. In its spectral doubling, the ghost-like procession of "baroque phantoms" produces an uncanny effect on the poet and reader. As Susan Buck-Morss claims, both the "'broken' old man" and the "woman-as-commodity" constitute repetitious urban types, exemplifying the eternal recurrence of the new under high capitalism.[39] What is particularly interesting about the revue (from *re-voir*, to look over or see again) is that it symbolically overdetermines the notion of the eternal recurrence of the same. Benjamin's description of novelty as a "semblance of the new [which] is reflected, like one mirror in another, in the semblance of the ever recurrent" finds its formal manifestation in the performance of the girls.[40] Despite its constantly changing elements, the revue always remains identical to itself. Not only do the girls in a troupe mirror one another, but each troupe resembles each other ("Nothing resembles a girl like another girl, if it is not a troop to another troop.")[41]

Like Benjamin, Kracauer interprets the performances of the revue girls allegorically, as a symbol of the system in which they are embedded. Establishing a formal analogy between the hands of the factory worker and the legs of the Tiller Girls, Kracauer claims that the mass ornament represents the rationalized industrial processes under high capitalism. In "Girls und Krise," Kracauer's review of the performance of the Alfred Jackson Girls at the Scala in 1931, Kracauer compares the revue as a whole to the "ideal of the machine." The revue constitutes a "marvelously precise apparatus," a "girl contraption" composed of individual parts whose existence is intricately bound to the life of the machine.[42] As a sign of the system, the joyful kickline represents the functioning of a thriving economy, capturing the optimism and prosperity of the 1920s:

> They were not merely American products but a demonstration at the same time of the vastness of American production. (. . .) When they formed themselves into an undulating snake, they delivered a radiant illustration of the virtues of the conveyor belt; when they stepped to a rapid beat, it sounded like 'business, business'. (. . .)[43]

MILITARY MACHINES

As Peter Jelavich points out, the aesthetic of the revue called to mind not only the image of the machine, but also that of the military corps.[44] The press was replete with military metaphors, labeling the revue an "army of girls'" and a "military organization."[45] The girls were subject to a militaristic discipline and training. Considered a "troupe" or "battalion," each dance company was under the strict surveillance of a "captain," an older girl in command who directed and disciplined the girls. M. F. W. Jackson, one of the "chiefs" of the girl troops, remarks in an interview: "In our organization, we devote ourselves [to the music hall] as one would devote oneself to military life, with honor, happiness, a spirit of sacrifice and a consciousness of dignity."[46] In their engagements abroad, the members of the troupe were organized according to a precise hierarchy corresponding to that of a military apparatus. Much like in the army, they led an entirely collective existence, living in communal lodgings and practicing and performing as a cohesive unit. "A healthy discipline holds the group together," maintains an article that appeared in *Comoedia* in October 1923. "At the head the 'captain' whose imposing 'Hello girls!' precludes the least stumbling, the slightest delay. Then, in order of size, weight, or hair color, the others take their places. (. . .) [E]ach of their movements is seconded by an energetic command: one! . . . two! . . . one! two! three! four!"[47]

The collective nature of the girls' existence was reflected in their formal aesthetic, evoking images of a military parade. The notion of the "revue" itself, which signifies a theatrical production consisting of satirical sketches, is a derivation of the military review, a military inspection or parade.[48] Levinson describes the girls as a "phalanx" whose steps resound with a distinct military beat. The girls themselves often appeared in uniform on the Paris and Berlin stages in the interwar period. In the 1929 *Folies-Bergère* show, "*De la Folie Pure*," the Alfred Jackson girls appeared in full military attire and in nautical dress. For the Casino de Paris' 1928 production, "*Tout Paris*," a troupe of girls outfitted in military uniform stood at strict attention, their hands lifted in a salute.[49] For Levinson, the cadenced step of the parade march evokes the glory of military victories of the past, the enthusiastic return to the barracks amidst beating drums and flaming flares.[50] Referring to a performance of the Jackson Girls in Berlin, Levinson writes: "The other day, when the Jackson Girls, helmeted and be-plumed, descended the great staircase of the German *Reichstag*, hands on hips, in a goose-step, were they not alluding to the pomp of the vanished Empire, to the solemn splendor of its *Wachtparade?*"[51]

Re-Membering the Body

On an allegorical level, the revue reflects the dual aspects of modern technology in the industrial age. While the aesthetic of the revue evoked the military and the machine, the girls themselves were manufactured like factory goods in a production process that combined the assembly line principles of Fordism and the discipline of the military. Through this parallel process, modern production finds its formal reproduction on stage. In *Berlin Cabaret*, Peter Jelavich makes the compelling claim that the revue provides a critique of the dominating forces of modernity that it appears to support. According to Jelavich, the revue reinforces and *aestheticizes* the fundamental elements of order and control that stand behind technological production.[52] At the same time, the formal aesthetic of the revue brings into stark relief the principle components comprising the modern industrial complex: the reduction of individuals to functioning parts of a whole, the dehumanization of the subject, and the submersion of the individual into the collective. Jelavich writes:

> [M]ore fundamentally, [the Girls] revealed—or perhaps disguised?—an underlying sense of economic and military order that demanded the dissolution of all personality and the dismemberment of the person. The bodies of the Girls embodied a critique of the modernity that they ostensibly represented.[53]

If, as Jelavich points out, the aesthetic of the revue seriously undermines individual subjectivity and personhood, it also restores the collective. Girl production in the interwar period provides a striking quotation of the military production of soldiers and arms in the war. In its collective discipline and order, the aesthetic of the revue draws on the aesthetic of the military corps. The little wooden soldier-girls "linked together by an invisible thread commanding an invisible spring" in *Le Petit Journal* recall the rows of military youth marching on the offensive on the Western Front, themselves lined up like "cardboard soldiers" and "shooting-gallery targets." As is so effectively demonstrated by the famous send-up in Mel Brooke's *The Producers*, featuring chorus-line girls forming a swastika, the kicklines of "girl-soldiers" in the revue radically trivialize the reality of the war. In this way, the revue rejoins a host of other forms of war trivialization which arose during and following the war, such as popular war cinema and theatre, board games, children's toys, picture postcards, and everyday artifacts.[54] George Mosse maintains that such trivia support the Myth of the War Experience, the transformation of the reality of the war into a sacred or mythological event. While war trivia serve as the counterpoint to the monumentalizing forces of public shrines and memorials, they contribute to the Myth of the War Experience in that they disguise and displace the actual experience of war. By rendering the experience of war familiar and commonplace, Mosse suggests, war trivia play the dual role of infusing people with a false sense of control over events and of inuring them to reality.[55] As I shall discuss further in my examination of the impact of trauma on postwar performance art, it is precisely a sense of control and domination over the forces of modernity that is enabled by the militaristic representations in the revue.

Not only does the mechanic aesthetic of the revue trivialize the reality of the war, but it significantly alters it. In its symbolic representation of the military corps, the revue puts the body back together again. The individual body is made whole again and the military body is made whole again. In this way, the revue moves beyond allegorical reflection to perform a "productive" operation, undertaking a formal reconstitution and restoration of the social body. The notion of sacrifice to the whole so fundamental to the Myth of the War Experience finds its physical embodiment here, albeit in trivial form. It is the vision of corporeal integrity in the "imagined" body of the revue that, I would suggest, accounts for the popularity of the cabaret in the interwar period.[56] The revue girls are a kind of disciplinary body in the Foucauldian sense, one of modernity's many "docile bodies" constitutive of a particular form of discursive arrangement. The *mise en scène* of revue girls in the interwar period presents an unusual sort of commodity fetishism. Like Marx's dancing table which stands on its head, these human commodities perform a mystical operation. Through the production of images of health and wholeness, the revue symbolically re-members the body, magically restoring the fractured parts of the social body into one machine-like whole.

II. Dada and Surrealist Machine Art

The representation of the *femme-machine* in avant-garde art and cinema provides an important counterpoint to the troupes of girls that stormed the stages of Paris and Berlin in the interwar period. The visual emphasis on fragmentation, montage, dysfunction, and shattering in much of the art of the period gives expression to a *fractured* body rather than a restored one. The icon of the woman-machine that emerged after the war grows out of a longer literary history. E. T. A. Hoffman's *Der Sandmann* (1816), which features a beautiful, lifelike wooden doll named Olimpia, serves as a romantic precursor to fin de siècle texts, in which female simulacra play a predominant role.[57] In Hoffman's tale, Nathanael, the romantic young hero with a "tempest-tossed soul," falls in love with Olimpia, only to go mad upon discovering that his loved one is an "inanimate puppet."[58] In line with Hoffman's tale, the figure of the automaton in turn-of-the-century texts makes a transition from male to female form.[59] The robotization of the female form marks a curious reversal of the conventional pairing of the masculine with the technological and the feminine with the "biological" and "natural." Taking on a role which is at the same time divine and maternal, the male creator replaces biological reproduction with technological production, creating a de-naturalized, nonreproducing woman-machine. In "The Vamp and the Machine: Fritz Lang's *Metropolis*," Andreas Huyssen makes the compelling argument that the appearance of the woman-machine at the turn of the nineteenth century reflects deep-seated anxieties concerning both the forces of modern technology and female sexuality. Huyssen argues that a distinctive shift in our understanding of technology occurs at the turn of the century. While the android was perceived as a liberating force in the eighteenth century, as "testimony to the genius of mechanical invention," it takes on ominous features in turn-of-the-century literature, becoming a "demonic, inexplicable threat," a "harbinger of chaos and destruction."[60] The creation of a woman-machine thus points to a psychosocial process of projection and displacement which reflects this shift in our perception of technology. "The fears and perceptual anxieties emanating from ever more powerful machines are recast and reconstructed in terms of the male fear of female sexuality," Huyssen writes, "reflecting, in the Freudian account, the male's castration anxiety."[61]

The prototype of the *femme-machine* can be found in Fritz Lang's *Metropolis*, in which the threatening power of female sexuality and modern technology is embodied in the figure of Robot Maria. In the film's most famous scene, a cabaret party organized by the mad scientist Rotwang, Robot Maria performs a seductive dance in a diaphanous gown to an audience of upper-class men. As Maria is lifted onto the ornamental urn, the mesmerized male mass rushes forward and surrounds her with upraised arms. Robot Maria's orgiastic dance unleashes a primal instinct in the spectators, propelling them to a Dionysian dance of their own in the city streets. The crowd of revelers that Maria gaily leads into the city streets echoes the mass of laborers that she incites to destroy the machines in the catacombs. This parallel process, by which Maria uses her libidinal power to provoke the laborers to revolt below and the industrialists to wild abandon above, underscores the link between technology and sexuality, both of which contain dangerous libidinal potential ready to break loose at any moment. In his reading of *Metropolis*, Huyssen argues that Robot Maria represents female sexuality as "technology-out-of-control," reflecting male fears of female sexuality, technology, and the gendered urban masses.[62]

The *femme-machine* appeared across the artistic landscape in the interwar period. Automated figures were a central feature of the First International Dada Fair held in Berlin in 1920, whose signature piece was a stuffed officer-dummy with a plaster pig's head hanging from the ceiling. In Rudolf Schlichter's 1920 "Dada-Dachatelier," the cabaret dancer-as-automaton assumes the significance of an urban type. A watercolor and ink drawing of a series of mechanical metropolitan types on a rooftop terrace, the piece features an automated Tingel-tangel dancer on a podium, her face locked in an alluring smile, her gestures frozen in the motion of the dance. Surrealist art exhibits following World War I also revealed an obsessive fascination with dolls, mannequins, wax figures, and automata. In the late 1920s, a series of photographs devoted to mechanical dolls and mannequins appeared in the surrealist magazine *Variétés*.[63] The "Exposition internationale du surréalisme" held at the Galerie des Beaux-Arts in Paris in January 1938 featured an exhibit entitled "Les plus belles rues de Paris," a city street peopled with mannequins created by surrealist artists Jean Arp, Salvador Dalí, Marcel Duchamp, Max Ernst, Joan Miró, Man Ray, and others. According to Georges Hugnet, these "beauties," which incarnated the "Eternal Feminine in a cardboard vision," were the realization of a Pygmalion dream: "In the presence of these svelte stars (. . .), before their tranquil immodesty, the surrealist artists, who had taken the care to idealize them in materializing their desire, sensed all the soul of Pygmalion."[64] The fascination with female dolls took on life-sized proportions in the work of the expressionist painter and poet Oskar Kokoschka, who had a life-sized doll fashioned in the image of his former lover, Alma Mahler. Much like Nathanael and Olimpia in *Der Sandmann*, Kokoschka accompanied the doll on carriage drives, shows at the theater, and meals at restaurants.[65]

As a number of critics have noted, the experience of the war seriously informed Dada and surrealist photo-montage. The problem of trauma became particularly important after World War I, when the psychic consequence of trench warfare became visible in the large numbers of soldiers experiencing neurasthenia, commonly known as "shell shock." Essentially a phenomenon of the First World War, the condition of shell shock was characterized by motor disturbances, confusion, convulsions, sleeplessness, intense fear, and recurring nightmares.[66] In her article, "'See: *We are all Neurasthenics!*' or; The Trauma of Dada Montage," Brigid Doherty makes the compelling claim that Dada photomontage, particularly the objects exhibited at the First International Dada Fair in the summer of 1920, constitutes a *materialization* of trauma. According to Doherty, Dada photocollage, which conveys trauma both in its discordant form and its politically and sexually volatile content, expresses in artistic form the hysterical manifestations of psychic shock arising on the body of the shell-shocked soldier.[67] The trauma of the war also provided the point of departure for the surrealist movement that grew in the aftermath of Dada. André Breton's and Louis Aragon's interest in a "surreality" was induced by their observations of shell-shocked soldiers in neuropsychiatric clinics in Paris during World War I. The delirium of traumatized soldiers suggested an alternate psychic dimension, prompting the young surrealists to probe deeper into the realm of the unconscious and the surreal.[68] In *Compulsive Beauty*, Hal Foster suggests that the trauma of the war makes itself felt in surrealism not as an outright expression, but rather in the form of a return of the repressed. "The effects of the trauma of the World War I dead and wounded on the postwar imagination of the body are not yet fully appreciated," Foster writes. "This damaged body is magically restored in some classicisms, aggressively prostheticized in others. In some postwar modernisms it seems repressed; in others—i.e., surrealism—this repressed damaged male body seems to return as an uncanny dismembered female body."[69]

As it is out of the scope of this study to examine the artistic vista of the *femme-machine* in depth, I will focus here on the works of two artists who were central to the surrealist movement: the American photographer Man Ray and the German painter and sculptor Hans Bellmer.

My reading centers on Man Ray's *Dancer/Danger* (1920) and a number of photographs from Hans Bellmer's first doll series (1934). In both *Dancer/Dancer* and the *Doll* (*La Poupée*), female sexuality and technology are collapsed in the figure of a mechanical woman. While the works function differently, they both provide instances of a figuration of trauma in a displaced form. A *rapprochement* between Man Ray and Hans Bellmer can be found in the seventh edition of the surrealist organ *Minotaure* (1935), in which the two artists collaborated on the illustrations of a short story by the poet Paul Eluard entitled "Appliquée." Inspired by the figure of Bellmer's *Doll*, Eluard's story features a perverse and narcissistic mechanical girl named Appliquée and her companion Animère. In line with Bellmer's fascination with the inner life of adolescent girls, the work explores the insatiable desires of the little girl, who steals her companion's mask in order to be closer to her and devours the lips in a blind and senseless rage. The narcissistic doubling of the doll-girl is reflected both in a photograph by Bellmer entitled "Composition," an assemblage of two sets of dolls' legs in a cotton-candy setting of children's trappings, and a print by Man Ray of two inverted Chinese masks surrounded by a mass of strawlike black hair.[70]

Like a number of American expatriates, Man Ray's career as an artist flourished in the Paris of the Roaring Twenties. When he joined Marcel Duchamp and Francis Picabia in Paris in July 1921, he was embraced by the Dada group there and became the leading photographer for the French surrealists. His photographs appeared regularly in the three main surrealist periodicals (*La Révolution Surréaliste* from 1924–1930, *Le Surréalisme au service de la Révolution* from 1930–1933, and *Minotaure* from 1933 to 1937) and served to illustrate works by André Breton, Tristan Tzara, and Salvadore Dali, amongst others.[71] The mechanical woman is a recurring topos in Man Ray's work, of which central examples include *Portemanteau* (1921), *Woman* (1920), and *Explosante-fixe* (1934). *Portemanteau* is Man Ray's signature Dada piece. A silver print photograph of a nude model-mannequin, it was originally published as "Dada-photo" in April 1921 in the one and only edition of Duchamp's and Man Ray's *New York Dada*.[72] *Woman*, which was exhibited at the *Salon dada* in Paris in 1921, is Man Ray's first Readymade, a mechanical eggbeater outlined by its longer shadow.[73] *Explosante-fixe* presents a volatile shot of a tango dancer in a whirl of movement, capturing the contained energy and the imminent force of the dance. Reprinted in Breton's *L'Amour fou*, the photograph served as an illustration of one of the three components of Breton's notion of "convulsive beauty," the experience of the marvelous rendered in a shock of recognition: "La beauté convulsive sera érotique-voilée, explosante fixe, magique-circonstancielle ou ne sera pas" [Convulsive beauty will be veiled-erotic, fixed-explosive, magic-circumstantial, or it will not be].[74]

Most pertinent to the subject at hand is Man Ray's *Dancer/Danger*, a drawing that was inspired by the movements of a Spanish dancer Man Ray had seen in a musical.[75] The work was first exhibited at the museum of the Katherine Dreier Société Anonyme in New York in 1920 and later served as inspiration for André Breton, who kept the drawing in his study where it was visible from his desk.[76] An airbrush drawing on glass, the composition consists of two interlocking sets of cogwheels. The shadow of a blueprint and the exactitude of the wheels convey architectural precision. Etchings on the glass suggest shattering. The title, which is lettered into the composition, carries polyvalent meanings. A slight curve in the letter "*C*" allows the word "dancer" to transform into "danger." The drawing implies impossibility. While the roundness of the gears and the fluidity of the interlocking structure suggest the female form and the incessant movement of the dance, the interlocking wheels check one another, freezing the mobility of the dance. Man Ray didn't intend to create a functioning machine. "I asked a mechanic to assemble the three wheels I wanted to include in this work," Man Ray explains. "'Oh, you're crazy, these wheels won't work!' he said."[77] Man Ray's *Dancer/Danger* abets the fear of technology/sexuality in the form of a dysfunctional machine. As Arturo Schwarz suggests, the interlocking wheels form a triangular *vagina dentata* that is permanently locked into place, unable to function.[78]

Like Man Ray, Hans Bellmer found his artistic milieu in Paris. From 1933 to 1937, Bellmer created two series of articulated dolls that were subject to a continual dismantling and remantling. "Plastic anagrams," in the words of the author, the dolls were photographed in a variety of disturbing poses and unlikely settings.[79] Bellmer created the first *Doll* in 1933 with the help of his brother. The armature of the doll was composed of a wooden framework which was often exposed, giving the doll the anatomy of a female automaton. The hollow plaster limbs and the pelvis were attached by ball joints, which allowed the author to disassemble and reassemble the doll at will. The stomach of the *Doll* was fitted with a panoramic device containing photographs designed to provide the viewer with a voyeuristic entry into the inner thoughts of a little girl. The second *Doll*, of which Bellmer produced a more elaborate and symbolic series of photographs, was composed of a more sophisticated system of ball joints and multiple body parts, allowing for more radical reconfigurations of the female anatomy. While Bellmer's work was castigated as "degenerate" in Nazi Germany, the French surrealists embraced the work, publishing a spread of photographs of Bellmer's first *Doll* in the sixth edition of *Minotaure* in the winter of 1934. Paul Eluard composed a series of prose poems to "illustrate" the second *Doll*, which appeared in *Messages* in 1939 and later as a work entitled *Jeux de la poupée* (1949). According to Bellmer's biographer Peter Webb, the *Doll* was the "ideal Surrealist object," effecting, in the words of surrealist artist Jean Brun, "the conjunction of the everyday and the imaginary, the animate and the inanimate, the natural and the artificial."[80] Within months, claims Webb, all of the surrealists had succumbed to the "doll-making craze."[81]

A number of political and personal forces stood behind the creation of Bellmer's first *Doll*: the rise of a repressive state mirroring a repressive father and the recollection of the "secret garden" of his childhood, where he played with adolescent girls "with wide eyes which turn away."[82] The *Doll* was directly inspired by Max Reinhardt's production of Offenbach's *Les Contes d'Hoffmann* (1881), of which *The Sandman* is the first act.[83] Shortly after viewing the three-act opera, Bellmer announced his decision to construct "an artificial girl" with infinite anatomical possibilities.[84] *The Sandman* provides a literary paradigm for Freud's notion of the uncanny (*das Unheimliche*), something which was once familiar (*heimisch*) and has since been repressed.[85] The uncanny is associated with the impression made by "wax-work figures [and] ingeniously constructed dolls and automata" whose uncanny nature lies in their resemblance to human form.[86] Freud attributes the uncanny in the text not so much to the existence of a female simulacrum, but rather to the repressed infantile castration complex, the female genitalia serving for Freud as the "uncanny" place *par excellence*, the place which was once *heimisch* and from which the (male) subject is now estranged. In Hoffmann's tale, the threat of castration takes shape in the figure of the Sandman, the bad father figure Coppelius/Coppola who threatens to rob Nathanael of his eyes.[87] The terrifying childhood tale is psychically reenacted throughout the novella—in the formative scene at Nathanael's childhood home in which the diabolical lawyer Coppelius rearranges the limbs of the little boy as one would a mechanical doll, in Nathanael's poem in which Clara's eyes leap out of her head and trace a burning hole in the boy's chest, and in the climactic scene in which Nathanael discovers gaping black holes in the place of Olimpia's eyes. It is the same symbolic reenactment of castration as dismemberment which comes to the fore in Hans Bellmer's series of dolls. As Rosalind Krauss points out, Bellmer's doll series, which she calls "construction *as* dismemberment," reenact the scene of castration in their continual dismemberment of the figure of the *Doll*.[88] According to Krauss, the *Doll* provides a dual function, the multiplicity of phallic symbols in a disfigured female form both summoning forth the threat of castration and providing a defense against it.[89]

Dismemberment is the central process at work in the ten photographs that comprise *Die Puppe* (1934), all of which were reproduced in a larger spread in *Minotaure* 6 in 1934 under the heading, "Variations sur le montage d'une mineure articulée." The fourth plate shows the doll entirely disassembled, a montage of disconnected parts—a plaster leg, a wooden torso, a face mask, a jointed leg, an uncanny skeletal hand. A number of plates in this series distinctly recall the figure of the dismembered soldier. In the third plate, which features the wooden doll at the side of her maker, aspects of the doll's framework are exposed. The revealed wooden armature of the leg recalls a prosthetic limb, the singular papier-mâché leg a plaster cast, the missing arms a dismembered torso, the hole in the stomach a gaping wound. In Bellmer's fetishistic and ritualistic dismemberment of the dolls is expressed a deep anxiety concerning the integrity of the body.[90] Castration in Bellmer's work becomes a sign that figures mechanical destruction and biological reproduction. A 1937 sculpture entitled *Machine-Gunneress in a State of Grace* makes the connection between technology and sexuality explicit. The "machine gunneress" in the wood and metal sculpture appears in the form of a praying mantis composed of disjointed parts of the female anatomy (breasts, two vulvas, buttocks and genitalia). The mantis stands in a predatory position, the "state of grace" referring to the prayer-like position the mantis assumes while lying in wait for its prey. The round genitalia recall the head of the mantid that can turn in all directions, the breasts the protruding eyes of the voracious insect. Here the sexual organs stand in for military organs, both of which serve as organs of destruction threatening to devour and consume the male.

Man Ray's *Dancer/Danger* and Hans Bellmer's doll series meet in a process of displacement and disfiguration, both works symbolizing the machine in female form and effecting a de-construction of the woman-machine. If Man Ray's dancer is, in effect, a mechanical still life, Hans Bellmer's doll series provide a more active variation on the theme of dysfunction. In both works, the trauma of the war can be felt. Man Ray's airbrush drawing is embedded in a setting of broken glass. The dead machine appears in the aftermath of a shattering, of a fracturing beyond repair. It is this moment of shattering to which Bellmer's work constantly returns. The artistic process at work in Hans Bellmer's doll series is an incessant and compulsive return to a phantasmatic primal scene staged as a battleground of desire. While Bellmer's dolls arose in relation to a rising Fascist state, the stark evocation of the dismembered soldier in the first doll series emphasizes the extent to which the carnage of World War I (in which Bellmer's authoritarian father proudly served) impacted the artist's imaginary. But in the tone and artistic processes, these works radically diverge. The *jeu de mots* in the title of *Dancer/Danger* suggests play and ironic distance. In the distance that the artist takes from this work is an implicit critique of mass production and a self-critique as well. Hans Bellmer, on the other hand, is directly and actively involved in an artistic reenactment of trauma. Plagued by personal childhood dramas and the rise of a tyrannical state, Bellmer effects an unmediated violence on the body of dolls, the expression of a dual revolt against the rule of paternal authority and the reign of his unconscious desires.

III. Repetition and Trauma

"At a certain point in time," Walter Benjamin writes in *Das Passagen-Werk*, "the motif of the doll acquires a sociocritical significance."[91] Benjamin's remark has particular resonance in the interwar period. The pervasive character of the mechanical woman in art and mass culture indicates the existence of a sociopolitical dimension in *Girlkultur*, one which is informed both by the mass production of arms and the mass production of goods. The disjunction between many of the images of the *femme-machine* in avant-garde art and entertainment suggests that the revue effects an operation beyond that of traumatic expression or allegorical reflection. The most widely accepted explanation for the popularity of the revues in the interwar period is a desire for distraction. Called by one critic a "grand bazar de distraction pour tous,"[92] the revue was seen as an opiate for the masses, an escape both from industrial work processes and the recent experience of the war. According to André Sallee, the kaleidoscopic explosion of the revue provided a temporary escape from the years of "mud and death" which remained etched in the memories of the public: "From Médrano's *Boum Boum* to Trenet's *Boum!*, from the revue *PaRiKiRi* to *Tout va très bien, Madame la Marquise* circulates the same overexcited current, the same speculation on the market of illusions. We throw ourselves into multicolored ephemera in order to forget the years of mud and death."[93]

While the desire for distraction is certainly a significant factor in the overwhelming popularity of the revues, I would suggest that the phenomenon of the revue marks not only a desire to escape the memories of the war, but also a need to work through the trauma of it. According to Freud, repetition compulsion, or the "daemonic compulsion to repeat," constitutes a formative moment in the "working out" of a trauma. The subject, fixated to the incident of shock, repeatedly returns to and replays the moment of trauma. For Freud, the repetitive nightmares suffered by shell-shocked soldiers constituted the most remarkable symptom of neurasthenia in that the content of their dreams was not subject to conscious recall. The event in essence returned against the will of the subject. It was this central problem of repetition that led Freud to revise his notion of dreams as wish fulfillments and to posit the existence of a death drive.[94] In his discussion of traumatic neuroses in *Beyond the Pleasure Principle* (1920), a significant number of which arose from World War I, Freud understands these neuroses as a result of a "breach" in the individual's protective shield. Repetitive dreams by trauma victims constitute for Freud retrospective attempts to master the large quantities of excitation to which they were exposed through the development of the anxiety necessary to shield them from the shock they already received.[95]

The "Fort-da" (gone-here) case, Freud's classic example of a traumatic neurosis, illustrates the process by which mastery over a traumatic experience is achieved through the course of repetition.[96] This case centers around the repetitive game of an eighteen-month-old boy, in which the boy throws away a wooden spool attached to a string and retrieves it with satisfaction. This recurrent game of disappearance and return stages the boy's anxiety at the distressing absences of his mother, to whom he is emotionally cathected. In the boy's active command of the situation, by which he symbolically provokes his mother's disappearance and her subsequent return, the boy makes himself master of it, rendering the traumatic experience a pleasurable one.

In its constant *mise en scène* of the machine, does the revue serve as a forum for the reenactment of trauma? Does it point to a kind of collective attempt to "work through" the trauma of modern technology induced by World War I and the industrial age? On one level, the reiterative staging of traumatic material in the revue mimics the *mechanism* of repetition compulsion. Like the spool and thread in the "Fort-da" case, the dancers on stage take on symbolic proportions, embodying the strength, order, and efficiency of the modern machine. Like the little boy's attempt to make himself master of a traumatic event through the active staging of it, the revue marks an attempt to gain control over the processes of industrialization through the repetitive staging of these processes. In its endless generation of symbols of mass production in the safe and controlled environment of the music hall, the revue (and by extension the spectator) serves both to control and contain these images. The threatening power both of female sexuality and modern technology is harnessed in the figure of female automata. In the trivialization and aestheticization of modern technological forces, the revue renders them pleasurable and innocuous.

However, the traumatic aspects of the war appear to be lost in this representation. Rather than representing the dangerous and destructive aspects of technology, the revue projects a utopic vision of the machine, producing illusory images of wholeness and productivity. Physical beauty takes on the strength and replicability of the mass-produced machine. The dancers on stage represent physical perfection in accordance with an industrial model, in which progress results in the production of perfect copies. This cult of physical perfection in the interwar period has reactionary overtones, which is perceptible in some of the social commentary on dance in the 1920s. In the program for the 1926 Charell revue, "Für Dich," Ola Jansen's commentary anticipates Nazi discourse in a startling way: "Firm the smile on their young lips, strictly controlled the play of the muscles in their slim bodies. The whole thing one movement, their will one thought that demands only beauty, perfection, polish in the movement—triumphant revue."[97] Levinson echoes this statement, referring to the symbolic role played by the "blonde Barbarians" on stage, who reflect the supremacy bestowed upon biological and mechanical forces in the modern age. "For [the Girls] are pure symbol, the living image of our life, which substitutes for the glamour of the mind and the quest of the sublime the worship of biological forces and mechanical forces," Levinson writes. "That is the lesson we should take to heart, as we watch—like the Romans of the Decadence—the parade of these 'sturdy, blonde Barbarians.'"[98]

The deployment of machinic images in the revue reveals a significant disjunction between avant-garde art and mass culture in the interwar period. Following World War I, the trauma of the war found its artistic expression in many of the fragmented bodies prevalent in the machine art of Dada and surrealist photocollage. Through the production of images of wholeness, the revue serves to mediate the anxiety of the industrial age. The counterpoint to psychic and social fragmentation, the woman-machine in the revue is a uniform whole which can reproduce *ad infinitum*. Unlike the violently dismembered dolls in Hans Bellmer's *Poupée* series or the disjointed images in Dada photomontage, the militarized body of the revue girls embodies notions of strength, integrity, and purity. Unlike Man Ray's gridlocked *femme-machine*, the revue girls represent productive, fully functioning units. Given the utopic vision of the machine deployed in the revue, one can question whether it constitutes a "working through" of the trauma of the war or a denial of it altogether. In its creation of illusory images of wholeness, the reenactment of the machine in the revue is ultimately a form of disavowal.[99] In this sense, re-membering is forgetting.

NOTES

Walter Benjamin and Bernhard Reich, "Revue oder Theater," *Der Querschnitt*, Band 5, no. 2 (1925): 1043. Translation modified from Peter Jelavich, *Berlin Cabaret* (Cambridge: Harvard University Press, 1993), p. 180. All translations are the author's unless otherwise indicated.

1. I am grateful to the curators at the Bibliothèque de l'Arsenal in Paris; the Zentrum für Berlin-Studien at the Zentral- und Landesbibliothek

Berlin, the Landesarchiv, the Akademie der Künste, and the Märkisches Museum in Berlin; and the Deutsches Kabarett Archiv in Mainz for their generous assistance in my archival research into the cabaret. I have retained the word "girl" throughout this article in order to remain consistent with the terminology of the period as well as the age of the revue dancers, who were often quite young.

2. Siegfried Kracauer, "The Mass Ornament," trans. Barbara Correll and Jack Zipes, *New German Critique* 5 (spring 1975): 67.

3. Siegfried Kracauer, *From Caligari to Hitler* (Princeton: Princeton University Press, 1947), p. 301. In his later work, Kracauer makes a direction connection between the cultural and the political mass ornament, referring to the "living ornaments" and "tableaux vivants" of Nazi spectacle. The ornamentalization of the masses in the Nazi era can be seen in the mass gymnastics display of ten thousand female bodies in Leni Riefenstahl's *Fest der Schönheit*, the second part of her documentary covering the 1936 Olympic Games in Berlin, as well as in the visual parade of Nazi soldiers and Hitler Youth at the 1934 Nazi Party Congress in Nuremburg captured in *Triumph of the Will*.

4. Alfred Polgar, "Girls," in *Auswahl: Prosa aus vier Jahrzenten* (Reinbek bei Hamburg: Rowohlt, 1968), pp. 186–87. Cited in Detlev J. K. Peukert, *The Weimar Republic*, trans. Richard Deveson (New York: Hill and Wang, 1987), p. 180.

5. George L. Mosse, *Fallen Soldiers* (New York: Oxford University Press, 1990), p. 4.

6. Modris Ecksteins, *Rites of Spring: The Great War and the Birth of the Modern Age* (Boston: Houghton Mifflin, 1989), p. 139.

7. Ibid., p. 145.

8. Roger Campana, *Les Enfants de la "Grande Revanche": Carnet de route d'un Saint-Cyrien, 1914–1918* (Paris: 1920), p. 204. On the effects of machine gun warfare, the Frenchman Roger Campana wrote: "The Germans fell like cardboard soldiers" while the Englishman Herbert Read described the German soldiers as falling like shooting-gallery targets. Herbert Read, "In Retreat: A Journey of the Retreat of the Fifth Army from St. Quentin, March 1918," in *The Contrary Experience* (London: Horizon Press, 1963), p. 248. A similar image was employed by a German machine-gunner in his description of a British offensive at the Somme: "When we started firing we just had to load and reload. They went down in the hundreds. You didn't have to aim, we just

fired into them." John Ellis, *Eye-Deep in Hell* (London: Fontana, 1977), p. 94. All examples drawn from Ecksteins, *Rites of Spring*, pp. 145–146.

9. Mosse, *Fallen Soldiers*, p. 4.

10. Ernst Jünger, "Feuer und Blut: Ein kleiner Ausschnitt aus einer großen Schlacht," in *Tagebücher I* (1926; reprint, Stuttgart: Ernst Klett, 1960), p. 465. Trans. in Anton Kaes, "Cinema and Modernity: On Fritz Lang's *Metropolis*," in Reinhold Grimm and Jost Hermand, eds., *High and Low Cultures: German Attempts at Mediation* (Madison, WI: University of Wisconsin Press, 1994), p. 24.

11. The International Labour Organization estimated the number of men disabled by the war at ten million in 1923. See Jay Winter, *Sites of memory, Sites of mourning: The Great War in European cultural history* (Cambridge: Cambridge University Press, 1995), p. 46.

12. See Joanna Bourke, *Dismembering the Male: Men's Bodies, Britain and the Great War* (Chicago: University of Chicago Press, 1996), p. 33.

13. Kenneth E. Silver, *Esprit de Corps: The Art of the Parisian Avant-Garde and the First World War, 1914–1925* (Princeton: Princeton University Press, 1989), p. 221.

14. Bourke, *Dismembering the Male*, p. 16.

15. See Andreas Huyssen, "The Vamp and the Machine: Fritz Lang's *Metropolis*," in *After the Great Divide: Modernism, Mass Culture, Postmodernism* (Bloomington and Indianapolis, IN: Indiana University Press, 1986), pp. 65–81.

16. See Jay Winter's *Sites of memory, Sites of mourning* for a discussion of the collective culture of mourning and commemoration that arose in France, Britain, and Germany following the war. See also Pierre Nora, ed., *Les Lieux de mémoire* (Paris: Gallimard, 1984).

17. *Von Mund zu Mund: Magazin und Programm*, Charell Revue 1926–1927, Grosses Schauspielhaus, Berlin.

18. Wolfgang Jansen, *Glanzrevuen der zwanziger Jahre* (Berlin: Edition Hentrich, 1987), p. 47.

19. André Levinson, "The Girls," in *André Levinson on Dance: Writings from Paris in the Twenties*, eds. Joan Acocella and Lynn Garafola (Hannover and London: Wesleyan University Press, 1991), p. 91. Reprint of translation by Ralph Roeder that appeared in *Theatre Arts Monthly* in August 1928.

20. Legrand-Chabrier, "Pistes et Plateaux," *La Presse*, 4 January 1925.

21. See Levinson, "The Girls," p. 91.

22. Ibid., p. 91.

23. Ibid., p. 92.

24. Legrand-Chabrier, "Pistes et Plateaux."

25. Levinson, "The Girls," p. 91.

26. The most important current criticism on cabaret culture in Berlin comes from Peter Jelavich, who devotes a chapter to the Weimar revue in *Berlin Cabaret*. For a discussion of military and machine metaphors in the German press, see Peter Jelavich's "'Girls and Crisis'" in *Berlin Cabaret*, 175–186; see also Detlev Peukert, "'Americanism' versus Kulturkritik," in *The Weimar Republic*, 178–190; and Karsten Witte's "Visual Pleasure Inhibited: Aspects of the German Revue Film," trans. J. D. Steakley and Gabriele Hoover, *New German Critique* 24–25 (fall/winter 1981–82): 238–263.

27. In his study of white collar workers, *Die Angestellten* (Frankfurt am Main: Societats-Verlag, 1930), Kracauer makes a similar association between mass entertainment and the modern industrial complex. He employs two principal terms to describe the entertainment industry: *Vergnügungsbetrieb* (entertainment companies) and *Pläsirkasernen* (pleasure barracks), incorporating both factory principles and military regimentation into the realm of mass entertainment.

28. See Maurice Verne, *Aux usines du plaisir: la vie secrète du music-hall* (Paris: Ed. des Portiques, 1929).

29. Maurice Verne, "Variétés," Enquête du *Paris-Soir* 6–30 (Dec. 1928): 13.

30. Jacques Lombard, "Dans les sous-sols d'un palais avec l'armée des 'girls' d'un cinéma permanent," *Paris-Soir* 25 (Feb. 1933). An article that appeared in *Paris-Soir* in 1933 maintains: "They are *femmes-machines*, each brought to life by the same bell, each executing the same gesture at the same moment, each having the same smile."

31. Adam Kuckhoff, "Größe und Niedergang der Revue," *Die Volksbühne* 3, no. 1 (April 1928): 6. Translation in Günter Berghaus, "*Girlkultur*—Feminism, Americanism, and Popular Entertainment in Weimar Germany," *Journal of Design History* 1, no. 3–4 (1988): 200.

32. For a discussion of "Fordism" and "Taylorism" in relation to the revue, see Jelavich, "'Girls and Crisis'," p. 181.

33. Roger de Lafforest, "Le Fabricant de Girls," *Voilà* 15 (June 1935); "La Fabrication Industrielle des Chorus-Girls," *Vu* 15 (Jan. 1930).

34. See Hervé Mille, "Je voudrais avoir l'âme comme elles ont le corps," *Paris-Soir* 29 (Aug. 1930).

35. Cited in Lafforest, "Le Fabricant de Girls."

36. Walter Benjamin, *The Arcades Project*, trans. Howard Eiland and Kevin McLaughlin (Cambridge, MA and London: The Belknap Press of Harvard University Press, 1999), p. 331, J56a: 10.

37. Ibid., p. 328, J55: 10.

38. Charles Baudelaire, "Les Sept Vieillards," *Les Fleurs du mal*, in *Oeuvres completes* I, Bibliothèque de la Pléiade, ed. Claude Pichois (Paris: Gallimard, 1975), pp. 87–88.

39. Susan Buck-Morss, *The Dialectics of Seeing: Walter Benjamin and the Arcades Project* (Cambridge, MA and London: The MIT Press, 1989), p. 191.

40. Benjamin, *Arcades*, p. 11.

41. Mille, "Je voudrais avoir l'âme comme elles ont le corps."

42. Kracauer, "Girls und Krise," *Frankfurter Zeitung* 26 (May 1931). Translation in *The Weimar Republic Sourcebook*, eds. Anton Kaes, Martin Jay, and Edward Dimendberg (Berkeley, Los Angeles, and London: University of California Press, 1994), p. 565.

43. Ibid. In Berlin, the revue flourished between 1924–1929, during the so-called period of relative stabilization. According to Kracauer, the Great Depression put an end to the success of the girls' ideological message: "One no longer believes them, the rosy Jackson girls!"

44. Jelavich, *Berlin Cabaret*, p. 181.

45. Levinson, "The Girls," p. 90; Jacques Lombard, "Dans les sous-sols d'un palais avec l'armée des 'girls' d'un cinéma permanent," *Paris-Soir* 25.

46. Pierre Lazareff, "M. F. W. Jackson le chef des girls du monde nous parle de ses enfants," *Paris-Midi* 24 (Jan. 1929).

47. Yvon Novy, "Les 'Dancing Girls' au travail," *Comoedia* 19 (Oct. 1923). An article entitled "La vie 'militaire' des girls" that appeared in *Le Jour-*

nal in 1933 writes: "For the moment, the British, American and German girls performing in Paris—there are at least 300 of them!—depend *militarily* on the schools of London, Manchester, Hollywood and Berlin, where they are subject to a severe training lasting a number of years. (. . .) Upon their incorporation into 'The Barracks-School,' a 'sergeant-impresario' commands them, directing them with utmost efficiency from the troupe's central instruction depot to the theatre, music-hall, cinema, cabaret, or circus. (. . .) There, their captain—a firm-handed colleague—takes charge of them and assures the slightest details of their intimate and artistic life." *Le Journal* 18 (March 1933).

48. Jelavich, *Berlin Cabaret*, p. 181.

49. For examples of cabaret performances in Berlin with explicitly militaristic characteristics, see Jelavich, *Berlin Cabaret*, p. 181.

50. See Levinson, "The Girls," pp. 90–91. While Kracauer recognizes formal elements of a military aesthetic in the disciplined order of the revue, he dismisses the connection on a meaningful level due to the lack of patriotic content and effect. In "The Mass Ornament," he writes, "Nor do the living constellations in the stadiums have the meaning of military demonstrations. No matter how orderly the latter appeared, that order was considered a means to an end; the parade march evolved out of patriotic feelings and in turn aroused them in soldiers and loyal subjects. The constellations of Girls, however, have no meaning outside of themselves, and the masses are not a moral unit like a company of soldiers." (Kracauer, "The Mass Ornament," p. 68).

51. Levinson, "The Girls," p. 91.

52. In *Berlin Cabaret*, Jelavich argues that the revue attenuates or "sweetens" the forces of order embodied in the girls: "They were a form of sexual bait, with a hidden hook: whoever consumed their image also internalized an appreciation for mass reproduction, replicability, and military discipline" (183).

53. Jelavich, *Berlin Cabaret*, p. 186.

54. See George Mosse, "The Process of Trivialization," in *Fallen Soldiers*, pp. 126–156.

55. Along similar lines, Jay Winter suggests that war films served both to humanize and mythologize the war. See Winter, "Films of the War" in *The Experience of World War I* (London: Macmillan, 1988), pp. 238–247.

56. Here I am using "imagined" in Benedict Anderson's sense. In *Imagined Communities* (London and New York: Verso, 1991), Anderson understands a nation as "an imagined political community" which sees itself as limited,

sovereign, and communal. To the extent that the girl troupes represent a larger, communal body, whether it be the body of the military corps, the factory worker, or the social body at large, they constitute an "imagined" community.

57. The most well-known example is Villiers de l'Isle-Adam's *L'Eve future* (1886), which centers around the creation of an ideal female android named Hadaly. Other fin de siècle texts include Jean Lorrain's *Monsieur de Phocas* (1901), in which an English collector and painter reveals a fetishistic fascination for dolls and wax figures, and Jules Bois' *L'Eternelle poupée* (1894), which features a "Bal des Poupées" and an ideal automaton Astarté. See Mireille Dottin-Orsini, *Cette femme qu'ils disent fatale* (Paris: Bernard Grasset, 1993), and Alfred Chapuis, *Les Automates dans les oeuvres d'imagination* (Neuchâtel: Ed. du Griffon, 1947).

58. E. T. A. Hoffmann, *Der Sandmann*, in *Sämtliche Werke* III, ed. Hartmut Steinecke (Frankfurt am Main: Deutscher Klassiker Verlag, 1985). Translation of *The Sand-Man* by J. T. Bealby in *The Best Tales of Hoffmann*, ed. E. F. Bleiler (New York: Dover, 1967), p. 214, 210.

59. See Huyssen, "The Vamp and the Machine," pp. 68–70.

60. Ibid., p. 70.

61. Ibid.

62. See ibid., pp. 77–81.

63. For a discussion of the figures of the automaton and the mannequin in surrealist art exhibits, see Hal Foster, "Exquisite Corpses," in *Compulsive Beauty* (Cambridge, MA and London: The MIT Press, 1993), pp. 125–154.

64. Georges Hugnet, *Pleins et déliés* (La Chapelle-sur-Loire: Guy Authier, 1972), p. 329. Quoted in *Man Ray: La Photographie à l'envers*, catalogue of the exposition of the Musée d'art moderne and the Centre de création industrielle held at the Grand Palais in Paris from April 29 to June 19, 1998 (Paris: Editions du Centre Pompidou, 1998), p. 52

65. See Frank Whitford, *Oskar Kokoschka: A Life* (New York: Atheneum, 1986), pp. 118–126, and Peter Wollen, "Cinema/Americanism/The Robot," *New Formations* 8 (summer 1989): 7–34.

66. Ruth Leys, "Traumatic Cures: Shell Shock, Janet, and the Question of Memory," *Critical Inquiry* 20, no. 4 (summer 1994): 624. See also Leys, "Death Masks: Kardiner and Ferenczi on Psychic Trauma," *Representations* 53 (winter 1996): 48.

67. See Brigid Doherty, "'See: *We are all Neurasthenics!*' or: The Trauma of Dada Montage," *Critical Inquiry* 24, no. 1 (August 1997): 82–132.

68. See Foster, *Compulsive Beauty*, 1–7, and Katharine Conley, *Automatic Woman: The Representation of Woman in Surrealism* (Lincoln and London: University of Nebraska Press, 1996), pp. 5–6.

69. Foster, *Compulsive Beauty*, p. 263, note 50. See chapter three of Foster's *Compulsive Beauty* for a discussion of the impact of trauma on surrealist works by de Chirico, Ernst and Giacometti, and chapter four for a discussion of Hans Bellmer's disfigured dolls in relation to the Nazi aesthetic of the armored male body.

70. Man Ray and Hans Bellmer collaborated on the illustrations of "Appliquée," but Man Ray's signature is lacking in the piece. As the images on the first two pages consist of a composition and a print attributed to Bellmer as well as a postcard of seven naked pubescent girls provided by Bellmer, we can assume that Man Ray assembled the four images on the third page of the spread. The Chinese mask print in particular would appear to be the work of Man Ray as the inverted white porcelain masks against a dark background are reminiscent of Man Ray's 1926 "Noire et blanche" mask series with Kiki de Montparnasse.

71. See Rosalind Krauss, "Corpus Delicti," in Krauss and Livingston, *L'Amour fou: photography and surrealism*, The Corcoran Gallery of Art, Washington, D.C. (New York: Abbeville Press, 1985), pp. 57–60.

72. Arturo Schwarz suggests the possibility of an influence of Villiers de l'Isle Adam's *Eve Future* in *Portemanteau*, as Man Ray had recently been introduced to the writer's works. Arturo Schwarz, *Man Ray: The Rigour of Imagination* (New York: Rizzoli, 1977), p. 160.

73. See Schwarz, *Man Ray*, pp. 158–159 and *Man Ray: la phographie a l'envers*, 8–9. *Woman* forms a unit with Man Ray's first Assisted Readymade, *Man*, an assemblage of two metal light reflectors and six clothespins attached to a plate of glass. The pieces were realized in 1918, with inverted titles.

74. André Breton, *L'Amour fou* (Paris: Gallimard, 1937), p. 21. Translation from André Breton, *Mad Love*, trans. Mary Ann Caws (Lincoln and London: University of Nebraska Press, 1987), p. 19.

75. Man Ray, *Self Portrait* (Boston and Toronto: Little, Brown and Company: 1963), p. 92.

76. See Conley, *Automatic Woman*, p. 28.

77. Cited in Schwarz, *Man Ray*, p. 214.

78. Ibid.

79. In an interview with Peter Webb, Bellmer claimed to be exploring the "physical unconscious" in his manipulation of the *Doll*: "I tried to rearrange the sexual elements of a girl's body like a sort of plastic anagram," Bellmer explained. "I remember describing it thus: the body is like a sentence that invites us to rearrange it, so that its real meaning becomes clear through a series of endless anagrams. I wanted to reveal what is usually kept hidden—it was no game—I tried to open people's eyes to new realities." Quoted in Webb, *Hans Bellmer* (London, Melbourne and New York: Quartet Books, 1985), p. 38.

80. Brun continues, "[The Doll] is the first and only surrealist object with a universal, provocative power." Quoted in Webb, *Hans Bellmer*, p. 41.

81. Webb, *Hans Bellmer*, p. 46: "No sooner had Bellmer's Doll made her scandalous début," writes Peter Webb in his critical biography of Bellmer, "than female dummies were to be seen everywhere in surrealist exhibitions. (. . .) For a while it seemed as if all the surrealists had succumbed to the doll-making craze: Ernst, Miró, Man Ray, Duchamp, Masson, Dominguez, Marcel Jean, Léo Malet and more besides."

82. In his introduction to *Die Puppe* (1934), Bellmer wrote: "Would it not be in the very reality of the Doll that the imagination would find the joy, the ecstasy and the fear that it sought? Would it not be the final triumph over those adolescents with wide eyes which turn away if, beneath the conscious stare that plunders their charms, aggressive fingers were to assault their plastic form and slowly construct, limb by limb, all that had been appropriated by the senses and the brain? (. . .) Would not this be the solution?" Translation in Webb, *Hans Bellmer*, p. 43.

83. Peter Webb writes of Bellmer and the German writer Unica Zürn, Bellmer's lover in the 1950s: "Suddenly here in Berlin he fell in love with a thirty-seven-year-old short-story writer. (. . .) Unica with her expressionless face, prominent nose and enormous eyes looked extraordinarily like the Doll. (. . .) They made a strange couple: both always wore black, and Unica usually walked rather stiffly, a few paces behind Bellmer, his head balding but with long hair at the back, so that one could picture them as Dr. Coppelius and his doll Olympia." Webb, *Hans Bellmer*, pp. 216–218.

84. Shortly after viewing Offenbach's *Tales of Hoffmann*, Bellmer declared to his wife, "I am going to construct an artificial girl with anatomical possibilities which are capable of re-creating the heights of passion even to inventing new desires." Quoted in Webb, *Hans Bellmer*, p. 29.

85. Freud writes, "[T]his uncanny is in reality nothing new or alien, but something which is familiar and old-established in the mind and which has become alienated from it only through the process of repression." Freud, "The Uncanny," in *The Standard Edition of the Complete Psychological Works of Sigmund Freud*, ed. James Strachey, vol. 17 (London: The Hogarth Press and the Institute of Psycho-analysis, 1955), p. 241.

86. Freud, "The Uncanny," p. 226.

87. In "The Uncanny," Freud delineates two orders of the uncanny: one arising from the impression made by objects whose animate/inanimate nature is uncertain and one arising from repressed infantile complexes, such as the castration complex and womb fantasies. In the second case, the return of repressed material evokes an uncanny impression as it reminds one of the inner "compulsion to repeat." See Freud, "The Uncanny," pp. 248–49, 237–38.

88. Krauss and Livingston, *L'Amour fou*, p. 86.

89. Ibid. According to Krauss, the dolls are phallic, both in their tumescence and erectile positions. In the perpetual process of dismemberment, the *Jeux de la poupée* "stage endless *tableaux-vivants* of the figure of castration." At the same time, Krauss argues, the dolls serve to mediate the anxiety of castration in accordance with the Freudian notion of the "Medusa effect," by which the multiplicity of phallic symbols serves to mitigate the horror of a lack. See Krauss, "Corpus Delicti," in *L'Amour fou*, pp. 85–86.

90. Foster, "Exquisite Corpses," pp. 120–122. Hal Foster reads the dolls in relationship to the Nazi construction of masculine subjectivity, interpreting the disfiguration in the dolls as an assault against Fascist notions of integrity. Foster argues that the dolls are expressly posed against the Nazi imaginary, which fears invasion of the "feminine" (Theweleit), of that which exceeds borders and boundaries. In their sadomasochistic expression of a fear of the feminine, Foster suggests that Bellmer's dolls participate "deeply in the Fascist imaginary, only to expose it most effectively. For in the *poupées* this fear of the diffusive and the destructive is made manifest and reflexive, as is the attempt to overcome it vis-à-vis the feminine. Such is the scandal but also the lesson of the dolls."

91. Benjamin, *Arcades*, 694, Z1: 5.

92. Claude Berton, "Réflexions sur le music-hall," *La Revue de Paris* (Nov. 1, 1929): 675.

93. André Sallee and Philippe Chaveau, *Music-hall et café-concert* (Paris: Bordas, 1985), p. 27.

94. Freud, *Beyond the Pleasure Principle*, in *The Standard Edition of the Complete Psychological Works of Sigmund Freud*, ed. James Strachey, vol. 18 (London: The Hogarth Press and the Institute of Psycho-analysis, 1955), pp. 32–33. In *Beyond the Pleasure Principle*, Freud writes, "But it is impossible to classify as wish-fulfillments the dreams we have been discussing which occur in traumatic neuroses, or the dreams during psychoanalyses which bring to memory the psychical traumas of childhood. They arise, rather, in obedience to the compulsion to repeat. (. . .) If there is a 'beyond the pleasure principle,' it is only consistent to grant that there was also a time before the purpose of dreams was the fulfillment of wishes."

95. See ibid., pp. 31–32.

96. See ibid., pp. 14–16.

97. Ola Alsen, "Revue—Feuerwerk," in *Für Dich! Magazin und programm*. Charellrevue, Grosses Schauspielhaus, Berlin. Translation modified from Katrin Bettina Müller, "Cult and Wasteful Extravagance: Revue, Dance and Cabaret in 1920s Berlin—an Exhibition," *Ballet International/Tanz Aktuell* (January 1996): 33.

98. Levinson, "The Girls," p. 94.

99. Freud understood disavowal as a mode of defense in which the subject refuses to recognize the reality of a traumatic perception. In psychological terms, one could also think of the revue as a sort of "restitution fantasy." Like a phantom limb, which protects the individual against an irretrievable loss, the revue provides an illusory sense of wholeness.

Chapter 5

HYGIENE, HARD WORK, AND THE PURSUIT OF STYLE IN BAUDELAIRE AND NIETZSCHE

Andrea Gogröf-Voorhees

"Hygiene: Must always be strictly observed. Protects from all diseases, when it isn't their cause."

—Flaubert, Madame Bovary

If a poet demanded from the State the right to have some bourgeois in his stable, people would be very much astonished, but if a bourgeois asked for some roast poet, people would think it quite natural.

—Baudelaire, Intimate Journals

When a human being resists his whole age and stops it at the gate to demand an accounting, this must have influence—Whether that is what he desires is immaterial; that he can do it is what matters.

—Nietzsche

Baudelaire's and Nietzsche's critique of the modern age, which they essentially saw as utilitarian, inartistic, hypocritical, weak, and blind to the deeper implications of its course, articulates itself in paradoxical fashion through their respective examination and consecutive reevaluation of decadence. Mostly French writers have noted the affinities between the two poet critics since the early twentieth century, and only sporadically.[1]

More recently, the connection between Baudelaire and Nietzsche, as foremost representatives of a modern ironic consciousness that knows itself marked by what it opposes, has gained in scope and depth in Europe and the United States. The growth of Baudelairian and

Nietzschean scholarship signifies a revived interest, at our turn of the century, in cultural decline and the search for new directions or reforms.[2] The following reflections address an aspect that so far has not been subject to a closer look.

I concentrate on Baudelaire's and Nietzsche's similar strategies of opposition and (self)-representation in regard to decadence and I argue that Baudelaire's own contribution to and relation to decadence in his concern with hygiene, his work ethic, and pursuit of style not only anticipates and reflects Nietzsche's, but also is crucial to the development of the latter's own position in regard to decadence. Baudelaire's intimate journals, which Nietzsche read, constitute, as Nietzsche admits, a veritable treasure of "psychologics of decadence" helping him from without to deepen his understanding of the phenomenon of modern decadence. Yet, I believe also that Baudelaire's sharp and disillusioned self-analysis provides Nietzsche with a mirror that strikes his own chords from within.

Baudelaire's and Nietzsche's intense immersion in work and their preoccupation with the threat of disease, contamination, and disintegration on the aesthetic, ethic, and physiological level are symptomatic of the larger nineteenth century concerns. From this point of view, Baudelaire and Nietzsche are representatives of and contributors to that which they endeavor to oppose and expose. Their keen attention to physical and mental hygiene as self-discipline necessary for self-protection from the onslaught of what they perceived as cultural decline, and to ward off personal depression, induced by illness, strife, and excess. Their preoccupation expresses an urgent need to exhibit the crisis underlying and fueling modernity. This crisis is, according to both, a symptom of a certain type of decadence issuing from a delusionary overconfidence in scientific and moral progress supported by a suspiciously outdated moral value system, resulting inevitably in global aesthetic and moral "decadence" that is dissolution, dissipation, indifference, and loss of existential purpose. Baudelaire's insight that "civilized man invents the philosophy of progress to console himself for his abdication and decline"[3] anticipates Nietzsche's statement that "'progress' is merely a modern idea, that is to say a false idea."[4] Their particular understanding of work as an essentially creative and nonutilitarian activity is not only part of their particular hygienic measures, but also indubitably indicative of their personal crisis which they not only recognized, but also explored and literally incorporated into their respective works. Their pursuit of style in turn is equally forcefully linked to an obsessive need to expose this crisis by lending it an appropriate "modern" form. Baudelaire and Nietzsche's originality lies in their genius to discover and uncover the manifold aesthetic resources decadence reveals to the poet and the critic. Their minds and senses wander where angels and bourgeois fear to dread. Baudelaire's and Nietzsche's works function as mirrors to the reader who, when beholding his reflection, may be shocked, repulsed, revolted, intrigued, yet forced into recognition all the same. As has been so justly pointed out, one of Nietzsche's greatest appeals to the modern reader is that he writes "exclusively for you. Not at you, but for you."[5] The same can be said of Baudelaire, who seduces the "hypocrite reader," his "alias," his "twin" into his poetic orbit.[6] Baudelaire's search for new and strange forms of beauty, and Nietzsche's demand for a stronger and more courageous, committed valuation of life from the perspective of art and death, are all the more relevant to today's discussion, not least because their concerns are not purely theoretical, but powerful expressions of characters and lives lived exclusively in the service of art as the representation of the underlying conditions of existence.

Both knew themselves to be "products" of their times, yet their attitude of resistance and their literary and philosophical contributions represent an heroic effort to counter and overcome what they felt as the deadening impact of a declining culture which viewed itself with what Baudelaire and Nietzsche felt as dangerous self-complacency. Positivism, utilitarianism, historicism, and materialism relentlessly pursued in what they saw as a naïve, if not hypocritical and blind, faith in the notion of progress were uncovered by Baudelaire and Nietzsche as decadent in themselves. What they rejected was a misdirected humanitarianism that under the cloak of a progressively scientific Christianity promotes the diseases it seeks to control and destroy. Baudelaire and Nietzsche not only bring these diseases into the light, but most importantly, they also represent them personally and in their style of writing. Both challenge what they saw as the aesthetic and moral decline of their times, demanding and performing a reevaluation of art and life as an expression of original sensitivity and temperament curbed and strengthened by an unblinking lucidity combined with perfect "technical" mastery. Paradoxically, both Nietzsche and Baudelaire valued and defended the classical notions of "unity" and "wholeness" in art and character, yet they also knew, as the first conscious and conscientious representatives of modernity, that the forces which promote inevitable disintegration and fragmentation were those that ironically carried the seeds of renewed creativity. Baudelaire's prose poems and his praise of the sketch, and Nietzsche's aphoristic style, testify to their experience with and subsequent predilection for the sketchy, the fragmentary, and the discontinuous. This tension between a will to unity and the necessary exploration of new means to achieve it in and as effect lies at the core of Baudelaire's and Nietzsche's works. Baudelaire's struggle to find a balance between the "centralization and vaporization of the ego" corresponds to Nietzsche's exhortations to self-overcoming, and his relentless efforts to encourage and practice the reminting of one's weaknesses into strength.

That Nietzsche saw himself as the first and foremost connoisseur in questions of decadence is a well-known fact. On October 18, 1888, he writes to Malwida von Meysenbug:

> Dearest friend,
> I will not tolerate contradiction on these things. In questions of decadence, I am the highest authority on earth: those people of today, with their pitiful degeneration of instinct should consider themselves lucky to have someone, who, in darker matters, gives it to them straight.[7] [*Verehrte Freundin, das sind keine Dinge, worüber ich Widerspruch zulasse. Ich bin, in Fragen der décadence, die höchste Instanz, die es auf Erden gibt: diese jetzigen Menschen, mit ihr(er) jammervollen Instinkt-Entartung, sollten sich glücklich schätzen, Jemanden zu haben, der ihnen in dunkleren Fällen reinen Wein einschenkt.*]

His interest in and understanding of decadence is situated in the larger context of his analysis of pessimism, nihilism, and the unfinished project of "revaluation of all values." Nietzsche's attention begins to focus on decadence as a physiological and aesthetic occurrence around 1883 while residing in Nice. There he reads the French authors, writers, and critics, representative of "French Decadence," such as Gustave Flaubert, the Goncourt brothers, Guy de Maupassant, Ste Beuve, Théophile Gautier, and Paul Bourget,[8] the latter two guiding him into the works and character of Charles Baudelaire, poet and cultural critic, who in time will be for Nietzsche not only "the first intelligent adherent of Wagner," [9] (that is a decadent), but also "the first lucid decadent,"[10] a spiritual kinsman, hopelessly dedicated, like Nietzsche, to a life lived against the grain with the ambition to leave his mark on the future.

The question of mastery and self-overcoming, recognizing and taming one's weak, unhealthy inclinations by translating them into strong and healthy ones is Nietzsche's formula against decadence. As one of his central thoughts, it is illustrated in *The Gay Science*, where already the most necessary task of the human being is "to give style to one's character—a great and rare art."[11]

This is precisely what Baudelaire hoped to master, although Nietzsche never publicly acknowledged it. This "three quarter fool," as Nietzsche more or less humorously called him in a letter to Peter Gast (KSB, 8: 263) is, however, also, in this letter recognized as providing "invaluable psychologics of decadence," occupying no less than fourteen pages (seventeen entries) in Nietzsche's notebooks from the years 1887–88.

When Nietzsche first discovered Baudelaire, he had drawn a close connection between the poet and Wagner. As we shall see later, Nietzsche will extend this connection also to himself. According to Nietzsche, in the summer of 1885:

> The poets who flourish at this time in France do so under the influence of Heinrich Heine and Baudelaire. . . . As for the pessimistic Baudelaire, he belongs among the almost unbelievable amphibians who are as German as they are Parisian; his poetry has something of that which one characterizes in Germany as "soul" or "infinite melody," and sometimes "hangover" (*Katzenjammer*). Apart from that, Baudelaire is a man of perhaps corrupt, but also very distinct, sharp, and self-assured taste: with this he tyrannizes over the indecisive ones of today. If in his time he was the first supporter of Delacroix, perhaps today he would be the first "Wagnerian" in Paris. There is a lot of Wagner in Baudelaire. [*Was den pessimistischen Baudelaire betrifft, so gehört er zu jenen kaum glaublichen Amphibien, welche ebensosehr deutsch als pariserisch sind; seine Dichtung hat etwas von dem, was man in Deutschland unter Gemüth oder "unendliche Melodie" und mitunter auch "Katzenjammer" nennt. Im Uebrigen war Baudelaire der Mensch eines vielleicht verdorbenen, aber sehr bestimmten Geschmacks: damit tyrannisiert er die Ungewissen von heute. Wenn er seiner Zeit der erste Prophet und Fürsprecher Delacroix' war: vielleicht,*

dass er heute der erste "Wagnerianer" von Paris sein würde. Es ist viel Wagner in Baudelaire.][12] (KSA, 11: 600–01)

Striking is Nietzsche's recognition of Baudelaire's dual nature which he detects, explores, and justifies in himself in *Ecce Homo* a few years later: on the one hand Baudelaire is a "decadent," connected to that pessimism out of weakness which promotes "nerves," like Wagner's music. That Nietzsche himself was not impervious to nerves himself is, however, also a fact, and the warning he emits against nerves ("One must not have any nerves." EH, 258) is immediately preceded by his admission to hysterical fits when reading his own masterpiece: "When I have looked into my Zarathustra, I walk up and down in my room for half an hour, unable to master an unbearable fit of sobbing" (EH, 246).

On the other hand—and this is the part Nietzsche never publicly acknowledges—Baudelaire is also and foremost an independent and highly original "man," strong and determined enough to impose his "distinct, sharp, and self-assured taste," which according to Nietzsche is the very prerequisite for style, on those who are too weak or mediocre to pursue their own. Nietzsche had found in Bourget's article on Baudelaire a definition of the style of decadence which he adapted to his own purpose in *The Case of Wagner*: "What is the sign of every literary decadence? That life no longer dwells in the whole. The word becomes sovereign and leaps out and obscures the meaning of the page, the page gains life at the expense of the whole—the whole is no longer a whole."[13] The emancipatory activity of the part to the detriment of the whole, however, is not so much regretted by Nietzsche as affirmed. Indeed, one of the central points of his philosophy is his discovery that "unity" in itself is only a fiction, an artifact.

It is precisely Nietzsche's insight that unity "in itself" does not exist but that as idea or in the Freudian sense as a wish, the concept represents the underlying motivation and goal for any kind of valuable creation. If unity and wholeness are not, as Nietzsche says, existent in the "nature of becoming, " if unity can be conceived only as "organization and co-play," he thereby legitimizes the modern aesthetics of decadence whose energy deploys itself in an ever renewed and increasingly desperate effort to lend form (unity) to a reality which it experiences as fragmentary and chaotic if not violent. For Baudelaire, the value of an artwork lies in its power to impose unity of character and vision. Before Nietzsche, he had criticized his age's mistake to promote and to hold on to the Enlightenment inspired conception of the world as a naturally rational whole, in spite of ample evidence to the contrary. To this conception, he opposes an aesthetic creed which refuses to elevate natural organic unity by stating that nature (the world, the street, etc.) is nothing but a vast dictionary or storehouse, devoid of beauty and meaning in itself. The creation of beauty and meaning, according to Baudelaire, cannot issue from the sterile imitation and naïve idealization of nature, but depends entirely on the artist's strength of will and magic ability to select, combine and alloy elements into an whole that exists only in his imagination.

To achieve the desired unity of impression, the painter of modern life needs to fight against the threatening assailment of details during the creative process:

> An artist with a perfect sense of form but particularly accustomed to the exercise of his memory and his imagination, then finds himself assailed, as it were by a riot of details, all of them demanding justice, with the fury of the mob in love with absolute equality. Any form of justice is inevitably infringed; any harmony is destroyed, sacrificed; multitude of trivialities are magnified; a multitude of little things become usurpers of attention. The more the artist pays impartial attention to detail, the greater does anarchy become (SW, 407). [*An artiste ayant le sentiment parfait de la forme, mais accoutumé à exercer surtout sa mémoire et son imagination, se trouve alors comme assailli par une émeute de détails, qui tous demandent justice avec la furie d'une foule amoureuse d'égalité absolue. Toute justice se trouve forcément violée; toute harmonie détruite, sacrifiée; mainte trivialité devient énorme; maintes petitesse, usurpatrice. Plus l'artiste se penche avec impartialité vers le détail, plus l'anarchie augmente.*][14]

Furthermore, the true artist, like Delacroix, for instance, never creates works " to please timorous souls who are easy to satisfy, and [who] find adequate nourishment in flabby, soft, imperfect works." The two most distinguishing marks of genius are "an immense thrust of passion coupled with formidable will-power" (SW, 363).

In this light, Baudelaire anticipates Nietzsche's own resistance to the style of decadence and his ideal of the "grand style":

The greatness of an artist cannot be measured by the "beautiful feelings" he arouses: leave that idea to the females. But according to the degree to which he approaches the grand style. This style has this in common with great passion, that it disdains to please; that it forgets to persuade; that it commands, that it wills—To become master of the chaos one is, to compel one's chaos to become form.[15]

It has been noted that "Nietzsche shares with Baudelaire in particular the temperament of a decadent and Dandy."[16] This temperament furthers an unusual need for distinction achieved through particular hygienic measures which both writers undertook and worked hard to maintain in the face of a common need to fend off what Baudelaire would call "ennui," "spleen,"[17] and the "pull from below." For Nietzsche it was his "his nausea over man" (EH, 234). The contraction of syphilis by both writers plays no small part in their sensitivity for decadence. Nietzsche obviously shared with Baudelaire a grave concern when he transcribes the poet's disquieting experience in the following terms: "*like* Baudelaire who one day felt the wind of the wing of madness pass over him" (KSA, 13: 86).[18]

Baudelaire's health problems were further increased by many years of financial stress and excessive alcohol consumption. Nietzsche had carefully read all his hygienic measures to remedy inclination to excess and fear of disintegration in one of the sections in the *Intimate Journals*, significantly entitled "Hygiene": "Fish, cold baths, douches, lichen, pastilles occasionally, together with the abstinence from all stimulants."[19] "Inclination to wastefulness ought, when a man is mature, to be replaced by a wish to concentrate and produce." (29) "Many friends, many gloves—for fear of eczema" (B, 45). "To heal all things, wretchedness, disease or melancholy, absolutely nothing is required but inclination for work"(B, 101).

Nietzsche's physical constitution was always frail with frequent migraine attacks and gastric pains, which forced him to pay particular attention to climate and diet. As Nietzsche says in *Ecce Homo*: "in the choice of nutrition, of place and climate, of recreation—an instinct of self-preservation issues its commands, and it gains its most unambiguous expression as an instinct of self-defense. . . . The usual word for this instinct of self-defense is taste" (EH, 252).

Disease and illness set Nietzsche and Baudelaire apart from the common herd, by which they in turn did not want to become infected further, and explain, in part at least, their need of and suffering from solitude. Baudelaire's "painter of modern life," like Baudelaire, always returns alone, producing his art far from the crowd, in the middle of night when the bourgeois sleeps, under a feverish spell in his garret. Nietzsche often claims solitude-"which is to say, recovery, return to myself, the breath of a free, light, playful air"(EH, 233).

Of course, Baudelaire's and Nietzsche's concerns inscribe themselves also in the historical context of large sanitary measures, moral and physical, undertaken in the big European cities and the scientific discoveries such as Pasteur's germ theory of infection in France and Robert Koch's bacteriological culture techniques in Germany. Emily Cohen describes the situation as follows:

> The battle in the name of hygiene, as much a battle in the name of morality, was first waged in the cities and coincided with the rise of capitalism and industrialization. City air and water were the two elements to be reckoned with. Though hygienic practices were often first developed for and practiced by the middle class and upper classes, the working class, the poor, prostitutes, often women in general, were eventually the prime targets, feeble and feminized, in the effort to make society function as efficiently and waste-free as a successful industry.[20]

Baudelaire and Nietzsche dealt with their personal condition embedded in this particular context in different ways, yet a common trait is their resolution to respond to and incorporate, literally and metaphorically, the general hygienic discourse into their own. As Emily Cohen has pointed out, "the poet's self-designation as "parfait chimiste" aligns him with the various bourgeois state functionaries, who in the beginning of the second half of the eighteenth century and especially through the nineteenth century, elaborated corrective measures, regulations, and institutions based on new conceptions of cleanliness" (Cohen, 239). Unlike the state functionary, however, Baudelaire worked without either respite or remuneration at extracting beauty from the common and ugly; he transformed mud into gold. Nietzsche, the doctor, joins Baudelaire the chemist. As Eric Blondel has convincingly argued, the interpretative basis of the "philosopher doctor's" text is "the body." Listing the many instances in Nietzsche's works, which use the faculties of the senses as metaphors for a critique of culture, Blondel asserts, that "style, for Nietzsche the genealogist, is the body speaking."[21]

However, while Baudelaire melancholically and passionately dives into the themes of decay, despondency, evil, and death in *The Flowers of Evil*, extracting from these the modern kind of artificial beauty for which he is famous now but that then earned him censorship and a trial, Nietzsche makes his entire philosophy contingent upon the necessity of his physiological handicap and he insists that life was easiest when it made the hardest demands on him (EH, 257). One entry in his *Intimate Journals* testifies to Baudelaire's effort to see hardship also from a positive side: "My humiliations were a grace from God."[22] Mostly, however, Baudelaire did not express much gratitude for his condition.

Unlike Nietzsche, he had to dirty his hands on a daily basis in the business of finding work that pays. Whereas Nietzsche had the advantage to receive pensions from the State for his injuries contracted during his short draft in the war and from his professorship, which allowed him the luxury to seek the right places and follow the necessary diet he prescribes in *Ecce Homo*, Baudelaire was caught up in Paris, faced with the necessity to deal with the business world, debts, and creditors; he had to practice what he called the "saint prostitution," the exchange of his art for a pittance and misunderstanding.

Baudelaire's Dandy is a wish-fulfillment; he is "the superior man, . . . not a specialist, [but] a man of leisure and of liberal education." His precondition is "to be rich and to love work" (B, 75). The Dandy-figure is the antithesis of utilitarian mediocrity, and the apotheosis of self-affirmation and self-abnegation in the light of necessary prostitution. He is representative of the poet's intention to push decadence to its final conclusion, being "the last flicker of heroism in decadent ages"(SW, 421). Whether he prefigures Nietzsche's "overman" as has been suggested, is a question, which exceeds the scope of this investigation.[23] But it is clear that Baudelaire, in this figure, has anticipated Nietzsche's insight that "one has to go forward, which is to say, step by step further into decadence,"[24] yet not in the service of "progress" as Nietzsche in this context ironically defines decadence, but in his refusal to be "useful," in the bourgeois, capitalist sense: "The vileness of any sort of employment. A Dandy does nothing. Can you imagine a Dandy addressing the common herd, except to make game of them?" (B, 69). Also, the Dandy stands for "opposition and revolt." He is "representative of what is best in human pride, of that need, which is too rare in the modern generation to combat and destroy triviality" (SW, 419). The Dandy embodies the two foremost characteristics of aesthetic and physiological decadence, the passion for beautiful form and sterility. "These beings have no other status but that of cultivating the idea of beauty in their own persons, of satisfying their passions, of feeling and thinking" (SW, 419). The Dandy is superficial out of profundity: "The specific beauty of the dandy consists particularly in that cold exterior, resulting from the unshakable determination to remain unmoved; one is reminded of a latent fire, whose existence is merely suspected, and which, if it wanted to, but it does not, could burst forth in all its brightness" (SW, 422). To be a Dandy is hard work, for it demands constant self-control: "The Dandy should aspire to be uninterruptedly sublime. He should live and sleep in front of a mirror"(B, 62). As E. Cohen concludes: "In the Dandy, volonté masters volupté" (Cohen, 251). The Dandy is the high priest of the religion of style.

In him, Baudelaire glorifies the "cult of images," his "great," "unique," and "primitive" passion (B, 90), and through him, Baudelaire elaborated his theory of artificiality, which attempts, through the systematic negation of nature, to "make up" with "Make-up" for the flaws the same inflicts on us, to impose style when the threat of the mud of the city, spiritual mediocrity, formlessness, and disintegration becomes painfully acute.

As it has been pointed out, Nietzsche's hermit in the high mountains offers as a countermodel to Baudelaire's urban Dandy.[25] Less aggressive and shocking perhaps in Zarathustra's floating Nietzsche's hermit and Nietzsche the hermit show signs of claustrophobia in his constant demand for "fresh air," and an almost paranoid concern for cleanliness. In *Ecce Homo*, Nietzsche speaks of his highly sensitive "psychological antennae" with which he smells the "entrails" of every soul, detects "the abundant hidden dirt at the bottom of many a character." The presupposition of his existence is "extreme cleanliness," contact with others always a threat to his integrity: "I constantly swim and bathe and splash, as it were, in water—in some perfectly transparent and resplendent element. Hence association with people imposes no mean test on my patience: my humanity does not consist in feeling with men how they are, but enduring that I feel with them" (EH, 233). The cool and smooth surface of the mirror in front of which Baudelaire's Dandy makes his home corresponds to the glaciers of Nietzsche's ascetic who opts for a living "among ice, [rather] than among modern virtue and other south winds"(A, 115).

The distinguishing features of Baudelaire's aesthetics, as we see, anticipate and reflect those of Nietzsche (and to Nietzsche, when he starts reading Baudelaire) in an uncanny way. Self-discipline, hygiene, hard work, and the question of style are not only symptomatic of their underlying sickness, but were also for both a means of self-assertion and self-defense against the Christian, capitalist/socialist value system, which, in fact, under the banner of moral integrity, progress, and the scientific pursuit of truth reveals itself to be for both decadent.

Although Baudelaire and Nietzsche agreed that matters of art should be only treated among "aristocrats," they were also ambitious, anxious to be printed and read. While Baudelaire endeavored to obtain a chair in the French Academy,[26] Nietzsche's pride and joy in finding "devoted admirers, all high-positioned and influential people in St. Petersburg, in Paris, in Stockholm, in Wien, and in New York," has no bounds as the many letters in his correspondence shows (KGB, 8, 531, 533, 537, 543). Yet, their work ethic defines itself in opposition to their age.

Baudelaire observes a hastening decline through society's delusionary overactivity in scientific, technological and utilitarian work to the detriment of what matters, namely, the undervalued and seldomly remunerated pursuit of beauty, which, according to Stendhal, whose definition both Baudelaire and Nietzsche adopted, is the only "promise of happiness." In the Salon of 1859, Baudelaire observes that

> . . . Mediocrity has always dominated the scene in every age, that is beyond dispute; but what is also true as it is distressing is that the reign of mediocrity is stronger than ever, to the point of triumphant obtrusiveness. . . . Our exclusive taste for the true . . . oppresses and smothers the taste for the beautiful. Where only the beautiful should be looked for . . . our people look only for the true. They are not artistic, naturally artistic; philosophers perhaps, or moralists, engineers, lovers of instructive anecdotes, anything you like, but never spontaneously artistic. They feel, or rather judge, successively, analytically. Other more favored peoples

feel things quickly, at once, synthetically.²⁷ [*Que dans tous les temps, la médiocrité ait dominé, celà est indubitable; mais qu'elle règne plus que jamias; qu'elle devienne absolument triomphante et encombrante, c'est ce qui est aussi vrai qu'affligeant. . . . Le goût exclusif du Vrai . . . opprime ici et étouffe le goût du Beau . . . notre public ne cherche que le Vrai. Il n'est pas artiste, naturellement artiste; philosophe peut-être, moraliste, ingénieur, amateur d'anectotes instructives, tout ce qu'on voudra, mais jamais spontanément artiste.*] (PL, 2: 610, 616)

And Nietzsche read in Baudelaire's journal the apocalyptic yet lucid analysis of a man devoid of any illusions about the present, the future, or himself:

. . . As fresh victims of the inexorable moral laws, we shall perish by that which we have believed to be our means of existence. So far will machinery have Americanized us, so far will Progress have atrophied in us all that is spiritual . . . [that justice] will deprive of their civil rights those citizens who are unable to make a fortune. . . . For myself, who feel within me sometimes the absurdity of a prophet, I know that I shall never achieve the charity of a physician. Lost in this vile world, elbowed by the crowd, I am like a worn-out man, whose eyes see, in the depths of the years behind him, only disillusionment and bitterness, ahead only a tumult in which there is nothing new, whether of enlightenment or of suffering. In the evening, when this man has filched from his destiny a few hours of pleasure, when he is lulled by the process of digestion, forgetful—as far as possible—of the past, content with the present and resigned with the future, exhilarated by his own nonchalance and dandyism, proud that he is less base than the passers-by, he says to himself, as he contemplates the smoke of his cigar: What does it matter to me what becomes of these perceptions (B, 52, 54, 55). [*Nouvel exemple et nouvelles victimes des inexorables lois morales, nous périrons par où nous avons cru vivre. La mécanique nous aura tellement américanisés, le progrès aura si bien atrophié en nous toute la partie sprituelle, que [la justice] fera interdire les citoyens qui ne sauront pas faire fortune. . . . Quant à moi qui sent quelquefois en moi le ridicule d'un prophète, je sais que je n'y trouverai jamais la charité d'un médecin.Perdu dans ce villain monde, coudoyé par les foules, je suis comme un homme lassé don't l'oeuil ne voit en arrière, dans les années profondes, que désabusement et amertume, et devant lui qu'un orage où rien de neuf est contenu, ni enseignement, ni douleur. Le soir où cet homme a volé à la destinée quelques heures de plaisir, bercé dans sa digestion, oublieux—autant que possible—du passé, content du présent et résigné à l'avenir, enivré de son sang froid et de son dandysme, fier de ne pas être aussi bas que ceux qui passent, il se dit en contemplant la fumée de son cigar: Que m'importe où vont ces consciences?*] (Pl, 1: 665–6–7).

Although Nietzsche followed this remark with the exclamation "A little fresh air" (KSA, 13: 92) it must have been difficult for him, as Pfotenhauer concludes, "to surpass this intransigent attitude, which plans to endure life without illusions, or to settle the matter as mere decadence" (Pfotenhauer, 109).

Nietzsche's own observation of the decline in spirituality produced by the infectious influence on "old Europe" by "the American lust for gold" can be heard as an echo, and seen as a complement to and development of Baudelaire's analysis. In the aphorism of the *Gay Science* entitled "Leisure and Idleness," Nietzsche, reflecting on the misuse of society's energy-economy, paints a picture that comes eerily close to our situation today:

> Even now one is ashamed of resting, and prolonged reflection almost gives people a bad conscience. One thinks with a watch in one's hand, even as one eats one's midday meal while reading the latest news of the stock market; one lives as if one always "might miss out on something." "Rather do anything than nothing"; this principle, too, is merely a string to throttle all culture and good taste. Just as all forms are visibly perishing by the haste of the workers, the feeling for form itself, the ear, the eye for the melody of movements are also perishing. The proof of this may be found in the universal demand for gross obviousness in all those situations in which human beings wish to be honest with one another for once—in their associations with friends, woman, relatives, children, teachers, pupils, leaders, and princes: One no longer has time or energy for ceremonies, for being obliging in an indirect way, for esprit in conversation, and for any otium at all. Living in a constant chase after gain compels people to expend their spirit to the point of exhaustion in continual pretense and overreaching and anticipating others. Virtue has come to consist of doing something in less time than someone else. Hours in which honesty is permitted have become rare, and when they arrive one is tired and does not only want to "let oneself go" but actually wishes to stretch out as long and wide and ungainly as one happens to be. This is how people now write letters, and the style and spirit of letters will

always be the true "sign of the times." If sociability and the arts still offer any delight, it is the kind of delight that slaves weary of their work, devise for themselves. How frugal our educated—and uneducated—people have become of all "joy"! How they are becoming increasingly suspicious of all joy! More and more, work enlists all good conscience on its side: the desire for joy already calls itself a "need to recuperate" and is beginning to be ashamed of itself. "One owes it to one's health"—that is what people say when they are caught on an excursion into the country. Soon we may well reach the point where people can no longer give in to the desire for a vita contemplative (that is, taking a walk with ideas and friends) without self-contempt and a bad conscience (GS, 259–60). [*Man schämt sich jetzt schon der Ruhe; das lange Nachsinnen macht beinahe Gewissensbisse. Man denkt mit der Uhr in der Hand, wie man zu Mittag isst, das Auge auf das Börsenblatt gerichtet—man lebt wie einer, der fortwährend Etwas "versäumen könnte." "Lieber irgend Etwas thun, als Nichts"—auch dieser Grundsatz ist eine Schnur, um aller Bildung und allem höheren Geschmack den Garaus zu machen. Und so wie sichtlich alle Formen an dieser Hast der Arbeitenden zu Grunde gehen: so geht auch das Gefühl für die Form selber, das Ohr und Auge für die Melodie der Bewegung zu Grunde. Der Beweis dafür liegt in der jetzt überall geforderten plumpen Deutlichkeit, in allen den Lagen, wo der Mensch einmal redlich mit Menschen sein will, im Verkehr mit Freunden, Frauen, Verwandten, Kindern, Lehrern, Schülern, Führern und Fürsten,—man hat keine Zeit und keine Kraft mehr für die Ceremonien, für die Verbindlichkeit mit Umwegen, für allen Esprit der Unterhaltung und überhaupt für alles Otium. Denn das Leben auf der Jagd nach Gewinn zwingt fortwährend dazu, seinen Geist bis zur Erschöpfung auszugeben, im beständigen Sich-Verstellen oder Ueberlisten oder Zuvorkommen: die eigentliche Tugend ist jetzt, etwas in weniger Zeit zu thun, als ein Anderer. Und so gibt es nur selten Stunden der erlaubten Redlichkeit: in diesen aber ist man müde und möchte sich nicht nur "gehen lassen" sondern lang und breit und plump sich hinstrecken. Gemäss diesem Hang schreibt man jetzt seine Briefe; deren Stil und Geist immer das eigentliche Zeichen der Zeit sein werden. Gibt es noch ein Vergnügen an Gesellschaft und an Künsten, so ist es ein Vergnügen, wie es müde gearbeitete Sklaven sich zurecht machen. Oh über diese Genügsamkeit der "Freude" bei unseren Gebildeten und Ungebildeten! Oh über diese zunehmende Verdächtigung aller Freude! Die Arbeit bekommt immer mehr alles gute Gewissen auf ihre Seite: der Hang zur Freude nennt sich bereits "Bedürfnis der Erholung" und fängt an, sich vor sich selber zu schämen. "Man ist es seiner Gesundheit schuldig"—so redet man, wenn man auf einer Landpartie ertappt wird. Ja es könnte bald soweit kommen, dass man einem Hange zur vita contemplativa(das heisst zum Spazierengehen mit Gedanken und Freunden) nicht ohne Selbstverachtung und schlechtes Gewissen nachgäbe.*] (KSA, 4, 557)

Baudelaire's sharp self-analysis, his pitiless insight into and groundbreaking reformulation of modernity as a historical reality and aesthetic concept, his complex relation to a world he had no illusions about, and whose illusions he did not tire to lay as bare as his heart, his self-assuredness and originality in taste, his nonconformity to bourgeois morality, and not last his own aesthetic and philosophical revaluation of values, for example, good and evil all find a ready sounding board in Nietzsche. If an objection can be made as to Baudelaire's Catholicism, which was one of the "decadent" traits Nietzsche vehemently condemned, it is answerable with Walter Benjamin's following proposition:

> The heroic bearing of Baudelaire is akin to that of Nietzsche. Though Baudelaire likes to appeal to Catholicism, his historical experience is nonetheless that which Nietzsche fixed in the phrase "God is dead." In Nietzsche's case, this experience is a projected cosmologically in the thesis that nothing new occurs any more. In Nietzsche, the accent lies on eternal recurrence, which the human being has to face with heroic composure. For Baudelaire, it is more a matter of "the new" which must be wrestled heroically from what is always again the same.[28]

The image Benjamin conjures up is convincing, yet astonishing too: both Nietzsche and Baudelaire share the tragic insight into the void underlying the human condition while confronting their experience from opposite ends: Nietzsche's stoic composure contrasts with Baudelaire's tenacious, aesthetic athleticism. Nietzsche did not confront decadence with poise, however. It is significant and ironic even that his composure crumbles when he is at the peak of his critique of decadence. The philosopher's complete immersion into the subject of literary and physiological decadence during his last productive phase in the year 1888, when he wrote no less than two books and three lengthy polemics (*Twilight of the Idols, Ecce Homo, The Anti-Christ, The Case of Wagner, Nietzsche Contra Wagner*) is indeed a stunning phenomenon. As his correspondence and the testimonies of friends and acquaintances show,

Nietzsche was a hard worker all his life.[29] Yet, during this particular period he seems to have engaged in a literal working frenzy, a fact that is all the more astounding considering his increasing illness. With his final collapse in 1889 all creative activity stops suddenly forever. Keeping in mind that Nietzsche defined the "other" of decadent, the "healthy" as someone who knows "the measure of what is good for him" (EH, 224), one cannot help but wonder, whether Nietzsche had—for his own sake—that "subtler sense of smell for signs of ascent and decline" which he attributes to himself over "any other human being before [him]" (EH, 222).

Then again, Nietzsche had readily admitted to being a decadent, yet only to a certain degree, namely, "as an angle, as a specialty" (EH, 224). In opposition to the "real" decadents, he is not *only* a decadent, but also and *mainly* "summa summarum" it's contrary, a "healthy," "well-turned out person," made stronger by every blow he receives (EH, 224–25). Perhaps, Nietzsche, in this last phase chose to run amok.

Baudelaire, furiously, yet not resignedly always admitted that the study of the beautiful (which is the world transformed aesthetically) "is a duel in which the artist shrieks with fright before being defeated."[30] This shriek can be heard throughout all of Nietzsche's last texts, yet he seems to be holding on to a self that goes down, like the sunset, in a flash. Baudelaire's and Nietzsche's knowledge of eventual defeat by the body, and their tenacious will to live on in the body of their texts, makes them take up the challenge again and again until final paralysis ends, in both cases, their ordeal.

Notes

1. The earliest text referring to Nietzsche and Baudelaire is by Charles Andler, *Nietzsche, sa vie et sa pensée*, 6 vols. (Paris: n.p., 1920–31). See also Georges Blin, *Baudelaire* (Paris: Gallimard, 1939), Marcel Raymond, *De Baudelaire au surréalisme* (Paris: J. Corti, 1940); Marcel Ruff, *Baudelaire*, trans. Agnes Kertesz (New York: New York University Press, 1966); Albert Camus, *The Rebel* (New York: Vintage, 1960); Georges Bataille, *Literature and Evil* (New York: Urizen, 1973); Paul de Man, *Blindness and Insight* (Minneapolis: University of Minnesota Press, 1971); Walter Benjamin, *The Arcades Project*, trans. H. Eiland and Kevin Mc Laughlin (Cambridge: The Bellknap Press of Harvard University Press, 1999).

2. See Henri Thomas, "Les Notes de Nietzsche sur Baudelaire, " *Nouvelle Revue Française* (Oct.–Dec. 1953): 1124–1127. The seminal article on the relationship between Nietzsche and Baudelaire is by Karl Pestalozzi, "Nietzsches Baudelaire-Rezeption," *Nietzsche Studien* 7 (Berlin: de Gruyter, 1978): 158–178; Stéphane Michaud, "Nietzsche et Baudelaire," *Le surnaturalisme français, Actes du Colloque organisé à L'Université de Vanderbilt, W.T. Bandy Center for Baudelairian Studies* (Neufchatel: Editions de la Baconnière, 1979), pp. 133–161; Philipp Rippel, "Die Geburt des Uebermenschen aus dem Geiste der Décadence," *Der Sturz der Idole. Nietzsches Umwertung der Kultur und Subjekt*, ed. Philipp Rippel (Tübingen: Konkursbuchverlag, 1985), pp. 21–49; Mazzino Montinari, "Aufgaben der Nietzsche-Forschung heute: Nietzsches Auseinandersetzung mit der französischen Literatur des 19. Jahrhundersts," *Nietzsche Heute: Die Rezeption seines Werkes nach 1968* (Bern: Francke Verlag, 1988), pp. 137–148. Robert Kopp, "Nietzsche, Baudelaire, Wagner. A propos d'une définition de la décadence," *Travaux de littérature* 1 (Paris: Klincksiek, 1988): 203–216; Jacques Le Rider, "Nietzsche et Baudelaire," *Littérature* 86 (1992): 85–101; Antoine Compagnon, *The Five Paradoxes of Modernity*, trans. Franklin Phillip (New York: Columbia University Press, 1994); Geoff White, "Nietzsche's Baudelaire, or the Sublime Proleptic Spin of His Politico-Economic Thought," *Representations* 50 (spring 1995); Andrea Gogröf-Voorhees, *Defining Modernism: Baudelaire and Nietzsche on Romanticism, Modernity, Decadence, and Richard Wagner* (New York: Peter Lang, 1999).

3. Charles Baudelaire, "Further Notes on Edgar Poe," *Selected Writings on Art and Literature*, trans. P. E. Charvet (London: Penguin, 1992), p. 194. References to *Selected Writings* are designated SW followed by page number.

4. Friedrich Nietzsche, *The Anti-Christ*, trans. R. J. Hollingdale (London: Penguin, 1975), p. 116. Refernces to this text are designated A followed by page number.

5. David B. Allison, *Reading the New Nietzsche* (Lanham: Rowman and Littlefield, 2001), p. vii.

6. Charles Baudelaire, *Les Fleurs du Mal*, trans. Richard Howard (Boston: David R. Godine, 1982), p. 6.

7. Friedrich Nietzsche, "To Malwida von Meysenbug," 18 (October 1888), *Sämtliche Briefe, Kritische Studienausgabe*, eds. G. Colli and M. Montinari, vol. 8 (Berlin: de Gruyter, 1984), p. 452. References to this edition are designated KSB, followed by volume-and page number. Translations are author's.

8. It is after reading Paul Bourget's text on Baudelaire that Nietzsche employs the term decadence, and it is also from Bourget that Nietzsche takes

the specific phrase "style of decadence." See Paul Bourget, *Essais de Psychologie Contemporaine*, 2 vols. (Paris: Plon, 1931–33), 2: 20. Traditional scholarship has not expressly challenged the repeated charges of Nietzsche's plagiarism of Bourget, yet the fact that Nietzsche did not plagiarize but rather appropriated and reinterpreted Bourget's theory of decadence to serve his own reevaluation of the concept has recently been established by Karin Bauer, *Adorno's Nietzschean Narratives* (Albany: State University of New York Press, 1999), pp. 130–31. Also see on the topic Matei Calinescu, *Five Faces of Modernity* (Durham: Duke University Press, 1987), p. 186.

9. Friedrich Nietzsche, *Ecce Homo*, trans. W. Kaufmann (New York: Viking Press, 1969), p. 248. References to this text are designated EH followed by page number.

10. Robert Kopp, "Nietzsche, Baudelaire, Wagner. A propos d'une définition de la décadence," *Travaux de littérature*, vol. 1 (Paris: Klincksiek, 1988), pp. 203–216.

11. Friedrich Nietzsche, *The Gay Science*, trans. W. Kaufmann (New York: Viking Press, 1974), p. 232. References to this text are designated GS followed by page number.

12. Friedrich Nietzsche, Sämtliche Werke, Kritische Studienausgabe, eds. E. Colli and M. Montinari (Berlin: de Gruyter, 1980), 11: 600–1. The following text appears as KSA followed by volume and page number. Translation author's.

13. Friedrich Nietzsche, "The Case of Wagner," *Basic Writings*, trans. W. Kaufmann (New York: The Modern Library, 1969), p. 626.

14. Charles Baudelaire, *Oeuvres Complètes*, ed. Claude Pichois (Paris: Gallimard, La Pléiade: 1976), 2: 699.

15. Friedrich Nietzsche, *The Will to Power*, trans. W. Kaufmann (New York: Random House, 1967), p. 444.

16. Geoff Waite, "Nietzsche's Baudelaire, or the Sublime Proleptic Spin of His Politico-Economic Thought," *Representations* 50 (spring 1995): 25.

17. Walter Benjamin, in the Arcades Project explains spleen as "the feeling that corresponds to catastrophe in permanence" (346).

18. Emphasis author's.

19. Charles Baudelaire, *Intimate Journals*, trans. Ch. Isherwood (Westport: Hyperion Press Inc., 1978), p. 104. References to this text are designated B followed by page number.

20. Emily Jane Cohen, "Mud into Gold: Baudelaire and the Alchemy of Public Hygiene," *The Romantic Review* 87 (1996): 239.

21. Eric Blondel, *Nietzsche, The Body and Culture*, trans. S. Hand (Stanford: Stanford University Press, 1991), p. 108.

22. Charles Baudelaire, "Journeaux Intimes," *Oeuvres Complètes*, 2 vols. ed. Claude Pichois (Gallimard, La Pléiade: Paris, 1975), 1: 671. References to this text are designated JI, followed by page number. Translations are author's.

23. Jacques Le Rider, "Nietzsche et Baudelaire," in *Littérature* 86 (1992): 89.

24. Friedrich Nietzsche, *Twilight of the Idols*, trans. R. J. Hollingdale (London: Penguin, 1975), p. 96. References to this text are designated TI followed by page number.

25. Helmut Pfotenhauer, *Die Kunst als Physiologie. Nietzsche's ästhetische Theorie und literarische Produktion* (Stuttgart: J. B. Metzlersche Verlagsbuchhandlung, 1985), p. 108.

26. Joanna Richardson, *Baudelaire* (New York: St. Martin's Press, 1994), 341.

27. Charles Baudelaire, "Le Salon de 1859," *Selected Writings on Art and Literature*, trans. P. E. Charvet (London: Penguin, 1992), p. 287, 294.

28. Walter Benjamin, *The Arcades Project*, trans. H. Eiland and Kevin McLaughlin (Cambridge: The Belknap Press of Harvard University Press, 1999), p. 337.

29. Sander L. Gilman, ed. *Conversations with Nietzsche*, trans. David J. Parent (Oxford: Oxford University Press, 1987).

30. Charles Baudelaire, "The Artist's Confiteor," *The Parisian Prowler, Le Spleen de Paris. Petits Poèmes en Prose*, trans. E. K. Kaplan (Athens: The University of Georgia Press, 1989), p. 4.

Works Cited

Allison, David B. *Reading the New Nietzsche*. Lanham: Rowman and Littlefield, 2001.

Andler, Charles. *Nietzsche, sa vie et sa pensée*. Paris: n.p., 1920–31.

Baudelaire, Charles. *Selected Writings on Art and Literature*. Trans. P. E. Charvet. London: Penguin, 1992.

———. *Intimate Journal*. Trans. CH. Isherwood. Westport: Hyperion Press, 1978.

———. *Les Fleurs du Mal*. Trans. Richard Howard. Boston: David R. Godine, 1982.

———. *Oeuvres Complètes*. Ed. C. Pichois. 2 Vols. Paris: Gallimard, 1976.

Bauer, Karin. *Adorno's Nietzschean Narratives*. Albany: State University of New York Press, 1999.

Benjamin, Walter. *The Arcades Project*. Trans. H. Eiland and Kevin Mc Laughlin. Cambridge: The Belknap Press, 1999.

Blondel, Eric. *Nietzsche, The Body and Culture*. Trans. S. Hand. Stanford: Stanford University Press, 1991.

Bourget, Paul. *Essais de Psychologie Contemporaine*. 2 Vols. Paris: Plon, 1931–33.

Calinescu, Matei. *Five Faces of Modernity*. Durham: Duke University Press, 1987.

Cohen, Emily Jane. "Mud into Gold: Baudelaire and the Alchemy of Public Hygiene." *The Romantic Review* 87 (March 1996): 239–255.

Compagnon, Antoine. *The Five Paradoxes of Modernity*. Trans. Franklin Phillip. New York: Columbia University Press, 1994.

Gogröf-Voorhees, Andrea. *Defining Modernism: Baudelaire and Nietzsche on Romanticism, Modernity, Decadence, and Richard Wagner*. New York: Peter Lang, 1999.

Kopp, Robert. "Nietzsche, Baudelaire, Wagner. A propos d'une définition de la décadence." *Travaux de littérature* 1. Paris: Klincksiek, 1988.

Le Rider, Jacques. "Nietzsche et Baudelaire." in *Littérature* 86 (1992): 85–101.

Michaud, Stéphane. "Nietzsche et Baudelaire." *Le surnaturalisme français. Actes du Colloque organisé à L'Université de Vanderbilt. W.T. Bandy Center for Baudelairian Studies*, 133–161. Neufchatel: Editions de la Baconnière, 1979.

Montinari, Mazzino. "Aufgaben der Nietzsche-Forschung heute: Nietzsches Auseinandersetzung mit der französischen Literatur des 19. Jahrhunderts." *Nietzsche Heute: Die Rezeption seines Werkes nach 1968*. Bern: Francke Verlag, 1988.

Nietzsche, Friedrich. *The Anti-Christ*. Trans. R. J. Hollingdale. London: Penguin, 1975.

———. *Basic Writings*. Trans. W. Kaufmann. New York: The Modern Library, 1969.

———. *Ecce Homo*. Trans. W. Kaufmann. New York: Viking Press, 1969.

———. *The Gay Science*. Trans. W. Kaufmann. New York: Viking Press, 1974.

———. *Sämtliche Werke. Kritische Studienausgabe*. Eds. G. Colli and M.Montinari. 15 Vols. Berlin: de Gruyter, 1988.

———. *Sämtliche Briefe*. Kritische Studienausgab. Eds. G. Colli and M. Montinari. 8 Vols. Berlin: de Gruyter, 1984.

———. *Twilight of the Idols*. Trans. R. J. Hollingdale. London: Penguin, 1975.

———. *The Will to Power*. Trans. W. Kaufmann. New York: Random House, 1967.

Pestalozzi, Karl. "Nietzsches Baudelaire-Rezeption." *Nietzsche Studien* 7. Berlin: de Gruyter, 1978.

Pfotenhauer, Helmut. *Die Kunst als Physiologie. Nietzsches ästhetische Theorie und literarische Produktion*. Stuttgart: J. B. Metzlersche Verlagsbuchhandlung, 1985.

Richardson, Joanna. *Baudelaire*. New York: St. Martin's Press, 1994.

Rippel, Philipp. "Die Geburt des Uebermenschen aus dem Geiste der Décadence. In "*Der Sturz der Idole. Nietzsches Umwertung der Kultur und Subjekt*. Ed. Philipp Rippel. Tübingen: Konkursbuchverlag, 1985.

Thomas, Henri. "Les Notes de Nietzsche sur Baudelaire. "*Nouvelle Revue Française* (October-December 1953): 1124–1127.

Waite, Geoff. "Nietzsche's Baudelaire, or the Sublime Proleptic Spin of His Politico-Economic Thought." *Representations* 50 (1995):14–52.

Chapter 6

PIERRETTE, ASSASSINE ASSASSINÉE[1]
The Portrait of Lulu in Two Tableaux

Jennifer Forrest

In his preface to *Idols of Perversity: Fantasies of Feminine Evil in Fin-de-Siècle Culture*, Bram Dijkstra justifies his lumping together of important fin de siècle painters with the multitude of their "virtually forgotten" contemporaries by citing how, more often than not, "great artists have been intellectually in tune with their own time rather than in advance of it in any significant fashion." The tendency, however, is to consider these "cultural icons" in isolation without linking them with the "dominant ideological movements of the time" (ix). The effort to take Frank Wedekind at his word on what he was trying to do in his creation of Lulu (e.g., the eternal woman), combined with that of associating his ideals with both the era's great philosophical dialogues (Nietzsche, Schopenhauer) and Western literary and artistic archetypes (Pandora, Eve, Antoine Watteau's paintings depicting Gilles) has lead to grand pronouncements on his often awkward yet earnest treatment of "weighty and abiding problems concerning the meaningfulness of pleasure and human dignity" (Hibberd 1984, 355). However, failure to analyze seriously Wedekind's Lulu, first, in conjunction with the earlier version of the plays, and second, in terms of fin de siècle culture and aesthetics, leaves critics unsatisfactorily scrambling for ways to reconcile the multiple stylistic and ideological currents composing the plays. Although many scholars have initiated studies of the influence of popular art—notably those forms to which he was exposed during his impressionable years in Paris—on Wedekind's conceptualization of Lulu and of his Lulu plays, the majority soon either abandon them altogether as peripheral or discuss them only in their appropriations by high art. The confluence of genres (farce, grotesque, satire, melodrama, horror, pantomime, comedy, tragicomedy—scholars refer to many of these styles in the same sentence), however, continues to resist such endeavors.

In *Art as Spectacle: Images of the Entertainer since Romanticism*, Naomi Ritter cites Félicien Champsaur's *Lulu, pantomime en un acte* (1888) as the source for the name of Wedekind's central character in the Lulu plays, *Erdgeist* (1898) and *Die Büchse der Pandora* (1905).[2] However, states Ritter: "she resembles Wedekind's Lulu only in her seductive dancing. Wedekind uses Champsaur's cruel Lulu as a mere springboard" (1989, 109). Like the majority of Wedekind critics for the past century, Ritter looks rather to literary archetypes to explain the multiple names to which Lulu answers in the plays: Lulu, Nelli, Eve, Mignon. Apart from Champsaur's purely formal inspiration, Lulu is the "talmudic first wife of Adam, Lilith, who gives Lulu her name," as well as the Lilith of Christopher Marlowe's and Goethe's *Faust*, in which she "practices magical powers that threaten men" (107).[3] Nelli, a derivative of Helen, recalls Helen of Troy, who exercises the same power over men, and Eve is the "ideal of innocence lured into evil," who, according to the image of the femme fatale, is also that first woman who tempts Adam to partake of the forbidden apple and incurs his, and all humanity's fall from grace (110). Finally Mignon recalls Goethe's *Wilhelm Meister*. Apart from her names, adds Ritter, Lulu's persona suggests the creation of a series of Galatheas by the Pygmalions with whom she is involved, while her portrait as Pierrot takes up and modifies to its purposes the decadent aesthetics of Oscar Wilde's *The Picture of Dorian Gray* (1891). But, however tempting it is to conjure formidable mythic predecessors to his Lulu, it is striking that Wedekind, through the mouth of the revised plays' Alwa Schön, clearly counsels the opposite effort:[4]

> That's the curse that weighs on literature today, that it's much too literary. We know nothing about any problems save those that arise among artists and scholars. Our horizon doesn't extend beyond the interests of our profession. To bring about a rebirth of a genuine vigorous art we should go as much as possible among men who have never read a book

in their lives, whose actions are dictated by the simplest animal instincts. (*Lulu Plays*, 113)

Alwa refers without doubt here to the popular classes. That Wedekind himself must resort to citing great literary precursors in his preface to *Die Büchse der Pandora* implies less a writer full of ideological contradictions, than a writer, whose work has been persecuted by the authorities for indecency, controverting their accusations by claiming to situate his work firmly within the moral scope of a long and venerated literary tradition. For example, he claims that, while Greek tragedies are "almost always beyond the pale of normality," no educated person would question their moral value. And, as according to classical literary traditions, if instructive art should also please, "then the presentation is lifted out of the realm of morality into that of art" (*Lulu Plays*, 104). In contrast, to the "great mass of normal readers," whose sensibilities the courts were ostensibly protecting, belongs "above all the uneducated person who appears in the drama itself as a strong man and against whose strident mockery the piece is directed." While the spectator who belongs to the popular classes "cannot be made sensible . . . by the *written* word alone," he cannot help but be edified when he "notices that cultivated persons find his counterpart [Rodrigo Quast] on the stage both contemptible and ridiculous" (*Lulu Plays*, 105). The preface's concluding paragraphs, however, make an about-face and refute art's duty to instruct and please by appealing first, to the legacy of Goethe, the great father of German literature, and his justification for some far from exemplary characters, and second, to the stories of Christ, the great father of Western civilization, whose justice reflects not the "bourgeois morality" of fin de siècle Germany, but that "human morality which transcends all earthly justice," a justice destined "for the weary and the heavily laden, not for the rich; for the sick, not for the healthy; for the sinner, not for the righteous man" (*Lulu Plays*, 106). In short, then, the Lulu plays do seemingly embrace the popular, and, in harmony with the romantic heritage of the period's aesthetics, he claims that the artist's vision is not answerable to, but transcends, bourgeois propriety and materialism.

R. Peacock's persuasive and fascinating article, "The Ambiguity of Wedekind's Lulu," goes further than most Wedekind critics in linking the various strains constituting the complexity of the Lulu plays to

French sources.[5] Depending on whom one consults, Wedekind spent anywhere from three to five years in Paris, interrupted by a stay in London. Because of his prolonged stay and his immersion in Parisian popular entertainment and brothel life, Wedekind, says Peacock, "didn't have to think up Lulu as a pure adventure of his fancy; he only had to look around, and we know that he did that. He could see the models, and furthermore on the scale he envisaged for Lulu." The real historical and cultural conditions existing in fin de siècle Paris serve, therefore, as the "basis for the actual milieu and plot of these plays, and for the *social* image of Lulu, as distinct from her wider symbolism" (111). This significant Parisian model for Peacock, however, limits itself to French boulevard melodrama and to the courtesan. To the first model would belong the revised versions of the 1895 Lulu play, the original of which carries hardly a trace of melodrama. The same can be said of the latter model, the courtesan, of which he cites one in particular, Cora Pearl, who in her *Mémoires* recounts her spectacular rise as a seductress and tormentor of men, and her fall into abject prostitution. Lulu's career bears a similar, and according to Peacock, often uncanny, resemblance to hers. But one can push the Paris connection even more to reveal how much the original vision of Lulu, Wedekind's idealism, his antibourgeois stance, and his works' heterogeneity owe to fin de siècle Parisian popular entertainments: the Parisian stationary circus, and the nineteenth-century French transformation of commedia dell'arte pantomime (in particular Champsaur's *Lulu*). Eric Bentley points out in his translation of the first Lulu play, "Some of us prefer *The First "Lulu"* however, not because it contains all the raw and raunchy bits that could never have passed the censors of those days, but because it is superior in style and structure" (11). I would add that it is not only superior, but simpler and richer because of the French influences—however much these mediums themselves were in transition—on that style and structure. "Conversely," comments Bentley, "what Wedekind and others may have seen as an improvement in the revised text, was not that, but only an adjustment to a more conventional type of theatre" (11). This conformity explains criticism's exploration of Wedekind's revised plays in terms of loftier philosophical themes and literary archetypes. The revised text contains strong enough traces of that thoroughly unconventional first Lulu play, however, to warrant an examination of its origins in French popular entertainments and decadent aesthetics, and thereby reattach the strong Paris link in the chain of influences.

MISS LULU AU CIRQUE

The European stationary circus dominated in France roughly between 1840 and 1880, and from 1880 to 1940 in Germany (Thétard 1947, 1: 48). To these dates corresponds the literary and artistic use of the circus performer as a metaphor for the artist. During the French circus's reign, the figure of the circus acrobat, from aerialists to clowns, was celebrated in poetry, novels, and art. In literature, for example, Théodore de Banville published his *Odes funambulesques* in 1857, Edmond de Goncourt his *Les frères Zemganno* in 1879, and J. K. Huysmans his *À rebours* in 1884. In art, Edgar Degas painted his etudes of *Miss Lala au Cirque Fernando* in 1879, Auguste Renoir his *Au Cirque Fernando* in the same year, Henri de Toulouse-Lautrec his *Au Cirque Fernando* in 1888, and Georges Seurat his *Cirque* between 1890–91. French literary and artistic interest in the acrobat continued not only well into the twentieth century with the work of Guillaume Apollinaire, Jean Cocteau, Pablo Picasso, Fernand Léger, and Georges Rouault, to name a few, but also had assumed dimensions divorced from the lure of popular entertainment indicative of art and literature in the last half of the nineteenth century. To the heyday of the circus in Germany corresponds in German literature Kafka's "Auf der Galerie" (1912) and "Ein Bericht für eine Akademie" (1917), the fifth elegy of Rainer Maria Rilke's *Duineser Elegien* (1922), and Thomas Mann's *Felix Krull* (1954). In art, among Max Beckmann's many circus pieces are *Trapeze* (1923) and *Acrobats* (1939). The German literary and artistic community, however, never embraced the image of the acrobat as fully and as enthusiastically as the French, and it is perhaps for this reason that German criticism overlooks the significance of the circus's influence on the form taken by the Lulu plays.

In 1859, Jules and Edmond de Goncourt wrote in their *Journal*, "We go to only one theater. All others bore us and irritate us. (. . .) The theater where we go is the circus." In preferring the circus over the legitimate theater, the Goncourts were making an artistic gesture against a realist drama that comfortably reflects the bourgeois audience's image back to itself. At the circus, they claim, "there are no actors and actresses pretending to have talent. Either they fall or they don't fall. Their talent is a fact" (1989, 491). While initially almost exclusively patronized by the popular classes in the first half of the twentieth century, the circus and pantomime at the Théâtre des Funambules began to draw new adherents from the literary and artistic ranks.[6] Circus acrobats appealed to the romantic imagination through their marginalized existence. The circus acrobat's performance with his/her very life before (and often high above) unsympathetic audiences resembled the romantic hero's own metaphorical acrobatics and unacknowledged position in society. It didn't hurt the mental association that many performers belonged to circus dynasties, with great "aristocratic" families marrying their children with illustrious members of other families. The notion of aristocracy even lent itself to the intermarrying of legitimate nobility with circus notables. The romantic image of the artist as acrobat was still valid in 1859 when the Goncourt brothers note:

> We see them, those men and women risking their bones in the air to snatch some applause, with a stirring in the bowels, with a fiercely strange, and, at the same time, warmly commiserating *je ne sais quoi*, as if these people were of our race and that all of us, mugs, historians, philosophers, stooges, and poets, we were leaping heroically for that imbecilic audience.[7]

In the same year as their journal entry, however, began a new phase in circus entertainments with the introduction of the flying trapeze by Jules Léotard, a trick that would soon be dominated by lady aerialists.

The lady acrobat came into her own during the 1870s, benefiting unquestionably from the newly exploited capacities of poster advertising, which presented her in titillating skimpy costumes as she ascended towards the great upper expanses. More important, in the circus arena she effectively challenged social misconceptions about the shape and capabilities of the female body; her strong legs were covered only in flesh-colored tights, her flashy costume was minimalized to avoid potentially fatal obstructions during the execution of an act, and her necessarily muscular arms were bare. Although many scholars discuss the lady acrobat in terms of sexual ambiguity, of androgyny, J. K. Huysmans in *A rebours* may be closer to a more accurate assessment of the sexuality that she projected while performing a trick in his description of Miss Urania:

> Little by little, while he was watching her, strange ideas arose; as he was admiring her suppleness and her strength, he saw an artificial change of sex take place in her; her graceful leaps, her insipid and affected female charms increasingly faded away, while there developed in their place, the agile and powerful allure of a male; in a word, after having been at first a woman, then, after having hesitated, after having bordered on the androgyne, she seemed to make up her mind, to take shape, to become completely a man. (1977, 210–11)

Far from being androgynous, the lady acrobat becomes decidedly male during her act. However, she was not alone in effecting this transformation. Turn-of-the-century American reformers were deeply troubled by travestied burlesquers' "horrible prettiness" (their legs and arms were also bared), and wondered how these women were able to reassume their "female" identities once they left the stage (Allen 1991, 134). Equally disturbing was the gaze these seemingly brazen women returned to the audience: "the burlesque performer made no pretense that her relationship with the audience was distanced by her absorption within another persona. She was aware of her own 'awarishness'" (Allen, 148). The lady acrobat enjoys the same traits, not through her gaze, but through her seemingly masculine bodily strength and dexterity. In carrying out an acrobatic number where her very life is wagered, she appears momentarily like a "victim": "one imagines her the captive of a relentless tyranny: a cruel director sequesters and exploits her. Imprisoned princess, she waits to be set free." But, this seeming victim has "muscles of steel," and she draws upon "her superhuman resources," her "superb animality," and metamorphoses into a "torturer;" "in the suppleness of this feminine body actually hides an aggressive and dangerous virility. She has something in common with the animals that are exhibited in the same ring" (Starobinski 1970, 52). Wedekind's prologue to *Erdgeist* dramatizes such a scenario; an animal tamer exhibits Lulu as one of his beasts, a lethal viper.

Félicien Champsaur's Lulu in his novelistic expansion of the pantomime, *Lulu, roman clownesque* (1901), is an accomplished circus aerialist and clown, whose leotard and tights are so transparent that one perceives, among other things, the pinkness of her skin. The neckline that plunges down to her belt combined with her apparent nudity ostensibly make her the object of male (and often female) desire. The spectator soon realizes, however, that she is the object of a thoroughly unsatisfiable desire, for Lulu . . .

> . . . so desirable, enigmatic, sphinx made of flesh, marvelously beautiful, Lulu, clownesse, Lulu, mime, Lulu, exquisite, whom Paris didn't know to have a lover, among the desires of men whose senses beat wildly, became, tamer of pigs and of males. (1901, 74)

The multimillionaire Baron Alphonse de Rothschild, ostensibly the most powerful and revered man in Paris, whose attempts to woo Lulu like one would a courtesan have failed miserably, offers her through the intermediary of a procuress 100,000 francs for one hour with her. His reasoning likens Lulu not to just any courtesan, but to one who, knowing her current value, has her price; he is grossly mistaken. While she accepts, arrives at the appointed bordello, dresses revealingly, gestures provocatively, and taunts the hideous Rothschild, her very smile and her parody of brothel language render him impotent: his desire had died, knocked down by Lulu's impenetrable smile and her "cold banter" (214). For Jean Starobinski, J. K. Huysmans, and Charles Baudelaire, the lady acrobat's victory is merely the result of circus illusion; beyond the circus arena, she behaves just like any other woman. In Baudelaire's *La Fanfarlo*, for example, Samuel Cramer's hopes for the confluence of the stage Columbine with the flesh and blood actress portraying her are dashed when she appears to him entirely out of character. For Champsaur, however, there is no deception: Lulu's offstage behavior differs not a whit from her clown persona. Concluding her rendezvous with Rothschild as if she were in the circus ring with her pig Râmbo, she was "With a somersault . . . at the bottom of the bed, still nude, dazzling with grace, supple and muscled beauty, with youth, with springtime" (1901, 216).

While not muscled like Champsaur's Lulu,[8] Wedekind's Lulu in Eric Bentley's translation of the reconstituted "monster tragedy" possesses her disorienting "awarishness," which is also that of the lady acrobat and the burlesquer. In the first act when Schoning and Goll reel from her alluring beauty during her exit from the dressing room as Pierrot, Lulu comments on their reaction using precisely that word: "And *I* am fully aware of it" (40).[9] She plays the roles handed to her—Nelli, Eve, Mignon—, indeed parodies them, but never becomes absorbed by them. In the second act, in Schoning's efforts to rid himself of Lulu, he tells her to take control of her husband Schwarz because, "That's what any wife has to do." Her response could come from the mouth of Champsaur's Lulu: "I didn't have to get married to be in that position" (81). She draws her power, as Schoning will understand in the following act, from other sources, not from assuming roles like that of wife. Karin Littau calls Lulu's ability to shift roles evidence of her deception, "precisely [because] she plays with the roles projected onto her" (900). But while the figure of the courtesan may be often deceptive, while she may have an ulterior motive for all her actions, this is not the case with Lulu. She shares her "monstrousness" with Manet's courtesan, *Olympia* (1863), who, while not being academically beautiful (as we assume Lulu is), looks uncompromisingly back at her viewer, a hint of mocking amusement at the corners of her mouth and in her eyes. The academic nude, says T. J. Clark, "could hardly be said to do its work as a painting at all if it did not find a way to address the spectator and give him access to the body on display." The form of address assumed by the nude was a "dreamy offering of self," a "looking which was not quite looking" and sometimes not even a looking at all (1984, 132–33). *Olympia* violated the rules of the nude's gaze, because her look . . .

> appears to be blatant and particular, but it is also unreadable, perhaps deliberately so. It is candid but guarded, poised between address and resistance—so precisely, so deliberately, that it comes to be read as a production of the depicted person herself; there is an inevitable conflation of the qualities of precision and contrivance in the way the image is painted and those qualities as belonging to the fictive subject; it is *her* look, her action upon us, her composition of herself. (133)

In addition, *Olympia* imitates the composition of the nude as established by Titian in his *Venus of Urbino* (1538), in which "the woman on the bed is Venus as well as wife" (94). She is the model for beauty against which painters during succeeding generations will match themselves. "The past was travestied in *Olympia*," and I cannot help but find in Wedekind's Lulu; however much he claimed that she represented eternal woman, a travesty of both traditional and mythical woman (95). Lulu wasn't scandalous simply because she was brazenly sexual; Lulu didn't offend merely by the obscenities suggested by her body; she disturbed above all by her "awarishness."

Wedekind's Lulu does not achieve, however, the degree of disruptiveness possessed by the burlesquer and the lady acrobat, who, without using their jobs as platforms for advancing the emancipation of women, effectively proved that traditional modes of defining women's place in society were nothing more than social constructs. Lulu, however, belongs to the era of the taming of these unruly women. For example, by the 1890s, the burlesque dancer's power to trouble underwent a twofold transformation. First, she lost mastery of projecting her "awarishness" with her body. She became an "exotic other, removed from the world of ordinary women," whose body once again went on passive display so as to provide unhampered arousal of the male spectator. Second, she was stripped of that speech which had made possible her claim to the subjectivity of her body (Allen, 237–38). Similarly, by the early 1890s, the lady acrobat's ability to disconcert was redefined by the competition of the trapeze striptease. Rather than undergo the strange metamorphosis from female to male in the execution of a trick, the trapeze stripper's body works hardest to confirm her inherent femininity. Champsaur's Lulu reflects the ambiguity created during this transition from humiliator to humiliated, and it is perhaps for this reason that Mireille Dottin-Orsini calls this novel, "the most bizarre text ever to be dedicated to the glorification of the feminine with a capital F" (1901, 363). If the novel strives to celebrate "Lulu-absolute woman" (164), it is to wrest femininity from the notion of social construct and recapture it for innate biology. And characteristically, Champsaur's Lulu is subordinated by the novel's end to the transcendence of her painter-lover, Georges Decroix. Wedekind's Lulu, however, is simply destroyed.

Pierrot Assassin Assassiné

Each act of Wedekind's early "monster tragedy" is dominated by the portrait of Lulu as Pierrot, accompanying her through a series of husbands and her flight, first to Paris, then to London.[10] However much unchanged in essence from one act to another, the portrait signals its function as a sort of title, providing clues how to situate and, in my opinion, interpret the play's title, its generic structure, its characters' names, and each act's events. While it is entirely possible that the physical presence of the portrait itself is a veiled reference to Oscar Wilde's *The Picture of Dorian Gray*, since most critics attribute Wedekind with some degree of indebtedness to Champsaur in the use of the name "Lulu," the image the portrait contains can also represent at the least an acknowledgement and encoding of the play's source as pantomime. Our understanding of the play's structure is enriched, however, if we consider the portrait of Pierrot, first, as drawing upon the generic codes of commedia pantomime in general, and second, as registering fin de siècle pantomime as an aesthetic and political satire against the legitimate theater and bourgeois social institutions. A third consideration is the death of professional pantomime in the 1890s, its mutation into an amateur salon entertainment, a form which itself will degenerate into a boudoir amusement, or *soirée déshabillée* (Rémy 1514). Like the striptease trapeze's stripping away of the lady acrobat's power to disconcert, the *soirée déshabillée* and related entertainments will redefine the Pierrot of spontaneous appetite as a courtesan of uninhibited promiscuity. This transformation of a male figure into a female was perhaps the result of Pierrot being played increasingly by actresses like Sarah Bernhardt. Wedekind was living in Paris during this transitional period, and his first *Lulu* reflects the uncertainty and instability of the genre and of the clown's ability to communicate recognizable character traits: Lulu is this Pierrot.[11]

Mime, the great ancestor of pantomime, says Tristan Rémy, goes back to Greek antiquity, and has retained its quality as a "genre of imitative comedy," or parody (Rémy, 1493). Having much in common with the carnivalesque, "The serious, the abstract, the noble were always brought down to earth with a bang" (Jones 1984, 19). The genre was particularly marked by a physicality in which the "body parodied both mind and spirit: all heroism ended in buffets and kicks in the pants" (20). Pantomime in the nineteenth century—the form which concerns us here are the harlequinades—was primarily a silent medium. In 1810, pantomime was permitted more or less for the first time since the French Revolution, and assumed the nonliterary form imposed on it by government ministers. In order to eliminate pantomime's competition with the legitimate theater, the authorities prohibited any production that would feature logical connections or actions between scenes, hence pantomime's nonsensical productions. But, as Louisa E. Jones points out, commedia productions had traditionally courted the irrational and the fantastic (1984, 18):

> Anything might happen on this stage: it was a world of dreams come true, repressed desires satisfied. *Commedia* action celebrates violence and desire without harm, guilt or consequence; even murder is ineffectual against characters who, like cartoon characters or jack-in-the-boxes, just pop back up. *Commedia* violence is at times like carnival violence, linked to patterns of ritual sacrifice and rebirth, even in 19th-century pantomime. (20–21)

The commedia dell'arte-inspired productions of the boulevard du Temple, in particular the Théâtre des Funambules during the romantic era, mark the beginning of a fruitful exchange between the "popular art forms of circus and pantomime and the ever more elite forms which assimilated, adapted and interpreted them" (Jones, 11). High art adopted and adapted popular figures, structures, and themes from the circus and pantomime only for low art to reappropriate them for exploitation in their new guise. In the last years of the century, however, the efforts of aesthetes and society people to interest the general public in a dying art came to nothing. The feminine monomime—a striptease mutation of commedia pantomime—probably drew its inspiration from productions of the kind found in Champsaur's *Lulu* and at the Cirque Molier (Champsaur wrote many pantomimes for this amateur circus). Most important, pantomime in the 1890s no longer featured acrobats, and devolved into the boulevard entertainment featuring "the most beautiful women in Paris" in states of undress considered daring for the times. (Rémy 1514). It was pantomime in the latter stages of its evolution that Wedekind saw in Champsaur's *Lulu*.

In the spring of 1888—the year in which Champsaur's *Lulu* was performed at the Nouveau Cirque (October 1, 1888)—a group of writers formed the Cercle Funambulesque[12] with the ambition of resuscitating the spirit and the scenarios of the "primitive" pantomime of the romantic era, and creating new works in the same vein and providing them with a theater and an audience (Jones, 167; Storey, 1985, 286). According to Robert Storey, the Cercle actively pursued only the second of these aims, finding the earlier pieces much too quaint (287). But while the Cercle found the old scenarios from the great Deburau's time ill-suited to fin de siècle Paris, there was a faction among its members that gave the physical violence of the old form a particularly decadent twist.

In much of the first half of the nineteenth century, as Jones notes, commedia stock characters who were victims of violence just as easily sprung back to life. The humor of the violence was lighthearted, slap-sticky, and, according to some, vulgar, indicative of the class that patronized the entertainment. As more and more novelists and poets became involved in the writing of funambulesque scenarios, the stories and gestures reflected the period's ideological trends, in particular the characterization of Pierrot. It was during the romantic period that Pierrot, as incarnated by Jean-Gaspard Deburau at the Théâtre des Funambules, deposed Harlequin as central character in pantomime repertory.[13] However much critics search for stock character traits in the sad-faced, aristocratic Gilles of Watteau's paintings, in reality, before Deburau, Pierrot was essentially the "lumpish valet," "the butt and messenger of who-ever happens to be onstage; a rustic, good-for-nothing dullard, credulous and sceptical by turns, and always at the wrong time, or frankly imbecile or feigning imbecility to avoid the stick" (Lehmann 1967, 210). While Deburau's Pierrot is still very much the buffoon, he is more active and willful: "Pierrot, transformed from cringing zany, delights the crowds by surrendering to every mad or ignoble impulse—as well as displaying the most touching pathos on occasion" (212). In other words, Pierrot is all appetite, whether for food or for women. But still, if a character dies, as when Pierrot saws Harlequin in half, s/he can be brought back to life. As Pierrot evolved after Deburau, the violence remained, but the scenarios took on a darker cast. Pierrot became more introspective, more melancholic, was increasingly the victim, and murdered characters stayed murdered for the duration of the pantomime. At the end of the century some of the Cercle's more avant-garde faction presented perfectly disturbing morbid tales in the blackest of decadent humor. In *Doctoresse!* (Hugounet and Villeneuve 1890), Pierrot's wife, Isabelle, the doctor of the title, murders her philandering husband and his lover, Columbine, by electrocution, and then proceeds to dissect the pair of them. Jones notes that, even in their more mainstream productions, "Cercle pantomimes inevitably end in murder" (1984, 168).

Like many other decadent writers, J. K. Huysmans shunned the legitimate theater as the "genre most saturated with bourgeois *bêtise*" (Jones 1984, 208). In 1880, he saw a performance (probably of *Le Duel* [Storey 1985, 219]) at the Folies-Bergère by undoubtedly the most imaginative and disconcerting group of acrobatic clowns of the nineteenth century: the Hanlon-Lees. Their typically dizzying and macabre act, described in Huysmans's *Croquis parisiens* (1880), began in a cemetery and ended in a general massacre. The Hanlon-Lees had reinvigorated the parody that is part and parcel of pantomime and infused Pierrot with a moral and physical blackness of the darkest sort. Huysmans responded with a travesty of bourgeois *bêtise* of his own in the equally savage *Pierrot sceptique* (cowritten with Léon Hennique, 1881), a pantomime published—not performed—as a rare edition book with illustrations by the father of the modern poster, Jules Chéret. Robert Storey finds that Huysmans's Pierrot is "form without substance, untouched by his own acts of terror" (222), qualities that are reminiscent of the "innocent" Pierrot of appetite, but whose appetite has taken on diabolical proportions. Asked if his Pierrot was a tragic figure, he responded that "His acts are tragic, not he himself" (qtd. in Jones, 211). This is a tragic, however, in which "no fall is involved, no justice, no pathos, no guilt" (Jones, 211).

Whether or not Wedekind read Huysmans's *Pierrot sceptique*, whether or not he saw a performance of the Hanlon-Lees, his contact with the Parisian stationary circus and pantomime would have impressed him with similar, if not quite so extreme, scenarios and representations of Pierrot. Pierrot's "familiar lack of conscience and consciousness" as seen through peculiarly fin de siècle eyes resurfaces in Lulu's idiosyncratic behavior, particularly in her impulsive need to satisfy her appetites, whether for food or men, and her sudden, and seemingly inexplicable, decision to change clothes with each "dramatic" reversal (Jones, 211). But all of the play's characters have something of Pierrot in them. Wedekind's trapezist/strongman Rodrigo Quast and the Marquis Casti-Piani resemble more primitive versions of both Pierrot and Harlequin. Rodrigo's belly will make his decisions for him before his libido: when Lulu finally succeeds in motivating him to make love to the Countess Geschwitz, his immediate thought is not the task he has been assigned, but to eat a caviar sandwich. Caught alone in the salon with Casti-Piani, Rodrigo reverts to the clumsy and stupid Pierrot of old who is the perpetual target of Harlequin's baton; Casti-Piani shakes him, knees him in the gut, hits him again, and draws a revolver, ostensibly in a fit of jealousy over Lulu, the woman he will denounce to the French police just moments later out of greed. Almost all the characters are victimizers who in turn become victimized and meet with nasty ends: Goll collapses in an apoplectic fit, Schwarz cuts his own throat, Lulu guns down Schoning, Schigolch tosses Rodrigo into the Seine, Kungu Poti strikes a mortal blow to Alva's head, and Jack the Ripper knifes to death Geschwitz. In a pantomime of have or not have, thrive or starve, kill or be killed, each opts for personal survival and will do the necessary to achieve those ends. Alva Schoning sleeps with his father's new wife on their wedding day. Schoning tries to have Lulu commit suicide, she shoots him instead. Rodrigo attempts to extort from Lulu, she has him killed. When Casti-Piani's attempts to sell Lulu on the white slave trade market in Cairo founder, he informs on her to the French police to break even financially. For a mere 500 francs and a roll in the hay with Lulu, Schigolch throws Rodrigo from his apartment into the treacherous Seine. They are all no less monsters than Jack the Ripper.

Huysman's claim that his Pierrot's "acts are tragic, not he himself," above all pertains to an uncannily id-driven Lulu, whose attachment to people and things lasts only as long as her interest in them. If Lulu the assassin ends assassinated by Jack the Ripper at play's end, her gruesome demise is tragic only in that the act has restored no moral order, nor has it established any "justice," "pathos," or "guilt." This is made especially clear in the Countess Geschwitz's apparent dying words ("Oh, shit"), which are also, ironically, the last words of the play; her death is just another annoying obstacle in her pursuit of Lulu.

Wedekind's first Lulu denounces not only bourgeois morality, but the bourgeois social order as well. It revives the topsy-turvy world of carnival in which all that is generally held sacred becomes the object of ridicule. The portrait of Pierrot framing each of the play's acts issues in this state of carnival. Lulu is many things to different people; she is Helen of Troy, the first woman Eve, Goethe's Mignon, and Dostoevsky's Katya, names associated with canonical texts, but names which are dragged through the mud when attributed to Lulu, the courtesan of monstrously unbridled appetite. Wedekind denounces not only naturalist theater, he upends all high art and philosophy; Schwarz, the conformist academic painter, in *Erdgeist* recalls Watteau by association with the latter's treatment of commedia subjects, and Goll calls him first Apelles, then Raphael, Velasquez, Brueghel, and Michelangelo. In the earlier monster tragedy, Alva makes a popular pantomime of Nietzsche's *Zarathustra*, an adaptation perhaps of Champsaur's mocking of Schopenhauer in his Lulu pantomime. The Pandora's box of the first Lulu's title suggests Greek mythology, only to become the vulgar expression referring to female sexual reproductive organs, the ones that Jack the Ripper summarily removes in the last act.

The ideal woman of romantic literature, who guaranteed by the example of her beauty transcendence to the artist, becomes an "inverse and complementary image" in the fin de siècle;

> Woman, according to this myth, is the great temptress because her nature dooms her to not get away from her body. That which makes her attractive and dangerous is that she represents tepid and guilty inherence in her body, opulent carnal immanence. (Starobinski 1970, 69)

Lady acrobats exercise "a splendid mastery over their bodies," "multiply through movement all kinds of seductions," and by this knowledge of their bodies epitomize supremely organic materiality (1970, 70). So, too, travestied Pierrots whose appetites anchor them firmly in their bodies. But where lady acrobats triumph in their "awarishness," in their ability to disconcert, travestied Pierrots manipulate and grasp almost instinctively. As representative of both, Wedekind's Lulu exults in her power to create desire in men; at the same time innocent and schemer, she taunts mercilessly Goll, Schoning, and Schwarz with her words, "I'm equally beautiful from all angles" (*First Lulu*, 41). The man who aspires to escape the prison house of his body becomes its victim: "the neglected body becomes deformed, begins to stoop, gets a potbelly; one had wanted to forget it, it returns to the charge in an obscene and grotesque fashion" (Starobinski, 67–8). His body announces itself emphatically with "a ridiculous fatality" (68). Woman, victorious in her physicality, finds her partner and victim in the wealthy bourgeois who is miserably and irrevocably trapped in his body. Champsaur's Lulu in the novel has an act she does with her pig, Râmbo, in which she rides upon his obese back, kisses sensuously his muzzle, and makes him jump through paper hoops. The pig, full of desire for Lulu, offers her flowers, then money, then his heart, all of which Lulu refuses, encouraging him on the contrary to do away with himself. With a rigged gun, the pig pulls the string attached to the trigger, and falls dead, only to be revived in true pantomime style by a repentant and caressing Lulu. This is the "Beastly Couple" composed of the beautiful, but treacherous, woman and the "odious," "fat," "ugly, disgusting, ignoble, filthy, rich" minister or banker (Jones, 149; Champsaur, 72). It is no coincidence that Wedekind's Lulu and her first husband Goll form such a beastly couple; unlike Champsaur's Râmbo who miraculously comes back to life, she wishes in all sincerity, but nevertheless in vain, that Goll's "burial was all a misunderstanding," and she sometimes thinks with nostalgic regret that she sees "his fat red head above [her]" (1901, 81).

According to many fin de siècle narratives, the romantic muse had freed herself from her ethereal bonds to take up with the very men against whom the romantic artist struggled to distinguish himself: the rich and fat bourgeois. During his sojourn in Paris, Wedekind would have been regaled with the lush images of their coupling in the rash of art posters bombarding Paris hoardings and walls such as Henri de Toulouse-Lautrec's *Reine de Joie* (1892) advertising Victor Joze's novel: a repulsive yet positively alluring woman in red décolleté kisses a grotesque, balding bourgeois on his bulbous nose. The process of stepping down off her pedestal is perhaps best exemplified by Baudelaire in "La femme sauvage" where he describes his beloved with her feet in the mud, while her eyes are turned up towards the heavens (154). Decadent scenarios, such as Huysmans's *Pierrot sceptique*, portrayed the artist taking up with substitute muses; Pierrot woos first a wax mannequin, and when she proves recalcitrant, he sets fire to her and elopes with a more docile cardboard model. Wedekind, more extreme, has his Lulu eviscerated by Jack the Ripper, the common man's answer to those respected medical men who located the source of all female ailments, most notably hysteria, in her sexual reproductive organs, and to those surgeons who promoted routine ovariotomies and hysterectomies to cure all ills manifesting themselves elsewhere in her body.[14]

Françoise Gaillard tells how the reporting of the catastrophic fire at the Bazar de la Charité in 1897, in which 121 people perished, most of them high society women, led to a flood of newspaper articles denouncing the male audience members who had unchivalrously saved themselves by trampling on, tearing through, and crawling over the bodies of those unfortunate women.[15] Men, journalists cried out, had become morally weak, flabby, feminized. But blame did not finally rest on these men, but moved on to the mothers who had raised them, and ultimately held all women responsible for male devirilization, the moral counterpart to the putrefaction of the flesh. Retaliation had begun much earlier than 1897, however, against those women whose bodies behaved as male bodies. A female body possessing a male body's physical prowess did not immediately, as Starobinski contends, reduce her to the materiality of her flesh. On the contrary, the equation of the lady acrobat to her body was the result of efforts to *make* her body signify femininity and a restored social order where the difference between the sexes was unambiguous. The circus *écuyère*, whose reign directly precedes that of the lady aerialist, faced a first threat to her dominance when travesties like Miss Ella jumped through more than fifty paper hoops and performed aerial somersaults off the saddle "like a masculine colleague." "Emulation produced miracles," and the *écuyères* found that they too could repeat the same feats (Thétard, 2: 179). After the 1860s, when the *écuyère* successfully rivaled the *écuyer* in acrobatic stunts, the clown was introduced into the ring during her performance. Seurat's *Cirque* depicts this couple, in which the *écuyère* must remain silent while the clown moons helplessly over her, "sometimes parodies his unwilling lover, and in one version, after being ignored by her, he regularly beats up the dummy" (Jones, 148). The clown, James Boswell, pulled hoops away just as the equestrienne was about to jump, yelled at her in English, and abused her in both gesture and look. Louisa E. Jones likens their relationship to that between "*femme fatale* muses" and their poets (1984, 147), because the equestrienne continued to perform, seemingly unresponsive to the imploring clown. But the regulation against her speaking suggests a dynamics similar to that set up in burlesque in the late 1890s, in which the female performer was joined by a male comic:

> To be sure, the woman performer did sometimes figure in burlesque sketch humor, but frequently her revealingly costumed body occasioned humorous remarks by male comedians or her words provided the comic situation that, through riposte and reaction, they could exploit. They were funny; she gave them something to be funny about. (Allen 1991, 238)

The introduction of the clown into the equestrienne's act, a person whose only purpose seems to be to constantly comment on her activities, to make her the object of his humor, served to emphasize with a vengeance her feminine social-sexual role, to direct attention away from her feats and toward her sexuality. It matters little that in a solo performance in the ring she would never have addressed the audience; the fact remains that the ban on her voice within the context of new performing conditions radically transformed her signifying abilities. Little wonder that around 1900, "Léris Loyal, daughter of the clown Gougou, created the number about the socialite who strips while on horseback." Henri Thétard adds that, "She was a great success" (1947, 2: 179). Alva Schoning's vitriolic comments to Lulu in Wedekind's play's final act—he calls her a virago, a she-wolf, a hyena, a bloodhound bitch—contrasted with the shrewish, stupid, and yet ever-lusting woman that Lulu has become recalls these comic fin de siècle pairings of abusive clown and silent equestrienne, and I can't imagine it played in anything but a brash farcical style.

In the finishing strokes to the portrait of Lulu, we return to those interpretations (including Wedekind's own explanations) that link her to myths and archetypes. Echoing the arguments of the majority of Wedekind scholars, Claude Quiguer says that Lulu, "the most vivid and the most haunting creation of Wedekind's theater, is not an *individual* with her own past and personality, but, in interchangeable costumes and names—Lulu, Nelli, Eva, Mignon—*allegory*—the animal tamer says: "*archetype*" and Schigolch: the "principle" of Desire." (Quiguer 1979, 79)

He finds that the names of Wedekind's plays, *Earth Spirit* and *Spring Awakening*, are "*without age*," and that they "indicate a deliberate will to understand the present through the *eternity* of *cycles* and *myths*" (Quiguer 1979, 78). When examined in conjunction with the majority of Modern Style era texts, he argues (and provides a convincing list of titles in support of that argument), Wedekind is treating the same eternal themes as his contemporaries: Nature and Life. But the abstraction and idealism of those titles lose their claim to innocence when one considers at the same time the overwhelming number of Liliths, Eves, Salomes, Judiths, Delilahs, Ophelias, and Ledas that figure in the paintings and novels of the fin de siècle. In this insistence on recovering the myths of an eternally perverse or fallen feminine, Lulu represents less a return to an unchanging symbol through the mask of the present than an effort on the part of the period's artists and intellectuals to impose the constraining traits of a timeless mask on an unstable present, here figured by the woman who poses a challenge to accepted social-sexual roles. Lulu as fin de siècle heroine, we are told, is intended to lead us to Lulu as "allegory," "archetype," or "principle of Desire." But how much more revealing of the period's preoccupations when we work in reverse, and move from the principle to the fictional character, and from high art to popular entertainment. Late-nineteenth-century circus and pantomime, two mediums in transition, furnished Wedekind with both the model for the fin de siècle "awarish" woman and the means for cutting her wings.

Notes

1. In mid-nineteenth-century French pantomime, "Pierrot becomes more and more polarized: one of his modern selves will be noteworthy above all for his capacity to suffer, the aristocratic pierrot; another will become above all brutal and remorseless, a criminal, proletarian pierrot. Fin de siècle authors spill much ink over this seeming separation of *assassin* and *assassiné*, black and white pierrots, as they are often called—though in fact they are not so distinct as is often assumed" (Jones, 106). For example, in *Marrrchand d'habits!* (1842), Pierrot kills a peddler, but is himself killed with the same sword he used to kill the merchant. As I will show in this paper, Frank Wedekind's Lulu plays draw heavily upon the tradition of French pantomime, and Lulu, in particular, embodies many of the character traits of Pierrot.

2. The bulk of my references will come, not from the revised versions, but from the first Lulu, to use the expression of *The First Lulu*'s translator, Eric Bentley. The earlier manuscript reflects more pronouncedly the influences here discussed, whereas the later versions bear the mark, not only of the passage of time, but of the censorship which first, the publication, and second, the performances, received.

3. It is interesting to see how different is the approach of French critics from their Germanist colleagues to the same material. Mireille Dottin-Orsini sees a desacralization, not a sacralization, of Lulu, commenting that, "One can see in the name 'Lulu' a humorous actualization of Lilith. For others, Wedekind named his heroine Lulu to take his revenge on Lou Salomé" (164, n1). Unless otherwise indicated, all translations from French texts are the author's.

4. There has been much critical discussion about whether Wedekind mocks Alwa's words regarding German literature, or if he is expressing his own

views on the subject. Supporting the latter view is the aim of this paper. For bibliographical references to the aforementioned articles, see Ward B. Lewis, *The Ironic Dissident: Frank Wedekind in the View of His Critics* (Columbia, SC: Camden House, 1997), p. 37.

5. A Wedekind critic who acknowledges French boulevard melodrama as a source for the Lulu plays is Elizabeth Boa, *The Sexual Circus: Wedekind's Theatre of Subversion*, (Oxford: Blackwell, 1987). In addition to Félicien Champsaur's *Lulu, pantomime en un acte*, Sol Gittleman cites a Grand Guignol dramatization of Jack the Ripper in Paris, *Frank Wedekind* (New York: Twayne, 1969), p. 66. Wedekind may also have visited the Musée Grévin in Paris and/or Madame Tussaud's in London, where great crimes and criminals were figured in wax. Wedekind's Jack the Ripper, who sells the uteri he excises, is particularly reminiscent of Mme Tussaud's wax casts of Messrs. Burke and Hare, who were hung for murdering people and selling them as fresh cadavers to medical research.

6. Pantomimists from the first half of the nineteenth century were usually accomplished acrobats and would have been equally comfortable at the circus as at the Funambules. Towards the end of the century, both Pierrot and the circus clown (and Auguste) were less and less associated with the type of accomplished acrobatics required of aerialists and equilibrists.

7. Goncourt, Edmond and Jules de. *Memoires de la vie littéraire, 1851–1865*. Ed. Robert Ricatte. 1989, I: 491.

8. Although Wedekind may not have read Champsaur's novelistic expansion of his pantomime, his familiarity with the latter's pantomimed Lulu is sufficient for an understanding of the complexity of her character, since it virtually passes unchanged in the transition (unlike Wedekind's *Lulu* in her various incarnations through the early 1900s).

9. In Stephen Spender's translation of the revised version, she says, "I'm perfectly aware of myself" (19).

10. To the later versions Wedekind added new acts in which the portrait does not figure.

11. For Naomi Ritter, Lulu "assumes the role of a literally heartless Columbine" (1989, 109). So too, for Tristan Rémy, is she a Columbine "in the fashion of the day" (1513). But for Champsaur's Lulu as a little girl mapping out her future, she is a combination of all commedia characters, but especially of Pierrot, the ancestor of the circus clown: "Now, it was a question, for the little girl, in whom circus memories and the faces of the buffoons, the masks of

the *ingénues* and the *coquettes* of old mixed together—to realize a type that she created after the fashion of the clown, different, however, by the nature of her sex itself: *Lulu, clownesse*" (1901, 14).

12. The group lasted only ten years, folding in 1898 (Storey, 286).

13. Louisa E. Jones' *Sad Clowns and Pale Pierrots* discusses in great detail nineteenth-century artists' embracing of the more romantically heroic Pierrot, especially chapter one.

14. For a detailed history of women and nineteenth-century surgery, see Ann Dally, *Women Under the Knife: A History of Surgery* (London: Hutchinson Radius, 1991).

15. "L'obsession de la pureté: misogynie, antisémitisme, décadence," paper presented on October 24, 1998 at the Twenty-Fourth Annual Nineteenth-Century French Studies Colloquium.

References

Allen, Robert C. *Horrible Prettiness: Burlesque and American Culture*. Chapel Hill: University of North Carolina Press, 1991.

Baudelaire, Charles. *Oeuvres complètes*. Ed. Marcel A. Ruff. Paris: Editions du Seuil, 1968.

Bentley, Eric. "The First 'Lulu': Nine Notes." *The First Lulu*. By Frank Wedekind. Trans. Eric Bentley. New York: Applause, 1994: 1–29.

Champsaur, Félicien. *Lulu, roman clownesque*. Paris: Charpentier et Fasquelle, 1901.

Clark, T. J. *The Painting of Modern Life: Paris in the Art of Manet and His Followers*. Princeton: Princeton University Press, 1984.

Dijkstra, Bram. *Idols of Perversity: Fantasies of Feminine Evil in Fin-de-Siècle Culture*. New York: Oxford University Press, 1986.

Dottin-Orsini, Mireille. *Cette femme qu'ils disent fatale*. Paris: Grasset, 1993.

Goncourt, Edmond et Jules de. *Mémoires de la vie littéraire, 1851–1865*. Ed. Robert Ricatte. 3 Vols. Vol. 1 of *Journal*. Paris: Robert Laffont, 1989.

Hibberd, J. L. "The Spirit of the Flesh: Wedekind's Lulu." *The Modern Language Review* 79, No. 2 (1984): 336–355.

Hugounet and Villeneuve. 1980. See Louisa E. Jones. *Sad Clowns and Pale Pierrots*. French Forum Publishers, 1984.

Huysmans, J. K. *A rebours*. Ed. Marc Fumaroli. Paris: Gallimard, 1977.

Jones, Louisa E. *Sad Clowns and Pale Pierrots: Literature and the Popular Comic Arts in 19th-Century France*. Lexington, KY: French Forum, 1984.

Lehmann, A. G. "Pierrot and Fin de Siècle." *Romantic Mythologies*. Ed. Ian Fletcher. London: Routledge and Kegan Paul, 1967.

Littau, Karin. "Refractions of the Feminine: The Monstrous Transformations of Lulu." *MLN* 110, No. 4 (1995): 888–912.

Peacock, R. "The Ambiguity of Wedekind's Lulu." *Oxford German Studies* 9 (1978): 105–18.

Quiguer, Claude. *Femmes et machines de 1900: Lecture d'une obsession Modern Style*. Paris: Klincksieck, 1979.

Rémy, Tristan. "Le Mime." *Histoire des Spectacles*. Ed. Guy Dumur. 1493–1519. Reprint, Paris: Editions Gallimard, 1965.

Ritter, Naomi. *Art as Spectacle: Images of the Entertainer since Romanticism*. Columbia: University of Missouri Press, 1989.

Starobinski, Jean. *Portrait de l'artiste en saltimbanque*. Geneva: Albert Skira, 1970.

Storey, Robert. *Pierrots on the Stage of Desire: Nineteenth-Century French Literary Artists and the Comic Pantomime*. Princeton, NJ: Princeton University Press, 1985.

Thétard, Henry. *La merveilleuse histoire du cirque*. 2 Vols. Paris: Prisma, 1947.

Wedekind, Frank. *The First Lulu*. Trans. Eric Bentley. New York: Applause, 1994.

———. *The Lulu Plays and Other Sex Tragedies: Earth Spirit, Pandora's Box, Death and Devil, Castle Wetterstein*. Trans. Stephen Spender. London: John Calder, 1977.

Chapter 7

BENJAMIN BETWEEN BERLIN AND PARIS
The Metaphorics of the City
Michael Payne

Having been born in Berlin in 1892, Walter Benjamin witnessed the simultaneous destruction of the old city and the realization of centralized plans for its rebirth, based on Baron Georges Eugène Haussmann's designs for the boulevards and avenues of Paris. At the turn of the century, Berlin was the quintessential modern city in the speed and noise of its life, it replacements of horses and cabbies with electric trams, and its loss of green parks and unexpected, unplanned places of tranquility that were once found in the heart of the old city. As Brian Ladd has shown, Berlin became at that time a city of ghosts, not only ghosts of its own urban past, but also ghosts of the history of Germany itself.[1] Behind the new streets and courtyards were hidden that other aspect of the modern city, the grim monotony of factory workers' tenements. What Walter Benjamin thought of this historical and modern Berlin is partly recoverable not only from such texts as "A Berlin Chronicle" and its derivative "Berlin Childhood around 1900" (1932), but also from his *Moscow Diary* (1927) and especially from his "Paris, Capital of the Nineteenth Century" (1937).[2] In 1913, Benjamin visited Paris for the first time, although he already knew the city in a sense before he went there from his experience of the new "Parisian" face of Berlin. No place was for him absolutely its own place, because he always brought to it related memories of someplace else. Furthermore, neither Berlin nor Paris had a fixed theoretical or ideological identity for him. Although Berlin is often depicted in his writings as the city of materialism that lends itself

most easily to Marxist critique, behind the aestheticism of Paris also—
or even down its labyrinthine streets—there awaits a surprising display
of the material brutality of the modern city, however beautifully alluring
its surface. Moscow, also, had for him no stable identity; much less was
it a synthesis of the materialism of Berlin and the aestheticism of Paris.
Rather, it offered the example of history simultaneously in one place
and of a cultural, East European otherness, not without profound connections with the capitals of the West. Tragically, it was Benjamin's publication of the first of his texts entitled "Paris Letter" in *Das Wort* in
1936, which denounced Nazi culture as "the playground of unqualified
minds and subaltern characters," that led to the order for his expatria-
tion and to his eventual suicide.[3]

Among the many pleasures that a visitor to a great city—such as
Berlin, Paris, or Moscow—can experience is the opportunity that such a
visit affords for reflection on the other city that is or was one's home. A
city, then, is not just a place to live or to visit; it is both a means of critically reflecting on the possibilities and limitations of living with others
in an urban setting and a means of productively distancing the traveler
from how he or she ordinarily lives, however much that may be living as
a global nomad or, in Benjamin's case, as a twentieth-century Diaspora
Jew. In cities, time is gathered together in one place. Benjamin's Berlin,
Paris, and Moscow were for him what we might now call "post-struc-
tural" places, structures displaced by the passing of time. They were
and are temporally after history yet also structurally—then and now—
always in the present. For example, to enter the Kremlin in Moscow
through the gates in Troitskaya Tower is to recall Napoleon's triumphal
entrance and later flight through those gates in 1812; and before that the
unification of Russian lands around Moscow in the last years of the long
rule of Ivan III, and earlier still the Kremlin's destruction during the
thirteenth-century defense of the city against the Tartars. No wonder,
then, that Benjamin writes of the Kremlin that "All the colors of Moscow
converge prismatically here, at the center of Russian power,"[4] even
though much of the rest of what he writes in his *Moscow Diary* about his
visit to that part of the city on January 4, 1927, is anything but imagina-
tively euphoric. His theoretical sense of urban layered time and sequen-
tial space, nevertheless, requires metaphorical expression. Throughout
his writings about Berlin, Paris, and Moscow, which are first of all about

his experiences of very real places, Benjamin reads those cities, nonetheless, as cultural discourses that have their own distinct metaphorics. Here there is a powerful—perhaps even foundational—instance of his distinction between ordinary, everyday experience (*Erlebnis*) and theoretical or philosophical reflection (*Erfahrung*).

The poetics (or theory) of the city has understandably produced an elaborate network of urban metaphors—a mythology of the metropolis—that is epitomized in such texts as the Genesis account of Cain's building of the first biblical city; Plutarch's life of Theseus and his description of the legendary founding of Athens; Freud's story in *Civilization and Its Discontents* of Eros's building the one out of the many (the collective civitas, the heart of civilization, which Freud tentatively bases on the archaeology of Rome.) These texts alternate between two related images: the city as polis and the city as labyrinth.[5] Not only for Plato but also for Plutarch, ancient Athens is the ultimate embodiment of the polis. Thus, according to Plutarch:

> After Aegeus's death Theseus conceived a wonderful and far-reaching plan, which was nothing less than to concentrate the inhabitants of Attica into a capital. In this way, he transformed them into one people belonging to one city, whereas until then they had lived in widely scattered communities, so that it was difficult to bring them together for the common interest, and indeed at times they even quarrelled and fought one another."[6]

In his dream polis, Theseus, according to Plutarch, instituted a constitutional democracy in which his own role was to be reduced to commanding the army and guarding the city's laws. Any post-Shakespearean (or post-Freudian) reading of this story of the origin of the city, however, cannot help but take note of how systematically it ignores the vicissitudes of Eros, which are central to Shakespeare's depiction of Theseus and his Athens in *A Midsummer Night's Dream*. Plutarch assumes that once the diverse interests of Attica are bound together for the common good, inscribed by law, and celebrated in a seasonal Pan-Athenaic festival, then the waywardness of desire will be tamed.[7]

Hebraic tradition, on the other hand, associates the origin of cities with the wanderer and outcast, Cain. Furthermore, a single, powerful sentence describing the city Cain builds (Genesis 4:17) associates it specifically with eros: "And Cain knew his wife, and she conceived and bore Enoch; and he built a city, and called the name of the city after the name of his son, Enoch." Eros, as Marcuse recalled by way of Freud, is not only the instinct to combine but also, therefore, a key to understanding everyday life in the city, in all its pleasures and discontents.[8]

The alternative (or perhaps complementary) image of the city to that of the polis is that of the city as labyrinth: a place to wander, to be an exile, to get lost, to lose oneself. This image is Benjamin's favored one, which he associates with the *flâneur*, the stroller or urban wanderer. For Benjamin, as an exile from Berlin, the epitome of the *flâneur* is Baudelaire in Paris. Although I am not aware that Benjamin explicitly associated the *flâneur's* labyrinthine city with Cain, Baudelaire comes close to doing so in his poem "Abel et Caïn" in *Les Fleurs du mal*:

> Race of Cain, on the roads dissembling
> Trail thy progeny that cry for blood!
> [*Race de Caïn, sur les routes*
> *Traîne ta famille aux abois.*]

Gerald Bruns, in his important contribution to the theory of cities, describes the labyrinthine antinomy to the polis this way: "Over against the polis theory there is a metaphorics of the city which stresses wandering, vagrancy, anonymity, randomness, the underground, the outlaw, the fugitive, the slave, the alien, the streetwalker, the begger, the trader, and the exile."[9] Understandably, then, in his magnificent, though unfinished text, "Paris, Capital of the Nineteenth Century," Benjamin identifies Baudelaire as the essential modern man, the ultimate *flâneur*:

> Baudelaire's genius, which is fed on melancholy, is an allegorical genius. In Baudelaire Paris becomes for the first time a subject of lyric poetry. This poetry is not regional art; rather, the gaze of the allegorist that falls on the city is estranged. It is the gaze of the *flâneur*, whose mode of life still surrounds the approaching desolation of city life with a propitatory luster. The *flâneur* is still on the threshold, of the city as of the bourgeois class. Neither has yet engulfed him; in neither is he at home. He seeks refuge in the crowd. Early contributions to a physiognomics of the crowd are to be found in Engels and Poe. The crowd is the veil through which the familiar city lures the *flâneur* like a phantasmagoria.[10]

Several things are of particular note in this passage: First, Benjamin finds in Baudelaire not only an urban poetic genius, but also someone who looks on the city with the gaze of the allegorist. Second, for Benjamin the city becomes the subject of lyric poetry precisely in the sense that it takes the lyricist inside himself; his exploration of the city leads him not outward but inward. Third, the *flâneur* is in a fundamental sense a challenge to the bourgeois urbanite: his freedom of movement, his critical mobility is new, challenging, and perhaps even threatening. Fourth, the *flâneur* resists becoming a part of the city (perhaps at his best he is a foreigner or an ethnic alien); neither Berlin nor Paris has yet engulfed him, which gives him a critical purchase on both places. Fifth, the social world of the *flâneur* is not the polis, not the constitutional community of Plato and Plutarch; it is instead the impersonal crowd of the arcades, as charted by Engels and Poe. The crowd, thus, lures the *flâneur* like an hallucinated (and consequently untouchable) image of the object of his desire. It is tempting to see in this image an analogy to Lacanian desire (as well as the phantasmagoria of Marx): that lure of the possibility of human fulfillment and integration that is just always beyond reach, like some mirage or vision in a mirror, as, for example, in one's reflection in a department store window. Benjamin would seem to anticipate this example, too, when he writes: "The department store is the *flâneur*'s last practical joke."[11]

The city—but perhaps especially Paris at the end of the nineteenth century—offers the lure of identifiable coherence that not only binds its citizens together—as Parisians or moderns—but also, by providing a sense of belonging, insinuates an always delayed promise of subjective wholeness into each person, a sense that is again a tantalizing lure that is always beyond reach, not unlike Koheleth's complaint in Ecclesiastes (3:11) that God's curse is to put a sense of immortality in the hearts of mortal human beings, a simultaneous wanting and lack. Christopher Prendergast, in his wonderful book, *Paris and the Nineteenth Century*, finds in Victor Hugo's prefatory text written for the *Paris-Guide* (1867), which came out in time for the Exposition Universelle, the exemplary expression of this ideological sense of Paris as the ultimately civilizing and integrating place.[12] Such a unifying vision of Paris, however, requires, as the art historian Tim Clark has convincingly argued, either the "high view" or the "blur"; the viewer must either be looking down (as from the tower of Notre Dame) or, by whatever means or vantage, be witnessing a blur. The serious point here is that the Impressionists captured Paris's resistance to an intelligible representation of its ideological desire.[13]

Just one part of the great sadness of Benjamin's longing for Paris was his being knowingly captivated by that desire. For example, in the opening pages of "A Berlin Chronicle" he recalls his reluctant wanting as a child to enter the labyrinth of his native city: ". . . Not far away were the haunts of that Ariadne in whose proximity I learned for the first time (and was never entirely to forget) something that was to make instantly comprehensible a word that at scarcely three I cannot have known: Love." In the present time of his writing this text, he recalls his early reluctance to enter the city's center with his mother, a resistance, he suggests, that continues to underlie "my present intercourse with the city's streets."[14] Almost imperceptibly this text moves from the streets of Berlin to those of Paris; but in place of his maternal Ariadne he is now accompanied by a "form" that is essential for his abandoning himself "to the shifting currents of these memories of [his] earliest city life." That ghostly form is Marcel Proust, sections of whose *Remembrance of Things Past*, Benjamin had recently translated and whose metaphorical imagination opens for him like a "fan of memory": "No image satisfies him, for he has seen that it can be unfolded, and only in its folds does the truth reside."[15] Now it seems to him that it is only through the images of Proust's novel that he is able to recall his own earliest memories of city life. Thus, Benjamin remained transfixed between Berlin and Paris, cities he recalled in texts of continuous revision that remained necessarily unfinished.

Tragic lover of cities that he was, Benjamin entered the labyrinth without Ariadne's thread. For him there was no proper exit from the city, and his story, thus, has no proper end. As to whether the center of his labyrinth was the place of his nurse or his mother, or whether he was a precursor of the deconstruction of centrality in both the personal and cultural sense, he offers only ghostly hints. John Ruskin, however, provided a commentary on an inscription beside the figure of a labyrinth on the door of the cathedral at Lucca, and his inscription may serve here as a coda, rather than a conclusion:

This is the labyrinth which the Cretan Dedalus built,
Out of which nobody could get who was inside,

Except Theseus; nor could he have done it, unless he had been
Helped with a thread by [Ariadne], all for love.[16]

Perhaps the recent fascination with Benjamin's work has rescued him
from the labyrinth after all.

Notes

1. Brian Ladd, *The Ghosts of Berlin: Confronting German History in the Urban Landscape* (Chicago: The University of Chicago Press, 1997).

2. Because of Benjamin's complex processes of revision, compositional dates are approximate. I follow Momme Brodersen's chronology in his *Walter Benjamin: A Biography* (London: Verso, 1996), pp. xiii–xvi. I also rely on this book more generally for a sense of the contour of Benjamin's life.

3. Brodersen, *Walter Benjamin*, p. 240.

4. Walter Benjamin, *Reflections*, ed. Peter Demetz (New York: Harcourt Brace Jovanovich, 1978), p. 100.

5. Here I am especially indebted to Gerald Bruns, "The Metaphorical Construction of Cities," *Salmagundi* 74–5 (spring-summer 1987): 70–85; and Tony Tanner, *Venice Desired* (Oxford: Blackwell, 1992), esp. pp. 1–16. This paper is dedicated, in memoriam, to Tony.

6. *Plutarch's Life of Theseus*, trans. Ian Scott Kilvert (London: Heinemann, 1967), 24: 1.

7. Cf. Leo Strauss: ". . . In the good city *eros* is simply subjected to the requirements of the city: only those are permitted to join each other for procreation who promise to bring forth the right kind of offspring. The abolition of privacy is a blow struck at *eros*." *The City and Man* (Chicago: University of Chicago Press, 1964), p. 111.

8. "The Affirmative Character of Culture," in *Negotiations: Essays in Critical Theory* (Boston: Beacon Press, 1960); *Eros and Civilization: A Philosophical Inquiry into Freud* (Boston: Beacon Press, 1966).

9. Gerald Bruns, "The Metaphorical Construction of Cities," p. 79.

10. Benjamin, *Reflections*, p. 156.

11. Ibid. Benjamin's *The Arcades Project* has recently been issued in an excellent English translation by Howard Eiland and Kevin McLaughlin (Cambridge, MA: Harvard University Press, 1999).

12. Christopher Prendergast, *Paris and the Nineteenth Century* (Oxford: Blackwell, 1992), esp. p. 7.

13. T. J. Clark, *The Painting of Modern Life: Paris in the Art of Manet and his Followers* (New York: Alfred A. Knopf, 1985), p. 35.

14. Benjamin, *Reflections*, p. 4.

15. Ibid., p. 6.

16. Quoted by J. Hillis Miller in *Ariadne's Thread: Story Lines* (New Haven: Yale University Press, 1992), p. 260n. Miller discusses Benjamin briefly on pp. 61–63. "Adriane," the spelling I have altered in this quotation, is an alternative for "Ariadne."

Chapter 8

À FLEUR DU DIALOGUE

Georges Bataille, Karl Blossfeldt, and the Language of Flowers

Kimberley Healey

In memory of Charles Bernheimer

Franco-German dialogues were becoming increasingly difficult in 1929. Political relations reached a crucial point in that year with the renegotiations of German reparations for World War I leaving many French public figures resentful and suspicious. Within a few years entire issues of popular French magazines like *Lu* and *Vu* would present the French view of "the German problem." The traveling journalist, André Siegfried, would express a common view about Germany's postwar challenges: "*Ce pays n'a pas trouvé en lui-même les forces de reconstruction morale que possède une civilisation de structure plus équilibré comme la France*" [That country has not found within itself the forces of moral reconstruction possessed by a civilization like France with a more balanced structure].[1] Damning national stereotypes were well on their way to becoming accepted truths. Germans appeared in French magazines as poor and desperate peasants or as corrupt aristocrats refusing to acknowledge social change. Positive aesthetic representations like the young German bodies so admired by a Stephen Spender or a Christopher Isherwood appear rarely in the French popular press. Rather, the French press attributes the German enjoyment of sports and nudism to the low cost of these pastimes. According to a reporter for *Lu* in 1932: "*Des romantiques allemands très bourgeois ont voulu, dans ce mouvement, se rapprocher de la nature*" [Very bourgeois German romantics wanted to get closer to nature by engaging in this movement (sports and nudism)]. The growing anti-German sentiment would preclude any aesthetic value being attributed to Teutonic culture. Even Goethe, in 1932, is praised as a French writer.

In French literature and magazines, French intellectuals and reporters portray Germans as non-Cartesian primitive subjects incapable of freeing themselves from their umbilical cord with the earth, with dirt and with all that is dark. In the January 1929 issue of *La Revue des Vivants*, Emmanuel Bourcier characterizes the Germans as not knowing how to dress, being sexual beasts, loving flags and chemical products, liking to sing in groups but not alone, and wearing shoes made for thick ankles. This is one of many examples from the period revealing a French preference for the curious German detail rather than journalistic attempts to analyze the greater, and constantly changing, social and cultural whole that was Germany. As the 1930s progressed, the French popular press included more reports on German police activities, anti-Semitism, the closing of the Bauhaus school and the strange social effects of the rise of National Socialism. However, the tone is more often curious and dismissive than condemnatory. Occasionally, these articles included anecdotes about the sudden disappearance of Jewish bankers in small towns. However, placed in a context of trivial notes about sausages and swastikas, the contemporary reader could be tempted to read disappearance as a mere *fait divers* rather than as a sign of impending catastrophe.

Stepping into this fray of questionable national stereotypes of 1929 Paris, the Berlin photographer Karl Blossfeldt (1865–1932) published his first book of images, *Urformen der Kunst* (1928), or *La Plante* (1929), in its French translation.[2] That same year Georges Bataille chose Blossfeldt's photos to accompany an article on nature, aesthetics, and culture, "Le langage des fleurs," in the short-lived French magazine, *Documents*. Five full-page photos by Blossfeldt appear interlaced with Bataille's four pages of text. Bataille does not specifically mention Blossfeldt in his text and the credits for the photos appear only in a note after the author's signature. The note runs: "*Les photographies inédites qui sont publiées avec cet article sont dues à M. Blossfeldt. Elles sont reproduites avec l'autorisation des éditions Ernst Wasmuth de Berlin*" [The [as yet] unpublished photographs published with this article are by Mr. Blossfeldt. They are reproduced with the authorization of the publisher, Ernst Wasmuth of Berlin (Bataille, 164)]. Bataille's text appears interspersed with Blossfeldt photographs depicting a bared campanula stamen (6x), some Bryon Alba tendrils (5x), a horsetail (20x), a barley head (3x) and a fern (12x). The photographs are very stark and bear only headings with the common and Latin plant names and the degree of magnification.

These particular images did not appear in Blossfeldt's first book. Thus, Bataille must have had access to the greater body of Blossfeldt's work. Bataille's text is by no means a review or even presentation of Blossfeldt's images. In contrast to other articles in *Documents* on Alberto Giacometti, African sculptures or Pablo Picasso, "Le langage des fleurs" does not take as its primary aim a commentary on the accompanying full-page images. Nor can one read Blossfeldt's images as illustrations of Bataille's text since by 1929 the photographer was at the end of his career and had already produced the photographs that Bataille would select for publication. A very particular relationship thus appears between the thematically related text and images. This unwitting collaboration is nonlinear in that it is not based on cause and effect; the text did not require the images as illustration nor is the text dependent upon said images. Although this concurrent publication of text and image is a relatively chance encounter of two men's lifelong attempts to understand the hidden qualities of the visual world, it also represents an intersection of French and German aesthetics.

During the two years of *Documents*' publication, 1929–1930, this consciously eclectic publication included in its subtitle the words: *doctrines, archéologie, beaux-arts, ethnographie* and *variétés*. Founded by Georges Bataille and Pierre d'Espezel, but apparently chiefly edited by Bataille, the magazine included articles by Michel Leiris, Carl Einstein, Paul Rivet, and Marcel Griaule to name but a few. Articles appeared on subjects as diverse as ancient African cave paintings, Hollywood, Picasso and Greek coins. Like many avant-garde revues, it was a forum for international collaboration. However, from the beginning conflict arose between those who envisioned the magazine as a site for ethnographic discovery and research and those, including Bataille, who contributed articles of a heterogeneous nature, such as his article on the big toe and shorter pieces on topics like spittle, slaughterhouses, and crustaceans.[3] Bataille's shorter and more disturbing pieces would eventually be relegated to a section called "*dictionnaire critique*." Although not fully documented, the editorial conflicts between Bataille and the major financial backer Georges Wildenstein may well have precipitated the magazine's demise.[4]

Documents as a whole had a somewhat ambivalent attitude towards things German. In several issues of the magazine, German ethnographers come under critical fire for what French scholars consider inferior methodologies. Despite these misgivings, German research continues to appear in the magazine and some vocabulary even remains in the original German. According to Alastair Brotchie, Carl Einstein, a major German contributor, may even have had his articles translated and possibly rewritten by Bataille. The power play is subtle but apparent as both German and French intellectuals struggle to gain acceptation for new visions of ethnography, anthropology, and cultural history. Despite the contributing presence of both French and German intellectuals, *Documents* never turns its ethnographic and highly curious eye to the state of Franco-German relations in 1929–1930.

Today, *Documents* is increasingly the object of scholarly analysis. In 1992, the Parisian editor J. M. Place published a complete reprint of the 1929–1930 issues. Although many researchers have focused on Bataille's exact position and influence in the journal, none have discussed the intertextual and international dialogue occurring between the photographs by Blossfeldt and the article by Bataille. In a similar fashion, Blossfeldt's biographers are far more interested in tracing the specific chronology of his work in Germany rather than in documenting the photographer's international influence—this despite the fact that translations of his first book appeared and sold internationally within less than a year of the original German publication. Unlike the photographs by Jacques-André Boiffard that accompany Bataille's better-known piece on the big toe, Blossfeldt's photos were not the result of lengthy discussions with Bataille. As Blossfeldt had already produced well over six thousand images by this time, Bataille simply used that which was available whether or not the photos had a specific relationship to his own text.

As James Clifford points out in *The Predicament of Culture*, "The journal's [*Documents*] basic method is juxtaposition—fortuitous or ironic collage. The proper arrangement of cultural symbols and artifacts is constantly placed in doubt" (Clifford, 132).[5] By taking the juxtaposition of images and text as our object, we can carry out a close analysis of how both Blossfeldt and Bataille question and refigure a very simple cultural symbol, the flower. This in turn reveals a larger and more problematic dialogue between French and German aesthetics and between visions of the natural and the human that fed contemporary national stereotypes. International perceptions of a nation will often either glorify or condemn that culture's particular relationship to nature. As ethnography developed as a science, intellectuals like Marcel Griaule would proclaim in *Documents*, "ethnography is interested in both beauty and ugliness, in the European sense of these absurd words."[6] Beauty and ugliness, for the writers of *Documents*, would depend on an object's location on the supposed continuum between nature and civilization. Post-World War I aesthetic ideologies in Paris and Berlin both reject and embrace nature and the natural. Bataille and Blossfeldt's textual and visual images call into question the symbolic and aesthetic aspects of the natural world in 1929.

The theories of juxtaposition apparent in *Documents* allow us to read between the lines, between the stamen so to speak, of what Bataille and Blossfeldt presented to Paris in 1929. Georges Didi-Huberman reiterates the importance of juxtaposition:

> *à travers la pratique éditoriale où Bataille, d'article en article, mena un véritable travail de 'montage figuratif', créant sur toute l'étendue de la revue (et particulièrement, bien sûr, dans l'illustration de ses propres textes) un stupéfiant réseau de mises en rapports, contacts implicites ou explosifs, vraies ou fausses ressemblances, fausses et vraies dissemblances . . .*
> [throughout Bataille's editorial practices, from article to article, he carried out a true "representational assembling," creating a stupefying network of relationships, implicit or explosive contacts, true or false resemblances, false or true differences from article to article (and, of course, particularly in the illustration of his own texts.] (105)[7]

If *Documents*' message appears in its heterogeneous structure then the interstitial text, the article within the article, of "Le langage des fleurs" bears close reading. This is particularly relevant since Bataille's text takes as its theme the dismembering and deconstruction of symbolic social dialogue.[8]

Blossfeldt did not consider himself an art photographer or artist. He began photographing plants as models for some of the sculpted objects that he created and as a means to teach his art students. His first photography exhibit was in 1926 when he was already over sixty and from then until now the debate has continued over whether or not to consider him an artist.[9] In 1929, Moholy-Nagy featured Blossfeldt's photos in an exhibit of avant-garde film and photography in Stuttgart. Blossfeldt does not appear to have had a relationship with the Bauhaus school but once Moholy-Nagy had discovered his photos it is likely that they would have circulated in the school. In his two books, *Urformen der Kunst* (1928) and *Wundergarten der Natur* (1932), which consist mainly of photographic plates, Blossfeldt calls for turning a new eye to nature as the practical source of art forms. According to Rolf Sachsse, "his philosophy was part romantic view of nature, part critique of functionalistic design, and part reductive application of Darwinism to both social and aesthetic developments" (13).[10] Blossfeldt hoped that even in an age of industrial production researchers would realize that nature could still provide the greatest designs. However, his is a nature that man has thoroughly manipulated in order to reveal pure form.

By placing side by side the two aesthetic value systems using nature as their base, in the photographs and Bataille's writings, one witnesses a Franco-German aesthetic discourse, that even in the late-1920s and despite national conflicts, continued on the printed page through words and images. Intercultural encounters such as this could possibly, at that time in history, only take place in the margins of French or German culture. This type of forced dialogue between image and text may well have been the aim of surrealist texts like Raymond Roussel's *Nouvelles Images d'Afrique* (1932). However, in surrealist practice the links between the illustrations and text were so vague that a sense of the uncanny arose in the viewer rather than a questioning of the relationship between images and text that clearly took as their base the same topic. Bataille's juxtapositions of text and image in *Documents* are not surrealist. His troubled relationship with the surrealists, and André Breton in particular had reached a crucial breaking point by 1929. Throughout *Documents* Bataille chooses illustrations for his articles that may be curious or evocative but not absurd, automatic, or senseless.

In "Le langage des fleurs" Bataille begins with the seemingly innocent question of why particular flowers have certain meanings in human culture. He quickly moves to a discussion of the flower's primarily erotic and morbid symbolism. Bataille does not dispute the idea that certain concepts are inexpressible through language and require natural objects, like flowers, for their communication. However, the concepts that are difficult to communicate are not the customary gestures of love and friendship but rather death and erotic desire. The flower, in Bataille's view, is a temporarily disguised object of horror and abjection. Despite the universally acknowledged beauty of a rose's bloom, one can never fully escape the stem that leads down to the roots: slimy, probing, and greedy for rot. Thus, for Bataille, the hidden meaning of human symbols reappears in the material reality of the natural object from which the symbol came.

What many may see as the flower's metonymy is actually in Bataille's view a synecdoche. The flower no longer equals love but is rather a part standing, in his view, for the whole plant, a natural organism whose characteristics include slime, dirt, and base desires. The corolla, or petals, briefly, stands in for the true nature of the plant, a horrific, rotting and slimy rather than romantic vision of nature. This shift in reading a cultural symbol then begs the question of how national stereotypes, that is, shoes for thick ankles, stand in for a whole which requires new critical reading. However, neither Bataille nor any of *Documents'* writers directly take their practices of cultural dissection and suture to the state of Franco-German relations. Nor does Bataille ever question the universality of the language of flowers. At the beginning of his article he specifies: "*Ce qui frappe des yeux humains ne détermine pas seulement la connaissance des relations entre les divers objets, mais aussi bien tel état d'esprit décisif et inexplicable*" [that which strikes the human eye does not only determine knowledge of the relationship between diverse objects, but also a particular decisive and inexplicable state of mind] (Bataille, 160). The viewer thus adds to the interpretation of the cultural object. However, Bataille presents the language of flowers as a universal and not culturally specific human phenomenon. For him, roses, water lilies, and narcissi are not French, German, or Greek in their deeper meaning but merely human.

Despite the text's title, only one photograph from Bataille's article is actually of a flower, a Campanula Vidalii, whose petals have been torn off leaving the hairy pistil and the fingerlike stamen exposed to the viewer. A note informs the possibly confused viewer that the flower's petals have been torn off. As Bataille writes of the rose, ". . . *si l'on arrache jusqu'au dernier les pétales de la corolle, il ne reste plus qu'une touffe d'aspect sordide*" [. . . if one tears off all of the corolla's petals, nothing remains but a rather sordid tuft]. This is not an accurate description of Blossfeldt's particular photo. Rather than being sordid this flower hangs alone in denuded grace yet also in death. The fuzzy pistil may be obscene, but it is no tuft. The flower has an unnatural sheen and the stark black and white photograph emphasizes the morbidity of the image. Blossfeldt's photos reveal plants stripped down to purely aesthetic elements. If this flower were offered as a cultural symbol, its flaccid forms would indeed communicate Bataille's morbid eroticism.

Blossfeldt's plants were cut, bared, dried, pulled out of their growth and always placed in front of a neutral background. His photographs all greatly magnify the plants. Blossfeldt must have taken many of them fairly quickly, before the stripped stems and decapitated flowers had time to turn brown. Sensitive to the aesthetic demands placed on nature Bataille writes that flowers do not age gracefully, *"elle se flétrissent comme de mijaurées vieillies et trop fardées"* [they fade like so many old and overly made up ladies]. Like a faded beauty, Blossfeldt's deflowered campanula no longer has the power to produce seed after being clinically prepared for the photograph. Although imbued with a disturbing sensuality, verging on the sadistic, Blossfeldt's photos are not as latently fertile as, for example, later flower photographs by Imogen Cunningham or Robert Mapplethorpe.[11] As Walter Benjamin would write in his review of Blossfeldt's first book, the conflation of floral and human can verge on "graphic sadism."[12]

For Bataille, and much of Western culture, the flower is particularly powerful in the discussion and proclamation of love. He writes that since what one loves in another human is not their reproductive organs but the person who carries them, it is normal that one would offer flowers with petals, and not bared reproductive systems, just as human desire must necessarily focus on the clothed and dissimulated body. According to Bataille, this one parallel does not, however, explain the complex system of floral language that has developed over the centuries. For Blossfeldt, plants are praiseworthy for their practical nature rather than for the obscure sexual references they awaken in the human psyche. *"Neben einem ornametal-rhythmisch schaffenden Urtrieb, der überall in der Natur waltet, baut die Pflanze nur Nutz- und Zweckformen"* [Next to the ornamental and rhythmic basic creative drive that prevails in nature, the plant builds only effective and purposeful forms].

These purposeful forms, plucked and offered in the culture witnessed by Bataille, function primarily as reproductive organs. Form may follow function in the ideal world of modern design but for Bataille, "*Mais plus encore que par la salissure des organes, la fleur est trahie par la fragilité de sa corolle: aussi, loin qu'elle résponde aux exigences des idées humaines, elle est le signe de leur faillite.*" [The flower is betrayed by the fragility of its corolla even more than by the dirt stains of its organs: thus, rather than responding to the demands of human ideas, the flower is a sign of their failure] (Bataille, 163).[13] Plants, and more specifically flowers, thus represent the failure of the idea of pure form and the omnipresence of a morbid sexuality.

Bataille's article focuses on the absurdity of a system of correlations between emotional states and flowers, an imposed language that has little to do with the real nature of a flower. Blossfeldt was also aware of the limitations of language. He did not write much. Indeed, other people frequently wrote more for the prefaces of his books than he did. In his very brief introduction to *Wundergarten der Natur* he writes: "*Es ist nicht meine Absicht, den hier gezeigten Bildokumenten irgendwelche Deutung zu geben. Wortreich Erklärungen stören den starken Eindruck, den die Bilder auf den Beschauer ausüben*" [It is not my aim to give any particular meaning to the photographs shown here. Wordy explanations disturb the strong impression that the pictures work on the viewers].[14] By allowing the images to speak for themselves Blossfeldt is presenting high modern art but also engaging in praise of nature, who does not need words. Blossfeldt never shows an interest in seeking out the language of his plants. He does not wish to read his photos in a textual manner. They are simply there as design elements, arabesques, and well-balanced patterns. In 1928, revealing the aesthetic of the era, the German artist Johannes Molzahn declared: "*Das Bild wird eine der wirksamten Waffen werden gegen den Intellektualismus, gegen die Mechanisierung des Geistes. Nicht mehr lesen! Sehen! wird das Motto der Erziehungsfragen sein*" [The picture will be one of the most effective weapons against intellectualism, against the mechanization of the spirit. Read no more! See! will be the motto of educational issues].[15] This call for the visual cannot, particularly in our later reading, escape the political.

Throughout *Documents* Bataille also challenges his readers to see, to see death, sacrifice and orgiastic expenditure in an increasingly sanitized world. This privileging of the visual precludes intellectualism for Molzahn and certain German nationalists yet for Bataille it demands critical questioning of society's constructs. Bataille recognizes the incredible power in an image. Flowers work in Western culture to express the inexpressible, to act in lieu of language. Yet Blossfeldt claims that for him they express little other than form. Both German and French intellectuals of the early twentieth century yearn for a reevaluation of textual truth towards a more living and spontaneous moment. This appears in surrealism, in *Neue Sachlichkeit* and in contemporary film.

Blossfeldt's photos turn a new eye to common weeds much as French ethnographers of *Documents* sought to employ their aestheticized vision of other cultures as the means to re-perceive their own. By glorifying and stabilizing the lowly horsetail as a monument, Blossfeldt creates images that enter into dialogue with Bataille's articles, particularly those like "The Big Toe," that propose and illustrate a new, and base materialism. However, one could also propose that here lies the threat of a new nationalism: the glory of the German cowslip in the meadow as opposed to the more elaborate, artificial and pretentious art of foreign cultures. Barley, a necessary German grain, becomes monument in Blossfeldt's photos. Blossfeldt's early work was the photography of classical ruins. Like Hegelian nationalists he seems to wish to make the leap from the true art of the classical age to the truth of Germany's own essence, thereby bypassing the Oriental and symbolic art that overwhelms in its chaos. The acanthus plant, which Blossfeldt photographed in the form of Corinthian pillars and the actual plant stripped of its overelaborate leaves, refer to the classical ages. Yet his horsetail photos also call to mind a new and powerful architecture, a modern tower of Babel, a skyscraper, a water tower, a factory chimney. German nationalism at the time also emphasized the classical and the eminently modern as monuments to a universal and evolutionary national identity.

For Bataille, the child sees the double meaning of objects, but the adult seeks to hide this truth and perceive the functional rather than the spiritual or sacred aspects of that which surround us in the world. Bataille states the purpose of his controversial dictionary definitions in *Documents* as revealing what a frightened young boy thinks of the factory chimney, the great concrete tower surging out of the Earth, rather than the technician's perception of mere purpose and material function.

Bataille's materialism calls for a description of matter tied to nightmare and vision rather than to form and function. One of his dictionary definitions describes the slaughterhouse, and is illustrated by photos of blood-smeared concrete and neat lines of cow feet, all amputated at the same joint. The modern slaughterhouse is no longer a site of sacrifice but has been banished to the margins of the city, sanitized and removed from public discourse. For Bataille this is a modern tragedy, the exiling of oneself from all that is horrible, and preferring simply that which is bloodless and amorphous.

The powerful plant form that stands alone illustrates yet also challenges Bataille's base materialism, which appears in other articles in *Documents*. Blossfeldt's photos reveal a disturbing dichotomy between the elevation of the aesthetic glory of nature and the complete domination and manipulation of the organic fragment. In his few texts and the titles chosen for his books, Blossfeldt elevates nature to a higher status than art. By refusing to be considered an artist he thus constructs himself as a technician of nature or as an interpreter of true form. However, the plant forms he chooses to photograph are completely subjugated by the human hand in their stark reality, dismemberment, and evident morbidity. Blossfeldt's plant photos, in their own way, show no blood and are themselves extremely sanitized and very artful versions of nature. The pure forms that Blossfeldt extracts from the organic fragments in his photographs are themselves artificial manipulations of nature and do not reveal the orgiastic expenditure that Bataille posits as the true nature of flowers.

The traditional language of flowers links the passion connoted by the red rose to blood and its power. An 1866 work traces the meanings of the red rose back to the drop of blood falling from Venus's foot as she was "hastening to the relief of her beloved Adonis."[16] The color and the flower take on the meanings of love and beauty through the shedding of blood, the injury of a foot. The rose is conspicuously absent from Blossfeldt's oeuvre. He never photographed cultivated garden flowers, finding them too lush. In a 1901 letter to the board of directors of the art school where he worked, Blossfeldt wrote: "Since only simple forms lend themselves to graphic representation, I cannot make use of lush flowers such as a gardener raises and am dependent almost exclusively on wild plants." He may also have been aware that these flowers carried too many traditional cultural meanings to present new images to the viewer.

A geranium in Germany may have been too familiar to have the shock value that appeals to Bataille or to give the viewer a new perspective on the powerful forms of nature.

Reading Bataille's article "The Big Toe" brings one even farther into his materialism that cannot perceive a world of matter uncomplicated by mental, social, and cultural events. This article appeared in December 1929 and includes many of the questions raised in "Le langage des fleurs."[17] Several full-page reproductions of unappealing big toes photographed from above and filling up the entire page accompany the article. Here Bataille elaborates on his earlier remark in "The Language of Flowers":

> *Il y a d'ailleurs lieu de remarquer que la valeur morale indiscutée du terme bas est solidaire de cette interprétation systématique de sens des racines: ce qui est mal est nécessairement représenté, dans l'ordre des mouvements, par un mouvement du haut vers le bas.* (164) [It is worth noting that the undisputed moral value of the term base goes along with this systematic interpretation of the meaning of roots: that which is bad is necessarily represented, in the order of motion, by a movement from above to below.]

In contrast to the elevated organic fragments in Blossfeldt's photos, Boiffard's hairy toes point down, sliding towards the Earth, yet the photographic aesthetic is quite similar, a greatly enlarged organic object in front of a neutral background. As Bataille writes in this article, "Although within the body blood flows in equal quantities from high to low and from low to high, there is a preference in favor of that which elevates itself, and human life is erroneously seen as an elevation." Blossfeldt shot most of his plant photos from the side or from above and every single plant that stands alone does so in a monumental, elevated way.

The plant, however, like the foot, has a firm link to the ground, and cannot escape the dirt of the Earth except in death. In "The Language of Flowers," Bataille devotes an entire passage to describing the disturbing yet hidden nature of the root of a plant.

> *il ne faudrait pas moins, pour détruire l'impression favorable [of the flower], que la vision fantastique et impossible des racines qui grouillent, sous la surface du sol, écoeurantes et nues comme la vermine. En effet, les*

racines représentent la contre-partie parfaite des parties visibles de la plante . . . celles-ci, ignobles et gluantes, se vautrent dans l'intérieur du sol, amoureuses de pourriture. (164) [destroying the favorable impression requires no less than the fantastic and impossible vision of the roots which squirm beneath the soil's surface, nauseating and naked like vermin. In fact, roots represent the perfect counterpart of the visible parts of the plant . . . they are ignoble and slimy, worming into the ground, in love with rot.][18]

From the disgusting root, slimy and naked like a worm, one can thus move to the always dissimulated yet very necessary big toe. In the article, "The Big Toe," Bataille emphasizes the dual nature of the big toe as glorious distinction from the apes and also as a dirty, ugly, and low object.

Bataille writes of *"deux séductions radicalement opposées"* [the two radically opposed seductions] that find their locus on this humble toe. The flower seduces with its petals yet horrifies with its bare and dirty roots. This idea of base seduction returns to a greater degree in his article on the eye when Bataille writes that *"la séduction extrême est probablement à la limite de l'horreur"* [the most extreme seduction is probably at the outer limits of horror]. As Bataille writes in the conclusion of his article on the big toe,

un retour à la réalité n'implique aucune acceptation nouvelle, mais cela veut dire qu'on est séduit bassement, sans transposition et jusqu'à en crier, en écarquillant les yeux: les écarquillant ainsi devant un gros orteil. [returning to reality does not imply any new acceptation, but it does mean that one is basely seduced, without transposition and to the point of screaming while opening one's eyes so wide: opening them so wide at the sight of a big toe.] (302)

The article on the language of flowers calls for a similar awareness of what is seductive in a plant form. The real seduction that a plant can represent includes its root, its rot, its bruised petals and hairy stem rather than the superficial attraction of a uniform red rose bud. In this article, according to Bataille: *"On représenterait ainsi la fleur la plus admirable non, suivant le verbiage des vieux poètes, comme l'expression plus ou moins fade d'un idéal angélique, mais, tout au contraire, comme un sacrilège immonde et éclatant"* [One would represent the most admirable flower not as the old poets would say as the more or less bland expression of an angelic ideal but quite on the contrary as a disgusting and bright sacrilege]. That which attracts must also repulse. No longer supported by a stem the flower becomes a voracious yet impenetrable organ. Its apparent symmetry revealed by Blossfeldt may be soothing to the senses, but the hidden folds and the prickly hairs participate in the base seduction, perhaps not "*à la limite de l'horreur*" but in a very different manner than red rosebuds.

As Clifford writes: "Since culture was perceived by the collaborators of *Documents* as a system of moral and aesthetic hierarchies, the radical critic's task was one of semiotic decoding, with the aim of deauthenticating and then expanding or displacing the common categories . . . the hierarchies and meanings of collective life."[19] Bataille's "Language of Flowers" does exactly this and Blossfeldt's photographs participate in the dialogue. Bataille mourns the passing of all that was generous, orgiastic, and out of control. There was (or could still be) a time of pure, uncontrolled and dangerous expenditure, and this is what is missing from our society today. Blossfeldt also engages in a nostalgia for a long past or yet to be experienced moment. Blossfeldt bemoans the "*oft seelenlose Gegenwartsgestaltung*" [the often soulless forms of the present]. His vision, as presented in his few writings, is much more restrained. His call for a return to nature does not allow space for blood, baseness, or orgies of fertile and wasteful production. The nature presented in his photographs is a very denatured nature. The images are powerful in their unnaturalness. The flower, corolla intact, is already starting to wilt, yet the photograph freezes it in time, not allowing it to disintegrate into a stinking pulp. The camera frames and dominates nature, rendering it a social document or symbol.

Karl Nierendorf in his preface to "Urformen der Kunst" writes for Blossfeldt,

> As Nature, in its endless monotony of origin and decay, is the embodiment of a profoundly sublime secret, so Art is an equally incomprehensible second creation, emanating organically from the human heart and the human brain: a creation which from the very beginning of time and throughout the ages has had as its origin the yearning for perpetuity, for eternity, and in the desire to retain the spiritual face of its generation.[20]

The preface continues with ominous references to the new, healthy and athletic type of man who appears in union with nature, possessing an automobile and seeking out a new and brighter world. This spontaneous and unquestioned birth of art from human and human from nature once again demands from the viewer or reader a suspension of critical questioning in favor of simply absorbing visual stimuli. The conclusion to be drawn here is that if art is natural or incomprehensible for Molzahn, Nierendorf, or Blossfeldt, then they most likely perceive the world as containing a natural and universal order that cannot be influenced by humans. They seem to be endorsing the idea that this order, or truth, can be revealed but cannot be questioned through the workings of society and culture.

For Bataille nature also soothes the disturbed soul of modern humans by revealing that which we have lost. The last sentences of his article unearth the darker possibilities of the flower or beautiful plant form. Bataille concludes with questions,

> *Toutes ces belles choses ne risqueraient-elles pas d'être réduites à une étrange mise en scène destinée à rendre les sacrilèges plus impurs? Et le geste confondant du Marquis de Sade enfermé avec les fous, qui se faisait porter les plus belles roses pour en effeuiller les pétales sur le purin d'une fosse, ne recevrait-il, dans ces conditions, une portée accablante?* [Couldn't all of these beautiful things end up being reduced to a strange mise-en-scène destined to render sacrileges even more foul? And the Marquis de Sade's baffling gesture, locked up with the lunatics, who had the most beautiful roses brought in so he could scatter the petals on a manure pit, wouldn't this make his gesture all the more overwhelming?][21]

Bataille in his writing has uncovered the liquid manure where the stripped petals may well have landed, the base realities of human symbols. Blossfeldt has given us a carefully staged mise-en-scene of the flower and the formal truths that it reveals. By using Blossfeldt's photos, Bataille offers his reader images of orderly plants, allowing the reader to judge for him or herself whether the dialogue between the camera, the plant, the text and the French thinker and German photographer is sadistic or utopic in its desire to seek out new realities. The cultural symbols of shoes and sausages that often stand in for a more critical dialogue between Paris and Berlin should themselves now come under the critical dissection and analysis that Bataille and Blossfeldt performed on their plant forms.

Notes

1. In *Lu*, 15 April 1932. Translations are author's unless otherwise noted.

2. *La Plante; cent vingt planches en héliogravure d'apres des détails trés agrandis de formes vegétales* (Berlin: E. Wasmuth, 1929). By 1929 translations of Blossfeldt's book appeared in London and New York and in 1930 a Swedish version was published.

3. These compelling and diverse articles have all been reprinted in the *Encyclopedia Acephalica* (London: Atlas Press, 1995). Alastair Brotchie did not, however, choose to include "Le langage des fleurs" in this collection.

4. See Brotchie's introduction to *Encyclopedia Acephalica* (8–28) for more on this.

5. James Clifford, *The Predicament of Culture: Twentieth-Century Ethnography, Literature and Art* (Boston: Harvard University Press, 1988).

6. Marcel Griaule, "Un coup de fusil," in *Documents* (1930, no. 1).

7. Georges Didi-Huberman, "Comment déchire-t-on la ressemblance" in *Georges Batailles après tout* (Paris: Belin, 1995, 101–23).

8. Neither James Clifford nor Georges Didi-Huberman mention Karl Blossfeldt's accompanying images although they do discuss "The Language of Flowers."

9. This ambivalent identity would actually have pleased Bataille. Dominique Lecoq cites Bataille as writing: *"les photographes d'art spécialisés puissent produire autre chose que des acrobaties techniques assez fastidieuses. Les photographes d'information ou de cinéma sont beaucoup plus agréables à voir et beaucoup plus vivants que la plupart des chefs-d'oeuvre qu'on soumet à l'admiration du public"* (122) [specialized art photographers cannot only produce rather fastidious technical acrobatics. News or cinema photographs are much more pleasant to view and more lively than most of the masterpieces which the public must admire]. "Documents, Acéphale, Critique: Bataille autour des revues," in *Georges Bataille Actes du Colloque International d'Amsterdam.* (Amsterdam: Rodop, 1987, 117–30).

10. As Rolf Sachsse reminds us: "What is decisive for his [Blossfeldt's] contemporary followers is the consciousness that all plant catalogues are inevitably connected with the disappearance of what is catalogued" (15). Rolf Sachsse, *Karl Blossfeldt Photographs*, Angela Dunn, trans. (Cologne: Taschen, 1994).

11. In his essay on Blossfeldt, Christoph Schreier accuses Bataille of seeing sexuality where there is none. However, the ascetic sensuality of the plant photos cannot be ignored. According to Schreier: "Rather than sexual symbolism Blossfeldt's works document something quite different and more general, namely, the pathos of forms that are both natural and artificial to an equal degree" (17). "Nature as Art—Art as Nature: Karl Blossfeldt's Photography," in *Karl Blossfeldt: Photography* (Ostfildern: Cantz Verlag, 1994, 11–21). I challenge the reader to merely look at photos like that of *Cornus pubescens* or *Aristolchia clematitis* and deny the presence of any sexual symbolism.

12. Walter Benjamin, "Neves von Blumen," in *Gesammelte Schriften*, vol. 3 (Frankfurt: Suhrkamp Verlag, 1989).

13. Georges Bataille, "Le langage des fleurs," *Documents* (1929, no. 3, 160–164).

14. Karl Blossfeldt, *Wundergarten der Natur* (Berlin: Verlag für Kunstwissenschaft, 1932).

15. Johannes Molzahn, "Nicht mehr lessen! Sehen!" *Das Kunstblatt* 3, 1928: 78–82.

16. Henrietta Dumont, *The language of flowers: The floral offering: a token of affection and esteem: comprising the language and poetry of flowers* (Philadelphia: T. Bliss, 1866).

17. Georges Bataille, "Le gros orteil," *Documents* (1926, no. 6, 297–302) and "The Big Toe," in *Encyclopedia Acephalica*, 87–93.

18. Georges Bataille, "Le langage des fleurs," 164.

19. Clifford, *The Predicament of Culture*, 129.

20. Karl Nierendorf, *Unformen der Kunst* (Berlin: Verlag Ernst Wasmuth, 1928).

21. Georges Bataille, "Le langage des fleurs," 164.

Part IV
World War II and Its Legacy

Chapter 9

AN UNWANTED CONNECTION
Aristide Maillol and Nazism
William J. Cloonan

Abel Tiffauges is the main character in Michel Tournier's *Le Roi des aulnes*. Tiffauges is a gigantic, myopic auto mechanic, filled with delusions of secret greatness: *"Je crois aussi que je suis issu de la nuit des temps. . . . Et d'ailleurs l'antiquité vertigineuse de mes origines suffit à expliquer mon pouvoir surnaturel"* (1970, 11) [I believe that I have issued from the night of time . . . and that the dazzling antiquity of my origins suffices to explain my supernatural powers]. A man whose impressive physical strength belies his fundamental gentleness, his sexuality is as confused and confusing as is his sense of his origins. Midway through the novel he is falsely accused of molesting a young girl; it is the advent of World War II that saves him from prison. Tiffauges is one of the many victims of the *Blitzkrieg*, and as such he is soon a prisoner of war. Shipped off to Germany, this *"pays de noir et blanc"* (country of black and white), he claims to discover there his hitherto mysterious identity. Without embracing the Nazi ideology, he nonetheless collaborates with his captors, and in microcosmic, parodic, yet ultimately lethal ways, he participates in the worst excesses of the Third Reich.

At first glance there appears little in common between Aristide Maillol and Abel Tiffauges. By the advent of World War II, Maillol was anything but obscure. Already an elderly man, Maillol, on the basis of about twenty sculptures that deal primarily with the female nude (Slatkin 1976, 16), was arguably France's most prominent sculptor

(Dagen, *L'Art français* 1998, 199). Yet there remains one telling similarity. Were it not for World War II and his benighted participation in it, Abel Tiffauges would have rotted his life away in prison, filled with his delusions, but incapable of doing harm. Were it not for this same historical catastrophe, Aristide Maillol would have lived out his existence, creating additional allegories of fecundity and national pride, and reaping new honors with each new work. At the end of *Le Roi des aulnes*, which loosely parallels the war's end, Abel Tiffauges literally sinks into a swamp. Aristide Maillol died in an automobile accident in 1944 while trying to protect his son who had been imprisoned as a collaborator for his activities in the *Milice*.[1] Both the fictional character and the famous artist were victims, although severely compromised ones, of a historical event whose reality and implications neither completely understood.

The aim of this essay is not to exculpate Aristide Maillol by trying to minimize the sculptor's collaboration with Germans during the Occupation. Rather, I want to show how Maillol's aesthetic practices, and to the degree one can determine them, his political views, echo what was occurring in the Third Reich during this period. However, once these similarities are established, I will argue that the widespread artistic and political conservatism among many French artists and intellectuals of this period, of which Maillol provides a good example, does not imply a secret sympathy with, or openness to Nazism, particularly this group's racial policies. Nazism, as understood in this essay, is much more than the sum total of the currents that led up to it, and thus the genocide endorsed by the Third Reich represents a radical transformation of Western values, rather than their logical fruition. I will begin by placing the career of the sculptor in the context of conservative French aesthetic theorizing and artistic infighting that originated before World War II but which came to full flower in the period between the two world wars. Maillol may well have been the outstanding sculptor of his day, but, due to various circumstances including the accident of his origins and Nazi tastes in the visual arts, it was relatively easy for him to cohabit with his country's occupiers. In this respect he was sadly typical of many of his less well-known colleagues.

Aristide Maillol was born in 1861 in the little town of Banyuls in southern France. All his life he remained faithful to his origins, and as such shared the traditional nationalism and political conservatism of the *Midi*.[2] As a young artist in Paris, he studied in and then abandoned the

École des Beaux Arts, tried his hand at painting, worked with some success as a tapestry weaver, and only around the age of forty turned to sculpture. His paintings and tapestries were greatly marked by Paul Gauguin's work, whose "art was a revelation," he told John Rewald (1975, 8), but the early, decisive influence were the Nabis painters, and especially the artist/critic, Maurice Denis.

The Nabi movement was short-lived, but nevertheless made its contribution to French conservative art theory. Drawing inspiration from Gauguin and literary symbolism, the Nabi were less interested in depicting physical nature than in using the world as a stepping-stone to the depiction of the artist's inner reality. A comment Maillol made to John Rewald in 1941 reflects the lingering effects of this attitude: "The further one gets away from nature, the more one becomes an artist; the closer one sticks to it, the uglier the work becomes" ("Maillol Remembered," 27). Although essentially devoted to painting, and particularly the decorative panel (Bullock in Chassé 1969, 7), the Nabis conceived of themselves as men of superior mentality and culture" (Chassé, 12), capable of unearthing the great truths hidden behind appearances. Their emphasis on mysticism in an age of positivism conveyed a dissatisfaction with modernity that would remain with Maillol for the rest of his life.

After a bohemian period, Maurice Denis, at one point in his career a major Nabi figure, espoused a neotraditionalism: "*Le recours à la tradition est notre meilleure sauvegarde contre les vertiges du raisonnement, contre l'excès des théories*" [The recourse to tradition is our best safeguard against the dizziness of reasoning, against the excess of theorizing] (in *Art français*, 197). Denis is here sketching a distinction that will become increasingly pronounced and virulent in the interwar period: tradition will be French, natural, and somewhat mystical; the nontraditional will become intellectual, cosmopolitan, and eventually foreign. In an essay devoted to Maillol, Denis situates him squarely in the camp of the traditionalists. Denis maintains that art's aim "*est de faire du simple avec du compliqué*" (1920, 236) (create the simple with the complicated), and that Maillol's works "*sont robustes et harmonieuses comme des objets naturels*" (237) (are robust and harmonious like natural objects). Maillol, he claims, is a great artist in part because, "*par sa naissance, par sa race, il appartient au Midi de la France*" (237) (by his birth, by his race, he belongs to the south of France), and that the artist "*sait quelles profondes racines le rattachent à la chère terre de la patrie*" (238) (knows what deep roots attach him to the beloved earth of his native country).[3] Whatever one makes of Denis' evaluation of Maillol's talent, the implications he draws about the true nature of French art will receive an impetus in the aftermath of World War I, and will concern a generation rather than simply an individual.

As Romy Golan points out: "France suffered something drastic with its ethos, its culture, and its self-image in the wake of World War I" (1995, xiv).[4] The Great War traumatized a world that had never before witnessed such a high degree of fire power and mechanized forms of destruction. The artillery was bigger, more accurate and hence more deadly; airplanes, tanks, and poison gas made their appearances for the first time. However, the trauma created by these engines of carnage were certainly European and possibly international. What provided a uniquely Gallic instance of shock, was that World War I took place almost uniquely on French soil (Golan, 7). Nominally among the winners, France nevertheless had to deal with its devastated landscapes and cityscapes, not to mention its shattered economy.

In his *Le Silence des peintres*, Philippe Dagen details the sense of failure many French visual artists, as well as those of other belligerent nations, experienced before their inability to capture through their medium the peculiar horror of this conflict.[5] The myriad trenches which at times dissolved even the notion of "no-man's land," the omnipresent fog and gas that could make the act of seeing extremely difficult, and the absence of clearly demarcated and time-limited battles as opposed to the more customary battlefields, created the impossibility of capturing pivotal and heroic moments on canvas. Modern art, or so it seemed, was not up to the task of fulfilling one of its traditional responsibilities. Another aspect of the situation that would have some ugly future ramifications was that while most French artists of draft age had no choice but to participate as soldiers in one capacity or another, their foreign counterparts living in France were often able to avoid military service.

Conservative critics seized upon the situation to deride modernist experiments as un- French. Cubism became "Kubism," as this movement, started by a Spaniard (Pablo Picasso) and a Frenchman (Georges Braque) was suddenly revealed to have putative German origins. According to Dagen, Cubism, which was branded antinational in 1912, became *boche* (*kraut*) in 1914, as it would be stigmatized as "Jewish" during World War II (*Le Silence* 1996, 34). In this increasingly reactionary context, it is not surprising either that landscape painting enjoyed an upsurge in popularity in the immediate postwar era, since it linked France's cultural vitality to its rootedness in the soil (Golan 1995, 7), or that even an artist of Picasso's stature would appear to abandon Cubism in the 1920s and turn briefly to a Poussin-inspired neoclassicism.[6] Given the discomfort engendered by the present, dominated by France's feared and admired ally, the United States,[7] as well as the growing success of foreign artists within the Hexagon, the past, as much imagined as real, became increasingly attractive to the French artistic establishment. This was precisely the sort of climate in which Maillol was destined to flourish.

In a 1930 essay entitled, "*Les problèmes de la sculpture chez Rodin et chez Maillol*" [the Problems in Sculpture in Rodin and Maillol] Jules Romains elaborates on a distinction that was gaining increasing currency at the time. For Romains, Renoir is "*l'artiste, nuance esthète*" (the artist, nuance aesthete), while Maillol is "*l'artiste, nuance artisan*" (the artist, nuance artisan) [213]; Rodin "*avait porté à un point extrême l'idée du mouvement, . . . le dynamisme*" (had carried to an extreme point the idea of movement), which exists in opposition to Maillol's work which "*ramène . . . à la recherche de l'équilibre, et d'un équilibre stable. . . . Il fait un art statique*" (returns . . . to the quest for equilibrium and a stable equilibrium. . . . His is a static art (209)]. Rodin is the Parisian artist who embraces modernity in all its fluidity and potential chaos while Maillol is the peasant from the *Midi* whose art reflects order, tradition, and invites calm contemplation of eternal verities. Rodin challenges, but Maillol reassures. Romains' admiration for Maillol was deep and genuine, but what separates his essay from those of his more conservative contemporaries who praised Maillol, was that, despite his love for the sculptor's work, and his awareness that it stood in fundamental contrast to Rodin's, he recognized that Maillol's art was a return to an earlier, simpler era, and as such was not really an art of or for the present:

> . . . *une oeuvre quelconque, statue ou tableau, marquée de primativisme, ne saurait, quel que soit son succès actuel, témoigner plus tard de notre époque. . . . Le primativisme reste parmi nous un état d'esprit de réaction, un goût second et transitoire, une contre-tendance.* (217) [. . . any work, statue or painting, marked by primitivism, would not be able, no matter

what its immediate success, to serve later as a witness to our era. . . . Primitivism remains for us a spirit of reaction, a transient, less important style, an opposite tendency.]

Yet this *"contre-tendance"* would gain a growing ascendancy in the years leading up to World War II, as art criticism in particular became increasingly strident and jingoistic in tone.

If there is a single phrase that might characterize conservative art criticism in the 1920s and 1930s, it is *"le retour à l'ordre"* (return to order). In its more benign meaning it reflects a yearning for past French greatness, some new form of classicism. In terms of the actual making of art, it involves, to use Philippe Dagen's expression, a tendency to favor the *"comment"* over the *"quoi"* (*Le Silence*, 290) (how over the what), as a concern for beautiful construction begins to replace a preoccupation with subject matter. Whatever this might suggest about the unwillingness or inability of the artists to confront the present times, in its cultural manifestations *"le retour à l'ordre"* is far from anodyne. The desired order was French, not foreign, and as early as 1925, some critics decided it was salutary to confront the "problem" of Jews in the arts. Fritz Vanderpyl published in the prestigious *Mercure de France* an essay whose title, *"Existe-il une peinture juive?"* [Does Jewish Painting Exist?] leaves little doubt about the article's content. Vanderpyl asserts that "In the absence of Jewish art in the Louvre . . . we are nevertheless witnessing a swarming of Jewish paintings. In postwar salons the Lévys are legion . . ." (Golan, 138).[8] One of the leading exponents of anti-Semitism in the service of French art was Camille Mauclair who, in 1929, published his *La Farce de l'art vivant*. In the essays contained in this volume, Maucalir takes aim at, among other things, L'École de Paris, whose membership he characterizes as follows: *"la proportion des sémites est d'environ 80% et celles des ratés à peu près équivalente"* [The proportion of Semites is about 80 percent, and that of failed artists more or less the same] (Dagen, *L'Art français*, 231).[9]

The reference to L'École de Paris is illuminating, since it stands in contrast with L'École Française. As the name suggests, L'École de Paris is urban and cosmopolitan; it is the seat of the avant-garde. L'École Française is traditional, and its members of French origin. What might have started out as an academic effort to distinguish between two different groups of artists quickly became a means of contrasting the works of uprooted radical foreign painters and sculptors whose works were often judged bizarre and incomprehensible, with those of truly French artists, who celebrated national values in images that were easily accessible to French citizens aware and proud of their country's beauties and traditions. Maillol was, of course, numbered among the artists of the École Française. Yet, while his sculptures attest to his aesthetic conservatism and patriotism, what was to make him a problematic figure in the post-World War II era, were not the works he created before and within the wartime period, but rather the company he kept during the conflict.

It should not be very surprising that Maillol, like many other French citizens, would turn to Marshall Pétain after France's disastrously swift defeat. The artist's beloved village, Banyuls, was in Vichy France, and given Maillol's conservatism in life and art, as well as his sense of his humble origins, he would be drawn to the hero of Verdun who was often portrayed as "*le maréchal paysan*" (the peasant marshal) [Golan, 156]. What is more unique to Maillol is that before as well as during the war, his art received strong support in Germany. One of his earliest and strongest supporters had been the German Count Kessler (Slatkin 1976, 12). At this period in Maillol's young career (the late nineteenth-century), he was still involved with the Nabis, who were reacting to positivism, and thus their works borrowed a "distinctly German mystical attitude" (cited in Slatkin, 93). Karl Epting, the director of the German Institute in Paris during the Occupation, considered Maillol more German than French: ". . . the temperament of Maillol is not French. Although southern, Provençal, and pagan, it could be German" (Golan, 159).

Maillol, who was rather reticent about his aesthetic views,[10] nevertheless had strong words about the French and their reaction to art: "I hate them [most people], they are wretched beings. I prefer my cat or a frog. . . . The French? They don't give a damn about art" (cited in Golan, 165). In contrast, he had been treated kindly in the German press, and had a major showing of sculpture in 1928 in Berlin (Golan, 165). Maillol was genuinely grateful for this support, and had nice things to say about Germans at the expense of the French: "I am so famous in Germany. Much more so than in France" (Golan, 165). Maillol was "so famous in Germany," because his art unwittingly paralleled Nazi official art. His identity as someone with deep roots in his homeland's soil made it easy for Nazi ideologues to see him as a French version of German artists whose work reflected Hitler's *Blut und Boden* (blood and soil) philosophy, where monumental figures of voluptuous women and virile men exemplified love of the homeland the purity of the German race.[11] Certainly the massiveness and simplicity of Maillol's sculpture had much to recommend it to German critics who found in it numerous allusions to the Aryan people's ancestors, the ancient Greeks: "Maillol's sculpture . . . can be called popular art, meaning that it is not art that makes concessions to the miseducated [*sic*] taste of the time. It is an art for the people as Greek art was: naive, blunt, healthy, unromantic, true to nature" (cited in Golan, 165). Maillol's art, for Nazi critics, had none of the false profundity and obscurity characteristic of the École de Paris. It was direct, traditional, and as such had a healthy appeal to honest, pure-blooded Aryans.

Aristide Maillol was, of course, not the only French sculptor to find favor with the Germans during the Occupation,[12] but perhaps more than anything else, what made his presence at the side of the German occupier stand out during and after the war was his friendship with the German sculptor, Arno Breker. Breker was one of Germany's leading artists; he was much admired by Hitler and was the only German sculptor to have an exclusive exhibition in wartime France (Petropoulos 1996, 138). The friendship between Maillol and Breker, which began in 1927, was from all accounts genuine. Their artistic formation was similar (Cone 1992, 65), and Maillol had been on a committee honoring Breker in 1942 (Cone, 157). In his memoirs, *Im Strahlungsfeld der Ereignisse* (1972), Breker recounts how deeply he was touched by Maillol's making the difficult, and for an old man painful, journey during the war from Banyuls to Paris to attend his exhibition. In these same memoirs, Breker positively gushes over Maillol's sculpture, "*eine einzige Hymne auf die Schöpfungsgeschichte aus der Allmacht Gottes*" [a single hymn to God's creative history (235)]. Maillol responded in kind, praising his friend as the "German Michelangelo" (Breker, 1972, 236). Breker also proudly recounts that his is the only completed bust of Maillol (239).

What makes this friendship interesting in the context of the present essay is what it tells us of Maillol's political awareness during the Occupation, and, to a lesser degree, what it implies about the French sculptor's racial views. Breker reports that during a visit with Maillol in Banyuls, two letters arrived, one for each artist. In the letter Breker received he was told, by the Resistance, that he would not leave

Banyuls alive ["*daß ich Banyuls lebend nicht verlassen würde*"]. The contents of Maillol's letter was a typical gesture of the Resistance: the envelope contained a drawing of a coffin, (*einen Sarg*, 238). What makes this incident particularly noteworthy and perhaps revelatory of Maillol's mentality was the French sculptor's reaction. Speaking of the two letters they had just received, Maillol supposedly remarked: "*Das verdanken wir unseren lieben Kollegen . . . wir haben zuviel Talent*" [We owe this to our lovely colleagues . . . we have too much talent (238)].

Although Breker's memoirs are, to say the least, self-serving, Maillol's reaction to the death threat is worth considering. It would appear from his remark that Maillol had little or no awareness of the political implications of his consorting with the Germans. As an artist he had long resented that French critics who, after briefly praising him as a modernist early in his career, rapidly turned away from him as a "middle of the road artist" who was not advancing the cause of progressive sculpture (Cone, 165). By the time of the outbreak of the war he was an old man, and during the Occupation he enjoyed the flattering attention the Germans lavished on him. At the same time, his loyalty to Pétain may well have marked him in his own eyes as a French patriot, faithful to his country and its, in his eyes, legally invested leader. Most tellingly of all, whatever his general attitudes toward the "Jewish issue," in his dealings with individuals there is no record, to my knowledge, of active anti-Semitism. In fact, his model and mistress, Dina Vierny, was Jewish.

Dina Vierny was arrested by the Gestapo. Breker recounts this drama in his memoirs, and his word choice is illuminating. Vierny was a "Russian woman of the Jewish faith" (*Russin jüdischen Glaubens* [244]). Breker details his efforts to obtain her freedom, but, to read what he says, one might imagine that she was arrested, not because she was Jewish, but because she was helping some endangered politicians and a few Jews (*Gefährdete Politiker, flüchtende Juden* [244]), flee France. When she was finally released, the conditions were that she would no longer work with Communists and, when she was back in Banyuls, undertake no more political activities. The direct threat posed by her being Jewish is never confronted directly. Nor does Breker mention Maillol saying anything about his mistress's ethnic origins.

These two incidents underscore the ambiguity surrounding Maillol and perhaps other French artists who passively collaborated with the

Germans during the war. On one hand, the evidence for a more active sympathy with the occupiers is certainly available. Breker states explicitly that Hitler admired Maillol (*Hitler schätzte Maillol* [244]); the French artist's work found favor in the Reich, and might even be confused for examples of Nazi art. Certainly he expressed admiration for Germany and benefited from German support during the Occupation. One is surely justified in expressing doubt about Maillol's apparent indifference to a political situation from which he was profiting, and even his love for a Jewish woman in no way resolves the issue of his attitudes to Jews in general, especially those who were competing artists. Michèle Cone expresses these concerns most fairly and succinctly: "The idea that artists live by a politics different from that of anyone else was certainly not Maillol's alone. . . . But Maillol's continued relations with Arno Breker, his admiration for Germany, and his son's involvement in the despicable *milice* are too consistent to be merely coincidental" (1972, 166).

All this is undeniable. No serious argument can be made for Maillol as a secret resister, or even for his being somehow the equivalent of German artists, like Emil Nolde, who remained in Germany during World War II, but turned their back on Hitler and the Third Reich in a gesture termed "interior immigration," wherein they simply refused to recognize what was taking place around them. Maillol was pro-Vichy, and at least in cultural terms, "pro-German." As an inhabitant of an occupied country, it would have been simply impossible for him to be oblivious to the wartime situation. Yet, when one attempts to assess the degree of collaboration of artists, or for that matter anyone, during World War II, it is easy to forget that the true horror of this conflict, unlike that of other wars, was only fully apparent *ex post facto*.

As mentioned earlier, what made World War I different from previous bloodlettings was the heightened degree of mechanized carnage. The soldiers who experienced the ravages created by the gas, the artillery, the tanks, and airplanes were all too aware of what was happening as it occurred. What gave World War II its unique ugliness was not simply the increased level of sophisticated weaponry, but the Nazi Final Solution.[13] Yet, as Robert Paxton among others has pointed out, the full knowledge of these atrocities was not available until the war's end:

> The killings incidental to the German invasions of Poland in 1939 and the USSR in 1941 gave way to industrial mass murder by 1942. Well-

informed reports of mass killings reached the West as early as summer 1942. Their veracity was clouded by Nazi disinformation, by the profusion of conflicting rumors, and by an Allied reluctance to be duped again, as they had been in 1914, by atrocity stories. Many particulars were confirmed only when the murder factories were liberated, to almost universal shock, in 1945. (1995, 34)

It is important to keep this time frame in mind, to remember that a complete awareness of the unique horror of World War II was not apparent to most nonvictims until after the conflict, since this knowledge provides the basis for better situating people like Maillol, not simply in the history of French collaboration, but also in the framework of European anti-Semitism.

Maillol's essentially conservative art would place him in the mainstream of French and European intellectual life. The ugly underside of this positioning was an anti-Semitism, that in France found an active and virulent expression in the Dreyfus Affair. In his *French Literary Fascism*, David Carroll cites Léon Poliakov's assessment of the extent of anti-Semitism in nineteenth-century France: "If one wanted to gauge the strength of anti-Semitism in a country by the amount of ink used up on the Jewish question, France would win top honors in the nineteenth century" (1995, 171). However, scorn for Jews was never the exclusive prerogative of the French or for that matter the Germans. Nor was it confined to rabid racists like Léon Daudet, or, during the war, to hate mongers ranging in literary talent from Lucien Rebatet and Robert Brasillach to Céline.[11] Dislike and distrust for Jews were well-known European phenomena that spanned all social classes and occasionally surfaced in otherwise distinguished authors such as Charles Dickens, most notably in *Oliver Twist*. Even someone like Émile Zola, justly praised for his heroic defense of Dreyfus during the trial, was the author of an anti-Semitic novel, *L'Argent*. The presence of anti-Jewish sentiments was a long-standing presence in Western high culture up until the war. Yet the crucial distinction is that among artists and intellectuals during the interwar years, while anti-Semitism might take the form of attacks against Jews in the newspapers, or cruel caricatures in novels and the visual arts, it reflected a desire to discriminate against the Jews, not to exterminate them. As widespread as anti-Semitism might have been, it was considered bad form, except among a radical minority of intellectuals and artists, to manifest these feelings in physically violent ways.

The irony of Maillol, and artists like him, is that the very traditionalism that drew him to fraternize with Germans, and sympathize with the cultural orientation of people like Arno Breker, might have shielded him from being able to imagine what was, up until 1945, indeed unthinkable. Maillol might have harbored anti-Jewish sentiments, but in this respect he would have been scarcely different from many of his colleagues, living or dead. He was a man of the past, of tradition; as an artist he was ill at ease with his century's numerous experiments and innovations, and scarcely open to "new" ideas of any sort. Imagining the reality of the Final Solution would have been nearly impossible for artists and intellectuals during the war, whatever their aesthetic orientation; for Maillol it would have been absolutely beyond his purview.

If one can, for a moment, separate the notion of a "new idea" from any moral connotation, the implementation of Nazi genocidal policies might well be this century's most radical innovation. It is not the official anti-Semitism of the Third Reich that distinguished its policies from those of earlier governments, but rather Hitler's government's determination to act out its prejudice, to use the scientific expertise and capacity for mechanization of the modern world to slaughter not only Jews, but also gypsies, political opponents, and homosexuals as well. In intellectual terms, the Final Solution called into question the Enlightenment tradition, appeared to deliver the death blow to Western humanism, and, in the postwar literary climate, provoked a radical reassessment of the writing of literature. In Germany, the inception of the *Gruppe 47* was more of a direct response to that nation's disgrace rather than to its defeat, and the experimentation of France's *nouveaux romanciers* was a reaction, at least in part, to the postwar revelations of Nazi racial atrocities.[15]

Although the knowledge of the Nazi genocidal policies was largely hindsight, the shock it created was so great, and the mark it left on human consciousness so indelible that it tends to affect our judgment of all those who played questionable roles during the war. Over fifty years after the Armistice, France is still struggling to emerge from what Henry Rousso aptly termed "le syndrome de Vichy," and a modest, yet significant aspect of this ongoing reevaluation concerns the role of artists "compromised" during the war. Maillol was arguably more famous than many of his colleagues, but his behavior during the Occupation was probably emblematic of that of a good number of his fellow artists. Maillol might have been vain and overly responsive to the flattery of his country's occupiers; in wartime circumstances this might be unfortunate, but it was all too common. Conservatism in art and politics might not be fashionable among many of us who comment on such things; yet in a rational society such attitudes are an individual's right. What is really of concern about Maillol's role during the war has ultimately little to do with what might have been his thoughts about minorities or even the politics of the Third Reich, and in any case we have no means of knowing what his view in either instance might have been. What fascinates us today about Maillol is less his personal decisions or nondecisions, than the way he reflects a conservative stance that can appear at times so similar to intellectual positions rampant in the Third Reich, but which, by the very fact of its being a tradition that was, among artists and intellectuals at least, a largely passive one with regard to anti-Semitism, it would seem to preclude the undertaking of activities comparable to those of Nazi Germany. Tradition provides context; it does not supply explanations, and attitudes, particularly long-standing ones, do not necessitate acts. Just as the Third Reich was in no rational sense the culmination of Charlemagne's Holy Roman Empire and Wilhelminian Germany, Nazi genocide was not the only possible outcome of the sundry sources from which it fed. Also, while the philosophy of National Socialism certainly has antecedents in Western history, the passage from thought to act remains a shock, a caesura in human consciousness; reactionary views and a willingness to put them into large-scale practice are not the same thing. More significantly, searching for cause/effect explanations lessens the unique horror of places like Auschwitz by implying that these concentration camps were understandable, and perhaps even inevitable given the history of racial hatred in Western culture. It is sometimes easy to forget that the history of ideas is not the history of human conduct. What happened in Europe during World War II may have many intellectual origins, but given the careful planning, the meticulous implementation and the amplitude of the destruction of human life, the Final Solution remains unprecedented. Finally, to suggest as I am doing, that the political and aesthetic conservatism of artists like Maillol, however questionable and compromising it was, did not constitute some fundamental solidarity with the Third Reich, is not to exonerate them, to make them innocent victims of circumstances they did not understand. I think in this essay, I have demonstrated Maillol's general sympathy with Nazi aesthetic and cultural policies. My aim rather was to use someone like Maillol, whose aesthetic and political conservatism was typical of many artists in interwar France, to stress the vast dichotomy between widespread reactionary attitudes and the specific actions that the Nazis took. If ever there were a telling example of Foucault's notion of discontinuity in history, it is certainly the gap between a long-standing tradition of anti-Semitism and the actual implementation of the Final Solution.

Of course, to stress the uniqueness of the Nazi Final Solution in Germany raises the potential for another sort of misunderstanding. Nazism occurred in Germany, and the burden of that fact and its lingering heritage is something the citizens of that nation must bear. However, in no way does this imply that the racist manifestations of Nazism are somehow unique to the German character, that they constitute a peculiarly Teutonic disease. Genocide in World War II was indeed a German product, but as recent events in Bosnia and Africa illustrate, variations on the theme of the Final Solution have proven to be an international, rather than a national phenomena. Perhaps the worst ramification of the Nazi experience is that what might have once been considered unthinkable, has moved into the realm of the all too possible.

As I have attempted to show in this essay, Maillol was representative of a widespread aesthetic traditionalism in France which, in a period of turmoil, easily turned into a political conservatism that permitted him, and people like him, to accept the praise and support of German artists and intellectuals without having to consider themselves disloyal to *"la France éternelle."* Maillol's century's major innovative artistic currents passed him by, leaving him, at the time of his death in 1944, as a revered yet outdated proponent of late nineteenth century French aesthetic practice. He did not live to experience firsthand reports of Auschwitz and Buchenwald, but it is hard to imagine that had he survived the war, he would not have been, like many of his conservative colleagues, horrified by what he learned. Like Michel Tournier's Abel Tiffauges in *Le Roi des aulnes*, his brutal demise spared him the painful duty of attempting to assess, not simply his own behavior, but the future of a world that had lost, at least temporarily, its moral underpinnings.

Notes

1. There were rumors that Maillol had been killed by the *Marquis* (see Elsen, 1979, 150), but these are unfounded. For a description of the accident, and the events leading up to it, see Michéle Cone, *Artists Under Vichy* (Princeton, NJ: Princeton University Press, 1992), p. 158.

2. In an essay by John Rewald, "Maillol Remembered," that appears in Thomas Messer's *Aristide Maillol: 1861–1944* (New York: Solomon Guggenheim Museum, 1975), the author underscores the irony that while "Maillol himself was not exactly liberal, the monuments he did or had wished to do were all connected with fighters for great liberal causes: Adolphe Blanqui, a socialist and revolutionary who spent the greater part of his life in prison; Émile Zola, the commission for whose monument the artist was heartbroken not to obtain; and finally, Henri Barbusse, a work for which the necessary funds were subsequently stopped" (1975, 23).

3. Allowing for the requisite changes in geographical location, such encomiums might also have been directed toward Arno Breker, one of Hitler's favorite artist and Maillol's personal friend.

4. Romy Golan, *Modernity and Nostalgia* (New Haven: Yale, 1995).

5. Philippe Dagen goes so far as to suggest that "*peinture d'histoire a disparu avec le monde d'avant-guerre*" (1996, 105), as a result of the Great War.

6. Concerning the various deployments of the word "classicism" during and after World War I, Kenneth Silver makes an interesting observation: ". . . for all that 'classicism' is, and was, subject to manipulation, after the start of war in 1914 it always referred to a new national sense of self-identity" (*Esprit de corps*, 100)

7. For a discussion of France's mostly negative post-World War I reaction to the United States' increasing influence in Europe see Golan, *Modernity and Nostalgia*, pp. 79–83.

8. According to Remy Golan, the Jewish artist, Moïse Kisling is supposed to have been responding to Vanderpyl's essay when, in answer to a poll conducted by the revue *L'Art vivant*, which asked prominent members of the art world to name the ten living artists who should be included in a new museum of modern art, he provided the following list: "Simon Lévy, Léopold Lévy, Irène

Lévy, Flore Lévy, Isodore Lévy, Benoît Lévy, et Moïse Kisling" (138). Kisling's joke, of course, subsequently proved not to be as funny as he intended.

9. It would be a mistake to think that such racist views were limited to obscure essayists and frustrated artists. To cite but two examples: the onetime Cubist painter Albert Gleizes contributed essays to *Régéneration*, "a review openly admiring the racial policies of Hitler's new Reich" (Golan, 103). A more telling example is the playwright Jean Giraudoux who said that he was *"bien d'accord avec le chancelier Hitler pour proclamer qu'une politique n'atteint sa forme supérieure que si elle est raciale, car c'était aussi la pensée de Colbert et de Richelieu"* [in agreement with Chancellor Hitler about insisting that a politics does not achieve its fullest expression if it is not racial, because this was also the thinking of Colbert and Richelieu (cited in Dagen, *L'Art français*, 231)].

10. We do not possess a body of original statements by Maillol. From all accounts, he was not a man who expressed his ideas freely either in writing or conversations. (Slatkin, 1976, 4)

11. Anyone interested in exploring this parallel need only place side by side Arno Breker's *Bereitschaft (Preparedness)* and Maillol's *La Baigneuse aux bras levé*) to discover the portrait of the perfect Aryan couple.

12. A convenient but not inclusive indication of French artists admired by the Germans during the Occupation is provided by the list of those who accepted the invitation of the German Ministry of Propaganda to visit Germany in October and November 1941 to admire the artistic achievement of the Third Reich. The group comprised thirteen artists in all, and among them were well-known figures such as Maurice de Vlaminck, André Derain and Kees van Dongen. Maillol was excused because of his age (see Golan, 155–157).

13. In fact, while the Final Solution is often perceived as the most horrendous aspect of the war, the American unleashing of atom bombs on Japan, and the terror bombings of Canterbury and Dresden, also contributed to the moral disillusionment engendered by World War II. For a discussion of this issue, see William J. Cloonan, *The Writing of War: French and German Fiction and World War II* (Gainesville: University Press of Florida, 1999), pp. 1–18. However, for the purpose of the present discussion, which focuses on artistic collaboration in France, Nazi genocide is the most important element.

14. For an excellent discussion of anti-Semitism among the French literati, see David Carroll's *French Literary Fascism* (Princeton: Princeton University Press, 1995).

15. Cloonan, *The Writing of War*, pp. 40–53.

References

Breker, Arno. *Im Strahlungsfeld der Ereignisse*. Schütz: Preusslich Oldendorf, 1972.

Carroll, David. *French Literary Fascism: Nationalism, Anti-Semitism, and the Ideology of Culture*. Princeton: Princeton University Press, 1995.

Chassé, Charles. *The Nabis and their Period*. Trans. Michael Bullock. New York: Praeger, 1969.

Cloonan, William. *The Writing of War: French and German Fiction and World War II*. Gainesville: University Press of Florida, 1999.

Cone, Michèle. *Artists under Vichy: a Case of Prejudice and Persecution*. Princeton: Princeton University Press, 1992.

Dagen, Philippe. *Le Silence des peintres: les artistes face à la Grande Guerre*. Paris: Fayard, 1996.

———. *L'Art Français: Le Vingtième Siècle*. Paris: Flammarion, 1998.

Denis, Maurice. "Maillol." In *Théories: du Symbolisme et de Gaugin vers un nouvel ordre classique*, 235–243. Paris: Rouart et Watelin, 1920.

Elsen, Albert. *Modern European Sculpture: Unknown Beings and Other Realities*. New York: Braziller, 1979.

Golan, Romy. *Modernity and Nostalgia: Art and Politics in France between the Wars*. New Haven: Yale University Press, 1995.

Grosshans, Henry. *Hitler and the Artists*. New York: Holmes and Meier, 1983.

Paxton, Robert. "The Trial of Maurice Papon." *The New York Review of Books*. Vol. 46, No. 20 (December 16, 1999): 32–38.

Petropoulos, Jonathan. *Art as Politics in the Third Reich*. Chapel Hill: University of North Carolina Press, 1996.

Rewald, John. "Maillol Remembered." In *Aristide Maillol: 1861–1944*. Director Thomas Messer. New York: Solomon Guggenheim Museum, 1975.

Romains, Jules. "Les Problèmes de la sculpture chez Rodin et chez Maillol." In *Problèmes D'aujourd'hui*. Paris: Kra, 1931.

Silver, Kenneth. *Esprit de Corps*. Princeton: Princeton University Press, 1989.

Slatkin, Wendy. *Aristide Maillol in the 1890s*. Ann Arbor: UMI Research Press, 1976.

Tournier, Michel. *Le Roi des aulnes*. Paris: Gallimard, 1970.

Chapter 10

OF HEROES AND TRAITORS
Two Early Films by René Clément

Philip Watts

From the end of the Second World War to the late 1960s, French films rarely represented the most troubling aspects of occupation, the deportation of Jews, the betrayal of resistance fighters, and the collaboration of French men and women with the Nazi occupiers. The few films that even attempt to present these dark moments—Alain Resnais's *Night and Fog* (1955) for instance, and his *Hiroshima mon amour* (1959)—are significant precisely because they speak of the suppression of knowledge about this period. The problem had been not only what to show, but also how to show it, how to make a feature film about the Occupation that would avoid, given the subject represented, standard techniques of audience identification and the rhetorical excesses melodrama. In the immediate postwar years, however, a few members of the French cinematic industry did attempt to confront this problem, either directly or through the use of allegory. One of these filmmakers was René Clément, two of whose films from 1946–1947 can help us to think about France's roles during the occupation and the different aesthetic regimes in place for representing these roles.

Sylvie Lindeperg has recently made a strong case for understanding René Clément as a filmmaker who in the course of a thirty year career as one of France's leading commercial filmmakers consistently confronted France's difficult memory of the war (1997, 412–413). This may seem surprising at first blush. Since 1954 when Truffaut attacked him as a representative of *the cinéma de qualité*, Clément's status among cinephiles and film scholars has been ambiguous at best. Unlike Jacques Becker or Jean Grémillion who have both had major retrospectives in Paris in recent years, Clément has yet to undergo a serious rehabilitation. Still, his films set during the Occupation are useful for understanding questions of national memory and film style.[1] For the purposes of this study, I want to examine two films that, to my mind, are particularly significant in this regard. *La Bataille du rail*, released in 1946 and *Les Maudits—The Damned*—which came out the following year, not only pose the question of how to represent history, but they also ask us to think about the relation between aesthetics and politics in the films of a nation finding a cinematographic language to represent its past.

In their subject matter, their style and their reception *La Bataille du rail* and *Les Maudits* are a study in contrasts. Both films won a prize at Cannes, *La Bataille du rail* the prix du jury international in 1946 and *Les Maudits* the prize of the best adventure film the following year. Both represent events that took place during the last months of the war and have recourse to a voice-over technique. Still, the differences are startling: *La Bataille du rail* is about the Resistance, *Les Maudits* about fascists and collaborators. Both films take place around machines of locomotion, but *La Bataille du rail* centers on trains; *Les Maudits* takes place in a submarine. In *La Bataille du rail*, the main characters spend most of their time outdoors trying to stop the trains. In *Les Maudits*, the characters are inside the submarine desperately trying to get their boat to South America. *La Bataille du rail* uses unknown and nonprofessional actors to tell the story of an anonymous collective of resistants. *Les Maudits* relies on an international cast of well-known actors to portray a group of Fascist dignitaries. *La Bataille du rail* is a quasi-documentary; *Les Maudits* is much closer to a stylized film noir. But it is precisely the differences between the films that make them a rich source for understanding representations of the Occupation.

René Clément began his career as a documentary filmmaker, working during the occupation for the *Centre artistique et technique des jeunes du cinéma*. In 1944, while France was still occupied, he started filming a documentary on resistant railway workers, *Ceux du rail*. This project was then expanded and fictionalized to become *La Bataille du rail*, one of the most critically and commercially successful films ever made about the French Resistance. Traces of this evolution from documentary to feature are visible in the film itself. Indeed, many commentators have noted that the film seems divided into two parts. The first part is a series of sequences that show the mostly anonymous railway workers clandestinely carrying mail and people across the demarcation line and doing everything in their power to delay the German trains. The second part is dominated by more traditional elements of feature film: a linear narrative, metaphoric images such as the ink stain representing the arrest of a Resistant, and stock characters such as the febrile German officer, the portly station master, or the old *cheminot* who repeats the line "*C'est pas du boulot*," as he goes about his everyday resistance. Furthermore, as Michèle Lagny has pointed out, the film's two parts reveal a strikingly different montage. The first part uses an active montage reminiscent of early Soviet cinema, especially in the sequence where German soldiers execute French hostages, as railworkers kill a German soldier. As for the second part of the film, it reverts to a more traditional and linear montage that "tends to erase the breaks" in the narration (1984, 96).

In spite of this mixed tone, when *La Bataille du rail* came out in France in February 1946, it was one of the few films of the time to achieve a consensus, attracting enthusiastic reviews from film critics and filling movie theaters for several months. According to the film historian Jean-Pierre Bertin-Maghit, this consensus came from the fact that the film seemed to include the entire French nation in the heroic resistance of a few *cheminots*. *La Bataille du rail* presents what he calls a "double manipulation." First, the film extends the boundaries of the Resistance to include the entire "social body," thus transforming individual acts into a collective action, and second, the narrative voice-over subtly includes the spectator in the railway workers' resistance activity ("*Bataille*," 284). At a time when the Resistance was torn by internal strife, *La Bataille du rail* provided a comforting image of national unity and reconciliation.

This consensus was not simply political, however, at least not among film critics. A heroic and mythical portrait of the French Resistance did not guarantee a film good reviews. In fact, by February 1946, most films about the Resistance were regularly panned by French critics. André Bazin was being generous when, in his review of *La Bataille du rail* he wrote: "One cannot say that, up to this point, the resistance has favorably inspired French cinema" (*Le Cinéma*, 143). Other critics were much harsher. Jean Néry criticized the Resistance film *Peloton d'exécution* as "*detestable* [. . .] *mercantilism*" (1946, 7). And Henry Magnan, also writing in *Le Monde*, savaged Jean Renoir's Resistance film *Vivre libre* for what he called its "distressing lack of taste" and its "extremely flat direction." "The only remedy," Magnan concluded, was to shy away from this "odious and laughable spectacle" (1946, 6). The aura of the Resistance may have translated into political power, but it did not automatically extend to the art of cinema.

La Bataille du rail was exceptional among Resistance films in that, along with the political consensus, it also achieved what might be called an aesthetic consensus. Critics unanimously praised it both for the authenticity of its representation and for an innovative style that, according to some reviewers, heralded the rebirth of a French cinematic realism. Early reviews often mentioned Clément's initial project to make a documentary, as if the film's origin served as a guarantee of its authenticity. In almost all the reviews, from daily newspapers to journals of cinema aesthetics, the same terms keep coming back. Jean Néry claimed the film was a document "France had an obligation to show the rest of the world" because it brought "truth" and "sincerity" to the screen. Alain Spenlé called the film "the first legitimate [*valable*] document on the French resistance" (1946, 72–74). Everything in the film was real, he concluded, from the French railway workers to the enemy soldiers who were, Spenlé tells us, "chosen among German prisoners of war." And in *Les Temps modernes*, Jean Pouillon called Clément's film "a legitimate [*valable*] testimony to the real way that men died." Before all else, Pouillon writes, the film was "a testimony about men" (*un témoignage sur les hommes* [1946, 1510]).

Clément's film brought together two important aspects of postwar film aesthetics. As "document" and "testimony," *La Bataille du rail* participated in the representation and understanding of the events that had just shaken the world. Postwar audiences saw cinematic realism as an important step in the reconstruction of Europe, a form through which the "social body" could both relive the events and establish a safe distance from them. Some critics even called upon these films to participate in the postwar purge of Fascists and collaborators. The journalist Madeleine Jacob, who covered the Nuremberg Trials for *Franc-Tireur*, published an article in the December 26, 1945 issue of *L'Ecran français* on the importance of the documentary evidence that film provided against the war criminals on trial in Germany. For Jacob, only film could truly bear witness to the Nazi crimes, only film could bring irrefutable proof of their guilt (1945, 10). In order to participate in the reconstruction of Europe, feature films would also have to bear witness to the immediate past. Clément himself saw this. In December 1945, two months before the official release of *La Bataille du rail* he declared: "After Buchenwald one can no longer make vapid films" (1945, 8–9).

While *La Bataille du rail* was seen as providing filmed testimony of the war, for many critics it also represented an aesthetic ideal and even what might be called the aspiration for a national film style in the immediate postwar years. One of the defining characteristics of the discourse on film in France at this time was the positive valorization of an aesthetic of simplicity, sparseness, purity, asceticism even. For a few brief years after the end of the war, French film criticism seems to have been intent upon defining a new classicism. Classical doctrine developed in seventeenth-century France through renewed interest in Plato's commentaries on art and Aristotle's *Poetics*. This interest was most famously formalized and codified in Nicolas Boileau's 1635 treatise on classical *Art Poétique* in which the author recommends precisely to "avoid excess" and rhetorical "brilliance" and to "be simple with art, sublime without pride, agreeable without artifice." Reviews of *La Bataille du rail* overflow with this classical vocabulary. Critics praised Clément for the sparseness of his technique. He had produced what one critic called "an extremely spare work" (*une oeuvre très dépouillée* [Barrot, 1946, 9]), and another labeled it a film of "grandiose simplicity" (qtd. in Lindeperg, 87). André Bazin praised Clément for his "tact" and "simplicity"—two key words in his later writings on Roberto Rossellini and Victorio De Sica (*Le Cinéma*, 146). Indeed, critics were just as likely to label *La Bataille du rail* the stylistic equivalent of Rossellini's *Rome Open City* or Georges Rouquier's *Farrebique*, a semidocumentary about rural life in France, as they were to compare it to other Resistance films. As it turns out, few French films in the postwar years would meet these criteria of sparseness and sobriety. Indeed, as we will see, Clément's next film *Les Maudits* seems to reject this aesthetic. But classicism, understood as a rhetoric of formal elegance, simplicity and restraint, became a national aesthetic ideal among critics in postwar France.

Classicism in France is not just a set of aesthetic rules, however. To evoke rhetorical simplicity, to praise a film for its sobriety is also to draw upon a discourse of stoicism, virtue, righteousness, and national identity. From the seventeenth century and the debates between Jesuits and Jansenists, the classical rhetorical ideal became inseparable from an ethical ideal, even if the practical application of this ideal remained somewhat vague.[2] Simplicity, sparseness and tact are terms that quickly took on an ethical dimension to accompany their aesthetic value. *La Bataille du rail* is certainly a spare and frugal film, but the overwhelming critical and public responses to it make clear that, after 1944, realism in France drew upon the moral imperative with which the classical aesthetic had long tried to associate itself.

For these aesthetic terms to make sense, they depend upon a series of contradistinctions: spare and overwrought, pure and impure, tact and lack of taste, French and foreign. There is no doubt that this return to a historically marked French aesthetic also served to distinguish French films from the American films that were, as of 1944, once again playing in French movie theaters. No better case can be found than in a small book published in 1947 by Henri Colpi, who would later become the editor of Alain Resnais's *Hiroshima mon amour*. In his essay, Colpi promoted the new European realism, of which he believed *La Bataille du rail* to be France's most representative work, as the continent's answer to American film. Hollywood still remained the "master of [film] technique" but a film such as Clément's produced, according to Colpi, an alternative to "Hollywood, this savage defender of artifice, Hollywood this promoter of bubble gum (*guimauve*), of *l'eau-de-rose*, of the final kiss, of the most false of falsities" (1947, 16). Colpi's tone is hardly measured, but the opposition he strikes resonated throughout postwar France. The economic battles waged by some French filmmakers and critics against Hollywood, often took on the form of an opposition between a European classicism and an American baroque, between French authenticity and the artifice of Hollywood. The national communion that took place around *La Bataille du rail* was thus a result not only of the political consensus it created around the Resistance, but also of a sort of aesthetic consensus where rhetorical simplicity was a marker for political virtue. *La Bataille du rail*, the film that "France had an obligation to show the rest of the world" not only portrayed the Resistance triumphant over the Nazi occupiers, it had become, for some critics at least, France's riposte to what was already being called "Hollywood's cultural hegemony."

This detour through the responses to *La Bataille du rail* shows the ways in which Clément's film fulfilled the expectations of postwar viewers and created a national consensus. Clément's next film *Les Maudits* seems, at least in certain respects, to answer to these same expectations. However, it does so in a way that reveals the social, political, and aesthetic tensions at work in the filmic representations of the occupation of France. In an article published on the occasion of the 1946 Cannes film festival, René Clément had declared that the world would soon witness what he called "the renaissance of French cinema" (1946, 6). Written after the completion of *La Bataille du rail*, but before *Les Maudits*, this declaration reveals Clément's desire that French cinema rebuild from the devastation left by the Nazi occupation to compete with American films. Neither Berlin nor Hollywood is named, but they remain the forces against which, according to Clément, "French taste" must assert itself. *Les Maudits* thus seems to respond to what might be called a double anxiety. While continuing the project initiated by *La Bataille du rail* of bearing witness to the war, *Les Maudits* must initiate a French commercial cinema that could compete in the newly reconfigured international market.

After *La Bataille du rail*, it was inevitable that spectators and critics expected Clément to repeat the success of his first film, and in one respect he did. By choosing a contemporary subject, Clément seemed to position himself on the side of the new postwar realism. *Les Maudits* is about a group of Fascists and collaborators fleeing Europe for South America in a submarine at the end of the war. The passengers on board this submarine are representative figures of European fascism: the *Wehrmacht* officer Van Hauser, a paragon of Prussian rigor; Forster, a sadistic SS official; Willy his acolyte, described in the film as "a pale little punk from Berlin;" Carousi an Italian Fascist businessman; Hilde Carousi, his wife, a "militant Nazi" and Van Hauser's mistress; Erikson a bland Scandinavian scientist; Couturier, a French collaborationist journalist who wrote for a sheet called *La Vraie France* and who, we are told, frequented Maxim's during the occupation; and the narrator, Dr. Guibert, kidnapped by the Fascists and forced to cross the Atlantic with them.

Before the film's release the press described *Les Maudits* as another realist venture, as if Clément were continuing the same project as in *La Bataille du rail*. On several occasions, journalists spoke of the realist settings, the minimalist technique, the nonprofessional actors in the film. Perhaps in order to capitalize on the success of *La Bataille du rail* and certainly because realism was the order of the day, the film's prepublicity cast it as another authentic fiction about the war.

Upon the film's release in October 1947, however, the reviews tell a different story. Critics almost invariably pointed to the film's artifice, its inauthenticity and its spectacular aspects. Reactions to the film were mixed, though there was little discussion in the reviews of the time about Clément's decision to make a film about Fascists and collaborators. Rather, it was the film's style, its apparent rejection of the realist aesthetic, that caused dissension among the critics. The ambiguity of the critical response can be seen in André Bazin's reactions to the film. Bazin, who remained a supporter of Clément all his life, even as young critics at *Cahiers du cinéma* excoriated the director, nonetheless seemed to be of two minds about *Les Maudits*. In his account of the films at the 1947 Cannes film festival, published in *L'Ecran français*, Bazin concluded that Clément was, along with Georges Rouquier, "the best representative of the new French realist school. Characters die in *Les Maudits* as precisely as characters peal potatoes on the farm in *Farrebique*" ("Cannes," 7). Two years later, in a long article published on the occasion of the release of Clément's 1949 film *Au-delà des grilles*, Bazin mentions *Les Maudits*, but this time his assessment is less favorable. The directing in *Les Maudits*, Bazin writes, was often excessive; a series of "bravura pieces" (*morceaux de bravoure*) that Bazin contrasts with the "intense and invisible sobriety" of Clément's other films (*Le Cinéma*, 150).

What Bazin characterized as "bravura," other critics rejected outright. A typical reaction is that of Jean Vidal, the critic at *L'Ecran français*: "The fiction remains evident (. . .) our emotion is not duped by [the film's] artifice" (1947, 4). The harshest review I encountered came from the *Revue du cinéma* which also emphasized the artifice of the film. Comparing *Les Maudits* to René Clair's 1945 *And Then There Were None* ("without Clair's sense of humor"), Jean Talleray writes: "We obviously cannot believe in this overly fabricated story. It is not even implausible (*invraisemblable*). It isn't true (*vrai*). (. . .) a contemporary subject, a good idea, a realist setting highlighted by an excellent technique are not enough to make a true film" (*un film vrai*) [1948, 80]).

From one film to the next, Clément seems to have changed aesthetics. But the artifice that critics of the time condemned, may have come precisely from Clément's attempt to make a film that simultaneously reflected upon some of the most difficult elements of Europe's immediate past and attempted to define the cinema of France's future.

Like *La Bataille du rail*, *Les Maudits* is a testimony, and both films use the voice-over technique. *La Bataille du rail* uses a third person narration whose function is to establish the film's authority as a documentary and to include the audience in the acts of resistance represented on screen. In *Les Maudits* the voice-over is more complicated. The film's narrator is the French doctor played by Henri Vidal, and his voice-over serves a dual function. On the one hand, the voice-over serves to establish the verisimilitude and documentary authority of the film. In one of the first scenes we are told the date—"April 19, 1945. A few days before the fall of Berlin"—and introduced to the passengers on board the submarine. This is the voice of testimony, and as with other films of the war, it fulfills a juridical function. *Les Maudits* was released during the purge trials of Fascists and collaborators in France, and in part it mimics the rhetoric of these trials. The doctor's narrative has all the elements of a testimony in the juridical sense. It takes the form of a flashback, told by a witness to a figure of authority, in this case the American Navy officer who rescues Dr. Guibert. It appeals to the audience's judgment, and indeed treats the audience as a jury. The doctor even calls his narration *"le procès-verbal de cette aventure"* (the sworn testimony of this adventure) and guarantees that every word is true. Among the many roles it plays, the narration of *Les Maudits*, like other films about the war, provides cinematographic evidence against fascism.

Alongside this authoritative voice, however, is a much more ambiguous testimony. The doctor's first person narration also at times resembles the ideologically unstable voice-over associated with film noir. Contrary to the witness in a trial who, taking the stand before testifying, must state his or her name, age, profession and place of birth, the doctor tells us next to nothing about himself. We only know that he returns to Royan at the end of the war and that he speaks German. We don't know what he did during the war—was he a prisoner, a Resistant, a forced laborer in Germany? We know that before being kidnapped he was expecting to meet a woman, but we are never told why, or who the woman is. Furthermore, his testimony is not always clear. He misinterprets certain scenes, and misjudges certain passengers on board the submarine. It is almost as if this questioning and somewhat unreliable voice were in dialogue with the authoritative voice which gives us the facts. But without this second voice-over there would be no plot, no intrigue, and no film. Too much information about the doctor would have deterred from the film's suspense. Too little undermines his legal authority. The film noir narration of *Les Maudits* brings to the fore a problem that other more "authentic" documents on the war avoided: the tension between the realist film as document and the realist film as fiction.

Perhaps because of this confusion, the film never records the real crimes of European fascism. Rather these crimes are displaced onto moral indictments and the film's aesthetics. Thus, Hilde Carousi, the militant Nazi is also an adulteress. And Forster, the Nazi party official, is portrayed as a sadist engaged in a violent and erotic relationship with his assistant Willy. This rerouting of political crimes as illicit sexuality was commonplace at the end of the Second World War. Two of Roberto Rossellini's films from the immediate postwar years draw equivalence between fascism and homosexuality. In *Open City* (1945), Marina, a woman who loves one of the Italian partisans, is convinced to betray her lover by a Fascist woman, Ingrid, in whose arms we see her during one of the film's last scenes. In *Germany Year Zero* (1947), the former Nazi schoolteacher and current black marketer who convinces Edmund to kill his father, displays a pedophilic desire for the young boy. In France, it was Jean-Paul Sartre who most famously associated fascism and betrayal to homosexual desire. For Sartre, the French collaborator combined masochism with a homosexual desire for the German invader (1949, 58). Andrew Hewitt has shown how from the 1930s to the present, homosexuality has been used as allegory for fascism, designed to signify and often denounce fascism's alterity and its "nonreproductive function" (1966, 246). In Clément's film, homosexuality is made to stand as the mark of difference, as a form of marginalization and disunification in a society attempting to restore a political and sexual order after the devastation of the war.[3]

Somewhere among all these desiring glances is Couturier, the collaborator. Couturier is the antithesis of the authentic and anonymous working-class Resistants in *La Bataille du Rail*. Just as the Fascists Hilde Carousi and Forster were associated with a destabilizing sexuality, Couturier is associated with artifice and the spectacle. Couturier is a journalist, an intellectual and a dandy who could have been modeled upon the notorious collaborationist journalist and editor of *Les Nouveaux*

Temps, Jean Luchaire. He is aloof, well dressed, cynical, and ambitious. His manner of speaking is at once clipped and precious, and his hair is slicked back, a sure sign, in French film, that a character belongs to the bourgeoisie and has Nazi sympathies. French films about the war constantly rely upon a semiotic system in which collaborators sport the wet look and Resistance fighters wear their hair loose. In any case, Couturier is a recognizable type, but what makes him most recognizable is his artifice, his falsity. Couturier is played by Paul Bernard, an actor known for his mannerist acting style: Bernard played the role of the libertine and deeply deranged aristocrat in Grémillion's *Lumière d'été* (1943) and the role of the rake in Bresson's *Les Dames du bois de Boulogne* (1945). The interpretation Bernard gives to the role of Couturier is of a man constantly on show. This representation in *Les Maudits* coincides with other filmic representations of collaborators in the immediate postwar years. In Henri Calef's film about the Resistance, *Opération Jericho* (1946), Pierre Brasseur, another actor known for his theatrical performances, presents the rather elaborate portrait of a collaborator. He plays the role of an anti-Semitic black marketer, who distinguishes himself through his effusive, gushing, and practically campy performance. The Resistants in the film are silent. He, like Couturier in *Les Maudits*, is a voluble clown.

This link between collaboration and artifice is anchored in the political reality of the purge trials. Accusations of treason against collaborators were often supported by denunciations of the accused's outlandish or excessive behavior. To cite just one example from the film profession, in an account of the actor Robert Le Vigan's trial for collaboration, the journalist from *L'Ecran français* states that not only Le Vigan was a traitor, but that he had always been known for the "extravagance" "outrance" of his acting style. His appearance in court was nothing more than a botched finale. "*Il en fait trop*" the journalist concluded, and, unmoved by his performance, the jury declared him guilty.[4]

Again, however, the representation of the collaborator as an individual who confuses reality and performance might very well draw upon archaic aesthetic distinctions. In classical doctrine, rhetorical excess and artifice are signs of moral turpitude. Because he is a mere imitator, Socrates argues in Book X of the *Republic*, the poet knows nothing of and therefore cannot teach virtue. Now, one could argue that *La Bataille* is as much of a fictional construct as *Les Maudits*, but the reception of these two works shows that in the immediate postwar years, at a moment of economic and moral reconstruction, French cinema associates a rhetoric that foregrounds performance and excess with moral turpitude and the perceived sobriety of cinematic realism with virtue. Whether on screen or in the courtroom, the collaborator is cast as an agent of excess and inauthenticity. Through what we might call an "artifice effect," the spectators are reminded that they are witnessing a performance. This "artifice effect" is most evident in *Les Maudits* in one of the film's early scenes. Having just finished lunch, Couturier declares: "what is missing here [in the submarine] is a movie theater. I love the movies" [*Ce qui manque ici c'est le cinéma. J'aime beaucoup le cinema*]. The incongruity of the statement leads us in several directions. To be sure, Clément is criticizing a certain form of spectatorship that trivializes film. Couturier consumes movies as others consume desert. Furthermore, the scene creates a distance between the spectators and the characters on screen. Contrary to *La Bataille du rail* where the film technique attempted to make itself as transparent as possible in order to permit identification between audience and members of the Resistance, *Les Maudits*, and this scene in particular proclaims its artifice. The "artifice effect" is a prophylactic measure of sorts. Just as the collaborators are secluded in their submarine, they are quarantined by the screen. As the discourse of postwar France would have it, the collaborators were isolated, few in number and separated from the rest of the population. This "artifice effect" has become something of a commonplace in French cinematic representations of collaborators. As Lynn Higgins has noted in her analysis of *Lacombe Lucien*, "collaboration remain[s] in the sphere of the spectacle" (1996, 193). At the same time, however, Couturier's quip about his love of the movies also hints at the fact that films about the collaboration must include questions about the political responsibility of cinema itself. Clément may have been launching a subtle critique of the French cinematic industry's accommodation with the Nazis and the Vichy government during the Occupation. The same phenomenon may be at work in *Les Maudits*. The indictment of Fascists and collaborators passes through an indictment of their relation to film.

Clément might not have been entirely successful in his project, however. The critics who in 1947 denounced his film as "an overly fabricated story" were expecting another realist exploit. And while *Les Maudits* does include some of the techniques of cinematographic realism, Clément has expanded his scope. Unlike *La Bataille du rail*, *Les Maudits* is not a testimony about the heroism of the French Resistance. It is a film about the problems of representing traitors. *Les Maudits* is also about the relation of France's film industry to the film industries of Germany and America. This film about French collaboration with Nazi Germany allegorizes the director's desire to initiate what he called "the renaissance of French cinema," by looking back to German expressionism and forward to the postwar presence of American films in France.

Alongside its German actors, its reconstituted U-boat, and its several scenes of dialogue in German, through its title *Les Maudits* refers to one of the most famous prewar German films, Fritz Lang's 1931 *M*, known in French as *M, le Maudit*. Lang's *M* also acts as a sort of narratological grid for Clément's film. Both films are constructed around the desperate and ultimately unsuccessful flight of social outcasts: in *M*, it is Hans Beckert the killer, in *Les Maudits* it is the shipload of Fascists. Furthermore, both films associate sexual perversion with murderous impulses: in *M*, Hans Beckert is compulsively attracted to young girls, in *Les Maudits* Forster the SS is a sadist. To a certain extent, Clément's film even borrows from Lang's technique, in particular the extensive use of tracking shots, the confined spaces of the setting and the strong contrasts of light and shadow. This borrowing may be more incidental than actual, however, since certain elements of German expressionism had become standard techniques in France by the end of the 1930s, and Clément's cameraman, Henri Alekan, was an adept of the German style (Crisp, 1993, 376–380). One further element links the two films. In his 1947 study of German cinema, Siegfried Kracauer noted that films such as Lang's *M* prefigured the rise of fascism in Germany. Kracauer even relates how, according to Lang, members of the Nazi Party originally thought the film, whose working title was *Murderer Among Us*, was about them. (1959, 218–219). That Lang's *M* was on the minds of postwar audiences is born out by the fact that one of the few German films of the immediate postwar years to confront the question of Germany's guilt was Wolfgang Staudte's 1946 *The Murderers Are Among Us*, a film that draws heavily upon the legacy of expressionism and reclaims the original title of Lang's 1931 film.

Fritz Lang's *M* thus remains a matrix of sorts for postwar films about fascism, though it may have been a morally ambiguous matrix. In its portrayal of the killer Hans Beckert, *M* stages a trial but ends up foreclosing any possibility of coming to a stable judgment. By the conclusion of the film, everyone, including the mothers of the victims, seems contaminated by Hans Beckert's crimes. Instead of resolving a conflict Lang's film leaves us with questions: Who is pure enough to judge the killer? Who is really responsible for Hans Beckert's crimes? This is precisely the conclusion that Gilles Deleuze comes to about all of Lang's work, and about *M* in particular. While expressionist films often foreground the struggle between good and evil, Lang puts into question the very possibility of judging. Everything has been reduced to appearances (1985, 180). *Les Maudits* may not have any difficulty judging and condemning the Fascists and their French collaborators. Clément's film is a revision of *M* in a historically precise setting. Still, the references to *M* reinforce the "artifice effect" and confirm that *Les Maudits* is about the filming of appearances, the filmic memory of fascism and the "renaissance of French cinema" in the face of the influence that German cinema exerted, until 1944 at any rate, in France.

In the final sequences of *Les Maudits*, after Couturier, Forster, Van Hauser, and Hilde Carousi have all died, Dr. Guibert finds himself alone on the submarine. At once traumatized and bored he begins recording in a notebook the adventures he has just lived through. It is at this point that the American Navy rescues the French doctor, and he tells his story to a naval officer, who, like all American soldiers, chews gum and wears his cap titled at a forty-five degree angle on his head. The officer councils Dr. Guibert to write how he was rescued by Americans in the final chapter—and to find a good title. Guibert responds that his title will be *Les Maudits*. This ending speaks to us about America's role in rescuing France from fascism, and is an acknowledgement of a debt of gratitude. But the ending also speaks to us about a stylistic debt, for it is the American who tells the French narrator how to finish his screenplay. The American, both by his acts and by his words, furnishes elements for the story's commercial appeal, a title and an ending. Postwar French cinema was in a state of high anxiety about Hollywood's economic dominance and its stylistic influence. Clément himself wrote about the necessity of defending French artisanal cinema against a foreign onslaught. And yet, in a film destined to revive the French cinematic industry, Clément concludes with a Hollywood ending. America, in the guise of a smiling naval officer, provides the "happy end" for *Les Maudits*.

René Clément's first two films leave a lot unsaid about the occupation. Most importantly, they avoid questions of the Vichy government's responsibility in repressing the Resistance and in deporting Jews. Yet, when taken together, *La Bataille du rail* and *Les Maudits* bear witness to a nation's attempts to represent the complex roles it played during the war. Through the tensions that inhabit them, Clément's early films bring out fundamental problems of screening the war. Located somewhere between the mainstream and what the French aptly call a *"cinéma d'essai*," Clément's films ask audiences to think about the relation between aesthetics and ethics, and about France's position between Berlin and Hollywood.

NOTES

1. René Clément's four films about the Second World War are *La Bataille du rail* (1946), *Les Maudits* (1947), *Jeux Interdits* (1952) and *Paris brûle-t-il?* (1966). Between *La Bataille du rail* and *Les Maudits*, Clément was technical advisor on *Le Père tranquille*, about an ordinary Frenchman who controls a large resistance network from his backyard greenhouse. *Le Père tranquille*, written and codirected by its star Noël-Noël was shot and released in 1946. For a thorough analysis of this film see Sylvie Lindeperg, *Les ecrans de l'ombre* (Paris: CNRS Editions, 1997), pp. 181–189.

2. The literature on classicism is overwhelming but I have found a useful presentation of the links between aesthetics and ethics in an article by Marc Fumaroli. Fumaroli outlines how in the seventeenth century classicism came to be associated with a simple style, a pared down rhetoric, sincerity, righteousness and, in the end, national identity. Marc Fumaroli, *"Baroque et Classicisme: L'Imago primi saeculi societatis jesu (1640) et ses adversaries"* in *Questionnement du baroque* ed. Alphonse Vermeylen, pp. 75–111 (Bruxelles: Editions Nauwelaerts, 1986).

3. The other film with the same title as Clément's *Les Maudits* is Luchino Visconti's 1969 work *The Damned* which also allegorizes fascism as homosexuality through the character of Martin von Essenbeck. Luchino's recourse to a melodramatic and opulent style shows the extent to which fascism and rhetorical excess are linked in the public imagination.

4. The association of cinema and political corruption is also present, though in a slightly less elaborate way in Henri-George Clouzot's *Manon* (1948), a modern adaptation of Prevost's novel. In Clouzot's film Manon and Desgrieux meet in a town in Normandy a few weeks after D-Day. Desgrieux is a

member of the Resistance; Manon is about to have her head shaved by the townspeople for having "danced" with German soldiers. Manon's brother, played by Serge Reggiani, had probably dealt in the black market during the Occupation. He is, in any case, unscrupulous, and in the years after the war, when he can no longer sell his sister, he opens a movie theater.

References

Anonymous. "Le Procès de Goupi Grand-Reich" *L'Ecran français*, No. 74 (November 26, 1946).

Barrot, Jean-Pierre. "*La Bataille du rail*: une oeuvre poignante comme la vie." *L'Ecran français*, No. 35 (February 27, 1946).

Bazin, André. *Le Cinéma français de la Libération à la Nouvelle Vague*. Paris: Cahiers du cinéma, 1998.

———. "Cannes va aussi au cinéma." *L'Ecran français*, No. 117 (September 23, 1947).

Bertin-Maghit, Jean-Pierre. "*La Bataille du rail*: De l'authenticité à la chanson de geste." *Revue d'histoire moderne et contemporaine*, Tome 33 (April-June 1986): 280–300.

Clément, René. "Après Buchenwald on ne peut plus faire des films mièvres." *L'Ecran français*, No. 24 (December 12, 1945).

———. "Le Cinéma français cet artisan." *Cinémonde*, No. Spécial Festival de Cannes, 1946.

Colpi, Henri. *Le cinéma et ses hommes*. Montpellier: Causse, Graille et Castelnau, 1947.

Crisp, Colin. *The Classic French Cinema 1930–1960*. Bloomington, IN: Indiana University Press, 1993.

Deleuze, Gilles. *Cinéma 2: L'Image-Temps*. Paris: Editions de Minuit, 1985.

Fumaroli, Marc. "Baroque et Classicisme: L'Imago primi saeculi societatis jesu (1640) et ses adversaries." in *Questionnement du baroque*. Edited by Alphonse Vermeylen, 75–111 (Bruxelles: Editions Nauwelaerts, 1986).

Greene, Naomi. *Landscapes of Loss: The National Past in Postwar French Cinema*. Princeton, NJ: Princeton University Press, 1999.

Hewitt, Andrew. *Political Inversions : Homosexuality, Fascism and the Modernist Imaginary*. Stanford, CA: Stanford University Press, 1996.

Higgins, Lynn. *New Novel, New Wave, New Politics: Fiction and the Representation of History in Postwar France*. Lincoln: University of Nebraska Press, 1996.

Jacob, Madeleine. "Les accusés de Nuremberg devant la preuve de leurs crimes." *L'Ecran français*, No. 26 (December 26, 1945).

Kracauer, Siegfried. *From Caligari to Hitler : A Psychological History of the German Film*. New York : The Noonday Press, 1959 ed.

Lagny, Michèle. "Les Français en focalisation interne." *Iris* 2, No. 2 (1984): 85–98.

Lindeperg, Sylvie. *Les Ecrans de l'ombre: La Seconde Guerre mondiale dans le cinéma français (1944–1969)*. Paris: CNRS Editions, 1997.

Magnan, Henry. "Vivre Libre." *Le Monde*, 19 July 1946.

Néry, Jean. "*La Bataille du rail*." *Le Monde*, 5 March 1946.

Pouillon, Jean. "A propos des films de guerre." *Les Temps modernes*, No. 7 (May 1946): 1507–1516.

Sartre, Jean-Paul. "Qu'est-ce qu'un collaborateur?" *Situations III*. Paris: Gallimard, 1949.

Spenlé, Alain. "La Bataille du rail." *Revue du cinéma*, No.1 (October, 1946): 72–74.

Talleray, Jean. "Un jeu de massacre." *La Revue du cinéma*, No. 11 (March 1948): 80.

Vidal, Jean. "Les Maudits." *L'Ecran français*, No. 120 (October 14, 1947).

Chapter 11

BETWEEN COLLABORATION AND RESISTANCE
Ernst Jünger in Paris, 1941–44
Elliot Neaman

The forty-six year old German writer Ernst Jünger, highly decorated World War I hero, leader of the revolutionary nationalist youth in Weimar, chastened esthete and apparently a Christian convert in the 1930s, was a member of the occupation army in Paris from February 1941 until July 1944. He was peripherally involved in the Rommel conspiracy against Hitler, but not a member of the inner core of the activists.[1] He was opposed to assassinations and thought that the war would have to run its course until the bloody end when a new order would emerge. He returned to Germany after the Stauffenberg plot against Hitler failed (July 20, 1944) and the army command in Paris had been flushed out, its highest officers forced to commit suicide or return to Berlin to face the hanging judge, Roland Freisler. Jünger was put on trial before the People's Court, but his superiors refused to name him as a coconspirator and the case was dismissed for lack of evidence. It was a very close call.

Jünger was a highly accomplished diarist and chronicled the entire war period, first in a book, *Gardens and Paths*, published in France in 1942, and then in a set of secret notebooks, not published until 1949, entitled *Radiations,* or *Emanations (Strahlungen)*. The German army command in Paris was led by aristocratic Prussian officers who disliked the interference of the party into their business and who gradually turned against Hitler in 1942 as the Russian campaign floundered. Jünger's diaries reflected their position and mentality. But he was perhaps even more sensitive than most to the suffering of the Parisians under occupation, and eloquently expressed his contempt for the ideological warriors of the SS, whom he called "lemurs" and "sadistic monsters." On February 8, 1942, he received a report of the mass shootings and exterminations taking place on the Eastern Front and wrote, there "is no question that there are individuals who are responsible for the murder of millions" (Jünger, *Sämmtliche Werke*, 1979, hereafter SW, 2: 303). On June 7, 1942, he encountered for the first time the yellow star and noted being "embarrassed to be in uniform" (SW, 2: 336). On September 10, 1942 he feared that he would soon despise all of humankind, because the masses have abandoned free will (*SW*, 2: 375). These sentiments reflected elitist haughtiness, but were uncommon opinions for the majority of the German officer class, and were, needless to say, hardly the sentiments of the average German soldier, let alone of the hated "*boche*" whom the French regarded as a primitive barbarian in uniform.

The diaries endeared Jünger to the French reading public in the postwar years, and until his death in 1998, he was considered *le plus grand écrivain allemand*, despite the fact that Jünger's own countrymen hardly shared that enthusiasm. Why Jünger had such a different reception in his home country, why there was indeed a gulf of understanding, a mutual puzzlement over the treatment of this enigmatic writer, is a subject of continuing speculation among observers of the French-German cultural exchange during the war and its aftermath. My contribution here attempts to clarify the historical background of Jünger's activities in Paris and to offer some insights into the often contradictory and harshly polemical stands taken by critics on the subject of Ernst Jünger's work and person. In doing so, I wish to address the larger issues of the memory of the Holocaust in France and Germany and the persistent fascination in France with ideas that derive from the epoch of European fascism.

Let us begin by examining Jünger's role as an occupier comfortably lodged in Paris at the Hotel Majestic on Avenue de Kleber during the war years. He enjoyed the protection and patronage of two high-ranking cultural connoisseurs, Karl Heinrich von Stülpnagel, the commander of the occupying forces in France, and his chief of staff, Hans Speidel, (later to become chief general of the *Bundeswehr*). Jünger's had a plum job, because it didn't take up much of his time, was ethically unoffensive and it had to do with literature, or at least with writing: he had to sift through the daily correspondence of German soldiers and their mail from home. He even saved some soldiers from the grip of the SS by discreetly destroying letters that would have been viewed as seditious.

In Jünger's spare time, which was apparently considerable, he was a *flâneur*, casing the sidewalks of Paris, browsing through the museums, studying the urban architecture, and strolling through the galleries, antique shops, and bookstores. Every new book or art purchase was meticulously registered. The aura attached to objects that weathered the ravages of time fascinated him. Besides collecting art and books, Jünger also nurtured contacts with famous writers and artists. In the salon of Marie-Louise Bousquet, a writer for Harper's Bazaar, he came into contact with "l'Hitlerisme Francais," with Drieu la Rochelle, Marcel Jouhandeau, Paul Léautaud, and Henri de Montherlant (Burrin 1996, 342–357). Right from the beginning Jünger straddled both sides of the Occupation, threading ties to resistors and collaborators. He knew Alfred Fabre-Luce, a supporter of the *Pax Germanica*, (Luce, *Journal de la France*, 1939–40, 175ff.) and contributed several pieces, mostly from his World War I diaries, to Fabre-Luce's well-known collaborationist anthology (Luce, *Anthologie*, 1942). But he was also a favored guest of the "Thursday salon" where the avant-garde met, particularly one run by Florence Gould (alias Lady Orpington), the wife of Frank Jay Gould, a wealthy American businessman.[2] There Jünger rubbed shoulders with Jean Cocteau, Georges Braques, Pablo Picasso, Sacha Guitry, Julien Gracq, Paul Léautaud, and other luminaries, including Jean Paulhan, one of the founders of the Resistance newspaper *Lettres Françaises* (Jünger, *SW*, 14: 127). Jünger was also happy to be seen at the salon of Lucienne Didier, a Belgian sculptor. Her husband, Edouard Didier, in contact with the German ambassador Otto Abetz since 1933, had founded an association called "Jeune Europe" as a forum for Franco-German intellectual exchange. He introduced Jünger to Hendrik de Man, the famous Belgian neo-Socialist and collaborator (Plard, 1955, 148). The gathering at the Didier salon of progressive Catholics, socialists, as well as Fascist sympathizers organized by Otto Abetz and Max Liebe, contributed to what Thomas Fries calls the "unholy alliance of the first period of the occupation"(Fries 1987, 198).

The warm reception of Jünger in leading French literary and artistic circles contrasted sharply with the experience of most German intellectuals in France, in particular when one considers the enormous difficulties faced by the German exile community in prewar France. The French academy closed its doors to German professors and most exiles experienced a social *cordon sanitaire*. According to Arthur Koestler: "the great mass of refugees in France lived cut off from French contacts and led a kind of ghetto existence" (cited in Grunfeld 1995, 211).

A particularly unsettling aspect of Jünger's name-dropping and romps through the art and book world of Paris's cultural elite is the dissonance between his cultural exploits and the terrorization and starvation of Parisians under Nazi occupation. Beginning in the summer of 1942, the city was being plundered and Jews deported. Although Jünger expresses his displeasure at the treatment of the Parisians by the SS, he seems to be unaware that the German Army was also an object of hatred for most of the occupied population. On August 18, 1942, he entered a stationary store and was greeted by the cold, spiteful stare of a young salesgirl behind the counter. He notes with surprise that the hatred in the girl's face might spread like a virus or a spark "that would take a lot of strength to put out inside oneself" (Jünger, *SW*, 2: 367).

It is true that Jünger allotted considerable space to ruminations about his distaste for Hitler and the Nazis. But he was ambivalent about his position *vis-a-vis* the other *frondeurs*. The manner in which he characterized the members of the George V circle, "spiritual knights who meet in the belly of the Leviathan," (Jünger, *SW*, 272) points to an act of distancing, of displacement into an almost medieval fantasy, even though his precarious situation called for utmost discretion and cunning. He kept his journal notes hidden in a locked safe in his room, but with Gestapo agents and informers crawling all over the Hotel Majestic, the project was not without considerable risks. Hitler was always characterized in the diaries as "Kniébolo," (a word play on "diabolo,"), for whom he had nothing but sneering contempt. And the *Führer* appeared menacingly in his dreams (Jünger, *SW*, 3: 41–42).

On the Eastern Front, Jünger talked to officers who related stories of the brutal activities of the *Einsatztruppen*. Like many others he heard of atrocities committed in the concentration camps (Bargatsky 1987, 101). Though shaken by these events, his detachment is evident as well. Historical events have the force of nature, they sweep human beings along as if by the irresistible power of a hurricane or the destructive fury of an earthquake. As much as the barbarism of the Nazis was repellent to him, he could not help but interpret the persecution of the Jews and others as part of a fated, cosmological scheme. Particularly in the last books of the war diaries, where Jünger contemplated the issue of German guilt, what he called his "stereoscopic" vision searched for a metaphysical explanation behind the perplexing evidence of the senses. In the following example, Jünger invokes a biblical image, rendering literal the meaning of "sacrificial" in the term Holocaust: "Was our persecution the last birth pang before the appearance of the Second Messiah, the Paraclet, with whom the epoch of the spirit shall begin? It is impossible that such a sacrifice won't bear fruit" (Jünger, SW, 2: 415).

Jünger's question is troublesome because it provided a metaphysical justification for the suffering of the Holocaust, a kind of theodicy that survivors would vigorously disavow (Levi 1988, 167–197). Jünger's interpretation of death as the sole authentic experience of life, indeed as having a higher reality than life, is another recurring topic in the war diaries. The Nazi mass murders interested him not so much from the point of view of the victims, but rather the abstract historical significance of the method applied in committing the crime.[3] In a commentary on the concentration camps he noted that death had become standardized, mechanized, and sanitized, like everything in the technical world (Jünger, SW, 2: 448). He thereby linked the administration of death to the general impoverishment of the "modern world." In the final pages of the war diaries, Jünger varied this theme with a not-too-subtle attack on the thesis of collective guilt. The engineers of the atom bomb make Tamerlane and his atrocities look absolutely royal since death becomes cheaper and responsibility untraceable when millions are killed. The advancement of technology brings with it a concomitant impoverishment of the world, because rational calculation takes precedence over the higher faculties of the imagination. Finally, the collective guilt assertion is just a mantle the allies use to hide their real interests:

> The thesis of collective guilt has two strands which run together. For the defeated it means, I have to stand for my brother and his guilt. It gives the victor an excuse for undifferentiated plundering. If the bow is pulled too tightly, the dangerous question arises whether the brother was really so unjust. (Jünger, SW, 2: 510)

After Germany's defeat, Jünger was prohibited from publishing his books and remained on the blacklist until 1949, because he refused to fill out the infamous Questionnaire distributed by the allied occupation forces to classify the guilt of ordinary German citizens in the much maligned process of "denazification" (the big fish get away, the smaller ones get caught.) In the postwar years, Jünger retreated from the political battles of his youth and was content to write books about obscure topics for rather esoteric audiences. He published science fiction novels, a book about his strange penchant for insect hunting and collecting, and another about his drug experiences with LSD, mescaline, and other hallucinogenic substances. His grand project remained his diaries, chronicling world travels and daily reflections on books, insects, nature, and the cosmos. He also became a kind of good will ambassador for the Federal Republic to France, a surprising activity considering his distrust of the state and his suspicion of democracy. Jünger played the role with increasing satisfaction as his fame in France grew. Mitterrand invited him to Elysée on practically every trip Jünger took to Paris. The war hero and last surviving bearer of the *pour le mérite* (Germany's highest medal of valor), was constantly invited to openings of museum exhibitions and to military commemorations of World War I. Already in 1975, President Carstens invited Jünger to Bonn as an official expert on French culture to help him prepare for a state visit.

In June 1979 the "old German fighter of the First world war" was invited by the mayor of Verdun to address the annual commemoration of the famous battle of 1916. Five years later, Jünger returned to the cemeteries at Fort Douaumont and Consenvoye, near Verdun, along with the French president and the German chancellor, to lay a wreath at the war memorials. Although French newspapers reported that hardly a spectator ventured out to observe Kohl and Mitterrand clasping hands while the Marseillaise played, camera teams were omnipresent as an "eye witness"(Fritz-Vannahme 1984).

Although *Le Figaro* called the ceremony "clumsy" and some German commentators thought the event was consolation for the absence of an invitation to the fortieth commemoration of the landing at Normandy in June, it was without doubt an important gesture of reconciliation, contributing to a strengthening of Franco-German relations. This little-noticed event can be seen in hindsight as a prelude to the much more problematical reconciliation over the graves, in the blare of publicity, when Reagan and Kohl met at Bitburg in the fall of 1985 (Hartman 1986).

In May, 1985 François Mitterrand and Helmut Kohl met in Konstanz to iron out tensions emerging in the course of a recent economic summit in Bonn and because of divergent reactions to the SDI (Strategic Defense Initiative) of the United States. Before the meeting started, Mitterrand insisted on flying by helicopter to Wilflingen to visit Jünger. Kohl knew his visit would irritate the Left in Germany, but with Mitterand in attendance, how much could it protest? The story is told that Kohl and Jünger had a hard time starting a conversation. Finally the Kanzler asked, "how did you start your beetle collection?" and Jünger had an opening. Kohl tried to talk about literature, but the conversation was halting. Finally he asked about the Argentinean writer Jorge Luis Borges, whose photograph from a recent visit was within view. In the end they talked about the First World War. As a departing gift Jünger gave Kohl a copy of his just published novel, *A Dangerous Encounter*. In sharp, calligraphic letters, Jünger inscribed in the book "In memory of an un-dangerous encounter" (Busche 1998).

The meeting between Mitterand and Kohl failed to erase the fears of the French that the German support for SDI, and relative neglect of the European defense program, (Eureka) represented "the first step towards a Germanized Europe," (as the headlines of the newspaper *Liberation* claimed) (*Liberation*, 31 May 1985). The Parisian newspapers commented somewhat unfavorably on Mitterrand's Jünger visit. Jünger's inflammatory 1932 work *The Worker* had not yet been translated into French, it was speculated, so few knew of the role Jünger played as part of the Conservative Revolution and the intellectual mobilization against the Weimar Republic. Would Jünger's popularity be diminished, it was asked, if *The Worker* were to be published in French?[4]

Jünger's popularity, often bordering on adulation, in France, is an intriguing phenomenon. His relationship to French culture and history was complex, but one can point to a number of historical reasons why Jünger's past was seen in an entirely different light west of the Rhine. First, Jünger's attachment to French literature distinguished him from most right-wing intellectuals of the Weimar period, who generally disdained French civilization as inferior to Germanic *Kultur*. (Laqueur 1974, 79ff.) Jünger had been an avid and admiring reader of French literature ever since he read the works of Maurice Barrès shortly after the end of World War I. French writers, especially Stendhal, Baudelaire, J. K. Huysmans, the Goncourts, and the antimodern Catholic intellectuals

Leon Bloy and George Bernanos had a profound influence on him. Jünger cultivated relationships to French writers in the interwar period and was in turn regarded by them as an avant-garde artist of some stature. (Weber 1949) When the German writer Joseph Breitbach introduced Jünger to André Gide in 1938, Jünger obtained a crucial introduction to the inner world of French letters.

Second, the French have generally judged Jünger's role as a captain of the *Wehrmacht* at the eye of the storm in occupied France very positively. After the war, Jünger was looked back upon as "the perfect type of occupier," charming, cultivated, and cosmopolitan. He gained recognition as a cultivator and protector of French culture. He was on a first name basis with luminaries like Jean Cocteau and Sacha Guitry. Even Sartre's *Le Temps Modernes* called him a "dreamer of peace during the war" and a "critic of Kniébolo-Hitler" (Roy 1951). He was considered a mole in the system, someone who worked to save what could be saved. In particular, the protection from plunder of valuable manuscripts in the *Bibliothèque Nationale*, and the refusal to carry out orders to dynamite a medieval church in Laon endeared the German to many a French patriot. Even among former members of the French Resistance, Jünger's reputation was generally untarnished—in fact he was often revered (Nadeau 1951). Joseph Breitbach testified that the occupation officer passed on important information—the dates and times of deportations of Jews from Paris—to the maquis (Mühleisen 1986). Henri Plard has pointed out that Jünger represents for the French a kind of stereotype that can be traced as far back as Madame de Stael's search for the "good German" in contrast to the *boche* (Plard 1990, 142–43). Whereas Nazi propaganda denigrated French culture as decadent, weak, feminine, or "judaicized," Jünger's books displayed a deep indebtedness to French traditions.

Third, Jünger's circle of wartime admirers in France, including Julien Gracq, Antoine Blondin, Robert Poulet, Marcel Jouhandeau, and Denis de Rougemont, began immediately after 1945 to propagate the image of a "great" European writer of classical stature. Gide had famously called Jünger's war diaries the "most honest book ever written about the war" (Klett 1998). When André Malraux's *Oeuvres Complètes* were published in France in 1989, *Le Figaro* sought and won an exclusive interview with Jünger, "*le plus grand écrivain allemand*," to solicit his opinion on matters concerning Malraux's life and works (Brincourt

1989). One of the questions posed to Jünger would very unlikely have been phrased in the same way by a German intellectual: "Isn't the type of man that you represent, Malraux and yourself, a product of very exceptional epochs, and could such types still exist today?"

Fourth, one cannot overestimate the contribution made by Henri Plard to Jünger's success in France. His translations are almost universally regarded as brilliant productions, and Jünger responded to his increasing popularity in France by devoting more attention to his French publishers. In fact a late novel, *Eumeswil*, appeared in Plard's French translation before the original German version was published.

Finally, the case of Jünger in France deserves the kind of treatment that Jeffrey Mehlman has called the "politics of literary adulation" (Mehlman 1986, 1–14). Without addressing the thorny argument Mehlman makes about certain forms of contemporary literary criticism, relevant here is his interpretation of the writings of Jean Paulhan, an acquaintance of Jünger who had been an early recruit to Jacques Doriot's extreme right Parti Populaire Français (PPF), worked with the Nazi occupying forces and collaborators, and at the same time grounded the first resistance journal *Les lettres françaises*.[5] Mehlman established a connection between Paulhan's linguistic research into homonymic antonyms and his criticism of the postwar purge of collaborationist writers by the National Committee of Writers. The meaning of the words "resistance" and "collaboration" tends to slide from one pole to another, a reversal of direction, like the translated pun *Sauerkraut*, which becomes *choucroute* in French. Paulhan's dream was that France might one day forget the bitter divisions caused by this unfortunate period in French history. Mehlman also controversially suggests that the "radical forgetting" of the linguistic origins of deconstruction is proof of the success of Paulhan's call for amnesty (from: amnesia) of collaborationist writers.[6]

In this context Mehlman introduces the figure of Gerhard Heller, an "anti-Nazi Nazi occupant" like Jünger, who worked with the German Propaganda Service in Paris as a censor, allowing many good books, including *Gardens and Paths*, to be published (Heller 1981). After the war, Heller emerged as a strong proponent of Franco-German reconciliation and was awarded the Grand Prix by the French Academy. It is an intriguing to ask whether the accolades imparted to Jünger are perhaps part of the same complex process of repression of memory of collaboration that Paulhan worked out linguistically, and Heller's superficial papering over of differences in his double role as occupier and French culture enthusiast exemplifies. After all, beyond the factual basis for the French people's admiration for Jünger, there also existed psychological projection. Jünger's interpretation of the events of the war and the roots of fascism may have helped ease the shame of defeat and collaboration. They provided a basis for the illusion of shared suffering and the toleration of crimes by an imposed and unwanted regime. François Mitterand's own checkered past as an early supporter of the Vichy government may explain his attraction to Jünger and his government's eagerness to enlist the old warrior in symbolic acts of reconciliation.

One of the most fascinating aspects of the French reception of Ernst Jünger has been the role Jünger's writing have played in what Richard Wolin calls the "French Heidegger Wars," referring to the hotly contested debates between the French Heideggerian Left and its critics over Heidegger's purported attempts to shift the blame for his support of National Socialism from personal engagement to the depersonalized "fate" of Western metaphysics and the "forgetting of being" (Wolin 1995, 42–61). Jacques Derrida and some of his followers have attempted to interpret Heidegger's attraction to Nazism as a philosophical rather than a political mistake; he conceived of the movement, so the argument goes, as a spiritual and cultural return to a pre-Socratic, polis-based renewal of German and occidental culture that would shift theory and praxis away from the subject/object legacy of Western thinking and consequently away from the planetary domination of technology, modern science and the "flight of the gods" (Derrida 1989). Derrida argues in *On Spirit*, that the use of the term "spirit" in Heidegger's infamous rector's address of 1934 indicated a step backwards from his own critique of the German humanist and idealist tradition explicated so adamantly in *Being and Time* (1927). In this debate, Jünger's intellectual trajectory can help support such a vindication of Heidegger because Jünger had an important influence in the 1920s and 1930s, but put much greater distance between himself and National Socialism than did Heidegger. Jünger also "spiritualized" his revolutionary battle against the Weimar Republic in a way that was generally free of Völkish, nordic, and racial ideas.[7] Some French Heideggerians (along with the general French reception) have overemphasized Jünger's distance from National Socialism, or even turned him into a resistance fighter.

A good example of this spiritualization of politics can be found in *Heidegger, Art and Politics*, in which Phillipe Lacoue-Labarthe attempts to "think" Auschwitz in a Heideggerian manner against Heidegger, locating in the *Ereignis* of the Holocaust a caesura which reveals the "truth of the West" as *techné* (Lacoue-Labarthe 1990, 44–45). Thinking about the essence of Nazism is, of course, different from approving it, but Lacoue-Labarthe leaves himself open to misunderstanding when he calls fascism "no more aberrant or inadequate" than any other of the "age's possible political forms" (Ibid., 107). In another recent context, Michael Zimmerman has stressed the indebtedness of Heidegger's understanding of the rueful effects of "planetary technology" to Ernst Jünger's influential essays of the 1920s, including "The Total Mobilization" in which Jünger postulated that modern technology was a revolutionary force about to sweep away all the stable structures of bourgeois society (Zimmerman 1990, 28ff.).

Pierre Bourdieu, seemingly in the minority of contemporary French intellectuals not bewitched by the legacy of Nietzsche, has shown how important Jünger's work was to Heidegger and how the ambiguous ideological structure of Jünger's Weimar writings could function as a surrogate revolutionary philosophy both for the conservative revolutionaries of the 1920s and radical Heideggerians today (Bourdieu 1991). Whereas Bourdieu remains wary of the continuing appeal of the antitechnological metaphysics of the conservative revolutionaries, Jean-Michel Palmier argues against rejecting *The Worker* simply because of its intellectual affinities with the revolutionary right and applauds the "immense intelligence" of its analysis of modern life (Palmier 1995). Philippe Lacoue-Labarthe also stresses Jünger's social, rather than racial understanding of politics. Jünger's intellectual association with National Bolshevism leads Lacoue-Labarthe to claim, incorrectly, that Jünger "refused from the outset to have any truck whatever" with National Socialism (Lacoue-Labarthe 1990, 24).

The shock in France that greeted the publication of Victor Farías's book *Heidegger et le Nazisme* in 1986—an exposé of Heidegger's involvement in Nazi politics revealing some, but not much already known in Germany—showed how extensive the radical forgetting of the Nazi era had become in France. How else can one explain the fact that the collaborationist past of writers like Ferdinand Celine, André

Therive, Pierre Benoit, Jean Giono, and Abel Hermant have not been exposed to nearly the kind of scrutiny that comparable German authors have been treated?

The above five points summarize some important reasons for the success of Jünger's career in France. Beyond these verifiable contentions, many people have speculated more loosely about Jünger's popularity. These theories might better be taken as a kind of barometer that registers attitudes and inclinations, rather than factual arguments. It is important to remember that the French heroicization of Jünger, his lionization as a "great" writer, has been supported and propagated, on the whole, by the conservative press, Jünger's personal friends, and national-conservative circles in France.[8] As in Germany, the Jünger reception in France has been marked by deep divisions between critics and apologists (Dornheim 1987; Neaman 1999). Still, in comparison to Germany, where his books are read by a relatively small number of devoted readers, Jünger is a household name among the substantial French reading public. An article on Jünger in the French press rarely appears without the epithet "*le plus grand écrivain allemand contemporain*," or similar designations.[9] It seems just as self-evident to the French that Jünger was "anti-Nazi" and "defiantly opposed to Hitler."

German observers of French intellectual life have advanced, over the years, several explanations for the "fascination" that draws readers to Jünger. Opinions differ as to whether the French have been seduced by a kind of evil genius, or, on the contrary, if the Germans have resisted a real genius. Rolf Hochhuth has argued for over twenty years that the confused discourse about the past has made Germans blind to a "great living author" (Hochhuth 1987). For the author of the famous 1962 play *The Deputy*, (condemning the Catholic Church's involvement in fascism), Jünger is an example of a world celebrity who has been recognized everywhere except in his own country, condemned as a "Nazi or even an anti-Semite" by people who have never read his books or know anything about his personal history. For Hochhuth, Jünger is "by far the most interesting German author, and it is no coincidence that the French esteem him above all others" (Hochhuth 1975).

Armin Mohler attributes Jünger's popularity in France to the fact that in contrast to other German writers, Jünger is viewed as a homegrown author (*einheimischer Autor*), one who even the normally anti-German right can embrace (Madler, aka Mohler 1976).

Georges Schlocker has pointed to Jünger's advocacy of anarchism as another plausible explanation for the French embrace. The French harbor special reverence for the outsider and iconoclast, one might argue, and Jünger's notorious elitism and refusal to conform can easily become enshrined in the pantheon of French radical individualism: In the mind of the Parisian intellectual, Jünger's icelandic mysticism suddenly becomes transformed into enlightened individualism.

> Someone who says no to the majority, like Montaigne and so many writers after him. . . . They see in Jünger the man who can grasp the big themes and locate the place where the individual stands. It is a contradictory attitude which says, "The writer should not become a hostage to political parties," and "It makes no sense to revolt against the state." . . . Jünger's works seem to the French to represent a battle against logic and functionalism, an emancipatory goal that in the meantime has attracted even the left. (Schlocker 1978)

Schlocker clearly views the lionization of Jünger by some French intellectuals as a symptom of the yearning for a new radicalism, even if its origins are on the right. This question of the French attraction to German philosophy considered "tainted" in Germany (from Nietzsche to Heidegger) goes well beyond the Jünger reception. After Solzhenitsyn's disclosures on the Soviet gulags were published in the 1970s, not a few disillusioned French Marxists turned to German philosophy in search of a different language with which to speak about alienation and bourgeois politics.[10] Jünger even encouraged the conversions. He reported to Henri Plard in 1977 with satisfaction of being informed that a group of French philosophers, "meta-Marxists" as he calls them, were giving seminars in Paris on *The Worker*.[11] Clearly the alleged postmodern abandonment of the "grand narrative" has not stopped some intellectuals from searching for a reenchanting cosmology that would integrate mythology and Nietzschean postmetaphysics into a new antilogocentric synthesis.

The French reception of Jünger points to the enormous difficulties involved in coming to any final judgments about Ernst Jünger's literary and political legacy. Almost everything he said or wrote becomes interpreted in the context of a complicated web of contested memory and historical associations. It seems that a core difficulty with Jünger's worldview lies in the suspicion that he attempts, in multifarious ways, to exonerate the majority of perpetrators and bystanders alike from any responsibility for the rise of Nazism. Primo Levi has written of the concentration camps that

> "many knew little and few knew everything" about what happened, but that whatever the case, since one cannot suppose that the majority of Germans lightheartedly accepted the slaughter, it is certain that the failure to divulge the truth about the Lagers represents one of the major collective crimes of the German people and the most obvious demonstration of the cowardice to which the Hitlerian terror had reduced them. . . . Without this cowardice the greatest excess would not have been carried out, and Europe and the world be different today. (Levi 1988, 15)

Jünger's message was just about the opposite. Since the original root of Hitlerism was to be found in an exaggerated Enlightenment faith in reason and domination of nature, culminating in a series of catastrophes and civil wars in the twentieth century, the German people were victims of history, at least as much as anyone had a right to the claim: "all suffered and therefore all must share the fruits of peace" (Jünger SW, 7: 207).[12] Many Germans did in fact suffer under Hitler's tyranny, while just as many were intoxicated by Hitler's victories and the ideology of the Super Race. Jünger conflates these two attitudes by lumping the German experience under Nazism as heroic stoicism: "das Ausharren auf verlorenem Posten" or waiting out a hopeless situation.[13] Like many of the protagonists in Jünger's novels (the two brothers in *The Marble Cliffs*, Lucien de Geer in *Heliopolis*, and Martin Venator in *Eumeswil*), Jünger could only imagine a "spiritual" resistance to tyranny. His response to the rise of Nazism was to watch from a distance. As Jean Cocteau said, some had dirty hands, others had clean hands, but Jünger had "no hands" (cited in Nevin 1996, 160). Henri Plard has aptly described the World War II diaries as a log of a sinking ship, the daily observations of the catastrophe by a sober mind (Plard 1955, 110). Jünger's philosophy of male, aristocratic virtue valorized the tragic heroism of facing up to destruction and defeat with silence. For Jünger to be a victim becomes a kind of test of strength and honor.[14]

One way of interpreting the very different reaction of the French to Jünger is to consider their own difficulties with coming to terms with the occupation and their initial acceptance of, even at times enthusiasm for Pétain. I have emphasized how Jünger's impeccable posture and his adoration of French culture set him apart from the caricature of the ugly, boorish Nazi thug. Even more than that, collaboration with an enemy like Jünger can be made to appear reasonable, even civilized. Jünger never abandoned the notion that collaboration was in fact in the service of a noble cultural goal. As he wrote to Plard in 1975,

> Both the Resistance and the collaboration have shades of light and darkness. The history of the Resistance included a large number of murders, also of innocent people. I think of my friend Medan, whose friendship with me cost him his life. The youth movements in Germany and France found themselves in a circle called "Jeune Europe" standing for ideas that even today have not yet been realized. . . . Goethe says there is hardly a crime that he couldn't have committed; that is true, more or less, I think for everybody. (Jünger to Plard, Sept. 19, 1975)

Jünger's understanding of the history of the Occupation was read by many in France as a story of shared suffering in a situation that offered few good choices. When all are victims, there remains no moral basis for differentiating good from evil, the murderers from the murdered. These are soothing nostrums, but the more historians examine the epoch of fascism, the more clear it becomes that there were far more choices than courageous people willing to make them. Moreover, the Vichy government could depend on the attitude of a large number of the French people who thought that the Third Republic and the Popular Front had justifiably failed in its attempt to create a French version of secular republicanism. The deep resentment of the French Revolution and its aftermath, modern mass Democracy, remained very much alive in the tradition of French Catholic antimodernism and Junger's writings spoke directly to that constituency.

The reception of Jünger tells us much about the very different ways the memory of fascism is confronted in France and Germany. In France the memory of Vichy is still fraught with controversy, as became clear when the Vichy official Maurice Papon was convicted by a French court of complicity in Nazi crimes only many years after he had served as a high official in various postwar French governments. Many French still consider the Vichy regime to have been an honorable arrangement in a period of national humiliation and Papon's trial therefore an affront to the Resistance he claimed to have served. In a broader context, the French reception of Jünger throws into relief the continuing appeal of critiques of Western liberal civilization, held responsible for the planetary domination of technology, historical triumphalism, the destruction of the environment, and the homogenization of culture, among many other sins. After the death of Marxism, some self-regarding revolutionary intellectuals on the left and right have joined forces by distilling such a broad critique from radical conservative ideas of the Weimar period. For too long historians have denigrated Fascist intellectuals as mediocre, misguided, or naive and have conceived of the intellectual grounding of fascism as opportunistic, irrational, muddled, and anachronistic. The reception of Jünger (and Heidegger) in France shows that intellectual fascism can and is read as a potent critique of liberal humanism and modernity. I have argued that French intellectuals have the dubious distinction of being less burdened by the taboo of taking Fascist ideas seriously than in Germany, a difference that explains, along with other peculiarities of French culture and the French memory of fascism, why Jünger is so much more popular and his ideas have a broader forum than in his native land.

Notes

1. Field Marshal Erwin Rommel, the Desert Fox, was one of Hitler's best generals. He just about defeated the British in Northern Africa in 1942–43. But he turned against Hitler as the war on the Eastern Front turned into a rout for the Germans. He was counting on Hitler to make an inspection of the Atlantic Wall sometime in May, when the landing of the Americans was expected in Normandy. Inexplicably, Hitler continued to direct the war from Berchtesgaden. After the invasion of Normandy, Hitler made an unexpected visit to the Western Front and was planning to come to La Roche-Guyon on June 19. Rommel had a golden opportunity to strike. As so often in the history of assassination attempts against Hitler, uncanny fate intervened. The bombing of England with the V-1 had begun from French territory on June 15. On June 18, one of the rockets strayed off course and came down near Margival, just about hitting the bunker where Hitler was meeting with Field Marshall Rundstedt. Depressed and disappointed with the performance of his Wunderwaffe, he returned immediately to Berchtesgaden. After that, the conspiracy against Hitler shifted to the Stauffenberg plan to kill Hitler at his bunker in East Prussia.

2. See Jünger, *SW*, 14: 383 ff. Jünger used the pseudonym "Lady Orphington" to hide an affair with her from his suspicious wife.

3. There are no hints of anti-Semitism in any of Jünger's published writings after the Second World War. But after a thirty year friendship, Jünger's Belgian translator Henri Plard broke off their relationship because Jünger allegedly defended Pierre Laval's anti-Semitism. Henri Plard, interview by Elliot Neaman in Henri Plard's home in Brussels, March 7, 1990).

4. *The Worker (Der Arbeiter)* is still a very controversial book, which sets out, in programmatic fashion, the contours of a new Fascist order in Europe and beyond, brought about by the revolutionary transformations of industrial society. Jünger's answer to the political stalemate of Weimar Democracy as seen from the vantage point of the fateful year 1932 was a broad alliance between Catholic and independent trade unions and the Nazi labor organizations with the backing of the army, in other words, the kind of social revolution that Gregor Strasser and other radicals in the SA hoped to achieve.

Parliamentary Democracy would be replaced by a corporatist state and a benevolent military dictatorship. This was very close to the plan that General Kurt von Schleicher tried to enact in his capacity as the last Weimar chancellor before Hitler took power in January 1933. The plan failed because Hitler sabotaged it and crushed Strasser's power base in the party, but the program remained as an option until Hitler finally eliminated the power of the SA in the so-called Roehm Putsch of June 1934.

5. Paulhan was managing editor at Gallimard after 1945. See Michael Syrotinski, "Some Wheat and Some Chaff: Jean Paulhan and the Post-War Literary Purge in France," *Studies in Twentieth Century Literature* 16, No. 2 (summer, 1992): 249.

6. In the wake of the De Man Affair in 1987, Jeffrey Mehlman's linking of deconstruction in toto to French collaboration in World War II, and amnesty attempts afterward, has, of course, been met with indignation by many literary critics. See for example Ian Balfour, "Difficult Reading: De Man's Interaries" in Werner Hamacher, *Responses*, 6-20. See also Mehlman's contribution (324-33), and many other selections in Werner Hamacher, et. al., *Responses, On Paul de Man's Wartime Journalism* (Lincoln: University of Nebraska Press).

7. The distinction between "spirit" and "race" erases the large gray zone where plenty of room remained to support alternative, equally problematic "solutions" to Germany's Weimar dilemma. See Anson Rabinbach, *In the Shadow of Catastrophe* (Berkeley: University of California Press, 1997), esp. 97-128.

8. This is particularly true of readers who grew up in the 1930s and 1940s. See Georges Schlocker, *"Fernweh nach den Göttern: Was die Franzosen an Ernst Jünger fasziniert,"* Süddeutsche Zeitung, 4 July 1978. But in both France and Germany a new generation of the counterculture, interested in esoteric subjects, (and unbothered by the disputes over Jünger's past), discovered Jünger's mysticism and celebration of drug experiences. See Jacques Le Rider, *"Les nouveaux lecteurs d'Ernst Jünger,"* Le Monde, July 19, 1981. Currently forty-eight titles of Jünger's books are available in French translation, twelve of them in paperback. Albrecht Betz contends that Jünger's popularity in France has been exaggerated and points to the small influence he has had on other French writers. But does the testimony of writers constitute the decisive criterion? How does one explain the many official kudos, the lavish praise of politicians and a wide range of intellectuals, or the planned Pléade edition? See A. Betz, *"Qui lit Jünger?"* Le Monde Dimanche, 19 September 1982.

9. See *"L'autre Goethe: Jünger, le viellard inspire,"* L'Express, 19 May 1989. Other examples could almost be quoted at random. Variations include *"un très grand écrivan,"* Jean Louis de Rambures, *"L'enigma Ernst Jünger,"* L'Express, 11–17 February 1974; *"le plus Francais des écrivains allemands," "Ernst Jünger un veilleur solitaire,"* Telerama, 22 May 1978; *"En France, c'est le plus populaire des auteurs d'outre-Rhin."* Lèopold Sanchez, *"Jünger 87 ans: tous ses cheveux et la dent dure,"* S, 4 September 1982.

10. Jünger mentions a certain "Lévy," presumably the philosopher Bernard Henri Lévy, who coined the phrase "New Philosophy" and, like André Glucksmann, was at this stage reevaluating student radicalism after reading Solzhenitsyn's memoirs. Jünger to Plard, Aug. 15, 1977. On Lévy see Paul Berman, *A Tale of Two Utopias; The Political Journey of the Generation of 1968* (New York: W. W. Norton, 1996), pp. 278–79.

11. See Paul Berman, *A tale of Two Utopias.*

12. On the essential differences between the conservative critique of the Enlightenment and Adorno and Horkheimer's famous treatise, see Anson Rabinbach, *In the Shadow of Catastrophe*, pp. 166–198.

13. Jünger borrowed the phrase from Oswald Spengler, see *Der Mensch und die Technik* (Hamburg: Beck, 1931/1961).

14. The philosopher Alfred von Martin therefore called Jünger's heroism *"das schweigende Heldentum"* and pointed out that Jünger was particularly fascinated by cities like Cathargo and Jerusalem that had experienced fateful destruction in war. See *Der heroische Nihilismus und seine Überwindung* (Krefeld: Scherpe, 1948), pp. 169–70.

References

Bargatsky, Walter. Hotel Majestic. *Ein Deutscher im besetzten Frankreich.* Basel and Vienna: Herder, 1987.

Bordieu, Pierre. *The Political Ontology of Martin Heidegger.* Trans. Peter Collier. Stanford: Stanford University Press, 1991.

Burtin, Phillipe. *France Under the Germans; Collaboration and Compromise.* Trans. Janet Lloyd. New York: New Press, 1996.

Busche, Jürgen. *Helmut Kohl: Anatomie eines Erfolgs.* Berlin: Berlin Verlag, 1998.

Brincourt, André. "Malraux: La legende du siécle." *Le Figaro Littéraire* (May 2, 1989).

Derrida, Jacques. *Of Spirit; Heidegger and the Question.* Trans. Geoffrey Bennington and Rachel Bowlby. Chicago: University of Chicago Press, 1989.

Dornheim, Lianne. *Vergleichende Rezeptionsgeschichte: Das literarische Frühwerk in Deutschland, England und Frankreich.* Frankfurt: Lang, 1987.

Fries, Thomas. "Paul de Man's 1940–1942 Articles in Context." In *Responses: On Paul de Man's Wartime Journalism.* Eds. Werner Hamacher, Tom Keenan, Neil Hertz. Lincoln: University of Nebraska Press, 1987.

Fritz-Vannhame, Joachim. "Langer Händedruck zur Marseillaise: Die historische Geste von Verdun." *Mannheimer Morgen* (Sept. 24, 1984).

Grunfeld, Frederic V. *Prophets Without Honor.* New York: Kodansha, 1955.

Hartman, Geoffrey H. *Bitburg in Moral and Political Perspective.* Bloomington: Indiana University Press, 1986.

Heller, Gerhard. *Un allemand à Paris, 1940–44.* Paris: Editions du Seuill, 1981.

Hochhuth, Rolf. "Wir Deutschen hatten einen wie Ernst Jünger noch nie." *Welt am Sonntag* (November 8, 1987).

―――. "Der Dichter in Uniform." *Abendzeitung* (Hamburg) (March 29, 1975).

Jünger, Ernst. *Sämtliche Werke.* Stuttgart: Klett, 1979.

Klett, Michael. "Aristocrat, il rêvait d'autre chose." *Le Monde,* 19 February 1998.

Lacoue-Labarthe, Phillipe. *Heidegger, Art and Politics: The Fiction of the Political.* Trans. Chris Turner. Oxford: Basil Blackwell, 1990.

Laqueur, Walter. *Weimar: A Cultural History, 1918–1933.* New York: Putnam, 1974.

Levi, Primo. *The Drowned and the Saved.* New York: Simon and Schuster, 1988.

Luce, Alfred Fabre. *Anthologie de la nouvelle Europe.* Paris: Plon, 1942.

———. *Journal de la France.* Paris: Plon, 1939.

Madler (aka Mohler,) Anton. "Ernst Jünger ein Kennwort in Frankreich." *Die Welt* (February 2, 1976).

Mehlman, Jeffrey. "Writing and Deference: The Politics of Literary Adulation." *Representations* 15 (summer, 1986).

Mühleisen, Horst. "Im Segelboot über das Bermuda Dreieck." *Christ and Welt* (January 25, 1986).

Nadeau, Maurice. "Le combat d'Ernst Jünger." *combat* (September 20, 1951).

Neaman, Elliot. *A Dubious Past; Ernst Jünger and the Politics of literature after Nazism.* Berkeley: University of California Press, 1999.

Nevin, Thomas. *ErnstJünger and Germany: Into the Abyss, 1914–1945.* Durham: Duke University Press, 1996.

Palmier, Jean-Michel. *Ernst Jünger: Rêveries sur un chasseur de cicindèles.* Paris: Hachette, 1995.

Plard, Henri. "Ex ordine shandytorum." In *Freundschaftliche Begegnungen.* Ed. Armin Mohler. Frankfurt: Klostermann, 1955.

———. "Ernst Jünger in Frankreich." *Text and Zeichen* 105/106 (January, 1990).

Roy, Jean-Henry. "Journal." *Le temps Modernes* 74 (December, 1951).

Schlocker, Georges. "Fernweh nach den Göttern." *Süddeutsche Zeitung* (July 4, 1978).

Weber, Albrecht. *Ernst Jünger und der französische Geist.* Ph.D. diss., Universität Erlangen, 1949.

Wolin, Richard. *Labyrinths: Explorations in the Critical History of Ideas.* Amherst, MA: University of Massachusetts Press, 1995.

Zimmerman, Michael. *Heidegger's Confrontation with Modernity; Technology, Politics, Art.* Bloomington, IN: Indiana University Press, 1990.

Part V
Postmodern Reflections

Chapter 12

ROMY SCHNEIDER, *LA PASSANTE DU SANS-SOUCI*

Discourses of *Vergangenheitsbewältigung*, Feminism, and Myth

Nina Zimnik

> . . . *puisque le mythe est une parole, tout peut être mythe, qui est justifiable d'un discours.*
>
> Roland Barthes, "Le Mythe, aujourd'hui."

Myths, Roland Barthes, wrote in the decidedly secular world of the late 1950s, are ways people make sense of reality. Austrians, Germans, and French have recently been invited to explore a new one, "the Romy Schneider myth." On September 23, 1998, the actress would have turned sixty, and the public took note. Many art houses in Germany (*Kommunale Kinos*) screened retrospectives of her work, TV stations aired her famous films, and, in early 2000, the readers of the French newspaper *Le Parisien* together with TV channel *La Cinquième* elected her actress of the century—before Marilyn Monroe, Catherine Deneuve, and Brigitte Bardot. Lesbian feminist icon Alice Schwarzer published a Schneider biography subtitled *Mythos und Leben* (*Myth and Life*),[1] the usual coffee table and "remembering Romy" books came out, and even an exhibition, echoing the expectations of the curators who called it a "traveling exhibition," started touring in Vienna in 1998.

As any star, Romy Schneider answers to a multitude of dreams and desires—identification figure for the women's movement in the 1970s, draw for francophile art house clientele in Germany, gay men's icon, to name only a few. Yet, her last film could be seen as paradigmatic for the contemporary discursive positionings of the star in Germany, *La passante du Sans-Souci* directed by Jacques Rouffio (1982). Playing both in the Berlin of the 1930s and the Paris of the 1980s, the film condenses some of the topoi with which either Schneider herself or her biographers portray the vagaries and vicissitudes of her life and displaces them onto the heroine: emigration from Germany to France, premature tragic death, abusive relationships and unhappy love, financial problems, alcohol and substance abuse etc., intertwining individual decisions and fate with the greater political picture, that is, with National Socialism and its legacy. This article investigates representations of *Vergangenheitsbewältigung* (coming-to-terms-with-the-past, notably with National Socialism) set forth by the film and of feminism in popular discourses on Schneider.

When Schneider died of cardiac arrest at age forty-two in her Paris apartment, she had appeared in sixty films and worked with such acclaimed directors as Claude Chabrol, Luchino Visconti, and Orson Welles. But most often, Schneider is remembered for her cinematic *pas de deux* with Claude Sautet. Her work generally divides into two periods: critics like to contrast the three *Sissi* films and the few films surrounding them with her later work in France, work that is considered "serious"; and in this valuation of the French tradition, her stay in Hollywood comes off as an uneventful escapade, a misfit. To be precise: The early work in Germany is often considered reactionary. In the remake of *Mädchen in Uniform* (1958), for instance, Schneider as the lesbian student, takes the hand of the headmistress, a gesture that signifies an acceptance on the part of the younger generation of the Fascist powers represented by the headmistress—a sequence that ideologically resituates the anti-Fascist original significantly. Playing empress Sissi, Schneider ascended to early stardom as a teenager. The *Sissi* series is notorious because it offered the German public of the 1950s a stockhouse of redemptive fantasies: Sissi consolidates the Austrian-Hungarian empire—albeit to the German national anthem. For the German fans of the 1950s then, her move to Paris to live with her "gaulle cock" boyfriend, Alain Delon, presented a veritable scandal, "treason." Since Schneider developed a political consciousness in the wake of the 1960s and denounced German fascism, she became the star of a younger generation, of the children of the NS perpetrators, who didn't feel like extending their hands to criminals. The press followed her private life closely, and especially women were impressed with her: just as in the movies where Schneider played strong, emotional characters who fought for their personal fulfillment, Schneider led an often unconventional (love) life. Moreover, Schneider inserted herself into the German women's movement at a crucial point. In 1971, she supported the pro-choice activities launched by *Stern* magazine, where women confessed publicly to having had an abortion (*Ich habe abgetrieben* [*Stern*, June 6, 1971]). Thus, from a German vantage point, the Schneider revival tends to imply a reconsideration of the sociohistorical coordinates of Schneider's life as a woman as well as a German, to be more precise as a German woman who "emigrated" to France to come into her own—and who failed miserably.

In *La passante du Sans-Souci*, Schneider plays Elsa Wiener, a gentile Berlin woman married to Michel, a gentile German publisher, during the Third Reich. The story starts when they take in Max Baumstein, a Jewish boy who, after a group of Nazis killed his father and beat him up, suffers from a stiff leg. Eventually, Elsa flees with Max from Berlin to Paris where she works as a cabaret entertainer at *Le Rajah*. On the way to Paris, her husband is caught by the Gestapo and gets five years in a concentration camp. In order to free him, Elsa spends the night with a prominent regular of *Le Rajah*, a local Parisian Gestapo officer called Ruppert von Legaart (played by Mathieu Carrière as a melancholic Nazi dandy). Legaart promises her Michel's freedom in return for her favors but has them both killed on the spot as it were, namely, in front of the café Sans-Souci, when Michel finally arrives in Paris. This diegesis is framed by a contemporary, that is, early 1980s setting: Max (Michel Piccoli) is now a man in his fifties and loves his wife Lina, a woman who looks like Elsa (Schneider plays a double role). "*Inhaber einer der bedeutensten Schweizer Versicherungen*" (owner of one of the most important Swiss insurance agencies), Max is also president of "Solidarité Internationale," a leftist organization that he founded. Through his work on behalf of a Paraguayan prisoner and victim of torture, he inadvertently runs into Ruppert von Legaart again who now calls himself Federico Lego and is Paraguay's ambassador to France. Max kills him and has to stand trial, the perspective from which most of the film's flashbacks start. He gets five years probation. Shortly before the end of the film, during a sequence when Max and Lina take a break at the Sans-Souci after his release from prison, a text on a horizontal band runs through the middle of the screen, telling the viewer that Max and Lina were killed six months after this meeting:

Sechs Monate später wurden Max und Lina Baumstein im Erdgeschoss ihres Hauses erschlagen. . . . Zu dem Attentat hat sich nie jemand bekannt. . . . Die Attentäter wurden niemals identifiziert. . . . Sechs Monate später wurden Max und Lina Baumstein im Erdgeschoss ihres Hauses erschlagen. [Six months later, Max and Lina Baumstein were beaten to death on the first floor of their house . . . the assassins were never identified . . . Six months later, Max and Lina Baumstein were beaten to death on the first floor of their house . . .] The end

As the credits state, the film is based on the 1936 novel *La Passante du Sans-Souci* by Joseph Kessel, *Académie Française*, an author who also wrote the book that Buñuel turned into his famous *Belle de Jour* (the title role went to Catherine Deneuve after Schneider had turned it down). Joseph Kessel's text is a typical encountering the whore story in the tradition of the nineteenth-century French novel. While getting drunk at one of the places he frequents, the café Sans-Souci, the narrator, a writer, develops an obsession with *la passante*, an enigmatic woman whom he first spots through the foggy window panes of the Sans-Souci. He ends up meeting *la passante*, that is, Elsa Wiener, a number of times. Like later in the film, Elsa had to flee Germany because of Michel's work, takes Max with her to Paris, and tries to free her husband from the camp etc. The novel chronicles her decline into prostitution and drugs, tying, as the opening paragraphs already indicate in their poignant use of *"la vitre embuée"* (foggy window pane) onto which *"une très vague cendre crépusculaire"* (a very vague crepuscular ash), [11] falls when she walks by, the (already Baudelairian) themes of subjectivity and reflection as well as distance and proximity to decay.

In general, Kessel paints Elsa's life in much darker colors than Rouffio did. Rouffio also added the frame that extends Kessel's story into the Paris of the 1980s and clearly focuses the diegesis onto the characters' encounter with fascism. To that end, Kessel's story itself was changed. In 1936, Elsa and Michel Wiener are not assassinated by her Nazi lover. Michel continues his successful career in publishing, and Elsa dies a suicidal death because her husband ceases to love her, that is, at the moment when he sees that her beauty had faded during the relentless fight for his life. Further, the Legaart character is more pronounced. While Kessel describes Ruppert von Legaart as *"maniaque," "sadique"* (202), and *"[c]ocaïnomane par accès"* (207)—characteristics that might also sketch Rouffio's Legaart — , Kessel's Legaart is physically repulsive. In the novel, Legaart is entirely devoid of the master ingredient of that "fascinating fascism" whose "seduction is beauty" (Sontag 1981, 105), an air that Mathieu Carrière sets forth skillfully. And although Rouffio refrains from details of their fatal night, his Legaart imparts an act on Elsa that, as Susan Sontag would put it, is being "situated on the furthest reach of the sexual experience: when sex becomes most purely sexual, that is, severed from personhood, from relationships, from love" (105), that is, tied in with the psychology of sadomasochism.—For the literary French consciousness of the mid-1930s, it was obviously still possible to entertain certain fancies about life in a concentration camp. In the novel, the camp actually has a ward where patients enjoy some form of medical care; the camp doctor lets Michel go because he is sick. And the camp has a functioning, honest banking system where Elsa can send money to support her ailing husband—the reason why Elsa prostitutes herself shamelessly which in turn, makes her loose her beauty and fall prey to alcohol and drugs.[2]

Such stories were hardly plausible forty-six years later. Whereas Kessel's narrative unfolds around the relations the "I" entertains with *"la passante du Sans-Souci"*, namely, Elsa, the film drops this perspective entirely. The Sans-Souci is now merely an accidental place where the Wieners get assassinated, and, most important, the film an account of Max's first-person flashbacks and his life in the 1980s. Key is that Rouffio adds a character to the script, namely, Elsa's friend, Charlotte, a woman who is first her colleague at *Le Rajah*, and, as the viewer learns during the court hearings a good fifty years later, ends up working for forty years as a *Schlepper* (prostitute) at Place Pigalle. It was Charlotte who, in 1945, after she herself had been liberated from a camp, attached a commemorative table to the outside wall of the Sans-Souci. Shown briefly during the last sequence—except for the names and the word *allemands*, one cannot read it though—the table replaces the tomb stone that, as a hoary Charlotte recounts on the witness stand during Max's trial, French Nazi collaborators didn't grant the victims.

Charlotte's archival prosthesis for memory, defended by Max's act of murder and endangered by hate crime half a century later, presents the backdrop for Rouffio's last sequence, a monologue where Max passionately affirms his love for Lina. In this sequence, Delerue's film music underlines that indifference was killed at the Sans-Souci (*on a tué l'indifférence* . . . , are the lyrics that lead into the credits). The last words of the film thus celebrate the resistance of Charlotte who doesn't just have a heart of gold but also a good deal of *chutzpah*. First a victim of the Nazis, then, as a prostitute, disenfranchised by patriarchal structures of desire, Charlotte does, however, live to see some form of justice: Legaart's death, and the respect of Frau Präsidentin, the female prosecutor of the case, and the bravos in the courtroom applauding both her final statement and Max's deed *"Meist ist es so, daß diese Schweine wohlbehütet im Bett sterben. Diesmal hat's einen erwischt. Einen Scheißkerl weniger—das erlebt man besonders gern!"* [Usually, pigs like him [Legaart, N.Z.] die in the comfort of their bed. This time, someone got caught. One asshole less—one likes to see that!]. Extending the theme of mourning and remembering to real life, Schneider dedicated *La Passante* to "David and his father" in the credits, that is, to her son who had a fatal accident in 1981 and to her first husband, the German Jewish stage actor and director Harry Meyen, a camp survivor who committed suicide in 1979.

The point of the film is, of course, political and pedagogical: the deaths of Lina and Max show that Fascist powers continue to threaten humanity. Physically represented in the character of Legaart, the enemy remains the same; and vice versa, there is a continuity between old and new "anti-Fascist" causes. Even if the old Nazis aren't personally responsible for all the injustice and political brutality in this world, they are in spirit. At the end of the film, a respectable looking young man spits in Elsa's face and explains: " *Das war für deinen Juden, du Schlampe*" [That's for the Jew, you slut]. Thus, when *Solidarité Internationale* fights *"contre la repression and pour la défense des libertés"* [against repression and for the defense of liberties], Max's anti-Fascist struggle is linked to the gamut of leftist causes popular in France when Rouffio shot his film; support for victims of torture in Latin America "especially in Chile, Bolivia and Paraguay"; imprisoned workers "in Persia, Turkey and other countries"; and IRA prisoners who should be granted the status of "political prisoners."

However, precisely this last sequence where Max and Lina meet at the Sans-Souci was significantly altered when the film was shown on German TV, *Bayrischer Rundfunk*, on December 15, 1999. Cut out from the shot were the frames with the text band that informed the viewer about Max and Lina's imminent deaths. The programmers also omitted the frames of the bartender of the Sans-Souci who asks to shake Max' hand to congratulate him on his courageous deed, thus diminishing the anti-Fascist community and also reducing the potential approval of the masses of murder. *Bayrischer Rundfunk* went to even greater pedagogical length when it edited out the murder of Max and Lina. The result is a happy ending, affirming the resurrection of Elsa as Lina and uniting the old fighters with the next generation, that is, in the moving court scenes when Max, Charlotte, and Maurice meet again after fifty years (Maurice was Elsa's admirer who had taken in Max after her death).[3]

In short, the recent TV version is a classical redemption fantasy. Or, as Walter Benjamin explains in his "Theses on History":

> The kind of happiness that could arouse envy in us exist only in the air we have breathed, among people we could have talked to, women who could have given themselves to us. In other words, our image of the past is indissolubly bound up with the image of redemption. The same applies to our view of the past, which is the concern of history. The past carries with it a [secret, not "temporal," NZ] index by which it is referred to redemption . . . ("Aren't we touched by a whiff of air that has surrounded our ancestors, too? Isn't there an echo of muted voices in the ones to whom we lend an ear? Don't the women we woo have sisters whom they didn't know?") There is a secret agreement between past generations and our present one. Our coming was expected on earth.[4]

Within the logic of the film, Lina is the miraculously actualized past conditional of Elsa, Max' dream come true, the woman who "could have given herself" to him, the "sister" whom Elsa didn't know. Typical for a *nouvelle vague* male desire, little Max loved Elsa with all his Oedipal longing—staged by Rouffio with the obligatory Freudian prop, the soft brown fur coat, and from the traditional voyeuristic perspective (Max watches Elsa undress when she comes home from the club).

Casting Schneider in a double role allows Rouffio to "present" history, thus wresting its victims out of the hands of the enemy although this enemy has not stopped winning, as Benjamin put it in Thesis VI. Lina, a virtual Elsa, guarantees that the past coexists with the present it once was. Through the continuity of the double role, Schneider reconciles memory, the picture of Elsa, with perception, Lina in the now, promising a repeatable integration of the past and, therefore, happiness ever after—as long as she "lives"—which is the philosophical reason why the German programmers of *Bayrischer Rundfunk* had to elide her death. As long as Lina stays alive in film, lives ever after in the logic of the diegesis, the horror of the Holocaust is tamed, the *Vergangenheitsbewältigung* successful.

Schneider was, of course, perfect for this double role. She herself was dogged by a split identity of which the art house public of the early-1980s was well aware. The clean German Sissi had metamorphosed into a sensuous French *"actrice"* and lived out her own dream of *"vivre libre à Paris"* (lyrics of Rouffio's *passante*), away from her oppressive family and, in retroactive assessment, mining the epitomic space of heterosexual love for the political and aesthetic freedom it harbored. Just as the viewer follows Elsa who, in Delerue's film music, *"s'enfuiait devant sa vie à Berlin . . .pour vivre libre à Paris"* [fled from her life in Berlin . . . in order to live freely in Paris], the media has offered ample material to follow Schneider's own, albeit significantly different, *"triste voyage"* (sad voyage) to France. On the cinematic level, Rouffio sustains the *Doppelgänger* motif through his constant use of mirrors and reflection devices, suggesting that both Elsa and Lina are not truly "one," neither two self-identical characters, nor simply one character that extends through time in two different emanations, but refer to each other through time and space. Both as Elsa and as Lina, Schneider is, for instance, regularly shot before a visually split background, for example, when Lina combs her hair in her hotel room at the beginning of the film, the vertical line of the bed in the background runs right through her torso, or after the fated night with Legaart, Elsa sits down in her hotel room, turning her back to a mirror that reflects her image twice.

Similarly, one should note the repeated use of open doors in the background of the frames, see for example, Legaart at Le Rajah or the shot after Elsa had saved Max's life: first Elsa hovers over Max drawing him off the street; after the cut, we see Lina in a medium shot in front of an open door as if in a Deleuzian movement-image, Elsa had just entered from an adjacent space. This contiguous unfolding of space suggests that time is "in joint," and sustains a logic and an ethics where the present has a door to the past, the future emerges out the past and can be forged in a linear manner, thus articulating a political hope that the film sets forth.

In addition, most of the doors in the film are glass doors. Already the establishing shot shows Schneider first behind a car window, second behind a glass door, the Paris airport entrance, then shows her opening it and rushing on to pick up Max. An interior decorating staple of 1970s architecture, glass is a medium that conveys both distance and proximity and while it is transparent, can also become a mirror and offer multidimensional perspectives. In the second shot (medium to medium close-up), one sees Max walking by a glass partition that reflects surrounding activities onto his face, turning Max into a carrier of time. Announced by his limp, events both inscribe themselves onto his body and, as if his body were the taint of the mirror that defies historical sublimation, it enters into new historical contexts, fraught, however, with the horrors of the past that clamored, loudly and belatedly, for attention in 1982 France. Immediately after shooting Lego, Max opens a glass door that had reflected the environment onto his face, making his way, as it were, through the images that kept inscribing themselves onto him. Elsa, in contrast, is barely visible after she slept with Legaart. When Legaart drops her off in front of her hotel, the viewer can hardly make her out in his car.

Perhaps Schneider's reemergence in the late 1990s also has traumatic functions, this time broadening the discussions of fascism by feminist perspectives and reinvigorating well-known feminist tenets, serving, not unlike Max's and Elsa's in Rouffio's film, as a Lacanian petit a that precipitates a wealth of symbolic activity. Whereas Schneider's Elsa escapes some of the sexist brunt of Kessel's novel, in real life, Schneider was—the well-known ingredient of the Schneider myth—not all that adept in that aspect. Alice Schwarzer starts her 1998 biography of Romy Schneider with a description of a talk show that took place in the fall of 1974 on German TV, in a chapter entitled *"Die Schöne und das Biest"* [Beauty and the Beast]. "Beauty" Schneider, actually meets two "beasts," that is, first Bubi Scholz, the boxing champion, who in 1984 killed his wife but was able, despite feminist protest, to leave prison after two years. The third talk show guest was Burkhard Driest. Driest, enfant terrible of the 1970s, was a law school drop-out who became famous after robbing a bank and writing a book about his prison experience (*Die Verrohung des Franz Blum*). Infatuated with his macho habitus, directors offered him theater and film roles, the first being that of Kowalski in *A Streetcar Named Desire*, the Tennessee Williams character who rapes his aging, depressed sister-in-law. In 1979, Schwarzer relates, Driest was found guilty of violently raping the actress Monika Lundi. Now, despite the fact that Driest ignores her completely, Schneider tells him during the show: "*Sie gefallen mir. Sie gefallen mir sehr*" [I like you. I like you very much] tugging—the height of humiliation according to Schwarzer—at his elbow to obtain his attention (Schwarzer 1998, 16).[5] The point of Schwarzer's opening scenario seems to be that Schneider had a tendency to hook up with abusive macho men whom she tried to seduce, all the while locating herself or being located in a fantasy structure where when beauty only kissed the beast, love would be the answer. Thus, Schwarzer's description of the actress is reminiscent of certain feminist rhetorics that marked the beginning of the second women's movement, for example, Kate Millett's *Sexual Politics* (1969; 1971 in German translation *Sexus und Herrschaft*). Versed in both Freud and Marx and weaned on a Frankfurt School criticism that short circuits psychoanalytic and Marxist discourses, texts like that present a woman who desires an abusive man as a masochist.

To comment further on the memorable encounter of 1974, Schwarzer takes recourse to an article that appeared in the *ZEIT*, Germany's leading intellectual weekly:

> *Sie [ZEIT, NZ] befand, daß in dieser Phase der ausklingenden, "Politisierung" und der beginnenden, "Innerlichkeit" hier, "das vom Leben geschlagene feinsinnige Bewußtsein laut mit dem grobschlächtigen, kriminellen Unterbewußtsein in uns allen" gesprochen und geradeheraus gesagt habe: "Sie gefallen mir sehr."* [The ZEIT noted that in the phase of the decline in "politicization" and the rise of "interiority," the "consciousness beaten up by life had talked with the brutish, criminal subconsciousness that is inside all of us," and this consciousness had said: "I like you very much."] (17).

According to the *ZEIT*, in the wake of the 1960s and their "politicization," Schneider and Driest define the thesis and antithesis of a dialectically dehiscing German interiority, notably a female consciousness "beaten up by life" that, as if none of its painful experiences and refined thought processes had left a trace of reason, attempts to flirt with the destructive drives of masculinity. In 1974, "consciousness beaten up by life," is, however, on TV to promote her latest film *Le train* (Granier-

Deferre 1973). Here, Schneider plays Anna Kupfer, a Jew who flees the Nazis, and is brutally murdered. In an interview with the *Deutsches Allgemeines Sonntagsblatt*, Schneider declares:

> *Diese Rolle ist eine Rolle, der ich in all meine letzten Filmen am meisten zustimme. Das Mädchen handelt, denkt und liebt so, wie ich es auch tun würde. . . . Um ein Signal gegen die Nazi-Typen zu setzen, die in Deutschland noch immer etwas zu sagen haben, habe ich mitgemacht. . . . Ich identifiziere mich mit der Rolle.* [Out of all my latest films, this is the role I agree with the most. The girl acts, thinks and loves the way I do. . . . I accepted the role in order to set a sign against the Nazi guys who still have a say in Germany. . . . I identify with this role.] (Seydel 212, cites from the paper Deutsches Allgemeines Sonntagsblatt, December 15, 1974.)

Le train marks a certain break in Schneider's career since it was the first of a series of films in which Schneider plays a Nazi victim. Eight years later, *La passante* was the last one, and since it is also the last film Schneider made before her death on May 29, 1982, and rife with personal innuendos, the fan literature often portrays it as her legacy. Partially echoing Schneider's own declaration a propos *Le train*, Schwarzer writes:

> *Romys Identifikation mit den Opfern der Elterngeneration hatte unstreitig politische Motive—aber nicht nur. Vermutlich spielte auch ein ganz persönliches Motiv eine Rolle: Nämlich die Abrechnung einer Frau mit einer Männergeneration, für die in Romys Fall in erster Linie ihr späterer Stiefvater, "Daddy" Blatzheim stand. Und das war wohl nicht nur bei Romy so. Wie oft eigentlich haben auch die "Terroristinnen" der 70er und 80er Jahre nicht nur die fremden alten Nazi-Bonzen, sondern auch den vertrauten Vater oder Onkel gemeint? Wie oft war es nicht nur der allgemeine politische Haß, sondern auch der ganz persönliche auf den Mann, der sie mißbraucht hatte?* [No doubt, Romy's identification with the victims of the parents' generation was motivated by politics but not solely. Probably, a personal motif played a role as well: Namely, a woman's revenge on the generation of men who was first and foremost represented by "Daddy" Blatzheim. And Romy was not the only one who felt that way. Just how often did the "terrorists" of the seventies and eighties mean not only the unknown old Nazi functionaries, but also the familiar fathers and uncles? How often was it not simply general political hatred but also the strictly personal hatred for the man who had abused them?] (37/38)

While the *ZEIT* offers a glimpse at an ethics and aesthetics of male-female relations that marked the prevailing ideology in the 1970s, Schwarzer's and also Schneider's comments situate them further. The *ZEIT* article picks up on an intersubjective matrix of violence where the refined woman desires a brutish, criminal man. Just as Schwarzer describes Schneider sitting next to Bubi Scholz, the context of the remarks that she cites from the *ZEIT*, that is, the opening of *Le train*, relates this particular form of heterosexual desire to German fascism, indicating that such desire is often played out explicitly before this specific historical background. In Schwarzer's opening scene, a submissive Schneider begs for the attention of a rapist-to-be, facing in fact as the singular in the title indicates, only one male "beast," split into the old Scholz and the young, leftist macho Driest. This assumption of an intricate relationship between patriarchy and fascism seems to be the underlying premise of Schwarzer's argument. A good twenty pages after the representation of the 1974 talk show, Schwarzer jumps from "a woman's revenge" on the (NS) generation of her father, pars pro toto to Schneider's stepfather, and to the most notorious women of the 1970s, the "terrorists," uniting Schneider and, presumably, RAF women like Ulrike Meinhof and Gudrun Ensslin in their interests.

Thus, according to Schwarzer, Schneider's work as an actress ties the personal to the political in very specific ways. Through certain semantic elisions, patriarchal abuse of the daughters merges with Nazi crimes, the Holocaust, and as an aside, leads directly into terrorist activity. Let us look at the structure of the second sentence of the above quote: "No doubt, Romy's identification with the victims of the parents' generation was motivated by politics but not solely" Schwarzer writes and continues: "Probably, a personal motive played a role as well: Namely, a woman taking revenge on the generation of men who was first and foremost represented by "Daddy" Blatzheim." How can "a woman's revenge" be a "personal" motive of Schneider? that is, a cause for Schneider's "identification with the victims of her parents' generation?" Is "a woman's revenge" really her own "motive," that "something within a person (as need, idea, organic state, or emotion) that incites him [*sic*] to action" as Webster's dictionary puts it? If we assume that the use of the personal pronoun and the stress on a "personal motive" runs counter to the impersonal generalization expressed in "a woman's revenge," the question imposes itself just whose "personal" motives Schwarzer "probably" "means" and what they are. Be it as it may, the "victims of the parents' generation" have been clearly defined. And, by her own account, Schneider "identified" with the Jews. To Schwarzer then, daughters who retaliate, who punish their "fathers and uncles," or "the man" for "abusing" them, daughters who hate from a "strictly personal" vantage point, actually become the executives of a restitutive world politics given that at least their "fathers and uncles" are likely to have many skeletons in the closet. In short, "daughter" and "victim" and "father" and "perpetrator" are but two foils who often intersect in one and the same intersubjective constellation.[6] But whereas the victims of the Holocaust were just that, a generation later German gentile daughters are in a position to fight back.

However problematic the gesture of paralleling women and Jews, and thus of genocide and incest for instance, is, it does characterize some of the intellectual activities of the 1970s where German fascism provided the soundboard for analyses of sexual identities and relations. Indicated by Schwarzer's account of the 1970s talk show, these relations, insofar as they involved abuse, were often metaphorized as sadomasochistic.[7] What is behind such confluences? Romy Schneider is the daughter of Magda Schneider and Wolf Albach-Retty, both acclaimed Nazi actors who entertained close relations with high politicians and the *Führer* himself. According to an interview that Schneider granted Schwarzer on December 12, 1976 (21), Schneider believed her mother even had an affair with Hitler (36). And "Daddy Blatzheim," Magda Schneider's second husband, seemed to have "black boots" on as Schwarzer's ambiguous remark about his relation to his stepdaughter whose career as Sissi he had managed, indicates: "[M]ißbraucht?" (abused?)—but exactly what kind of abuse did Schneider suffer? The question is confusing when we look further down in Schwarzer's text. Supposedly, Schneider confessed to Schwarzer during the interview, that when she was a young girl presumably, Blatzheim had wanted to sleep with her ["*Il a essayé de coucher avec moi. . . . Et pas seulement une fois*" (80)]. Even if Blatzheim didn't entertain exactly what legal terminology would call incestuous relations with his stepdaughter—a point only recent biographies bring up—the biographers agree on the "fact" that Blatzheim violated her in another respect: he embezzled Schneider's money or at least made serious mistakes investing it, notably the rather large fees she received for her Sissi films.

When tracing the discursive figurations surrounding this actress, one often has the feeling as if they provide a forum where Sylvia Plath's poetic imagination coalesces with Klaus Theweleit's cultural studies. It was Theweleit who in his famous 1977–78 study *Male Fantasies* looked at the writings (autobiographies, letters, postcards etc.) of German Freicorps men, "the" paradigmatic proto-Fascist and Fascist subjects, and subjected them to psychoanalytical readings. He concluded that these men had to *"entlebendigen,"* to kill off "woman"—what she stands for metaphorically, for example, fluidity — in order to sustain their own subjectivity. In a second move, Theweleit interpreted anti-semitism as a collateral defense mechanism for the male German subject, thus formulating the influential theses that Fascist men seemed to feel the need for a mortification of the feminine and, since what is fascist about masculinity is its need to suppress femininity and the ensuing displacement of hatred onto third parties, this type of subjectivization was by no means limited to the specific historical time in question. In short, gender and fascism merge conceptually.[8]

This gesture does not only mark Schwarzer's text on Schneider. Margit Steenfatt, for instance, another one of Schneider's biographers, concludes à propos *La passante* in 1986:

> *Romy kommt mit dem Film ihrer Vergangenheit zwar näher, aber nicht aus ihrer Rolle heraus. Die Erkenntnis, dass Männer Gewalttäter und Frauen Opfer sind, kann keine Lösung sein und wird dem Faschismus in der Welt kein Ende bereiten. Romy hätte bei der Bearbeitung des Romans für den ersten und letzten Teil des Films andere Schlussfolgerungen ziehen können. Der Anteil der Frauen erschöpft sich heute ja nicht mehr darin, daß sie "Männer lieben" und "Verfolgte retten."* [Romy gets closer to her past with this film but doesn't leave her gender role. The insight that men are perpetrators of violence and women victims cannot be a solution and will not end fascism in this world. When Romy worked on the film script, she could have drawn other conclusions, especially for the first and the last part of the film. Today, the part of women is no longer limited to "loving men" and "saving refugees."] (119)

In short, the representations of Schneider are symptomatic of a plethora of feminist issues. Indicative of the prepoststructuralist (popular) discourses around 1986, Steenfatt would have liked to see a more activist approach on part of the actress and bemoaned her lack of role-modeling. Women and their specific problems are "made,"—one is not born a woman but becomes one in the force field of society as Steenfatt's title *"Eine gemachte Frau"* in the adjective's double entendre on "successful" and "fabricated" suggests in a good Beauvoirian manner. Further, while *"Innerlichkeit"* and *"Politisierung"* form the two poles between which Schneider has been located over and over, in their application to Schneider, these categories themselves are seldom subject to sustained critique, even when they are cited with an attempt at irony, as in Schwarzer's opening scene. Coming from the eighteenth-century German tradition, *"Innerlichkeit"* characterized much of the artistic and intellectual endeavors of the German 1970s. As a discourse that foregrounded the search for "authenticity" during the 1970s, it was related to the topics of the women's movement, which, in turn, were the concerns of many of Schneider's films. Stereotypically, however, in those films, woman's desire is reduced to leaving her men and finding true love or fighting for the one and only true love, as in *La passante*, gestures that, at least, already irritated Steenfatt.[9]

The feminist take on Schneider has, of course, been furthered. The flyer to the travelling exhibition in Speyer (December 5, 1999 through March 26, 2000) reads:

> *Vergebens versucht Romy Schneider zeitlebens die Sehnsucht nach einem geordneten Familienleben, und ihr Streben nach Selbstverwirklichung in ihrer Arbeit als Schauspielerin zu verbinden. Sie scheitert an einem zentralen Konflikt der berufstätigen und erfolgreichen Frau im 20. Jahrhundert.* [All her life, Romy Schneider tried to combine her desire for an orderly family life and her strife for self-realization in her work as an actress. She failed because of the central conflict of the successful working woman in the twentieth century.] (Mythos Romy)

Rather, say, than casting Schneider in psychologizing scenarios of addiction and possibly analyzing her "failure" as a function of alcoholism and substance abuse—her intoxicated fits and self-destructive amorous relations were not only a cinematic fantasy—but also the contemporary marketing strategy of the actress is based on the universalization of problems that West German bourgeois women have been articulating since the beginning of the second women's movement: Women—another 1970s expression that reverberates contemporaneous Marxist-feminist traditions—can't "realize" themselves in their work. Thanks to the general oppression by German patriarchy, one must assume, because Schneider was neither a victim of the decrepit state of government-funded child care, nor of the tamed German capitalism that, given its salary standards and intolerance of black labor, puts private child care out of reach for most bourgeois women relegates them to live in mommy tracks and traditional private structures. Yet, despite its particularity, the "central conflict" must have an appeal for the masses of German museum goers, decrying, qua Schneider as the identificatory nexus, the inadequate realization of women's rights in Germany. If myths, speaking with Roland Barthes, are ways to order reality semiologically and thus to make sense, the mythmaking and its uncritical reception indicate that people still identify with the representations of the sociohistorical coordinates of Schneider's life and the "central conflict."

In short, the plethora of texts on Schneider often raise the question whether her mystification isn't marked by feminist positions that have been differentiated. While pointing to deficiencies in the implementation of equal rights, as above, the authors tend to work on the assumption of a universal lot of women. Furthermore, some texts on Schneider abound with a retrograde or even hostile assessment of feminism. Let us hear Schneider's key biographer Michael Jürgs on the topic of the women's movement and feminism:

Was heute in den neunziger Jahren als Trend in der Frauenbewegung beschrieben wird,—daß die Frau selbst begehrt, auf die Männer zugeht und nicht mehr wartet, bis sie begehrt wird—, hat Romy Schneider immer schon gelebt. [The trend that is described by today's women's movement in the nineties—a woman desires, approaches men and doesn't wait anymore for them to desire her—was always already lived by Romy Schneider.] (1991, 199) *Sie war als Frau eigentlich viel moderner—nur eben zur falschen Zeit—und der herrschenden Moral weit voraus, vor allem der in Deutschland, als die meisten Theoretikerinnen des Feminismus, deren Bücher zwar erfolgreich sind, aber mit dem wahren Leben nichts zu tun haben.* [As a woman she was very modern—only at the wrong time—and was ahead of dominant morality, especially of the German morality of most feminist theoreticians whose books might be successful but bear no relation to real life.] (200)

Skipping the problematic implications of Schneider's libidinal strives that female authors have raised over and over, Jürgs uses Schneider for a quick sideswipe at "most feminist theoreticians," denigrating a putatively homogenous group, at once both mocking their "success" and, yet another atavism from the times of "authenticity," critiquing their supposed distance to "real life." Jürg's hostility toward feminist intellectual analysis is, however, characteristic for the literature on Schneider. This literature generally portrays her as intuitive but uneducated and graced with rather limited intellectual capacity, thus valuing her for something that the generic biographical attitude of superiority has to undermine at the same time that it, by being largely nonanalytical, restages the conflict it displaces onto its heroine.[10] Subsequently, the clichéd assessments of the actress raise the question whether part of her appeal consists in a melodramatic splitting of her persona into a somewhat dumb, yet sensitive and driven artist, in casting her as the artistic version of the woman-next-door who feels strongly but cannot articulate her problems or effect change efficiently.

While feminism certainly catalyzes the discourses about Schneider, they are also informed by other liberal and leftist positions. Mentioning the murder of Max and Lina, the director's cut doesn't limit itself to perspectives on history but offers a critique of both German and French attitudes in the early 1980s. Max's death obviously means fascism hasn't ceased plaguing France, a country that had hitherto cultivated the glory of its *résistance*. The film also rejects the francophile gaze of German leftists who—not unlike Schneider herself who had left the thicket of postwar Germany and gained entrance into Parisian high art circles—managed to ignore the details of French collaboration for a long time, buying instead into the presentation of France as an anti-Fascist refuge from German atrocities.[11]

To sum up, despite the fact that the ongoing making of the Schneider myth toys with her supposed lack of political insight, it is grounded in an assessment of the political importance of the actress' films and her life. Aside from the arguable figurations of "feminism" on part of people who seem hostile to it, the mythmaking process also suffers from incongruencies within feminist theory. Schneider has not only served as a feminine role model, but also as an icon for a "certain coming-to-terms-with-the-past" of her (German) generation, notably for women. It is a discourse where the will to face National Socialism merges into a hatred of patriarchy, positioning women as victims of men who, insofar as they act as oppressors, are always already Fascist.

The latest representation, a TV screening of *La passante du Sans-Souci*, adds to the retrograde touch of the Schneider revival. Schneider's last film is often hailed as her legacy, because it condenses and displaces the paradigms that serve to articulate both the artist's life and the concerns that thread through her films. The TV screening of *La passante du Sans-Souci* in December 1999 revitalized the romantic francophile gaze of Germans who might have wanted to escape the problems of postwar Germany, dreaming instead perhaps, as Schneider and the passerby she plays, of *"vivre libre à Paris."*

Notes

1. According to the weekly *Der Spiegel*, Alice Schwarzer's book was number thirteen in the category nonfiction of the German bestsellers January 11, 1999. http://ibiservice.com:80/best/shtml.

2. The narrator summarizes a letter from Michel to Elsa:

Il était malade. Surmenage. Cœur affaibli. . . . On l'avait expédié à l'infirmerie du camp. Mais la nourriture y était à peine meilleure que l'innommable bouillie que l' on servait aux internés. Le médecin lui avait accordé seulement deux semaines de repos—l'infirmerie était surpeuplée,—et conseillait la suralimentation. En même temps, il l'avait autorisé à recevoir, de l'extérieur, des colis ou une centaine de marks afin d'améliorer son ordinaire. C'était le secours que Michel . . . venait demander à Elsa. [He was sick. Overworked. A weak heart. . . . He was sent off to the ward of the camp. But the food there was hardly better than the unbearable soup that they served to the interned. The doctor had granted him only two weeks of rest—the ward was overcrowded—and recommended extra food. At the same time, he had also allowed Michel to receive parcels from the outside or about hundred marks to improve his rations.] (113/114)

3. Holier than thou, the Bavarian version also attempted to make the film more leftist and did away with Rouffio's tenuous attempts at rendering Max more ambiguous. The cutters threw out the scene where a radical journalist uses Max's impressive capitalist achievements in order to question his true dedication to the leftist revolutionary causes he supports.

4. The translation of Benjamin's text "Über den Begriff der Geschichte" is problematic in places. Since a few words are missing from the English translation of Thesis II, I added them to the English text. Here's the German original:

Glück . . . gibt es nur in der Luft, die wir geatmet haben, mit Menschen, zu denen wir hätten reden, mit Frauen, die sich uns hätten geben können. Es schwingt, mit anderen Worten, in der Vorstellung des Glücks unveräußerlich die der Erlösung mit. Mit der Vorstellung von der Vergangenheit, welche die Geschichte zu ihrer Sache macht, verhält es sich ebenso. Die Vergangenheit führt einen heimlichen Index mit, durch den sie auf Erlösung verwiesen wird. Streift denn nicht uns selber ein Hauch der Luft, die um die Früheren gewesen ist? ist nicht in den Stimmen, denen wir unser Ohr schenken, ein Echo von nun verstummten? haben die Frauen, die wir umwerben, nicht Schwestern, die sie nicht mehr gekannt haben? Ist dem so, dann besteht eine geheime Verabredung zwischen den gewesenen Geschlechtern und unserem. Dann sind wir auf der Erde erwartet worden. (693/4)

5. Dietmar Schönherr, the talk show host, recently published his own interpretation of Schneider's much maligned remarks: according to Schönherr, Schneider was first and foremost impressed by Driest's frank leftist statements and not by his virility (Steinbauer 1999, 145).

6. Schwarzer's text joins misogyny, fascism, and leftist struggles in a few places. In Germany, the second women's movement developed out of the anti-Fascist struggles of the 1960s when women noticed that even in these supposedly free and democratic fights, their position was still one of inferiority. Schwarzer also mentions that the terrorist Andreas Bader had earned a living as a pimp before founding the RAF (1998, 15).

7. . . . and also alarmed the public when they played themselves out in subcultural practices. "Today," Susan Sontag wrote in 1974, "it may be the Nazi past that people invoke, in the theatricalization of sexuality, because it is those images (rather than memories) from which they hope a reserve of sexual energy can be tapped" (1981, 104). Since it is no accident that the film ends with Max showering Lina with love in front of the commerative table at the Sans-Souci, we may well ask if politics don't serve to heat up romance for Rouffio.

8. In its modifications, differentiations, and displacements, Theweleit's argument has been floating through feminist theory for many years. Contemporary discussions of fascism and gender tend to be more differentiated, see, for instance, Sander Gilman's impressive study *Freud, Race, Gender*, (Princeton,

NJ: Princeton University Press, 1998), where Gilman has demonstrated the identification of the Jew as effeminate.

9. Bereft of any poststructuralist sense of irony, the patterns of passion that Schneider's films set forth tend to smack of a certain melodramatic co-option that is, however dated its aestheticization might feel to contemporary feminist sensibilities, alive in some German contexts. When, for example, the well-known literary critic Ulrich Greiner wrote the ZEIT comment on the Lewinsky affair, he called his article "Der Präsident und das Mädchen," echoing one of Schneider's greatest cinematic successes, namely, *Der Kommissar und das Mädchen* (*Max et les ferrailleurs*, Claude Sautet, 1970). *Der Kommissar und das Mädchen* is a film where Michel Piccoli plays a lonely, maladapted police officer who foolishly throws away the happiness he found with "the girl," that is, Schneider as the hapless whore Lili, when he delivers her and her petty thief friends to the authorities.

10. The press material of the exhibition "Mythos Romy" puts it this way: "*Sie leidet unter der Vorstellung, nicht ausreichend Bildung zu besitzen, um mitreden zu können*" [She suffers from the idea that she isn't educated enough to enter discussions].

11. Robert Paxton's influential study *Vichy France: The Old Guard and the New Order* (New York: Knopf) came out in 1972. One of the important deconstructions of France's self-stylization as anti-Fascist was Marcel Ophul's film *Le chagrin et la pitié*, a film commissioned for French TV but not actually shown until 1981.

References

Arnould, Françoise and Françoise Gerber. *Romy Schneider*. Trans. Sylvia Strasser. Bergisch-Gladbach: Bastei Lübbe, 1998; Reprint, Lausanne: Pierre-Marcel Favre, 1985.

Barthes, Roland. "Le Mythe, aujourd'hui." *Œuvres complètes*. Ed. Eric Marty. Paris: Editions du Seuil, 1993.

Benjamin, Walter. "Theses on the Philosophy of History." *Illuminations*. New York: Schocken Books, 1969.

———. "Über den Begriff der Geschichte." *Gesammelte Werke*. Vol. I, No. 2, 691–704. Frankfurt a. M.: Suhrkamp, 1980; dtv Brockhaus Lexikon, Vol. 2. Mannheim: Deutscher Taschenbuch Verlag, 1989.

Granier-Deferre, Pierre. *Le Train.* France/Italy, 1973.

Jürgs, Michael. *Der Fall Romy Schneider: Eine Biographie.* München, Leipzig: List, 1991.

Kessel, Joseph. *La passante du Sans-Souci.* Paris: Gallimard, 1936.

Schwarzer, Alice. *Romy Schneider. Mythos und Leben.* Köln: Kiepenheuer und Witsch, 1998.

Seydel, Renate. *Romy Schneider. Ein Leben in Bildern.* Berlin: Henschel Verlag, 1990.

Sontag, Susan. "Fascinating Fascism." *Under the Sign of Saturn.* 73–105. New York: Random House, 1981.

Steenfatt, Margit. *Eine gemachte Frau: die Lebensgeschichte der Romy Schneider.* Hamburg: Kellner, 1986.

Steinbauer, Marie-Luise. "Dietmar Schönherr. Romy und die Politik." *Die andere Romy. Momentaufnahmen.* 142–145. München: Marion von Schröder Verlag, 1999. http://ibiservice.com:80/best/shtml

Flyer of the exhibition *Mythos Romy. Verwandlungen, Filme und Leben der Romy Schneider.* Speyer Historisches Museum der Dompfalz (December 5, 1999 through March 26, 2000).

Chapter 13

History/Paris-Berlin/History

Sande Cohen

> ... the language of historical pathos ... really describes linguistic events that are by no means human.
>
> —Paul de Man, "The Task of the Translator."

Introductory: Historiography and the Strange

Writing this essay "in" Los Angeles involves acknowledging the strangeness of associational fields. Paris/Berlin, France/Germany have had aspects of their histories placed within representations of Los Angeles. I have read a critic who claims that California, with L.A. as its epicenter, became Germany, given the prevalence here of psychoanalysis, film noir, and surf. When Jean Baudrillard gave a paper in L.A. in 1982, he stayed at a seedy motel at the beach, and conjured up, in person, the atmosphere of Godard's *Alphaville*. The recent consecration of the Getty Museum atop the Santa Monica mountains cannot but churn up both Parisian architectural "modernism" and the German connoisseur type, or Aby Warburg and the intellectual tradition that sees itself as heirs of true European humanism, in resistance to Parisian radicalism and frivolity. Is it accidental that contemporary French radical criticism is better represented in California's art schools than at its universities—the humanities at Berkeley and UCLA remain more Frankfurt-oriented than anything else. In short, Paris and Berlin are always "in and about" L.A. Further back, we could draw on more associations—Paris and Cubism, Paris and 1968, Berlin/expressionism, Berlin/1933–45, so the question becomes "what can Paris/Berlin represent for an American intellectual in Los Angeles?" L.A.'s cultural guardians regularly announce L.A. to be the "new capital"—Paris/Berlin—of the twenty-first century—but what can that mean? Paris/Berlin *for whom?*

It is not an admission of failure or a lack of any sort to suggest that representations on the history of the twentieth century cannot be merged, synthesized, or placed "in context." To the point: can historical writing presume a notion of "context," exempt from the politics of discourse if for no other reason than representation performs its own "context?" And more than ever, is it not possible to affirm, necessarily, that conceptions of both "context" and "history" fit Levi-Strauss's formulation as set forth in *The Savage Mind* (1962): there are many types and modes of "history-for"—persuasion to believe and disbelieve, for dampening the spirit, for elevating the ephemeral, a "for" that is ad infinitum—and there is no such thing as history that is "not-for?"

Consider then the idea that history has become metaphysical again, in the precise sense that things have happened (e.g. a *chronicity* of disasters for Africa) that are so disruptive to representation that one must doubt every sense of telos, direction, aim, end, finality, truth? Doubt here is kin to a form of skepticism that has been called "classical," and for good reason: by what judgment can one *measure* "history" and through which comparisons does the telos of, say, the technological series (extension of life span in selected areas) subsume or not the series called the "*telos* of literacy" (falling-off in the West)? Representational synthesis has become a question of metaphysics: it discloses active and passive elements. And might one not also say that it is incumbent to account for experiences that are situational to the degree that it is not possible to invoke history as mediation of differences, that there is a new subjectification that unevenly accompanies metaphysics? In short, history has been *shifted*: from context-providing, the concept of history has become a trap of representation; from serving as the platform of truth, a condition of judgment's possibility, the concept of history is a stake in conflicts, the outcome, or even processes of which, might be unknown.

In this paper, I discuss the shift from history as context-supplier, providing belief in agreements, an important mechanism in the binary-machine of progress and regress, among other concepts, to that of trap—by making a sort of narrative, the episodes of which are Simone Weil's radicalism toward "history," Alexander Kojeve's Hegelianism of the futility of resistance, Walter Benjamin's messianism, and Hannah Arendt's recuperation of the Roman basis of culture, which, Arendt claimed, Nazism did not ruin. In response to the diversity of notions about *post-histoire* that have come out of Paris, I offer analysis of Alexandre Kojeve's and Simone Weil's theories of history that flowed into, respectively, American mass behavior (Kojeve), and Nietzschean cultural critique (there is a genealogy from Weil to Deleuze and Guattari's *Anti-Oedipus* [1972]). On the Berlin/Germany side, I analyze Walter Benjamin's philosophy of history for a "state of emergency" and offer a criticism of Hannah Arendt's idea of historical recuperation, which she invoked to protect European culture against its recent past, restoring a "history" that did not perish with Nazism. Again, for no other purpose than to bring out some of the strongest reactions to the conceptual difficulties of joining "history" and context, I read these texts as they ushered in a suspension of "normal" history; these writers offered forceful notions of "history" and are discussed as episodes, incidents, or otherwise "moments" in the dissolution of history into "history-for," which is what happens when the concept of "context" becomes disputable in and of itself. Again: to say that concepts of "history" today belong as much to intellectual, cultural and political traps as to any other offered relation is just to make an interpretation—not a "history."

Why bother with historiography at all?

In part, because "history-for" is like Jean-Francois Lyotard's notion of postmodernism—it registers a *shift in the rules*. The ancient author Clemens Galen noted that *historia* was the scrutiny of the records written by others, sign-work, and was related to the problem of how to read the signs, how to make *salient* the significance of temporal patterns out of different series of signs; postmodernism, history-for, looks more like Galen's epistemology than the theories of determinism and expectation that we have been fed in the twentieth century.[1] For if we can speak today of the politics of politics, as in micro-Statism included as an aspect of globalization; if we can speak of the politics of language, in the dissemination of ideas, Western apparatuses of review, control on representation; and if there is a generalized politics of culture, as in the autonomization of lifestyles, whereby lifestyle is an end in itself, then we are speaking of rule shifts. The rules sorted and resorted has become almost an end in itself, yet with bizarre consequences—who could have predicted the collapse of American intellectual criticism from the Left, self-territorialized in universities, a subset really of political correctness, which is capable of muffling anything *it* considers unsayable—indeed what to do with all the new *things* of the world, of which Bruno Latour tells us we must integrate?[2] I am simply saying that critiques of "essentialism" and "foundation" and "conditions of possibility" that cross every discipline and discourse are further indices that the intellectual stock that surrounded ideas of "context" has dissolved and, with it, any cohesive sense of history. Indeed, the very idea of coherence has been questioned.[3] What do the processes we make similar—the dematerialization of art, the idealization of culture, the overweening presence of politics—actually have in common such that "historical" representation becomes their shared form?

So the subject of this paper is "history and instability of history," perhaps an awkward formulation, but so is the thing evoked, for it challenges any concept of history that would mediate disagreements, particularly those judgments that claim to effect social understanding, intellectual coherence, and political guidance, among many other social relations. My hypothesis is that conceptualizations of "history" today have recourse to forcing the future into our arrangements; the expenditure of such force directed toward the future requires constant *historicization of the present*. Paradoxically: Western conceptualizations of "history" are outmoded just as the present historicizes itself in a furious competition to get into the future. Politicized all the way through—made available for the work of the negative, for the labor of including the negative in our representations—the concept of "history" was dissolved in the twentieth century—it is fair to ponder any affirmative function of historical knowledge in contemporary society. The "narrow defile" (Walter Benjamin) called "progress" now *excludes* the vast majority of humankind, and Westerners are in a scramble to maintain footholds of all sorts, even nameability—"I call this that," "We say that . . ."[4] The concept of "history" is no longer inclusive as a social relation or is only inclusive as a narrative Apollonian effect.[5]

Finally, the readings given below try to remain aware that appeal to history has conjured the widest possible divergences: Hitler endlessly declared the conjunction between "nostalgia" for the past and the elimination of rivals; by the late 1930s, writers such as Levi-Strauss were calling for "history" as something to escape from, if one wanted to think critically; the poet/doctor Gottfried Benn made his poetry echo with the *ritornello* of "Ecce historia," or the absolute, obedience to authority, required at all times; Gilles Deleuze and Felix Guattari have reminded us that historiography is the point of contact between Statist representation, culture, and politics; Jacques Derrida enjoins us to listen to the specters of history as "new scholars"; and Roland Barthes and Jean-François Lyotard, in different ways, argued that historical consciousness was sustained by an underlying linguistic protocol that was as much schizophrenic and psychotic as "normal." Every *new* group with a social stake requires a moment where it can *historicize itself or secure some future time.*

Alexandre Kojeve's Immobilization of History

In his exemplary book, *The College of Sociology,* Denis Hollier cites Raymond Queneau's comments on a lecture given by Alexandre Kojeve at the College de France in 1937. According to Queneau, Kojeve said that Georg Hegel's notion of history was correct except that "The man at the end of history was not Napoleon but Stalin."[5] Kojeve's updating of Hegel announced the theme of intellectuals placed "out of work"—deprived of the dialectic and the labor of strife, the negative, the "end of history" meant that the future had arrived, on time and so intellectuals, masters of the negative; were obsolete. In that lecture, Kojeve proposed a radical solution to the "burden of history" (*pace,* Hayden White), at least from the perspectives of philosophy and cultural ruminations. Kojeve insisted that one think of history in terms that are eternal, and have always been true: ". . . every Action is egoist and criminal, as long as it does not succeed—and Napoleon succeeded . . . judgment is sheer worthless chatter . . . utter inactivity . . . a *Sein,* hence a Nothingness."[6] At one stroke, Kojeve blessed the present as eternal and every eternal as present to itself. This Napoleon into Stalin configuration represents the achievement of "total integration with History" Hegel's presentation of Napoleon as "history" is an incarnate updated as the truth of philosophy's wisdom, of an identity between reality and the universal, and the homogenization of both. Homogenization here suggests total knowledge: all the processes and agencies of conflict, strife, from Darwinian survival to the most immediate events of culture, are "known" (hence positivism)—the real is the real is the real and therefore is the actual. In a phrase as dramatic as it is ludicrous, Kojeve simply declared: "History has ended." Artists and intellectuals can henceforth live only "a purely literary existence," for their effectivity is restricted to words/figures that are "interesting" to a society that tolerates differences simply because society can make all differences indifferent. Kojeve's *Introduction to the Reading of Hegel* is undoubtedly one of the most provocative "theories" of history produced in this century. Institutions such as the university and museums come to embody nothing more than "refuge . . . [in] the ivory tower."[7] And in terms that anticipate Jean Baudrillard's idea of simulation, culture is not merely bereft of "clothes," but in its transformation of strife into successes of cultural recognition, culture cannot but pursue the "beautiful death" that represents "total, definitive failure" insofar as one continues to believe in the difference of culture. More paradox: just as everything is declared to have a cultural dimension, "culture" vanishes. Kojeve's writing on all this is still a model of the more than ambiguous "stakes" in all cultural valuations.

The brutality of Kojeve's retrieval of Hegel is the sign of his text's significance. Despite Kojeve's writings and discussions about the "end of history,"[8] the text's brutality was faithful to its time—Kojeve's work on history, revolution and art in the 1930s insisted on what Vincent Descombes has called the metaphysics of a "nature [that] would be mastered and society appeased," that is, the termination or end of opposition between social groups. Kojeve's model was introduced so as to "oppose" opposition to history: it emphasized *success* as the sole criterion by which to evaluate the diversity of action and discord about ends and goals.[9] The radicalism here involves the introjection of a super-Puritanism of the "winners" and "losers": the "winners" of competition for the State and its prizes do not have to answer for the success of their "success," just as it is then incumbent on the slaves to revolt, logically speaking, but the slaves won't revolt any more. The very dynamic of mastery and revolt is closed—all the differences have been articulated so the world no longer requires differences sorted out by reference to models of history. What is perpetuated is society itself as another, better, nature. Again: when the slaves have revolted their failure is greater than what they opposed—the Soviet Union problem, that is, when was and was it not a "worker's state" and what then does that mean? What desire is there to be other—to critique the "system"—if one lives in a time that is so successful (or failed, and hence mixtures thereof) in being itself, that to call for opposition is moved to the position of the reactionary? It is not stretching it to say that Kojeve proposed that Hegelianism had become the only kind of "normality" the West would finally tolerate.

Kojeve's tactic in the cultural and philosophical wars of the 1930s was to include negativity within being or history. Negativity was shifted from a "motor" of history, where negation could create differences, and was instead absorbed by a sense of *totality* that now replaced history:

> If, then, Man's complete satisfaction is the goal and the natural end of history, it can be said that history completes itself by Man's perfect understanding of his death. . . . History perfected and definitively completed . . . [in which] Man attains fullness of consciousness of a self that no longer has any reason to negate itself and become other.[10]

Here indeed is the project of an idealistic and terroristic conception of history—to live and think historically has become rational so long as reason eliminates dissension. The usual sense of "to be historical" meant to be in opposition and to create differences; as this possibility has come to an end, we can now live the existence of *non-reason*, where one does not have to think oppositionally at all—in the name of what "X" might one rebel? Philosophically, there is nothing that is posited as able to bother the West; the West can absorb itself—this was Kojeve's great insight, the West as a Big Monad, as Lyotard might have put it, come into its own. At odds with Nietzschean premises, Kojeve affirmed *recuperation* of the negative, a recuperation which canceled any idea of a difference of difference, or affirmation of the future to be different.[11]

Simone Weil's Extremism

At about the same time that Kojeve was undoing the concept of history-as-strife and replacing it with a version of positive ignorance, "each of us God then, by our beatitude and knowledge" as Blanchot sarcastically put it, Simone Weil, the Red Virgin of Parisian radicalism, was hatching her own strong critique of historical thought, (still) neglected by most of those involved in theory of history. Unfortunately, historians have relegated Weil's writings to literature. Simone Weil tried to write a story of sorts about what she called the transhistorical problem of "uprootedness." *The Need for Roots* (1943), which concerns me here, is less a narrative than it is a verbal onslaught about such "uprootedness," and the interest of her text lies in the fact that it evokes this "superhistorical" condition as the name of a disastrous process and as a device to criticize the cultural and political configurations of 1940 Europe. Weil tried to connect present experiences and metaphysical historical process.

In the first place, Weil's problem was that of finding a way to organize and present the *processes* of deterioration that had produced Nazism and fascism. To make this connection, *The Need for Roots* assaults the pieties of progressives: Weil insists that 1943 was continuous with 1789, where the latter date signified the triumph of a social system in which rights had edged out transcendental obligations, the latter said to represent "eternal, universal, and unconditioned" obligations required for the "eternal destiny of human beings," a phrase evocative of some Heideggerian themes from the same period. In making 1943 Europe continuous with 1789, Weil placed history as such under the sign of failure: 1789's politicization of rights was itself unbroken with earlier acts of conquest and money power, both of which had demolished any other processes than those of discontinuity, and *The Need for Roots* drew the conclusion: history was subsumed by the continuity of "uprootedness," where progressive goals were merely a different adjustment to the same problem.

From the "onset" of history until now, money, control, and glory have undercut the places and zones of contact where people feel "inspired," as in creative labor, the enthusiasm of apprenticeship, the intensity of art. Uprootedness, analogous to what Marxists in the period called "reification" or existentialists called "bad-faith," is set against processes undertaken by "inspiration," hence the continuous process of disheartenment—those who benefit from "progress though discontinuity" make up various cohorts with a stake in the very negativity that Kojeve declared "unemployed." If, as Weil insists in a deeply conservatizing image, the "loss of the past" is the "supreme tragedy,"[12] this because "discontinuity" is self-perpetuating (accumulation of obstacles, as in systems theory, where clogs and blockages in a system determine limits, boundaries, even what can be affirmed) then, absurdly, *we* continue to act like Romans and their acts of "uprootedness" that stem from "self-idolatry." Meaning: "Hitlerism is a return to pagan Rome," and a return to Hebraic madness, and . . . and. . . . Again: starting from "the dual Roman-Hebrew tradition," a heresy in modern historiography, Weil insisted that 1943 should be understood as a "local" outbreak of a conflict that is at "one" with what we call "history." Metaphysically, what one could describe as the "oneness of discontinuity" is nihilism, the triumph of fear of new affects and connections, in every area of life, and was exactly a concept of "history" that challenged the rival intellectual perspectives of the period, with their various invocations of "historically" based resistance. For Weil there was nothing to go back to: "The past once destroyed never returns. The destruction of the past is perhaps the greatest of all crimes." As she notes, in perfect tranquility and calmness, Adolf Hitler read Sulla and learned exactly the *lesson of history*—to historicize is to dominate.[13] One cannot but "hear" a Nietzschean murmur in such words. Hitler, to Weil—before the name Holocaust appears—fulfills Western history. Hitlerism is no aberration but a logico-social product of the West.

In this, science, knowledge, and culture are so many indices of historical destruction, insofar as they have joined to palliate the *danger* of "human destiny," and the contemporary political rivals to Nazism have used up the resources attendant upon a strong sense of "roots." To make her point, Weil did not hesitate to draw upon historical analogies, of which the following gives the gist of her attitude toward history:

> The Romans were a handful of fugitives who banded themselves together artificially to form a city and deprived the Mediterranean peoples of their individual manner of life. . . . The Hebrews were escaped slaves, and they either exterminated or reduced to servitude all the peoples of Palestine. The Germans, at the time Hitler assumed command over them, were really—as he was never tired of repeating—a nation of proletarians, that is to say, uprooted individuals. . . . Whoever is uprooted himself uproots others. Whoever is rooted himself doesn't uproot others.[14]

Understanding history is congealed to the matter of allowing ourselves to be affected by this *continuity of discontinuity*; the avowed goal of Weil's reading is social upheaval toward the repetition of Western, malfeasant, "normality," echoes of which are to be found, among many writers, in Avital Ronell's discussions of Heidegger and the failure of "custodianship" toward self and others. One should not underestimate the radicalism involved here: Weil assumed that the West had already "killed" itself. There could be no point to the normal uses of "historical" thinking by comparison to the need for alternatives.

What meets then in Weil's *The Need for Roots* are Hegel's master/slave without the dialectic and Nietzsche's analysis of *ressentiment*—but these components, the dialectic as ideal and the process of psychologization do not meet as the culmination of Enlightenment surpassing politics and subjectivity, but as the "marriage"of schemas and structures that make things worse. The cures *are* the problem. Marxism is no alternative because it shares, with conservatism, the idealization of *false continuity*, for the Marxian perspective and its "imaginary picture" of workers and the social contract adds to the "loss of joy in one's work"[15] in the destruction that is history. Weil invoked a "metahistorical" criterion for assessing the continuity of discontinuity—the idea of *labor fastened to joy*, the only social bond that could ever matter. In the face of all the myriad ways in which labor and joy are unfastened, the disjuncts between work and joy, *The Need for Roots* calls for a total reorganization of society after the war, using the experiences of those few "historical atolls," like the life of the Carthaginians, a poetic people who, in their acts of self-creation, loved what they had created (there are only *islands* that remain in the wake of the West's destructions).

Resistance to what I have called the "continuity of discontinuity" can only begin, according to Weil, with the sense of suffering as it actually exists. Instead of asking for the *control* of the resources of socialization, Weil asks that we make different connections. For example: "Culture—as we know it—is an instrument manipulated by teachers for manufacturing more teachers, who in their turn, will manufacture yet more teachers," this according to the lines laid down by a despotic academic system.[16] Young people suffer not absence of connection, but the barriers of productive making; while privileging an optimism toward ordinary "people" that we may find unduly idealist today, Weil would have upended "uprootedness" in the cultural sphere by turning, for example, the academic system into the experience where "second-class works and below . . . are most suitable for the *elite*," and having those excluded from culture devour "first-class works most suitable for the people"; when workers experience that "Electra is hungry," they can engage the "intensity of representation" instead of a representation that is corrective, a truth-type of experience elites foist on the lower orders.[17] Jean-Francois Lyotard's *Driftworks* is an echo of Weil's notion—the insistence that there is more potential disruption in a Cezanne painting than in the entire discourse of the French Communist Party. In effect, Weil's philosophy of history is a plea for the *"spiritualization of work."* Instead of demanding of those who suffer, especially the proletariat, to connect with elite cultural life, as the French left did in the 1920s and 1930s in its attempt to popularize Marx, Weil offers a theory of resistance—the "spiritualization of work" (joy) or the injection of love in social relations.[18] Resistance to history acknowledges that Hitler learned history from historians,[19] and to resist such learning, acts that affirm the future as different are what matter. Here, too, Weil anticipates Deleuze's *Nietzsche and Philosophy* (1962) with its proposition that Eternal Return is strictly an issue of affirmation (negation does not have a future, even if it occupies life).

Hannah Arendt's Recuperation of Judgment

Turning now to a sense of history after World War II, I would like to discuss Hannah Arendt's postwar recuperation of the Roman-German negative continuity that Weil challenged. Hannah Arendt's sense of historical continuity and discontinuity is laid out in her essay "The Crisis in Culture," published in 1960. Arendt's argument slips in and out of a narrative, telling the story of the "rise" and "fall" and "rise" again of aesthetics and ideology, politics, and art. Her concern is exactly the concept of "culture" *after* the barbarism of history's most recent incarnation of disaster, Nazism.

In narrative terms, Arendt invokes a sense of historicity by recounting the emergence of "good society"—the triumph of the middle classes and the ambiguous position of the artist—that emerged out of courtly life and, because of its philistinism, reduced works of art to questions of utility; by the middle of the nineteenth century, this "good society" had managed to mobilize and integrate culture for reasons of status and position. Arendt locates in the trope of *euphemism*, saying something by not saying something, what is "disallowed" when members of "good society" congregate and spread their cheerfulness to each other, an "essential" conjunction of "good society" and philistinism. Artists are in a weird position, namely, society: the work of art straddles entertainment, philistinism, and immortality. Arendt raises these terms in a problematic similar to Simone Weil's critique of the present, and then, unlike Weil's strategy or move to the transcendental, turns to a history prior to this division between the artist saying/doing something that is not-useful, not-good, and society's rigid demand to make the not- into the useful and the good.

Arendt's conceptual model, structurally similar to Weil's notion of "spiritual work," was that the *desire for immortality,* which the Greeks attached to objects, proved unsustainable in the face of "good society" and its philistine criteria of demanding that objects testify to one's self-education, self-perfection.[20] First despised as "useless," the artist's work was quickly turned into a currency circulating in the networks of position and social esteem. Arendt certainly offered that the vast majority of art works (and texts, of all sorts) in the "modern" world were mostly shot through with philistine elements, if not totally subject to the form of philistinism, an amalgamation of *kitsch* (instantaneity, satiety) and something "higher," the "useful" raised to transcendental status. Objects, in a philistine world, are experienced *for the self* instead of *for the world,* and have "lost the faculty of arresting our attention and moving us." The "thread of tradition" was broken—objects aren't ruined by mass entertainment or by mass society (freshness, novelty, wasted time, decay, and more production), but by the function to which they are put. Every time a museum pitches a show of which the objects are "there" for any kind of edification, they have, in that presentation, been deprived *of* their objectivity in the world. It is clear enough to say that the process of philistinism is homologous with the process of "uprootedness"—they are different versions of each other, the cultural condition where "good society" sometimes turns to the right or the left, but always does so on the basis of "elites know best." What is showable in public life is hardly ever dangerous.

But Arendt's evocation of Rome stands in sharp contrast to Weil's use of Rome as an image of cultured barbarism. Where Weil denounced Roman brutality at every turn, allowing that Rome tolerated only amusement for the masses and a false politics of eloquence for the elites,[21] Arendt "turns back," as it were, to the Roman idea of culture. As is well known, Arendt credits "Rome" with effecting an attitude of love for the world by means of enculturation. Rome's contribution was to ignore the Greek admonition against fabricators and affirming the Greek ideal of making judgments that *beautiful* things matter in their own right—what matters is how the world looks, appearances in and of themselves. What

Arendt then proposed was a device that could be returned to us from the past; to Weil's sense of historical destruction as requiring severe and present action in the here and now, Arendt turned off such historical destruction—the strange place where Rome and Berlin intersect—this to salvage the *action of judgment* from the terrible history of Europe, judgments that join art and politics, subject and public.

Art, in Arendt's schema, is exactly what Weil called "rootedness": that which might not be withdrawn into the barbarism of a "good society" gone haywire. Arendt's device consists of a philosophical concept that is said to be universal and immanent to any notion of subjectivity—the insistence that there are pure judgments of "quality." This device is nothing other than the *ideal* that such judgments of "quality" distance us from philistinism, in any age, as well as from the horrors of Nazi-type attitudes (its joining of *kitsch*, utilitarianism, mythic ideology, and rank sentiment).

Where "history" showed to Kojeve the image of eternality, or repetitions of power, and to Weil history could not be returned-to, Arendt offers a mode of accommodation with history. The threat to culture as such, most violently signaled in Nazism, can be set aside: by considering the work of art as those things where politics, aesthetics, and judgment converge. In this, works of art are not subject to criteria of truth but rather to experiences of *taste*, where those making judgments can render statements about objects and where "quality is beyond dispute." With the evidence of cultural barbarism all around her, Arendt made "taste" the truth of a recuperable, affective world, modeled on "beyond dispute." "Beyond dispute" asserts faith in judgment, judgment as a retrieval of faith. Where Weil's faith in elite culture was taken to the point of complete rupture, Arendt pulls back—to Cicero's injunction against the specialization of experience, locating art works within humanist ideals. Arendt names "taste . . . the activity of a truly cultivated mind." Hence, philosophy of art survives European self-destruction, but survives as subjective taste raised to the power of connoisseurship—how else can the world be "humanized" except through the combined "qualitative judgments" performed by those who know? This humanist, who "knows how to choose his company," is also then a social type distanced from "good society" and mass society, but who, through "sensitivity to beauty" and "love of beauty," *adds* taste to the world, judgments of taste also things of the world.

Arendt crystallized this salvage operation on taste (a "diving" into the wreck, no doubt, *pace* Adrienne Rich) by saying that "the common element connecting art and politics is that they both are phenomena of the public world," mediated by "a mind so trained and cultivated that it can be trusted to tend and take care of a world of appearances whose criterion is beauty."[22] Cicero's admonition "to look for the sake of seeing only . . ." is taken as the activity that is super-historical, tending to the world, and is threaded to Immanuel Kant's notion that judgment, in aesthetics and politics alike, gives the conditions for "anticipated communication," art and politics intrinsically joined through the act of "potential agreement," the "perspective of all those who happen to be present" in experiences of art and politics.[23] Neither knowledge nor truth claims override culture and politics: the "activity of taste . . . judges the world." We can "woo" consent or persuade others—by "people talking," but what actually matters is that there is such a relation to the world as "the self-evidence of quality . . . the truly beautiful easily recognized," the beautiful brought into the fold of humanization. Hence, no determinate judgment must be made about philistinism or "good society" or worse—taste can humanize a culture, because it escapes the specialization of the scientist and the philosopher and, especially, narrow political ideologies. We can, Arendt says many times, "rise above" conflict by the exercise of judgments of taste and quality.

Weil's *The Need for Roots* establishes and anticipates history-as-delirium, in the sense that Rome/Jerusalem/Hitlerism render "history" as violent discontinuity of continuity, a world at war in every respect, requiring the utmost engagement or destruction of distance. By contrast, Arendt "went back" to sources that could be rehabilitated and, in that, anticipates recent "conversationalism" (e.g. Rorty, Habermas). Weil's work is but part of what has been called "attitudes of post-histoire," and Arendt's notion of the beautiful lie of agreements made by connoisseurs—I realize my statement is contentious—is continuous with German idealism.[24]

Walter Benjamin's Legacy

According to Arendt, Walter Benjamin's writings were obsessed with the destruction of cultural traditions and the concomitant loss of cultural and social authority. Destruction and preservation were the key terms of Benjamin's work, which locates this work close to Croce's historiographic question, "what is living and what is dead?" in cultural assessments.[25] It seems to me that Benjamin's *Theses on the Philosophy of History*, completed just before his death in 1940, joins the concern with engagement that Weil heralded (spiritualization of work) with Arendt's attempt to salvage a sense of judgment and quality, showing us some of the sharper edges and dangers of "history" becoming "history-for."

Benjamin's *Theses on the Philosophy of History* are premised on the idea that concrete objects embody past states of mind and world—material continuity—but these embodiments must be interpreted in a way that does not falsify the past's own "eventness." We are engaged with what comes forward from the past, to be construed as processes and products that have crossbred and reversed and interpenetrated each other to the point that befuddles ordinary historical understanding. Past objects are not pure and historical representation of things must pass through the "*hookah*," as the very first thesis has it, or the *medium*— "the story is told . . ."—so that perhaps there is no separation between "history" (writing) and "history" (act), which confounds to no end. The *Theses* make historiography, the analysis of historical writing, inseparable from what historical writing is concerned with, is *about*.

Benjamin's critique of European historicism is performed in the hookah-medium he called "historical materialism," Marxist but not only that, in which the historian in a "state of emergency" has to select "fitting emblems in which to anchor" modern experience. "Fitting emblems," Arendt's phrase, from her introduction to Benjamin's *Illuminations*, means working allegory and traditional historicism into something else, a method of reading open to minute differences within things, an application of analogical thinking oriented by awareness of "present dangers." As a way of approaching the persistence of past, Benjamin's method is exactly counter-symmetrical to Kojeve's "idea of history," and, cast in the rhetoric of desperation, it is an altogether different kind of desperation than that of Weil—Benjamin wants to make a device that can use "history" and "tradition" in *whatever modality they are transmitted*, rather than accept the death of the past as Simone Weil did.

"The past carries with it a temporal index by which it is referred to redemption. There is a secret agreement between past generations and the present one."[26] Traditional historicist "empathy" and its sometimes objectivist, sometimes subjectivist, biases, is what this "secret agreement" suspends. "Secret agreement" smuggles in irony toward Euro-Historicism, what Lyotard would later call *"metanarrative,"* and is a call for the value of redemption over that of mere "historical understanding." As did some Russian formalists, Benjamin insists that ordinary historical understanding diminishes connections with the past and the future; to narrate in its ordinary sense is to *historicize* or create a fact on the ground, which is exactly what Benjamin does not want to do, since a fact on the ground and as understood (not the same thing), produces a void filled, entropy not energy. In order to *activate* the present by means of the past, Benjamin calls on the concept of the messianic, which replaces the "historical" agency of messianism, the proletariat and its various representatives. Instead, the project of the *Theses* is to bring out this universal messianic power, however weak, yet still in us—"a power to which the past has a claim."[27] That the past has a claim—hardly reducible to a legal mode—can be interpreted as the past's *reach* toward us, barely imaged here, of the past in disturbance, of course giving the possibility that Benjamin has radically *personified history* through the meager yet potent image of suffering, perhaps a past that suffers from melancholy, an equally difficult notion, or the past out of joint to itself, waiting for us to "reach" it. Unlike historicism, historical materialism is the practice of connection—a fully mystical claim because, as the recent publication of the Arcades Project shows, Benjamin wanted to link the "crystals" of experience with "totality"—joined to terse apothegms, effecting a reflexive sadness about European history, humanism given a 1940 emblem, Paul Klee's *Angelus Novus.*

Rather than carry out the program of Rankean aesthetics with narratives whose subjects were made "immediate to God" via historical writing (a mad claim, always), the past is not fully citable—presentable—until there is a "redeemed mankind." If a first use of mysticism issues in "to reach," this second moment, to be "redeemed," suggests the past's messianic claim, a mystical junction of past-present, is already here, already concretized, and Benjamin's discourse calls this quasi-presence of claim/redeem *"heliotropism."* This figure calls its readers to evoke a naturalism that emanates from "redeemed" and "claim." Benjamin's syntax switches between naturalism and mysticism and antihistoricism, wherein past/present/future evince the "most inconspicuous of all transformations."[28] Directed toward the past, images "never seen again" recur as "flash"—bolts from the proverbial blue and that shock—where an "image of the past" in its "own concerns threatens to disappear irretrievably." Might history itself flame out?

Mystical yet based on a thoroughly rigorous attempt to translate the cultural state of emergency into political urgency, one must try to "seize hold of a memory as it flashes up at a moment of danger." Past and present have been reduced to tools of the ruling class where, in the mystical register, even the dead are unsafe from the victors. One can summarize all this by saying that the *Theses* offers a version of presentism that is as much Nietzschean as Marxian, recalling Nietzsche's famous statement that only those who are building a future have a right to judge the past; here, Benjamin recodes this by turning to the past as threatened with complete absorption, history run dry. The traditional method of historical empathy (Dilthey, hermeneutics) is unsuitable as a tactic of resistance, and only that method that attempts to grasp and hold "the genuine historical image as it flares up briefly" is of value as resistance to domination.[29] It's a question of, as the famous apothegm has it, history against the grain; the historical materialist carries out, enacts, an affirmation of a state of emergency, now "the rule." The point of Benjamin's antihistoricism is to help bring about a real state of emergency for those who would "lose" by virtue of belief in the false ideologies then dominant, which ruthlessly used history for purposes of murder. Once again: the image of this is to be found in Klee's *Angelus Novus;* the angel of history knows that "one single catastrophe" has already occurred, the madness of the false progress called the "storm of history."[30]

One could hardly ask for more as a concept of the engaged critic. But Benjamin's *Theses on the Philosophy of History* unfortunately veer toward an acceptance of binaries that are not very useful. For the *Theses* . . . also insist that historical knowledge belongs to the symmetry of revenge and liberation, making an equation of the two, making a logic that undercuts the more radical mysticism, or materializes the mysticism in the psychology of the oppressed. Benjamin insists that the working class has been restricted by social democracy to the role of redeeming the future, "cutting the sinews of its greatest strength," its "hatred and its spirit of sacrifice, for both are nourished by the image of enslaved ancestors rather than that of liberated grandchildren."[31] Nietzsche gives way again to Marx. Perhaps this idea is a retrospective obligation of loyalty to the past, a psychic debt, in Nietzsche's terms, or a payment to history's past victims.

Further, Benjamin's criticism of the formalism and emptiness of historicism—its ability to include events in stories that judged valuable by present victors, akin to Arendt's sense of philistinism—yields a second weakness. It was one thing to doubt historicism's conception of time as empty and homogeneous; but to propose a "dialectical" connection to time, a "leap into the past," into ". . . the open air of history," to evoke the experience of "awareness," of making the "continuum of history explode," is an enthusiasm caught in the word magic of the name "dialectic." Again, it is one thing for Benjamin to say that holidays are weakened reminiscences of past leaps, but to invoke a "dialectic" out of time/space *spiritualizes* past/present/future conjunctions (a "secret agreement") and idealizes the critic's ability to span differences. While the strength of Benjamin's notion is that the present is not a transition or switching station between past and future, his version and use of "dialectics" makes the present, conceptually speaking, "stand still," and presumes that "history" can be grasped in the present, possessed through those "fitting emblems," the critic having a "unique experience with the past," the critic "man enough to blast open the continuum of history."[32] In short, to historicism's additive method or one thing after another given narrative continuity, historical materialism is constructive—to think history "in a configuration pregnant with tensions," and which then requires a different kind of critic and historian, one who "gives that configuration a shock, by which it crystallizes into a monad . . . the sign of a Messianic cessation of happening . . . a revolutionary chance in the fight for the oppressed past."[33] Historicism's use of linear sequence, its unthinking use of the genetic method, tying origin and end to a *telos*, is set aside in favor of a procedure that can grasp "the constellation which his own era has formed with a definite earlier one." In short, Benjamin "lifted" history into cultural strife, a move that is both radical and reactionary—dissolving linearity is radical until it is fitted into a "dialectic" that is reactionary, because it is just another way of soothing a sensibility that judges itself radical.

Finally, Benjamin intended that his *Theses* would exemplify the possibility of interpretation, or translation, as something which can be culturally exhilarating and politically acute, connecting the postulate that there is a divine language in which names have magical powers with our debased use of signs, in which things have been overnamed, overcoded, as the semioticians would say. Since human history is very much the process of ruling class induced deceptions, (not unlike Weil's idea of the negative constancy of "uprootedness"), to mix life's connections between the "mud" and "heaven," the image of the historian is shifted to that of translator—to increase meaning, rather than demand that writing yield *the* truth of things.[34] And to increase meaning—"history" against the grain—one has to accept disjunctions on all the levels of language with which one operates—we have to think "history" beyond origin and end or, in a stronger register, understand, if we can, that history is potentially *not* humanizable, since our ordinary notions of "history" accept a false correspondence between historical writing and historical meaning.[35] In 1940, Walter Benjamin produced the *Theses on the Philosophy of History* that made it impossible for any particular group to find comfort or satisfaction in any ordinary version of "historical" knowing.[36] To use "history" to suspend "history"—is this not the labor of engaging the instability of history and its representations?

Conclusion

The twentieth century has given us as much terror as we can take, wrote Lyotard in *The Postmodern Condition*. The philosophies of history discussed above are a few of the versions, Kojeve excepted, of what today would be called "counter-history," ways of opening the events and processes of the past to our present situations, multiple and fragmented. The radicalism of Weil and the return to conservatism by Arendt are two sides of the same coin—"coming-to-terms-with" disasters of politics and social life as a whole. Benjamin's attempt to combine radical class politics and radical interpretive strategies has the merit of making the present absolutely contestable, but at the cost of mysticism and the overestimation of the individual counter-historian's literary skills—the poetics of imagining differences, a way of recuperating tradition and its vicissitudes.[37] Weil's version of "history" has the merit of shifting criticism toward the present engaged as "continuous discontinuity," neither aestheticizing history as Arendt's writings did, nor "bonding" with history via Marxist blending of mysticism and naturalism, as did Benjamin's *Theses*. Yet none of these strategies of engagement with historicism are available to us, except as *historical examples* and academic practices (not the same thing); again, reading these intellectuals, especially from places like Los Angeles, where "history" is mostly a question of bringing enlightenment to the "people" who seem, often, not to care about historical consciousness at all, is itself strange.

While on an ethical plane one can easily identify with Weil's extreme engagement, and understand the peace treaty Arendt made with European history by a return to "taste" and rhetoric, and the literary attractiveness of Benjamin, it seems to me that Kojeve's paradox is dominant—negation doesn't drive the "system" of advanced social structures by threats of shattering the course of movement; no, negation is a way the system maintains equilibrium. Weil and Benjamin's resistance, or the respective ethics of labor and poetics of representation, presupposed rupture was possible. Arendt's model did not, opting for an idealist resolution. Today, we're not sure what "historical" questions *to ask*.

NOTES

1. R. J. Hankinson, *The Sceptics* (New York: Routledge and Kegan Paul, 1995), pp. 226–229.

2. See Bruno Latour, *We Have Never Been Modern* for a statement of anthropology as the humanities last hope for synthesis.

3. Todorov, in *The Morals of History* (Minneapolis: University of Minnesota Press, 1995) has suggested that coherence often involves intellectual straitjacketing, producing not understanding, but misfiguration. Historians seem to still rely on coherence in an archaic manner—as an unproblematic concept, as "common sense," or a goal without problems.

4. These comments are drawn from Odo Marquard, *Farewell to Matters of Principle* (New York: Oxford, 1989), p. 94–95. Thanks to Elie During for giving me this book, and to Sylvere Lotringer, who provided an opportunity to give a paper on some of this material at Columbia University, November 1999.

5. I am drawing on Gilles Deleuze and Guattari's *What Is Philosophy?* (1994).

6. Denis Hollier ed., *The College of Sociology, 1937–39* (Minneapolis: University of Minnesota, 1993), p. 86.

7. Hollier, *College of Sociology*, p. 87.

8. Hollier, *College of Sociology*, p. 89.

9. Unlike Kojeve's correlation of realism equals brutality, I fail to understand how Fukuyama's model has any intellectual credibility. His argument in the *End of History* turns 1806 into 1989—"the fundamental principles of sociopolitical organization have not advanced terribly far since 1806"—and declares history "over" equals liberalism's eternalism, this by saying that liberalism *is* the State that realizes "universal to right to freedom . . . with the consent of the governed," ideas that are formalist, or legalistic, at best, and utterly destructive of critiques of ideology. See F. Fukuyama, "The End of History?," *National Interest* (summer 1989).

10. Vincent Descombes, *Modern French Philosophy* (London: Cambridge, 1980), p. 28ff.

11. A. Kojeve, *Introduction to the Reading of Hegel* (New York: Basic Books, 1969), pp. 258–259.

12. On this topic, see the work by David Krell, *Of Memory, Reminiscence, and Writing* (Bloomington, IN: Indiana University Press, 1990), preface.

13. Simone Weil, *The Need for Roots* (New York: Routledge and Kegan Paul, 1978), p. 114.

14. Weil, *The Need for Roots*, p. 225.

15. Ibid., p. 45.

16. Ibid., p. 77.

17. Ibid., p. 65.

18. Ibid., p. 67.

19. Ibid., p. 242.

20. Ibid., p. 216. This is an extraordinary section.

21. Hannah Arendt, "The Crisis in Culture," in *Between Past and Future* (New York: Viking), p. 203.

22. Weil, *The Need for Roots*, p. 259: Romans "disfigured the most beautiful things. They dishonored suppliants by forcing them to tell lies. They dishonored gratitude . . . love . . . for them meant either acquiring the beloved as one's property, or else . . . submitting oneself."

23. Arendt, "The Crisis in Culture," p. 219.

24. Arendt, "The Crisis in Culture," p. 222.

25. On this topic, see the forthcoming book by Kriss Ravetto, *The Making and Unmaking of Fascism*, (Minneapolis: University of Minnesota Press, forthcoming).

26. See her introduction to Walter Benjamin, *Illuminations* (New York: Schocken, 1969), p. 41.

27. Walter Benjamin, *Illuminations* (New York: Schocken, 1969), p. 254.

28. Benjamin, "Theses," p. 254.

29. Ibid., p. 255.

30. Ibid., p. 256.

31. Ibid., p. 258.

32. Ibid., p. 260.

33. Ibid., p. 262.

34. Ibid., p. 263.

35. See Jean-Jacques Lecercle's comments in his *Interpretation as Pragmatics* (New York: St. Martins, 1999), p. 19.

36. See the remarks by Paul de Man, *The Resistance to Theory* (Minneapolis: University of Minnesota, 1986), pp. 90–93.

37. Michael Taussig, *The Nervous System* (New York: Routledge and Kegan Paul, 1992), pp. 10, 24, 156. Some comments on the use of Benjamin's counter-historicism. Michael Taussig's *The Nervous System* wants to perform, to actualize, Benjamin's *Theses*. Taussig accepts that "terror" is everywhere ordinary, differently realized, differently resisted. He insists that the "whole world" is surreal. Out of this surreal/violence and ceaseless process of manipulation and destruction, the critic or writer needs "a mobile position that is resonant with the mobility of the Nervous System itself," nervous system standing in for society. He accepts the notion of the critic working within a "state of emergency," which is simply the State and its setting in motion conflicts that cannot be settled. The critic, Taussig writes, makes of critique and representations a practice ". . . giving oneself over to a phenomenon rather than thinking about it from above." Ones sense of the meanings of history are to come from divergent things. But this potential ambiguity of history and referent, language and sense, origin and end et al., is rendered unambiguously, for the critic/historian's real task is to grasp "the power of the image as bodily matter awakening memory,

awakening collective dream time in our era of mechanical reproduction . . . practical inquiry." One can ask how embedding criticism in "dream-time" can have any practical consequences. Further, Taussig misses Benjamin's use of disjunctive writing, focus on the gaps between object/discourse. To awaken here means to repeat, to stir, to mix, to insist on using "moments of danger" of the present so as to dislodge habits "deeply ingrained amid the corporeality of the Nervous System's being." Unfortunately, Taussig has the laudable act of to "dislodge" guaranteed by the need for a "healing image" and "healing of misfortune." The language of healing forgets Benjamin's warnings concerning historicist synthesis, which also claimed to "heal" social schisms. *The Nervous System* opts for "the power of the mental image to hold a history of nations," as in looking toward those places where societies practice "cures" on their troubles (like the Putumayo Indians). Taussig cites one of the Mothers of the Disappeared who has a dream in which her missing child's dream-presence leaves her with a feeling for reality that actually destitutes her; this experience of suffering confirms Benjamin's idea that "even the dead" aren't safe from historical manipulation. But Benjamin's leaving open the possibility of history-as-inhuman, without synthesis, is shunted by Taussig onto the "magical" side of the desire for "cure."

CONTRIBUTORS

AMINIA M. BRUEGGEMANN is Visiting Assistant Professor at Brown University in Providence, Rhode Island. She is the author of *Chronotopos Amerika bei Max Frisch, Peter Handke, Günter Kunert und Martin Walser* (New York: Peter Lang, 1996, and with Hubert Rast, *Assoziationen: Arbeitsbuch*. 2nd Year German Language Program, Communicative Approach (New York: McGraw-Hill, 1991). In addition, she has published scholarly articles and given lectures on contemporary authors such as Peter Handke, Günter Kunert, Hans Schädlich, Martin Walser, and Christa Wolf. Currently, she is working on a book-length manuscript on representations of computers and technology in contemporary German literature.

WILLIAM J. CLOONAN is Richard Chapple Professor of Modern Languages and Linguistics at Florida State University. He is the author of *The Writing of War: French and German Fiction and World War II* (Gainsville: University Press of Florida, 1999), and with Joanne James, *Apocalyptic Visions Past and Present* (Tallahasse: Florida State University, 1988). His other books include *Michel Tournier* (Boston: Twayne, 1985), and *Racine's Theater: The Politics of Love* (University, MSs: Romance Monographs, 1977). He is currently at work on a new project on Franco-American literary relations.

SANDE COHEN is a Professor in nineteenth- and twentieth-century European intellectual history at Cal Arts School of Critical Studies. He has published over twenty-five scholarly articles on historiography and critical theory, and the following books: *French Theory in America*, coauthored with Sylvère Lotringer (New York: Routledge and Kegan Paul, 2001); *Passive Nihilism* (New York: St. Martin's, 1988); *Academia and the Luster of Capital* (Minneapolis: University of Minnesota Press, 1993); and *Historical Culture: On the Recoding of an Academic Discipline* (Berkeley: University of California Press, 1986).

JENNIFER FORREST is professor of French at Southwest Texas State University. She is the coauthor with Leonard R. Koos of *Dead Ringers: The Remake in Theory and Practice* (Albany: State University of New York Press, 2002), and a forthcoming book on film sequels and series. She has written extensively on film, and representations of the circus in nineteenth-century French literature.

ANDREA GOGRÖF-VOORHEES is Associate Professor of Liberal Studies at Western Washington University at Bellingham, Washington. She is the author of *Defining Modernism: Baudelaire and Nietzche on Romanticism, Modernity, Decadence and Wagner* (New York: Lang, 1999). She has also authored essays on German and French romanticism and decadence.

TERRI J. GORDON is Assistant Professor of Comparative Literature at New School University, where she teaches in The New School B.A. Program and the University Humanities Program. Her research interests lie in the areas of ethics, gender studies, and the aesthetics of the body. She has published on the cabaret, post-war film, and performance art in the Third Reich and is currently at work on a book-length study of representations of the dancer in fin de siècle Paris.

BEATRICE GUENTHER is Associate Professor of French at the College of William and Mary. She is the author of *The Poetics of Death: The Short Prose of Kleist and Balzac* (Albany: State University Press of New York, 1996) and coauthor of *Générations*, a French textbook on oral and written forms of expression. In addition, she has published several articles in French and German literature. Her primary focus is on constructs of identity, with a focus on concepts of nation and gender. She is currently researching women's education in early nineteenth-century France and Germany.

KIMBERLEY HEALEY is Assistant Professor of French at the University of Rochester. She is the author of *The Modernist Traveler: French Detours, 1900–1930* (Lincoln, NE: University of Nebraska Press, 2003), as well as articles on aesthetics, exoticism, colonialism, and literary modernism in twentieth-century French studies. She is currently working on a book on contemporary women writers in French and their efforts to get beyond or challenge literary modernism.

ELLIOT NEAMAN is Associate Professor of late modern European history and Chair of History at the University of San Francisco. He has written widely on German right-wing thought and radical conservatism. He is the author of *A Dubious Past: Ernst Jünger and the Politics of Literature* (Berkeley: University of California Press, 1999), as well as articles and reviews in *Tikkun, New German Critique and German Politics and Society*. He is currently working on a book project on the European view of American foreign policy since 1945 and articles on German reaction to September 11 and the War on Terror.

MICHAEL PAYNE is John P. Crozer Professor of English Literature at Bucknell University. His recent books include with John Hunter, *Life after Theory* (London: Continuum, 2003), and with John Schad *Renaissance Literature: An Anthology* (Oxford: Blackwell, 2003). His earlier books include *Reading Knowledge: An Introduction to Barthes, Foucault, and Althusser* (Oxford: Blackwell, 1997), and *Reading Theory: An Introduction to Lacan, Derrida, and Kristeva* (Oxford: Blackwell, 1993).

SARAH JULIETTE SASSON is Visiting Lecturer at Sarah Lawrence College. She has published on Heinrich Heine and France, the figure of the parvenu in nineteenth-century texts, and the dialectics of hospitality. She is currently working on a project on Balzac.

HEIDI M. SCHLIPPHACKE is Assistant Professor of German and Codirector of European Studies at Old Dominion University. She has published on family and gender in C. F. Gellert, G. E. Lessing, and Goethe's *Wilhelm Meisters Lehrjahre* along with essays on Theodor Adorno and Max Horheimer and Bernhard Schlink. She is currently working on a book manuscript entitled *The Oedipal Divide: Family, Gender and the Postmodern*.

PETER SCHULMAN is Associate Professor of French and International Studies at Old Dominion University. He is the author of *The Sunday of Fiction: The Modern French Eccentric* (West Lafayette, IN: Purdue University Press, 2003), and with Mischa Zabotin, *Le Dernier livre du siècle: Deux Américains enquêtent sur l'intelligentsia française au tournant du siècle* (Paris: Romillat, 2001). He has also coedited two volumes of essays, *The Marketing of Eros: Performance, Sexuality and Consumer Culture* (Essen: Verlag Die Blaue Eule, 2003) with Frederick A. Lubich and *Chasing Esther: Jewish Expressions of Cultural Difference* (Santa Monica and Haifa: Kol Katan Press, 2003) with David Metzger.

PHILIP WATTS is Associate Professor of French at the University of Pittsburgh. His book *Allegories of the Purge: How Literature Responded to the Postwar Trials of Writers and Intellectuals in France* (CA: Stanford University Press, 1998) won the Aldo and Jeanne Scaglione Prize for French and Francophone literary studies in 2000. He has published articles and reviews in *French Forum, South Atlantic Quarterly* and *Esprit*.

NINA ZIMNIK is Assistant Professor of German and Cultural Studies at the University of Lüneberg, Germany. She has written extensively on film and media studies and has translated works by Slavoj Zizek into German.

Index

Académie Française, 5, 11, 36–38, 130, 232, 237
Aesthetic, 45, 69, 78, 88–89, 95–97, 115, 120, 125, 130, 174, 184, 194, 215, 218
Aesthetics 14, 38, 39, 44, 46, 89, 124, 130, 141, 143, 145, 166, 174–75, 177, 212, 214–15, 218, 220, 225, 262, 285–86, 288
Anti-Semitism, 7, 174, 198, 201, 204–6, 208, 221, 240, 245, 264
Arendt, Hannah, 15, 274–75, 283–87, 290–92
Aristotle, 38, 42–43, 46–47, 215
Authenticity 220, 222, 233, 267

Barthes, Roland, 251, 266, 277
Bataille, Georges, 173–89
Baudelaire, Charles, 5, 12–13, 93, 119–40, 148, 157, 168–69, 235
Baudrillard, Jean, 273, 278
Bauhaus, 174, 178
Bellmer, Hans, 12, 90, 100–5, 108, 115–16
Benjamin, Walter, 5, 13, 15, 87, 93–94, 105, 134, 165–71, 180, 257, 269, 274–75, 278, 286–92, 294–95

Berlin, 5–6, 9–10, 12–13, 37, 38, 90, 95, 97, 99, 111, 113, 116, 165–66, 170, 174, 177, 188, 199, 217, 219, 225, 229, 251, 253, 258, 273, 275, 285
Blossfeldt, Karl, 13, 173–89
Bonaparte, Napoleon, 6, 166, 276
Brecker, Arno, 14, 200, 201–2, 204, 207–8
Breton, André, 102, 178

Céline, Ferdinand, 7, 203, 239
Champsaur, Félicien, 142, 147–52, 156
Chateaubriand, F.-R. de, 4, 68, 161
Cicero, 285, 286
Classicism, 36, 39, 42–43, 45, 59, 100, 198, 207, 215–16, 225
Clément, René, 14, 211–26
Clichés (see also stereotypes), 3, 9, 71–72, 76, 267
Collaboration, 7, 14, 201, 203, 208, 211–16, 218–24, 231, 237–39, 243, 245, 255, 267
Corneille, Pierre, 38, 40–42, 46–48
Cubism, 196–97, 208, 273

Dada, 6, 12, 99–101, 108
Dandy, 126, 128–31, 253

Index

De Man, Paul, 245, 273
Decadence, 11, 22, 24, 37, 46, 50, 52, 108–26, 128–30, 132, 134–37, 145, 154, 157, 236
Delacroix, Eugène, 5, 123, 125
Deleuze, Gilles, 224, 258, 292
Denis, Maurice, 195–96
Derrida, Jacques, 238, 277
Diderot, Denis, 44–46, 48, 61

Education (*Bildung*) 19, 21–22, 24–26, 28, 31, 34, 270
Enlightenment (*Aufklärung*), 14, 19, 25, 30, 32, 35–37, 48–49, 58, 61, 125, 131, 204, 242, 246, 282
Europe, 3–4, 8–10, 19, 30, 68, 90, 92, 119, 127, 145, 166, 175, 196, 203, 205, 216–17, 219, 230, 235, 242, 280, 285, 287–88, 292
Expressionism, 99, 223–24, 273

Fascism, 14, 105, 219–20, 223–25, 230, 238, 243–45, 252, 254, 256, 262, 268–69, 280
Feminism, 32–33, 251–52, 259, 260, 263–67, 269
Femme-machine (see also machine), 12, 89, 90, 92, 97–99, 105, 108, 111, 112
Flâneur, 168–69, 231
Flaubert, Gustave, 119, 122
Folies-Bergère, 87, 90, 92, 95, 154
Fordism, 92–93, 95
Foucault, Michel, 97, 206
Frederick the Great, 4, 37–38, 63
French Revolution, 5, 33, 61, 151
Freud, Sigmund, 103, 106–7, 117–18, 124, 167–68, 260, 269

Gautier, Théophile, 67, 69–70, 72–74, 76, 79, 122
Genius, 29, 40–43, 45, 73, 79
Gide, André, 6, 236

Goethe, Johann Wolfgang von, 5, 68, 72, 142–43, 155, 174, 243
Goncourt, Jules and Edmond, 122, 145–46, 235
Gottsched, Johann Christoph, 37–40, 59–60

Hegel, Georg, 182, 274, 276, 278–79, 282
Heidegger, Martin, 238–39, 241, 244, 280–81
Heine, Heinrich, 5, 11, 67–83, 123
"History," 15, 274–77, 281, 286–87, 290–92
Historiography, 273, 275, 281, 287
Historization, 276, 283
Hitler, Adolf, 7, 200, 202, 204, 207–8, 229, 232, 240, 242, 244, 263, 276, 281, 283
Hitlerism, 231, 280–81, 286
Hoffmann, E.T.A., 72, 97–99, 103
Holocaust, 8, 15, 230, 233, 239, 258, 262–63
Hugo, Victor, 4, 68, 169
Huysman, J.K., 5, 125, 146, 148, 154–55, 157, 235

Idealism, 238, 286

Jelavich, Peter, 91, 94, 96, 113
Jünger, Ernst, 7, 14, 88, 229–46

Kant, Immanuel, 68, 286
Kessel, Joseph, 254–55, 259
Klee, Paul, 288–89
Kohl, Helmut, 234–35
Kojeve, Alexander, 15, 274–76, 278, 280, 285, 287, 291–93
Krakauer, Siegfried, 87, 94, 109, 111–13, 223–24

la Roche, Sophie von 11, 19–34
Labyrinth, 166–68, 170–71

Index

Lang, Fritz, 89, 98–99, 223
Lessing, Gottfried Ephraim, 11, 35–65
Levi-Strauss, Claude, 274, 276
Lyotard, Jean-François, 275–76, 279, 282, 288, 291

Machine, 4, 12, 43, 87–89, 91–92, 94–95, 97, 99, 102, 104–5, 107, 212
Maillol, Aristide, 13, 193–208
Mann, Thomas, 6, 145
Marx, Karl, 260, 283, 289
Marxism, 13, 68, 166, 241, 244, 280, 282, 287, 289, 291
Mitterand, François, 234–35, 238
Modernity, 96, 122, 134, 195, 197, 242
Molzahn, Johannes, 181–82, 187
Mysticism 241, 246, 288–89, 291
Myth, 15, 96, 97, 150, 156, 251, 259, 266–67, 270

Nabi, 195, 199
National characteristics (see also clichés, stereotypes), 9, 11, 42, 48, 52
National Socialism, 174, 205, 233, 238–39, 268, 275
Nationalism, 29, 182
Nazi, 14, 103, 107, 109, 115, 117, 193, 199–200, 202–6, 208, 211, 215–16, 220–23, 232–33, 236–37, 240, 243, 245, 252–53, 256, 261–62, 269
Nazism, 7, 94, 206, 138–39, 206, 242, 280–81, 283, 285
Nietzsche, Friedrich, 12, 13, 68, 119–41, 156, 239, 241, 275, 282–83, 289–90
Nihilism 15, 281

Paris, 5–6, 9, 11–15, 27–28, 38, 90, 95, 97, 99, 100–2, 123, 128, 130, 144–45, 148, 151, 153, 165–66, 170, 174, 177, 188, 198, 229–32, 234, 236–37, 251–54, 258–59, 273, 275

Pétain, Philippe, 199, 201
Picasso, Pablo, 175, 196, 231
Plard, Henri, 236–37, 241, 243, 245

Racine, Jean, 38, 40–43
Ray, Man, 12, 90, 99–102, 105, 108, 115
Resistance, 7, 200–1, 203, 211–16, 219, 220–23, 225–26, 231, 236–38, 242–44, 256, 267, 281–83
Riefenstahl, Leni, 88, 109
Rilke, Rainer Maria, 5, 145
Romanticism 19, 72, 143, 153, 156
Rouffio, Jacques, 15, 251, 254–59, 268–69
Rousseau, Jean-Jacques, 20–24, 27, 31

Sainte-Beuve, Charles-Augustin, 5, 69, 122
Sartre, Jean-Paul, 227, 236
Schneider, Romy, 15, 251–70
Schopenhauer, Arthur, 13, 141, 156
Schwarzer, Alice, 251, 259, 260–65, 268
Sensitivity/sensibility (*Empfindsamkeit*) 19, 24, 28, 31, 72
Seven Years War, 36–37, 53
Shakespeare, William, 40–42, 167
Sontag, Susan, 255, 269
Stael, Madame de 4, 5, 11, 19–34, 236
Stereotypes, 4, 8, 29, 36–37, 46–47, 49–50, 173–75, 179, 236
Surrealism, 6, 12, 89, 99–103, 108, 116, 178, 182

Theater 11, 36, 39–40, 45, 47–48, 60–61, 144–45, 151, 152, 154, 159
Third Reich, 193–94, 202, 204–6, 208, 253
Tournier, Michel, 193, 206
Truffaut, François, 3, 8, 211

Unification (of Germany in 1998), 9, 10

Vergangenheitsbewältigung (Coming-to-terms-with-the past), 15, 252, 258, 267
Vichy, 7, 8, 14, 202, 204, 222, 225, 238, 243
Voltaire (François-Marie Arouet), 4, 38, 42–45, 49, 59, 68, 72

Wagner, Richard, 5, 68, 123, 124
Wedekind, Frank, 12–13, 141–60
Weil, Simone, 15, 279–87, 291–92
Weimar, 91–92, 111, 229, 235, 238–39, 244–45
Wilde, Oscar, 77, 142, 151
World War I, 6–7, 14, 87–89, 99–100, 105–8, 173, 177, 196, 207, 229, 231, 234–35
World War II, 6–8, 13–14, 193–94, 197–99, 202–3, 205–6, 208, 211, 220, 225, 242, 245, 283